BROTHERHOOD
OF THE SEA
S.U.P.
ORG 1885

BROTHERHOOD OF THE SEA
S.U.P.
ORG 1885

IN MEMORY OF OUR BROTHERS WHO LOST THEIR LIVES IN WORLD WAR II

A

GEORGE ABBELA
ALEX ABRAHAM
JOHN ABRAHAM
KURT ACKERMAN
WILLIAM J. ADRIAN
FELIPE AGERO
THEOBERT AHLBERG
C. V. AIKENS
WILLIAM ALDERMAN
HARRY ALEXANDER
ORIN C. ALLISON
RICHARDO ALMODOVAR
JOHN ALOST
GEORGE W. ALTHER
DANIEL E. ANARINO
ARNOLD K. ANDERSON
HERBERT E. ANDERSON
JAMES ANDERSON
JOS. ANDERSON
THOMAS ANDERSON
WILLIAM ANDERSON
LEROY N. ANDREW
ISAIAS ANDUZE
CAROL O. ANGVIK
JAMES C. ARANT
JAAN ARBEITER
EDUARDO C. ARBOLEDA
EMILIANO ARCAY
EVARISTO ARENAS
ALBERT A. ARSENIAN
JOHN J. ASH
ANDREW ASP
JOHANNES AUSTIN
JOHN R. AVELLAR
ERNEST AVERETT

B

JOHN J. BABBIN JR.
ELMER E. BACON
JOHN BAGLEY
EDWIN B. BAGGOTT
JOHN BAHLS
ROBERT H. BAILER
ROBERT L. BAKER
JACOB K. BALDWIN
O. C. BANKS
ELMER D. BARKER
WILLIAM R. BARNARD
CARLOS BARNUM
JOHN W. BARR
ALLEN W. BARROW
ESTEL BARTON
WILLIS D. BARTON
WILLIAM BARTON
MIKE BASEL
STANLEY J. BATULES
ALBERT J. BAUGHER
ROBERT BAYLIS
JAMES BELL
MATTHEW BELL
ROBERT BELVIN
ERNEST L. BELFORD
H. G. BENN
CHAS. BERGHEN
JOHN BERGERON
ADRIAN T. BERNARD
LEO H. BERNSTEIN
CARL BENNETTE
JOHN BENNETT
SIGURD BENTSEN
JOSE A. BERMUDEZ
JENNETH BERRY
PRIMO BETANCOURT
R. BETENCOURT
BRUCE G. BIDDLE
ALEX W. BIGELOW
A. BIRD
CHRISTIAN BJORNSON
ROBERT BLACK
DONALD G. BACKMER
JAMES J. BLAKE
JACK E. BLANCHETTE
JOHN BLANTON
SAMMIE BLOCK
CORNELIUS F. BLOME
JOHN BLOMME
JOSEPH E. BLOMGREN
JAMES J. BLOSS
CARLO BOCCEDORA
STANISLAW BOCHULSKY
JOHN J. BOCZEK
J. BOND
FRANCISCO BONGCAK
WM. A. BORDON
UBERT BORGMAN
W. BORGMAN
N. L. BORREGARD
WALTER G. BORST
ANTOINE BOSCH
MARTIN L. BOWMAN
BOBBIE BOYKIN
JOSEPH B. BOYLE
EDWARD S. BOYLSTON
WYONE BOYNTON
A. BOZMAN
EDWARD J. BRADLEY
JAMES H. BRADY
THOMAS BREEN
MICHAEL BRAEMERT
ROY BRADGON
O. J. BRAND
VAY BRILL
JOHN BRITT
JULIUS BRITTAIN
B. T. BROOKES
P. J. BROUGHTON
OTHO BROUSSARD
BERNARD BROWN
EARL L. BROWN
FRANK S. BROWN
FRED W. BROWN
HAROLD H. BROWN
RALPH BROWN
ROBERT F. BROWNING
VERDO D. BROYLES
S. BRUCE
ROBERT BRUMIT
LEOZAIRE BRUNEAU
LEO A. BUBLITZ
JOSEPH BULLARD
SAMUEL T. BULLARD
JAMES H. BURKE
R. BURNS
EDWARD W. BURTON
MIGUEL A. BUSANET
WALTER L. BUTLER
WM. M. BUTLER
LEE D. BUCK
STEFAN BUTALA
E. BYERS

C

MARTIN M. CACIC
JACKSON CADENHEAD
FRANCISCO CAESPO
FILLIPO CALAFATO
JOSEPH H. CALDWELL
WM. M. CALDWELL
WILLIAM CALDWELL
ROBERT CALEY
LESLIE D. CALLAHAN
MAURICE J. CALLAHAN
STANLEY CALLAMAN
JUSTO CAMACHO
SANTOS CAMACHO
WILLIS E. CAMP
JAMES P. CAMPBELL
WILLIAM CANNON
THEODORE CARLSON
PETER J. CARNEY
GEORGE CARNEY
PAUL CARONIA
JACK E. CARSTAIRS
J. D. CARTER
WILMON R. CARTER
ROBERT E. CARPENTER
REUBEN S. CARROLL
CLARENCE E. CASSEL
JOHN CASSEL
WILLIAM P. CASSIDY
BERNARD CASTILLO
V. CASQUECENTE
ARISTON A. CAVINTA
EDWARD CEBULA
SVEN G. CEDERHOLM
FRANK CEMINA
FRANCIS CENTENO
LEONARD CHADWICK
ANDREW CHAMBERS
CURTIS CHANDLER
WILLIAM CHAPMAN
EDMOND CHARLEBOIS
SAMUEL CHARLES
HARRY CHASE
AMOS CHISHOLM
ELMO CHISHOLM
WM. B. CHISHOLM
WILLIE CHISHOLM
ALEX CHRISTIAN
W. A. CHRISTEN
EMIL CHRISTENSEN
SOREN CHRISTENSEN
CHESTER CHRISTOPHERSON
PETER C. CHUE
EMERSON W. CHURCH
RUPERT R. CHURCH
FRANK CIAMPI
FRANK CIMINO
DOMENIC CIPOLLONE
OWN L. CLAGETT
ARCHIBALD M. CLARK
JOHN S. CLARK
ROBERT CLARK
RAYMOND J. CLEARY
HOWARD CLEVELAND
FRED CLIFTON
ALBERT COLLINS
PERRY COLLIER
PATRICK D. COLEMAN
KASPER COLLWITZER
ADOLPH COLON JR.
ROBERT B. COMBS
CHARLES W. COMPTON
BERNARD E. CONNERS
HAYWARD COOK
HERMAN COOK
ALBERT COOPER
CLARENCE CORBIN
WILLIAM H. CORBIN
ROBERT COREY
A. CORIZIS
SHELDON CORKERN
PAUL CORONIA
WILLIAM CORRIGAN
DEMETRIO CORTEZ
JOHN COSCARELLI
ROBERT L. COSMAN
CARVILLE COUNSELMAN
RAOUL P. COURTIN
B. COVINGTON
DONALD COX
CARL V. COX
WILLIAM COX
THOMAS CRAWFORD
RAY CREIGHTON
WILLIAM CREWLAY
WALTER A. CRISTEN
MILFORD A. CROSS
CHARLES CROUSE
FORTUNATO CUARESMA
JAMES M. CUMMINGS
JOSEPH CUMMINGS
NESBETH CUMMINGS
P. W. CUMMINGS
HERMINGILDO CURETT
GEORGE CURMA
JAMES A. CURRAN
ODE G. CUSTER

D

R. J. D'ARTOIS
SAID DACHER
RALPH DAKIN
RICHARD W. DALY
EUGENE DAWSON
BYRL DANIELS
CARL DANLEY
GERONINO DAVID
STEPHEN DAVID
MANUEL DAVILLA
JAMES E. DAVIS
LEON DAVIS
WILLIAM L. DAVIS
VIRGIL H. DAWLEY JR.
JOHN S. DAY
PAUL DE BOLLE
THEO. P. DECKER
KAMAHA DEEN
ENRQUE DEL CAMPO
LOUIS DE GENNARO
RUFINO DE JESUS
ALBERT DE LAMONT
B. DE LOACH
PERCIVAL J. DE LEON
NATHAN DEMBOFSKY
WILLIAM DEMBOFSKY
JOHN C. DEMERETT
VALENTIN DERRICKS
MANUEL DE SILVA
HERBERT K. DEURSEL
LEROY F. DEUTCH
FRANK DE VITO
MICHAEL DE VITO
JOHN DEZIK
WARNER B. DINGER
LEWIS J. DION
FRANK S. DI LORENZO
A. DI SANTO
JOSEPH A. DISANZA
DENNY A. DIX
JAMES DIXON
RAY M. DIXON
B. A. DOBSON
ALAN L. DOHERTY
SCRIP D'OLIVE
HARRY M. DIMINEY
EUGENE DOMINQUEZ
PATRICK S. DON
THOMAS E. DORSEY
HAROLD J. DOSTIC
OLIVER DOVER
H. W. DOWLING
FRANK E. DOXTATION
JOHN S. DOYLE
PHILIP DOYLE
W. A. DRAWDY, JR.
K. DRUMWRIGHT
HERBERT DUERSEL
JOSEPH DUFFY
JOHN J. DUNN
CLYDE A. DUNNING
WM. J. DWYER

E

WILLIAM K. F. EADY
ROBERT EAGELSON
ROBERT EARNHARDT
MARIANO ECHANES
OLAN H. ECK

ARVID ELIASSEN
SAMUEL H. ELKINS
DANIEL ELLARD JR.
ROBERT ELLIOTT
T. W. ELLSE
JOHN T. ELMGREN
JESSE J. ELSHICK
W. E. EMANUEL
CECIL J. EMERY
GLENN L. EMMERSON
WILLIAM M. ENERBRETSON
GEORGE C. ENGLE
CARL L. ENGLISH
WILLIAM ENGELBRETSON
FRANK ERAZO
EUGENE H. ERICKSON
RAY L. ERWIN
THOMAS A. ERWIN
LEONCIO M. ESPIJO

F

HENRY C. FAHY
WILLIAM FAIRMAN
DANIEL E. FAISON
FRANK FALCO
JOSEPH F. FALESNIK
GEORGE H. FALK
WILLIAM E. FARRULLA
EUTAQUIO FARULLA
JOHN FAULKNER
GEORGE E. FELLMAN
CLARENCE FENTY
FRANK P. FERGUSON
LIONEL FERGUSON
JAMES H. FEURTADO
CLAUDIO FIGUERAS
ISMAEL FILOMENO
EUGENE FINCH
WM. FINDLAY
HARRY W. FINK
JOHN J. FINN
STANDLEY E. FISHER
JAMES E. FITZPATRICK
STANDLEY FLANDERS
RUSSELL B. FLIPPEN
JOSEPH FLYNN
WILLIARD J. FOGT
AKSEL FORSSMAN
PERCY FORSYTHE
W. O. FOUNTAIN JR.
WILMER FOX
FORNEY FRANKLIN
L. A. FREDERICKS
NELSON FREE
JACK FUNK
FREDERICK FUNKEN

G

CLOVIS D. GADBERRY
WILLIAM GADSON
WILLIAM GAJDOS
WILLIAM T. GALLIGAN
KASPER GALLWITZER
PETER GALBRAITH
LAURENCE GALLAGHER
JOHN GALLE
RILEY GANEY
RICARDO M. GARCIO
HAROLD W. GARDINER
L. A. GARDINER
EUGENE J. GARDNER
J. GARRIDO
ADAM S. GAYDOWSKI
JOHN F. GEARIN
OLIVER GEDMAN
FREDERICK E. GENTH
JETER GEORGE
PETER GEORGE
LIONEL GERGUSON
ARTHUR J. GERRY
WILBURT GERRY
RICHARD GEZAK
LEONARD E. GIBONEY
CLIFFORD G. GILBERT
ODUS GILLS
JAMES W. GILROY
JAMES R. GILSTRAP
ALFRED J. GIROURD
A. J. GIROWED
JOSEPH P. GLEASON
MAURICE M. GLEMBY
WILLIAM GOETHE
BENJAMIN GOLDSTEIN
LEO GONYA
L. GONZALEZ
CHARLES E. GORING
ALBERT R. GOTT
JOHN GOURDIER
JACK G. GOTTESMAN
GEORGE I. GOVING
EDWARD GRAHAM
CLARENCE E. GRAUL
EDWARD GRAY
WINIFRED GRAY
PAUL GRECH
GEORGE W. GREEN
HARVEY GREEN
ORVILLE E. GREEN
WILLIAM C. GREENE
MORRIS GREENFELD
JACK C. GRIFFIN
CHARLES W. GROOVER
SARAFIN GUEMES
JAMES GURRY
LOUIS GVANILL
WARREN GWALTNEY

H

MARVIN HADDOX
ALBERT HALBIG
JAMES HALE
ELMO HALL
H. HALL
H. M. HALL
JOHN E. HALL
WILLIARD HALL
GEORGE HALLENBECK
FRED HAMILTON
GEORGE HAMILTON
JAMES HAMILTON
JOHN HAMPTON
ARTHUR L. HAND
ANDREW HANRAHAN
AAGE E. HANSEN
ANDREA F. HANSEN
R. F. HANSEN
MAURICE P. HARDY
W. HARLEY
IRVING G. HARRINGTON
HARRY HARRIS
JAMES R. HARRIS
LLOYD A. HARRIS
HENRY M. HARRISON
MOODY HARRISON
WHITLEY HARRISON
ROBERT S. HART
JOHN W. HARTLEY
KING HARTLEY
WALTER S. HASKINS
ERNEST HAUGEN
ARTURO HAU LUCAS
JOHN W. HAUGEN
HENRY W. HAWK
DANIEL HAY
S. HAYBYE
FRED HAYES
J. J. HAYES
GEORGE W. HAYMAN JR.
WARNER M. HAYNIE
L. D. HEADINGTON
JOHN HEALEY
J. E. HEFFEMAN
DALMACIO HELERA
LOUIS HELLERBY
KENNETH HELSEL
JAMES HENDERSON
LLOYD R. HENDERSON
WARDEL HENDRICKS
FREDERICK A. HENDY
HARRY HENNING
RALPH R. HENRY
ALBERT E. HEPPNER JR.
RICARDO HERNANDEZ
STEVE D. HESTER
WILLIAM G. HESTER
CARL HEUBNER
RALPH HEWETT
CHESTER E. HIATT
GERALD F. HICKEY
A. J. HICKMAN
HARRY HIGBEE
RALPH B. HILDRETH
WILLIAM P. HILL
ROBERT H. HILLIARD
EDWARD N. HINTON
MAX HIRSCHJOWITRZ
ERNEST HISTING
HERBERT HODGES
JOHN HOFMAN
CARL J. HOFFMAN
CHRISTOPHER HOFFMAN
RAY HOGG
CHARLES HOLCOMBE
CHARLES HOLDER
EUGENE HOLLAND
BARRY HOLMS
ARTHUR HOLYOAK
LOUIS HONIGMAN
JOSEPH F. HOOKS
DAVID A. HORTON
HERBERT HOSSEIN
P. J. HOUSTON
FLORIN H. HOWARD
JOHN A. HOWARD
ROBERT E. HOWARD
WILLIAM T. HOWELL
JAMES HRONO
EDWARD HUBEWET
SHELBROWN W. HUDGINS
CARTER HUDSON
CARL HUEBNER
HERMAN HEUBNER
JUDE HUFFMASTER
WOODROW HUGGINS
JOHN HUGHE
JOSEPH HUGHES
RENO HUGHES
WILLIAM L. HUGHES
WILLIAM R. HUGHES
RAYMOND HUNA
JAMES H. HUNTE
RALPH E. HUPPER
MARION HURD
VIRGIL J. HURD
HARVEY L. HURST
JAMES H. HUSTEN
J. O. HUSTON
HERMAN HUTCHINSON
J. W. HUTSON
BASIL HYDE

J

JOSEPH JACKSON
EDWIN N. JAFFE
HJALMAR JANSEN
BISARI JANY
CHARLES O. JENKINS JR.
JOHN JENKINS
WILLIS J. JENKINS
CHAS. JEREMIAS
OLLIE JERNE
LE ROY JERNIGAN
PETER J. JOBLONSKI
KARSTEN JOHANSEN
RUSSEL J. JOHNNENEE
FRANK JOHNSON
JOHN JOHNSON
KYLE V. JOHNSON
LEIGH JOHNSON
OSCAR JOHNSON
WILLIAM JOHNSON
WOODROW JOHNSON
SAMSON JONDAL
A. JONES
CHARLES JONES
JAMES E. JONES
LEWIS JONES
RICHARD N. JONES
HAROLD S. JORDON
SHERMAN L. JORDON
ROBERT O. JORGENSON
TONY E. JOSATO
JAMES J. JUDGE

K

FRANK H. KACZUR
ROBERT J. KAEMPFER
EDWARD J. KALLI
WILIAM K. KAMAKA
EDWARD KAMONT
CHARLES KARDOS
HYRUN KARETTI
EMIL J., KATRENICK
RICHARD L. KEAN
EDWARD KEANE
JAMES D. KEARNS
JOSEPH R. KEHL
FRED KEITH
EDWARD KELLY
HERBERT N. KELLY
RAYMOND KELLY
CHARLES D. KENT
RAY P. KENT JR.
JOSEPH KICKLIGHTER
MELVIN KILEY
MARY KIMBRO
KENNETH K. KINES
FORREST R. KING
STANLEY KINKOWSKI
ALFRED KINNELL
VIRGIL C. KITTLESON
RONALD KLEINSMITH
CHAS H. KLEMM
ROBERT KLINE
STANLEY KLOSKOWSKI JR.
MARTIN KNUDSEN
KARL G. M. KOBE
MATHEW E. KOIVAL
WALTER J. KON
JOHN KOOL
CHAS W. KOSTEN
RALPH P. KROTZER
HENRY J. KRUPA
JOHN KUCH
HUGH KUHL
SEROFIN KUEMES

L

LOUIS LABIANO
DAVID LABOY
FRANK LA CASSE
CHARLES LA GAL
KARL G. LAGERGREN
HOLBLIMB LAMMON JR.
DONALD L. LA MONT
JAMES LANDWERMEYER
EDWARD E. LANE
G. W. LANE
H. LANE

(Continued back page)

BROTHERHOOD OF THE SEA:

A History of the Sailors' Union of the Pacific

1885-1985

San Francisco, Cal., April 17, 1901.

To the Shipowners of San Francisco:

Gentlemen:—We have the honor to submit the following draft of an

AGREEMENT BETWEEN

—THE—

Sailors' Union of the Pacific, Pacific Coast Marine Firemen's Union and Ship Owners of San Francisco, Cal.

1. Recognition of the Sailors' Union of the Pacific and the Pacific Coast Marine Firemen's Union—*i. e.*, employment of members of these unions exclusively, under the wage schedules and working rules to be mutually agreed upon.

2. A Nine-hour workday for all Sailors in all vessels in all ports on the Coast, with overtime pay for all extra work.

3. A Nine-hour workday for all Firemen in all ports on the Coast in all steam-schooners and steam vessels where only two men are employed, with overtime pay for all additional time.

4. Board-money of not less than sixty (60) cents per day for seamen and firemen in port, where crews do not board on the vessel.

5. Scale of wages (for Sailors):—

STEAM VESSEL RATES.

Coasting Steamers in freight and passenger trade, per month	$45 00
Overtime per hour	40
(Nine hours to constitute a day's work. Two hours' notice shall be given and received by men leaving or being discharged from these steamers.)	
Steam Schooners trading to Outside Ports, per month	50 00
Trading to Inside ports, per month	45 00
Overtime per hour	50
(Work performed on Sundays and Holidays on all steam vessels to be paid at "Overtime" rates.)	

SAILING VESSEL RATES.

Sailing Vessels trading to Outside Ports, per month	45 00
Overtime, per hour	50
(Work performed on Sundays and Holidays on sailing vessels trading to Outside Ports to be paid at "Overtime" rates, from April 1st to October 1st.)	
Sailing Vessels trading to Inside Ports of the State of California, Oregon, Washington, Alaska and British Columbia, per month	40 00
Overtime, per hour	40
Sailing Vessels sailing direct from any port on the Pacific Coast of the United States and British Columbia to the Hawaiian Islands, per month	40 00
Sailing direct to the Marquesas, Navigator and Society Islands and Mexico, per month	35 00
Sailing Vessels bound to Central America, South America, China, Japan, Philippine Islands, and Australian Ports, per month	30 00
Sailing Vessels trading to Siberia, per month	30 00
Sailing Vessels chartered in one port on the Pacific Coast of the United States to load in another port on the Pacific Coast of the United States and British Columbia for foreign ports, the wages to be the same as on the Coast until loaded and cleared, viz., per month	40 00

WORKING RULES (FOR SAILORS).

Dinner Hour—Dinner hour is to be from 12 to 1 P. M., but may be varied not to exceed one hour either way. Members shall have one hour for dinner while lying in any port or roadstead, and no work shall be performed during such hour, except (1), such work as is necessary for the immediate safety of the vessel, her cargo or passengers; (2), landing of passengers or mail and departure of vessel; (3), moving vessel to or from berth, which cannot be moved from or to except at high tide.

Working Hours—Working hours in all harbors on this Coast shall be nine hours per day—that is, from 7 A. M. to 12 M., and from 1 to 5 P. M. Any time worked beyond the regular hours shall be paid for at "Overtime" rates. Work in this case means loading or discharging of freight and coaling or cleaning vessel. When men work overtime to finish loading in order to get to sea, overtime shall count until one watch is sent below. Moving ships between any points lying inside of the line drawn from Alameda Point to Hunter's Point on the south and Point Richmond and Fort Point on the north, including Sausalito and Tiburon, if done outside the regular working hours, shall be paid for at "Overtime" rates.

SCALE OF WAGES (FOR FIREMEN AND COAL PASSERS).

Firemen, per month	$50 00
Coal Passers, per month	40 00
Overtime, per hour	50

6. For the purposes of this agreement the Hawaiian Islands shall be considered as included in the term "Pacific Coast."

7. This agreement shall hold good for one year from the date of signature, and shall be considered as violated whenever the seamen or firemen are requested to work with non-union men, or to accept freight from or deliver cargo to non-union men.

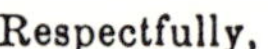
Respectfully,

Joint Committee } SAILOR' UNION OF THE PACIFIC, PACIFIC COAST MARINE FIREMEN'S UNION.

BROTHERHOOD OF THE SEA:

A History of the Sailors' Union of the Pacific 1885-1985

By Stephen Schwartz

Foreword by Paul Dempster
Preface by John F. Henning
Introduction by Karl Kortum

Published by the Sailors' Union of the Pacific, AFL–CIO
Distributed to the trade by

Transaction Books
Rutgers – The State University
New Brunswick (USA) and Oxford (UK)

Library of Congress Cataloging-in-Publication Data

Schwartz, Stephen.
Brotherhood of the sea.

Includes index.
1. Sailors' Union of the Pacific — History.
2. Trade-unions — Merchant seamen — Pacific States — History. 3. Merchant seamen — Pacific States — History.
I. Title.
HD6515.S42P337 1986 331.88'1138754044'0979 86-13940
ISBN 0-88738-121-9

Table of Contents

Illustrations will be found between pages 32 and 33, and pages 112 and 113.

Dedication

This work is dedicated to those who gave their lives in the cause of the Sailors' Union of the Pacific.

"To resist oppression in any and every form"

— Coast Seamen's Union Minutes, March 6, 1885

Foreword

By Paul Dempster

President/Secretary-Treasurer
Sailors' Union of the Pacific, AFL–CIO

The history of the Sailors' Union of the Pacific is not the story of one man, or even of a group of individuals; it is the "biography" of a labor organization and of the class — seagoing workers — that created it.

Seamen throughout the world came to the West Coast of the United States during the period of the region's economic growth and political rise, and it is fitting that this history should examine the seamen's labor movement as a global rather than a local experience. As the reader will discover, the Sailors' Union of the Pacific came to carry the banner for seamen the world over.

A reflection of the unique international status of the maritime labor movement comes from the congressional debates over the 1915 Seamen's Act, landmark legislation passed through the untiring efforts of S.U.P. leader Andrew Furuseth, with the support of U.S. Senator Robert M. LaFollette. In 1910, during the long fight for passage, Senator LaFollette submitted to the legislators a memorial on the history of the seamen's status before the law. This memorial became a key document for Furuseth, who often referred to it in conversation and print.

Furuseth was particularly given to quoting from the 15th century "law of Oléron," cited in the memorial, which affirmed that "the seamen of the North Atlantic and the North Sea coasts have never been slaves." Oléron is an island off the Atlantic coast of France and its maritime code became a major source for maritime law throughout the world. Under the code of Oléron, seamen were described as "companions of the vessel."

Before this, the best that seamen had gained in terms of legal standing had come when the commercial authority of Barcelona, a major Mediterranean port, recognized in the compilation known as the *Consolat de Mar* that seamen had the right to set the terms of their contract, if they were free men and not slaves. But slave sea labor had long prevailed in Mediterranean waters and this precedent was subsequently put to use by the U.S. Supreme Court.

Andrew Furuseth was forever true to the spirit of Oléron, of seamen who had never known legal bondage. The struggle not only for liberation and survival but also for improved wages and benefits was carried out in the same spirit by the generation led by Harry Lundeberg, through battles on the docks and the ships, in 1934 and in the other big strikes. This constructive spirit was furthered under the leadership of Morris Weisberger.

It was in keeping with that spirit that Stephen Schwartz approached the writing of this story of the Sailors' Union. Now that the book is available to our members and the general public, we look forward to new achievements as we enter our second century.

The fight goes on!

Preface

By John F. Henning

Executive Secretary-Treasurer
California Labor Federation, AFL–CIO

The romance of the sea flows deeply through history and never more strongly than in the lives of those who brave the waters of the world.

Labor history has a highly honored place for Union seamen and their wars against the violence of nature and the grasp of shipowners.

The Sailors' Union of the Pacific embodies the story of an organizational militancy that survived decades of combat to win the workers liberation.

Author Stephen Schwartz tells that story in daunting detail. He tells it in tribute to the S.U.P.'s century of struggle.

Those who would write history presume to interpret. It must be that way. The mere recitation of dates and places is almanac writing and nothing more.

Mr. Schwartz's task was to understand one hundred years of an often tumultuous Union in what was for so long an industry of primitive exploitation.

He faced first the pursuit of documentary history. Not an easy mission in the case of a Union that was fighting on the run, in times when members were outlawed and banned. Archives were hardly the preoccupation of officials then, when their documents of innocence might be cited as evidence of conspiratorial purpose.

Mr. Schwartz found S.U.P. records of almost countless meetings, and correspondence between officials on issues that shaped decisive policy.

With chilling impact he presents the reality of the brutalized lives suffered by seamen in the early decades of the S.U.P.'s existence.

The book balances leadership values against the economic elements upon which all history largely rests. Certainly, S.U.P. history reminds that not all institutions respond alike to the inexorable influence of economic causes.

However, he dismisses neither economic factors nor political ideology in his evaluation of the S.U.P. experience.

He emphasizes the awareness of European leftist thought in maritime unionism, particularly in the years that followed the Russian Revolution. The currents of revolution washed American shores in those years but American seamen, as with American workers generally, in the end molded Union life in accord with the economic and social dispositions of the United States.

The S.U.P. policy of picket line and job action militancy had no time for the dictatorship of the proletariat. Yet there has been more blood shed in American labor disputes than in all the history of the socialist unions of Europe.

The author sees two names dominating S.U.P. history: Furuseth and Lundeberg. This is not to minimize the work of those before or since their day, but simply to appreciate that the wheel of chance presented them with historic opportunities for which they were prepared.

Andrew Furuseth will be remembered always for moving the conscience of Congress and a President in enactment of the La Follette Seamen's Act of 1915. As a charter of freedom it stipulated rights and protections against industry tyranny.

Harry Lundeberg built the S.U.P. as it has been since the 1934 maritime strike. The union entered an era of unprecedented power with the Wagner Act and emergence of the Lundeberg leadership.

Under Lundeberg the S.U.P. became a fortress, a bastion against all enemies, domestic or otherwise.

In astonishing devotion to the least word spoken or least deed done, as well as to the dramatic times of conflict, Mr. Schwartz has left for all of us and those to follow a story of the Sailors' Union of the Pacific never before told. Certainly not as well nor as fully told.

Introduction

By Karl Kortum

Chief Curator
National Maritime Museum

The world's first permanent Sailors' Union, hardy enough to survive to the present day, was organized in San Francisco. In the year 1985-86 it celebrated its hundredth anniversary. This book is a part of the celebration — a permanent part.

The seamen who created the Union in rainy gatherings on the San Francisco lumber wharves and in night-time meetings in various "halls" ashore, had a homogeneity that was missing from their Eastern counterparts. They were in large percentage men of North Europe. In 1905, twenty years after its founding, the Union had a membership of 3,500 and 75 percent of these were from that part of the world. This figure may represent some variation from the founding days, but probably not much.

This is not to say that the activists and great spirits who launched the organization were all from the Baltic areas; Mr. Schwartz's text makes the actual mix clear. But there was an undergirding of men from Scandinavia and North Germany and these were the nations where social advance had reached farthest. (Women had the vote in Finland in 1907.)

A large percentage of our West Coast seafaring men came around Cape Horn in British square-riggers like the *Balclutha* and jumped ship in San Francisco. They were young men; sailing before the mast in a Cape Horner was a young man's game and so was humping lumber on the Pacific Coast. They stepped into an egalitarian system that they had undoubtedly heard about. The steps were in front of them for any ambitious sailor to take — become donkeyman in the sailing ships, or winch driver or quartermaster in the steam schooners and coastal liners. Rise from that level to second mate. Mate and master came next, and similar levels existed in the engine room.

The coastwise voyages were short and you could pile off if you didn't like the way the ship was run and get a berth in another vessel. A bad master got a bad reputation and it echoed up and down the Coast. It was an open system — communication was good and the foremast hand and the captain may have come from the same town in Norway and each was mentioned by the other in letters to the families back home. The social ferment back home came out to the Pacific Coast by return mail.

It was fine soil for the Sailors' Union movement to flourish in, to send down its roots and find nourishment.

In contrast, there is a mention in the *Coast Seamen's Journal* of November 9, 1889 of the conditions in the New England-owned, New York-registered square-rigged ships flying the American flag that then composed the bulk of this country's foreign-going merchant marine. These were the vessels called "down-Easters" and on some of them the "bucko mate" flourished:

"American boys do not go to sea as a rule, except they by reason of family ties, are assured of being in a short time the officers of vessels; and in the short time they do serve as boys they are kept aft. By such means they learn to look upon men in the forecastle somewhat in the same way as the young southerner was trained to look upon the Negro."

Not much communication there, not much egalitarianism, not much chance for solidarity!

The class of ship called down-Easters knew San Francisco well; in fact, it could be said that the carrying of our Central Valley wheat was the main reason that they came to be launched on the Penobscot and Kennebec and other new England rivers.*

The worst side of their coming cropped up from time to time in the San Francisco courtrooms — the excesses of the bucko mate.

The bucko mate was an extremist, his distorted view seemingly arising out of the conflict between the

* In a four year period in the early 1880s no fewer than 418 down-Easters took their departure from the Golden Gate wheat-laden. British iron ships in the trade on the style of *Balclutha* were even more numerous; 761 loaded California wheat during the same period. *Balclutha* carried grain around Cape Horn to North Europe on five different voyages.

down-East standard of a smart ship and insufficient real sailors to keep her that way. "At that time the American ship was the pride of the ocean," as a notorious hard case, the mate of the down-Easter *Louis Walsh*, put it.

But, sadly, this pride was an anachronism; the era of American *interest* in the sea was dwindling. The nation was turning inland — in not too many years the cowboy was the admired American man at work, not the sailor. The vastly different time when the ship *George* of Salem, built in 1812, produced forty-five captains from her forecastle was long gone.

"Yankee workmen built the clipper ships, but they were not manned by Americans," says Samuel Eliot Morison in *The Maritime History of Massachusetts*. He goes on: "The Yankee mariner with his neat clothes and perfect workmanship, had passed into history by 1850. Few Americans could then be found in the forecastles of merchantmen on deep waters. Why did this change take place? Why did New Englanders abandon the sea?"

There were even fewer Americans in the forecastles of the down-Easters, the next generation of square-rigger after the clipper ships.

Why? They weren't paid enough.

The world had never seen a mastery of seafaring equal to that of the Americans in the era of the ship *George* and extending three or four decades in either direction.

R. H. Thornton says in *British Shipping*, published by Cambridge University Press:

"More profoundly than any others, the American shipbuilders studied the basic principles of ship propulsion by the aid of sails, and in fifty years they contributed as much to the development of the sailing ship as the whole maritime world had contributed in three hundred. And their ships were not only well built. They were well handled. With all too few exceptions, the British master mariner was little more than an ignorant leading hand, while in American ships not only was the pay two or three times more than the British, but their officers were recruited from the grammar school, started their careers with a good grounding in mathematics, navigation and ship's husbandry and later, as captains with a financial share in their ship's trading, could not only afford to live as gentlemen, but if men of good character and fair manners were received into the best mercantile circles ashore.

". . . the sailing ship, like everything else, was conceived afresh from the standpoint of the new American hustle. While the lumbering East Indiaman relied upon her size and her armament to see her through, American shipowners discovered a cheaper and more effective method of avoiding capture, which was to design a vessel fast enough to show a clean pair of heels to anything likely to dispute her passage."

Good pay played a role in all this.

By the second half of the century the bucko mates (and the other, decent men who held that post) found themselves in a rearguard action. There was a more sizeable merchant marine than is generally realized — the historian John Lyman estimated the total number of down-Easters (full-rigged ships and barks), launched after the Civil War at nearly a thousand vessels. But there were few Americans before the mast. To repeat, the trend of the nation was inland. Much of the capital in New York, Boston, and Philadelphia that had been invested in shipping in the first half of the century and through clipper ship times* was shifting to railway building, manufacturing and real estate.

A parasitic new industry had sprung up — and nowhere was it worse than in San Francisco. The boarding house system — complete with boarding house masters, shipping masters, "crimps" and "runners" — now supplied the sailors to the ships. It was attacked with full vigor by the Sailors' Union once that organization had got fairly on its feet.

A consequence of this vicious system is given in Paul Taylor's short but excellent *The Sailors' Union of the Pacific*, published in 1923. The four ships mentioned are all well-known down-Easters:

"In 1884 the United States Consul at Hull, England, complained in a letter to the Commissioner of Navigation:

" 'The wheat ships arriving at this and other ports from San Francisco are manned by the most worthless set of men. Of the large ships here during the past four months, viz., the *Reaper, Amy Turner, Solitaire,* and *Tam O'Shanter*, the first named had but two, the second three, the third three, and the last, three men who could be trusted at the wheel to steer. These men were paid from $20 to as high as $40 per month, and, in addition to this a bonus or "blood-money" is called for by the boarding master to the extent of $15, and as high as $25 for each man. It is little short of a miracle that vessels so manned should safely reach their destination. The large majority of these men are green landsmen, and, as a matter of course, being but of little use on board the ship, they do not receive the best of treatment, and on reaching port desert and become chargeable on some of the consulates. Three months advance pay is demanded at San Francisco, and this as does everything else, goes to the boarding master. The men are put on board without clothing, and, according to many of them, in a state of intoxication, and without their own consent. Upon arrival here they are

* Almost all the clipper ships were built in the early 1850s. The *Annals of San Francisco*, published in 1855, claimed that, for all that they were built on the East Coast, "the clipper ship is virtually the creation of San Francisco." Present research indicates that there were scarcely more than eighty extreme clippers. Ten regular full-rigged ships were launched for every clipper that took the water. Some of these were medium-clippers. The clipper ship era was a brief but incomparable flowering that then and now seizes the popular imagination.

in debt to the ships, and aided by the crimps, and not opposed by the officers, they desert.' "

Are we to feel pity then for the bucko mate, stuck with greenhorns like the above and anxious that his paintwork be in a state of perfection? Of course not. But he *had* a problem. It was inherited from the time of the ship *George*, previously mentioned. The American down-Easter *still* set the seamanship standard for the merchant ships of the world.

Here is what Basil Lubbock has to say about this American phenomenon in the excellent essay formed by the first two chapters of an otherwise imperfect book, *The Downeasters* (1929):

"In all that pertained to a smart, shipshape appearance aloft and alow, the officer from Maine or Massachusetts always showed himself a super-seaman; and if he was called a (bucko) and a slave-driver he never spared himself, and his efforts were all for the honour of his ship.

"There was far more, however, to the make-up of the American deep-water mate than the picturesque belaying-pin and cruel knuckle-duster. He was a distinct American type, a virile type, in the same category and with much the same outlook on life as those frontiersmen, the cowboy and the miner and the lumberman. He was also a product of the times, obeying that law called 'the survival of the fittest,' for one must remember that he invariable began life as a ship's boy, a 'red-neck' or a 'greenhorn', a lamb for slaughter; surviving which he became an able seaman; then, through a show of initiative or powers of leading in times of stress was promoted petty officer, and finally by sheer character and driving force fought his way to the quarterdeck.

"There are two distinct grades of humans, positive and negative: the bucko mate was aggressively positive, and he was often a cruel, hard taskmaster, because his own struggle to rise out of the ruck had been so cruel hard that it had toughened the fibre of his nature and steeled his heart to an almost incredible degree.

"The sea undoubtedly makes character with a heavier tool than does the land. Old ocean uses the adze or the axe where Mother Earth uses the smoothing plane. But the man who backs the blizzard or the sea in its fury has often found that his greatest testing has come from his own species. It takes character to blaze a difficult trail successfully, just as it takes character to handle a ship in a hurricane, or steer one through a Cape Horn snorter; but, more than these, it takes character to hold one's own in the wilds where no law runs but the law of the six-shooter, or on the deck of a windjammer, where a knife thrown in the dark, or a block dropped from aloft, may mean a sudden exit from this world.

"The one quality that has been the making of the great American nation is that of nerve force, known under various slang terms such as 'grit'. . ."

"It is curious that, when a man holds an excess of nervous energy in his composition, he is in more danger of becoming an oppressor than a supporter of his weaker neighbours. More often than not it is just this excess of nervous energy — perhaps one should call it vital force — which has produced the bad men and the outlaws of the wild and woolly West, and the bullies and the buckos of the blood-boat."

It will be noticed that Lubbock describes the ship's boy who eventually became mate as rising through the ranks, that is "coming aboard through the hawse pipe" (to use the old expression). This in contrast to the 1889 citation from the *Coast Seaman's Journal*, previously given, which has him coming aboard "through the cabin windows." No statistics that I know of exist on the provenance of the bucko mate, but I tend to respect the contemporary citation from the *Journal*. Captain Fred Klebingat, a Pacific Coast sailing ship captain, affirmed the New England system in a conversation a few years ago: "A lot of East Coast skippers were never in the forecastle; they went second mate with Dad — with 'Pa' — after a few trips living aft as boys."

But let us not obscure the bucko mate with too much pedantry. In his rages, brought on by the cumulative pressures of a voyage and untrammeled in his power, he was a monster.

Felix Riesenberg in *Under Sail* describes a hardcase mate, Mr. Zerk, who the crew finally came to respect because of his seamanship. But Zerk in a single episode spoiled it all; for a small offense having to do with a ship's lamp he turned on the peaceful old ship's carpenter and bloodily beat him up. *Under Sail*, incidentally, in the scenes at the end of the voyage, portrays the degradation of a ship's crew by the boarding house system with more eloquence than anything I know of in print.

The classic description of a raging, uncontrolled tyrant on shipboard, cited on page 3 of Mr. Schwartz's text, is the flogging scene in *Two Years Before the Mast*. Richard Henry Dana was in touch with a shipmate after the book came out and in subsequent editions the original description is verified from this second source. The captain concerned had identified himself to the crew in grim, colloquial language in a previous confrontation on board:

"I'm Frank Thompson, all the way from 'down East'. I've been through the mill, ground and bolted, and come out a 'regular-built down-East johnnycake' — when it's hot, d---d good, but when it's cold, d---d sour and indigestible; and you'll find me so!"

Robert P. Tristram Coffin, in a knowledgeable book, *Captain Abby and Captain John*, tells about the coming of the third mate:

"One melancholy sign of change in the American logbooks after 1855 is the growing frequency of trouble among the crews . . . many of them were scoundrels of the first water. And captains had to use strong-arm methods to secure even these.

"So the third mate came into being. A child — and usually a tough one — of necessity. It was the third mate's chief duty to collect men and make them toe the line once they were aboard. That gentleman would ferret them out in ports and pay the debts they had contracted. Sailors, both the good ones and the bad ones, owed money to everybody. Then the mate would liquor them up and bring them aboard. Having usually been one of his quarry, he generally knew the ropes of the game. . . . When the men sobered off, they would find themselves far at sea with a job on their hands. The third mate might have to use his fists on them to make them go aloft. He was generally a good man with his fists, and had a big pair. He had to have, to live. Sometimes, too, it was a case of the biters being bit. For often when the new crew came to, they turned out an utter set of wild-cats, hyenas, and scalawags of the first magnitude and made the captain's and the third mate's lives a misery and a burden.

"With such crews aboard, mutiny began to be a frequent occurrence. Of course, captains themselves were often enough the cause as well as the men. A weak or an unfair captain was headed for trouble sure as he had a parting in his pants for the wind to go between his legs."

The verb "shanghai" had its origin in San Francisco and is not in the cloudy circumstance of the noun "martini", which *may* have originated here. What it meant was clearly defined as early as 1855 in a lecture in Portsmouth Plaza by the Reverend William Taylor. (A handsome, tapered skyscraper near City Hall was named for the reverend in 1930; it is now part of Hastings Law School, but was originally a Methodist hotel.) Taylor, author of *Seven Years Street Preaching in San Francisco*, published in 1856, explained to his listeners that sailors in San Francisco in the early 1850s preferred short voyages — they did not want to go to Shanghai. A run up to Oregon, or what were then called the Sandwich islands, or Callao or Valparaiso was fine, because they were at the moment miners and they needed a payday before they went back to the mines. Winter had come and they were down from the foothills and mountains — too much rain, mud, and flooding in the placers.

However Shanghai was increasingly becoming the destination of the big California clippers after they had arrived via Cape Horn and delivered their premium cargoes in San Francisco. Shanghai is at the mouth of the Yangtze river, 586 miles below Hankow, the center of a network of canals extending throughout China. The port handled a mass of varied cargoes, and became famed for speed in loading, a prime consideration in the battle of the British versus American clipper ships for the record passage to London each year. The tea trade paid a large premium to the earliest arrival.

The trouble with Shanghai as a destination — if you were a sailor turned temporary miner and on the beach in San Francisco — was that the big clipper ships kept on going. They went on around the world; they didn't come back to the Golden Gate short of another circumnavigation. So dirty work was necessary in sailortown to fill out their crews.

A quarter century later San Francisco had a new bizarrerie to boast of — except boast is not the right word. It too preyed on men of the sea. The San Joaquin valley had become bread basket to North Europe and sailing ships to almost rival the numbers that came in the Gold Rush, certainly to exceed them in tonnage, came to carry away the harvest.

"To San Francisco and Portland now flocked the largest and best sailing vessels of all the maritime nations of the world. Grain was a treacherous cargo, liable to shift to one side, if loaded in bulk, and always imposing a severe strain on the hull that conveyed it. Only the strongest and most powerful ships and the boldest and most experienced seamen were fit for the fourteen-thousand-mile voyage around the stormy Cape."*

Portland's role in the grain trade bloomed toward the end of the century, later than the period of which we are speaking; it was not on a scale to equal San Francisco's. No fewer than 547 sailing ships assembled within the Golden Gate to carry the grain harvest of 1881 around Cape Horn.

And where did the sailors come from to man this vast flotilla?

From the well-organized and brutal industry previously mentioned, dealing in sailor's live bodies. It was obscenely profitable, fleecing the sailor of his inbound accumulated wages, taking a mortgage on most of his outbound wages, and demanding of the captain $40 or so "blood money" per man to even put the sailor on board.

Five hundred and forty seven ships, each with a crew of, say, twenty five . . . sometimes half the crew in flux, "worked off", deserting, leaving the ship for one reason or another . . . money to be made on them, new men to be supplied at a price.

The sailor had economic slavery under the system and perpetual poverty. He was usually working to pay off a "debt".

San Francisco was the crimping capital of the world. Let's take a look at how the system worked. This is an account by Frederick Perry, mate on an arriving down-Easter, the *Continental*, in 1876. It was published in a little-known book called *Fair Winds & Foul*:

"We soon rounded Fort Point, opening up the Presidio on our right, and then headed over for our

* Winthrop L. Marvin, *The American Merchant Marine*, New York, Charles Scribner's Sons, 1902.

anchoring ground off Alcatraz Island . . . All fore and aft sails were now quickly hauled down, unbent and stowed away in the lockers. On the signal from the tug we let go our anchor and once more were tied fast to mother earth. A fleet of small boats quickly surrounded us, manned by a loud-mouthed lot of boarding-house runners, who swooped down like birds of prey, quickly to befog the brains of our crew by feeding them with a vile concoction of whisky that soon produced a half-drunken stupor, in which condition they were taken ashore and were soon robbed of the few hard-earned dollars they might have coming to them.

"When this was accomplished, and it was usually only a matter of two or three days, they shipped the men out again.

"It was one of the strict rules of the ship that no runners should be allowed on deck until all the work was finished and the crew dismissed, but it took a strong man armed with a heavy oak heaver to keep the more persistent ones from clambering over the side. When held in check they threw small packages over the side of the ship containing bottles of their vile stuff and a couple of cigars with a printed card attached, setting forth in glowing terms the superior quality of the accommodation to be obtained at their particular house over that of their competitors, keeping up in the meantime a running line of talk that would put a ballyhoo man at a side show to shame.

"Calling in the most endearing terms to the men as they worked aloft or passed along the deck, they begged them in the name of all that is holy not to forget that Jackson's or Chandler's as their respective home might have been designated, was next to the Garden of Eden — the nearest to a perfect Elysium for poor, tired, overworked sailors that could be found on earth. And the strange part of it was that, after being skinned or half flayed alive in every port they entered, darned if the poor fellows, with but few exceptions, didn't believe what they were told.

"We now laid our yards square in man-of-war fashion, having had the men aloft put every gasket and rope in a neat condition, and then the final order for the voyage was given: 'All hands pump ship.' There was a grand rush of all hands to the pumps; the lanyards were quickly strung out on each side of the deck, and with a shout of 'heave,' the pump wheels began to spin. As the sound of the clanking plungers mingled with the notes of the well-known chantey, *Leave her, Johnny, leave her*, floated out across the bay, passengers and crews on the various vessels lined the rails and waved and cheered to the most graceful object that ever sailed the seas — an American Clipper ship.

"'Avast heaving and the crew was dismissed. The hungry runners now sprang over the rails and made a grand rush for their victims like the lions in the Colosseum. Within fifteen minutes the last sailor and his dunnage had gone over the side and the fleet of runners' boats headed away towards the city front and 'Liberty.' "

Now let us regard a common aftermath of the above. Basil Lubbock cites it in his account of the down-Easter *John McDonald*:

"This splendid three skysail-yarder, which was built and owned by Flint, and named after the famous designer, was kept 'shining and sailing' by that most capable Captain Storer.

"The following story is a typical example of the treatment of sailors by the crimps and boarding-house runners of San Francisco in the eighties and nineties. One morning the *Joseph B. Thomas* arrived, in San Francisco Bay from Liverpool, and anchored close to the *John McDonald*, which, with a cargo of wheat, was awaiting her crew. The anchor of the *Joseph B. Thomas* was hardly on the ground before her fo'c'sle crowd were being plied with the contents of black bottles and offered well paid jobs 'up country' or 'in a bar' by the runners of Alec Jackson and Billie McCarty, with the result that they and their bags were soon on their way to the shore in the runners' boats.

"It so happened that Mrs. Lermond and Mrs. Storer were relatives, and on the following morning the third mate and two of the remaining hands on the *Joseph B. Thomas* rowed Mrs. Lermond and her children across to the *John McDonald* to visit her relation. The scene that greeted the visitors as they pulled alongside brought the blood to the face of the indignant third mate, for up the gangway of the outward bounder practically the whole of the *Joseph B. Thomas's* late crew were being bundled by the runners. Most of these unfortunate hands were Scandinavians, and were more or less unconscious, drugged or drunk, but two of them, Steve Brodie, of Yarmouth, Nova Scotia, and Charlie McDonald, of Prince Edward Island, two superb 'blue-nose' sailors, were not so far gone, and began to object to the rough handling of the runners, and there and then, in front of Mrs. Lermond and her children, these two fine sailormen had their faces pounded to a jelly with knuckle-dusters and slung shot. Later in the same day Mrs. Lermond waved a sad good-bye to her late shipmates as she went over the side. The *John McDonald* was getting under way, and the men, who had only just arrived after a long passage in the *Joseph B. Thomas*, were walking wearily round the capstan of the outward bounder, and bravely trying to put some warmth into the chorus, 'Good-bye, fare you well, Juliana, my dear.' "

High time for a Sailors' Union and that is the story Stephen Schwartz tells in this book. Interestingly, the Union gained its formative strength from the coasting sailors, not from the deep-water men described in the above incidents. The deep-water men were enrolled later. It was the coasting sailors with their acquaintanceship, short voyages, and ethnic similarity, who made solidarity possible.

Victory did not come easy.

Throughout the '90s, in particular, the war raged on the City Front:

"Broken heads, rainbow lined eyes and battered countenances are more numerous now along the bilgy byways of the docks than ever before. In fact one of the fraternity who does not sport a countenance that bears some sign of a melee or an arm supported in a sling is looked upon as one who takes but little interest in this business."

San Francisco Call, October 17, 1894

The depression of 1893 made slippery footing on which to fight a determined Shipowners' Association, 45 companies strong. The Association had employed a refined kind of thug by the name of Williams to destroy the union — Williams was crippled a bit when a letter he wrote found its way into the columns of the *San Francisco Examiner*. It said, "A dose of cold lead has a wonderful effect in quieting disorders . . ."

But the struggle took its toll. Seven years after its founding the Union was reduced to a quarter of its membership. However it was led by men of principle (and literacy) and Andrew Furuseth and Walter Macarthur fought back. Seven years later again saw the Union recognized by the shipowners — there was too much skill there, and stubborness, to destroy.

A word wants to be said about the life at sea, particularly on the sailing ships of the time. I cannot believe that these men of spirit found it untrammeled misery. Furuseth was a defender always of the craftmanship of the sailor — that is, of seamanship — from his time in these vessels. Macarthur wrote a useful handbook, *Last Days of Sail on the Pacific Coast; San Francisco Harbor.* He headed a committee in 1935 to preserve the bark *Star of Finland* as a memorial to the sailing ships. Macarthur had sailed before the mast in the down-Easter *Parker M. Whitmore.*

The effort to preserve the *Star of Finland* didn't work and six years later she made a passage around Cape Horn with a cargo of lumber and I was before the mast. I liked the life and after 127 days at sea was sorry in a way to see the voyage come to an end. Liking the life didn't prevent my organizing with a shipmate named Tom Soules a walkout over wages that saw the whole crew locked up in His Majesty's Gaol, Hobart, Tasmania.

I fancy the same spirit was to be found aboard the down-Easter *A. J. Fuller* making a voyage from new York to Honolulu in 1898 as recorded in Felix Riesenberg's *Under Sail.*

"Our oilskins were in shreds, boots leaked, and every stitch of clothing in the ship was damp, except when dried by the heat of our bodies. Had I been told of this before starting out — well, I suppose I would not have believed it — and, when I say that during it all we had a fairly good time and managed to crack jokes and act like a lot of irresponsible asses, it goes to prove that man was born to be kicked; be he on a sailing ship around the Horn, on the hard edge of the Arctic littoral, or in the bloody trenches; fate is always there to step in and deliver the necessary bumping."

Oilskins in shreds . . . and cracking jokes! A kick by fate is one thing. A kick by your fellow man is something else. That is the time to organize.

Acknowledgements

The writing of this book has been a humbling experience. To begin with, I have learned more than I ever thought I could about what a labor organization means to its members and to the community. Further, I have had to learn the lesson of the serious author — and the historian — in finding that many events, both dramatic and significant, could not be treated with the amplitude I would have liked. Those scholars who later take up this subject will find many themes that should be pursued in greater detail than was possible here.

The Sailors' Union of the Pacific history project began in 1983. With regard to the book itself, many individuals, both inside the Union and among the general public, helped in the writing and editing. To list all of them would mean, probably, the addition of a new chapter.

I regret I must therefore restrict my acknowledgements to those who played the most prominent roles in this effort. First, of course, was Paul Dempster, the current president/secretary-treasurer of the S.U.P., who proved a faithful friend and a trustworthy employer.

Karl Kortum, of the National Maritime Museum in San Francisco, who read the manuscript very closely and who provided innumerable suggestions for its improvement (nearly all of which have been accepted), as well as counseling me on illustrations and writing a valued introduction, was probably my most important direct collaborator.

The full manuscript was also read and, in effect, edited by Jack Henning of the California Labor Federation; I extend my thanks and my warmest regards to both these fine men.

I owe a great debt to Ottilie Markholt, the preeminent historian of Pacific Coast maritime unionism. Ottilie was a genuine inspiration for me.

Important expressions of support came from a number of leading scholars in the field of worldwide labor history. Professor Pierre Broué of the University of Grenoble kindly edited the two chapters on the 1934 strike, while preparing that section of the book for translation and publication in French. Professor Paul Avrich of Queens College, New York, read the first two chapters and gave needed advice on the direction of my research on the International Workmen's Association (of San Francisco and Denver). Professor Pietro Ferrua of Lewis and Clark College, Portland, Oregon, another student of the I.W.A., similarly helped. It is my sincere hope that the works of Professor Avrich on Sigismund Danielewicz and of Professor Ferrua on William C. Owen will gain the necessary opportunities for further development and publication.

Individuals who read sections of the work and offered significant commentary included Professor Robert Cherny, of San Francisco State University; Professor Bruce Nelson, currently of Dartmouth College, New Hampshire, and several members of the S.U.P. Thanks are also due John Durham, San Francisco's leading bookseller to the radical and labor movement, for help in obtaining research materials, and S.U.P. staff members Doris Prince, Betty Andrews, and Betty Tinsley, who retyped my admittedly abominable first drafts. Proofreading, indexing, and numerous other editorial "odd jobs" were handled with care and despatch by my dear friend Lawrence V. Cott. In addition, of course, Karl Kortum and I enjoyed the help of his staff colleagues at the National Maritime Museum in assembling the illustrations.

Acknowledgements must also go to the staffs of the following research institutions; the Bancroft Library, University of California, Berkeley; the Hans Kelsen Graduate Social Science Library, University of California, Berkeley; the Hoover Institution Library, Stanford; the Houghton Library, Harvard University, Cambridge; the Oregon State Historical Society, Portland; the University of Washington, Seattle; the New York Public Library; the Tamiment Library, New York University; the Institute for Contemporary Studies, San Francisco; the Anne Rand Memorial Research Library, International Longshoremen's and Warehousemen's Union, San Francisco, and the Paul Hall Library, Seafarers' International Union, Piney Point, Md.

Finally, thanks for encouragement in "the difficult hours" go, above all, to my companion Rebecca Long.

Stephen Schwartz

San Francisco, June 1986

CHAPTER I
The Lookout of the Labor Movement
(1885)

The Coast Seamen's Union, which was to become the Sailors' Union of the Pacific, AFL-CIO, was founded on March 6, 1885, with a call for labor organization — the "Sailors' Declaration of Independence" — from a lumber pile on the Folsom Street Wharf in San Francisco.

But the history of the Sailors' Union really should begin with the forebears of two leading ethnic groups among the seamen who have made up the organization; with the Polynesian seafarers who crossed the Pacific 3,000 years ago, in one of the greatest explorations of the human epic, and with the Scandinavians who, after adding a series of glorious chapters to European history, contributed a legion of tough, independent-minded fighters to the armies of the American working class.

The Polynesians

Polynesians were the first sailors in the Pacific. In his beautiful book *Voyage: The Discovery of Hawaii,* artist-historian Herb Kawainui Kane presents the probable chronology of the great Polynesian migration. Beginning around 1,100 years before Christ's birth, the ancestors of the modern islanders spread out from an unknown origin point, perhaps in the Indonesian region, to Samoa and Tonga, the cradle of Polynesian civilization.

Then, 2,000 years ago, a second surge carried the canoe-borne people to Tahiti and the Marquesas, which became, in turn, the new cultural and spiritual center of the race. Later yet, around 700 A.D., Rapa Nui (Easter Island), the Hawaiian chain, and New Zealand were settled. To the far west, people speaking a language related to the Polynesian family made landfall on Madagascar, off Africa in the Indian Ocean.

The Polynesians carried out these achievements thanks to their extensive and refined navigational technique. As explained by Kane, celestial navigation was preserved among the Polynesians by a *kahuna* brotherhood of experts, who kept star maps and used the major compass points, the horizon, the celestial equator, latitude, longitude, the zenith, star groupings, star names, lunar phases and the apparent movement of the sun.

At sea, the masters of Polynesian canoe navigation operated with dead reckoning by alignment with visible landmarks. They could guide a canoe by following starpath bearings, compensating for leeway and the set of the current; leeway was figured by the angle of the vessel's centerline and wake.

Polynesian starpaths were tracked along successive stars, rising or setting, toward which the canoe was steered in the direction of a known destination. As each star rose too far above the horizon to be used, or set out of sight, a following star was selected as a new reference point.

The island men also navigated by ground swells, generated by trade-winds and storms. Kane explains that "during a voyage, as the last guiding star faded, or the sky became overcast, Polynesian navigators noted the ratio of pitch to roll induced by the dominant swell, and they maintained their courses by keeping this ratio constant until the same familiar stars appeared."

(Swells from the bow or stern of a vessel cause the phenomenon of pitch, while rolling is produced by the action of swells abeam of a ship. When a vessel moves at a diagonal angle to a swell, pitching *and* rolling occur.)

Plotting latitude by zenith stars, the Polynesians made long north-south voyages between Hawaii and Tahiti. Stars passing directly over an island appear to pass directly over all positions due east or due west of that island, Kane points out. Since longitude cannot be determined without a chronometer, the Polynesians had to guess east-west bearings, allowing for error by sailing well upwind of the destination island. When the zenith star for an island passed directly overhead, they knew their latitude was correct. They then turned downwind, checking the star's position as it passed through the zenith each night until the destination was reached.

The Polynesian sailors continuously observed more than 150 stars. In addition to celestial methods, they also navigated by land signs, watching for birds, clouds, light effects, and other indicators.[1] Born of the sea and nourished by it, the Polynesian peoples produced descendants known as excellent seamen in modern ships — and proud Union men.

Dana: The Hawaiians in California

Richard Henry Dana, a New England university student, after shipping out in the hides trade to Mexican California in the 1830s, contributed an important record of the terrible conditions that could be suffered by seamen under the American flag, in his classic book *Two Years Before the Mast.* Although Dana enjoyed the seaman's life, and his book is hardly a cover-to-cover complaint, his description of a flogging aboard the brig *Pilgrim* was dramatic and horrible. But aside from his testimony against brutality, Dana's magnificent narrative is also valuable for its presentation of life on the California shore in the days when Mexico, Russia, and Britain, as well as the United States, were vying for Pacific domination. Among many interesting scenes, Dana describes the California colonies of Hawaiian boatmen, who also served as guardians for stored hides. "There are so many of them on the coast of California," wrote Dana, noting that they were "very good hands in the surf." The "considerable trade" that had been maintained for years between California and Hawaii, even then, saw "most of the vessels manned with islanders," who also "let themselves out to cure hides at San Diego, and to supply the places of the men of the American vessels while on the coast. In this way, quite a colony of them had become settled at San Diego, as their headquarters." Dana spent four months ashore as a hide-curer with the Polynesians. The traditional ethnic diversity of seafaring men was demonstrated at Dana's San Diego hide depot, where "we had now, out of forty or fifty, representatives from almost every nation under the sun: two Englishmen, three Yankees, two Scotchmen, two Welshmen, one Irishman, three Frenchmen, one Dutchman, one Austrian, two or three Spaniards (from old Spain), half a dozen Spanish-Americans, two native Indians from Chile, one Negro, one Mulatto, about twenty Italians, from all parts of Italy, as many more Sandwich Islanders [Hawaiians — SAS], one Tahitian, and one Kanaka from the Marquesas Islands."[2]

The Nordics

From the other side of the earth, the navigating tradition and exploring feats of the Scandinavian peoples are known world-wide; indeed, the name *viking,* originally meaning a "man of the creeks," according to the British historian T.K. Derry, has come to symbolize both the sea-rover and the Nordic. Every educated person today knows the story of Leif Eriksson, who explored the North American mainland in the period around 1000 A.D., sailing first to the wooded regions of "Markland," probably the Labrador coast, and then to the mysterious "Vinland," which has been identified with a range of sites from Newfoundland to Massachusetts. In the last two decades these semi-legendary exploits, as recorded in the *Vinland Saga,* have been given added support in the established history of the New World by the excavation of a Norse settlement at L'Anse-aux-Meadows in Newfoundland, thanks to the efforts of a Norwegian amateur archaeologist, Helge Ingstad.

During the nineteenth century, as the United States began to grow, Scandinavia contributed a major leaven of its sons and daughters to the new republic. Directly after the American Civil War and the opening of the Western prairies under the Homestead Act, one out of 10 newcomers to the United States was Scandinavian. In 1881-85 and 1901-05, during two crucial periods in the history of the Coast Seamen's Union and the Sailors' Union of the Pacific, Scandinavian immigration expanded, and by 1910 the U.S. Census showed 1,200,000 Swedes, 800,000 Norwegians, 330,000 Danes and Icelanders, and 200,000 Finns.[3] While many of the Scandinavians were attracted by free farm land in the American West, a large minority came as seafarers. For nearly all, the chief motive for leaving Europe was economic, with America promising opportunity for the manual worker and tradesman, as well as the farmer. In the "old country," a man often had little chance at any kind of decent work, to say nothing of a respectable compensation. Political and other great events, such as famines, also drove young Scandinavians to America. Some fled from military and other harsh obligations. Finns came across the sea to escape the Imperial Russian regime.

Derry outlines the progress of Scandinavian migration through the 19th century, from the rural areas, to the cities, and then across the seas. The Nordics who came to man the ships and to till the soil in America brought with them a distinct political consciousness, ranging from what today would be called liberalism to the radical theories of socialism and syndicalism. In the last half of the 19th century, the Scandinavian lands became a world center of progressive politics. The cause of Norwegian independence from Sweden influenced national movements among many other oppressed nations, including the Irish and the Poles. It is not surprising that Finland, while still Russian-controlled, was the first European country to extend the vote to women, in 1907. In the rise of the labor and social democratic parties in Europe, Scandinavia played a major role through the Norwegian Labor Party, and the Swedish, Danish, and Finnish Social Democratic parties. The Scandinavians, courageous, principled, and avid for their own and their children's education, were destined to provide the backbone of the Sailors' Union of the Pacific.

Similar to the Scandinavians in their strong working class consciousness was another ethnic group, prominent in maritime affairs on the West Coast, and likewise involved in the organizational affairs of the

[1]Data on Polynesian navigation derived from Herb Kawainui Kane, *Voyage*, Honolulu, Island Heritage, 1976. [2]Richard Henry Dana, *Two Years Before The Mast*, available in numerous editions. [3]T. K. Derry, *A History Of Scandinavia*, Minneapolis, University of Minnesota Press, 1979.

Sailors' Union: these were the Germans, who represented an important dynamic element in immigration to America. Many were political refugees, forced to leave their native land by the revolutionary events that took place there at the end of the 1840s; many others came across the Atlantic in disgust with anti-Socialist legislation imposed in Prussia in the latter decades of the 19th century.

A Meeting Place

The Polynesians and Nordics came together in California. The maritime exploration of the California littoral began with the conquest of Mexico by the Spanish. The conquistador Hernán Córtes marched to the Gulf of California, and the peninsula of Lower (Baja) California was soon extensively colonized by Spanish church missions, first administered by the Jesuits, and then by the Dominicans. The coast of Upper (Alta) California remained more or less neglected until the end of the 18th century, when the Russians, having established their Siberian imperial enterprise, began voyaging into the Pacific. In response to the threatened capture of the California Indians by the Russian Orthodox rather than the Catholic faith, the Spanish in Mexico decreed the establishment of missions and military outposts, or presidios, north from San Diego to San Francisco Bay. Missionary activities in Upper California were directed by the Franciscans.

As noted by Dana, by the 1830s the California coast, then controlled by the independent government of the Mexican Republic, was the scene of a thriving trade in hides and tallow, with the merchants of Boston trading in American bottoms. As early as the 1780s, New England navigators had sailed the Northwest Coast, opening an international fur trade, which continued for forty years. With discovery of the "Japan grounds" in the 1820s, American whalers started penetrating the Pacific, with hundreds of ships, and years before the Gold Rush, flocking to Lahaina and Honolulu. Hawaii became the "emporium of the Pacific," where all trade centered; the sea lanes between Hawaii and California were increasingly used by Yankee traders, smuggling as often as not.

Development of trade with China, always a leg in the voyages of Boston's "Nor'West men" (the Chinese paid a high price for furs), attracted even more American ships. Between 1846 and 1848, control of the northerly Mexican-held territories, including California, passed outright to the United States.

Condition of Seamen

In the hides trade, on the whaling ships, and in the trade with China, the lot of the American seaman was often unenviable. Wages were low, food was bad, and quarters were inadequate.

The deteriorating condition of stores (food supplies) on a long voyage and the cramped quarters on what we would regard as tiny vessels, were common and unavoidable. Carl Cutler, in his classic *Greyhounds of the Sea,* states that at the beginning of the 19th century, few of our ships "exceeded 300 tons burden or attained a length of 90 feet." Yet they regularly and in great numbers voyaged over the face of the earth's oceans. Another maritime historian, W.B. Meloney, notes that "on December 31, 1789 (six years since the end of the Revolutionary War), the U.S. had 123,893 tons of shipping in deep-water commerce, which was carrying 17 percent of its exports. (Seven years later) the tonnage had increased to 576,733 tons, and American bottoms were transporting 94 percent of the imports and 90 percent of the exports." Meloney further declares that "the growth of the American merchant marine during this period is without parallel in the history of commerce."

Poor food and cramped quarters may have been beyond alleviation, but that was not the case with wages, and the enterprising Yankee shipowners, who were showing the world what a merchant marine could be, were confronted with enterprising American sailors. The following account of a maritime strike is taken from the Baltimore *Federal Gazette* of April 11, 1800: "A large mob of sailors who had turned out for higher wages, and were parading the streets of Fell's Point on Monday, in riotous confusion, made an attempt after dark to board and rifle a vessel belonging to Messrs. David Steward & Sons, on board which it is said men had entered at $18 per month. Their design being learnt, several citizens put themselves on board, to defend her in case of necessity, from the ravages of the mob, who seemed bent on mischief, and approached with drums and fife, and colors flying. As they attempted to get on board they were opposed, when a severe conflict ensued, and notwithstanding the vessel lay close alongside the wharf, they were three times repulsed, with broken heads and bloody noses. Mr. David Steward, Mr. J. Beeman, and several others who were on board, we learn, were very considerably wounded, but — fortunately no lives were lost."

Dana's *Two Years Before the Mast* was the first widely-read book to expose the brutality of life aboard Yankee vessels. His unforgettable description of the flogging of the seaman Dana called "Sam," followed by that of Dana's friend, "John the Swede," who suffered only for having questioned Sam's punishment, scandalized the nation. Dana tells of the maniacal captain screaming, "If you want to know what I flog you for, I'll tell you. It's because I like to do it! — Because I like to do it! — It suits me! That's what I do it for!" To an America as yet unaccustomed to what would today be called a sadistic sexual perversion, such a spectacle was frightful. Dana's account of shipboard cruelty was the earliest major protest against the physical abuse of seamen under the U.S. flag. It was not to be the last.[4]

---

[4]Carl Cutler, *Greyhounds of the Sea*, New York, G.P. Putnam's Sons, 1930; W.B. Meloney, *The Heritage of Tyre*, New York, The Macmillan Company, 1916; the Baltimore reference is taken from Peter B. Gill (and Ottilie Markholt), *The Sailors' Union of the Pacific, 1885-1929*, unpublished manuscript, Bancroft Library, University of California, Berkeley, on which see, further, chapter II, note 8; Dana, op. cit.

Dana's *Two Years Before the Mast* first appeared in 1840. In 1846, the Irish-born writer J. Ross Browne published *Etchings of a Whaling Cruise,* another literary landmark in the struggle against shipboard brutality. Browne's account, which was a major source for Herman Melville in the writing of *Moby Dick,* includes a number of incidents of unjustified, capricious, violent punishment of seamen by apparently-crazed officers.[5] Melville himself commented eloquently on the life of the American seafarer under the rule of Yankee fists in his *Typee,* which appeared the same year as Browne's book: "The usage on board was tyrannical; the sick had been inhumanly neglected; the provisions had been doled out in scanty allowance; and her cruises were unreasonably protracted. The captain was the author of these abuses; it was in vain to think that he would either remedy them, or alter his conduct, which was arbitrary and violent in the extreme. His prompt reply to all complaints and remonstrances was the butt-end of a handspike, so convincingly administered as to effectually silence the aggrieved party."[6]

The labor historian Ira B. Cross, in his article on "First Coast Seamen's Unions" published in 1908, justly commented that "it is impossible to do justice to the brutality shown to the sailors in those days." Along with the reign of cruel mates and masters, known as "buckoes," the seamen were afflicted by a legal status that made them virtual slaves. Cross points out that in the years before the discovery of gold in California, sailors from the hide and tallow ships that tied up at the southern end of San Francisco Bay routinely jumped ship, an act deemed criminal, under the heading of "desertion," by the civil authorities in California ports, who were anxious to maintain good relations with the sailors' employers. An ordinance was passed in October 1847 in San Francisco, prescribing six months of hard labor for desertion, with a $50 bounty for each captured runaway sailor.

The discovery of gold in 1848 created a "marvelous change" in California, Cross declares. Hundreds of ships were abandoned in the ports as the men, often including officers, headed for the mines. Anti-desertion ordinances fell into disuse and sailors' wages rose on vessels heading back to the East. In August 1850, the first San Francisco seamen's strike took place, following a wage cut (to $25 per month) imposed as the ranks of prospective crew members filled with disillusioned miners anxious to return home. For three days, strikers marched through San Francisco, headed by a drum corps with an American flag. The strike was defeated by the excess number of failed treasure-hunters turned strikebreakers.

The first West Coast attempt at union organization of seamen came in 1866, with the setting up in San Francisco of the Seamen's Friendly Union and Protective Society, with Alfred Enquist as president and George McAlpine as secretary. However, the union could not be maintained for long because its members could not support a shoreside organization while they shipped.[7]

In addition to the "bucko" brutality visited on the American seamen, there were other grievous forms of oppression: "crimping", "blood money", and the practice of "shanghaiing". But the crimes of bucko officers were the sparks that first and foremost inflamed the mind of the sailor and, at times, the public. The violence of the officers has been explained away as the consequence of shipping with sailors who, having been shanghaied, might prove to be tailors, or butchers, or clerks, and whose uselessness aboard a vessel was often only exceeded by the danger they represented to others. The men couldn't or wouldn't work, the theory goes, and the officers duly vented their rage on them.

An answer to this false version of the story was definitively provided in 1895 by *The Red Record*, a publication listing notorious cases of brutality aboard U.S. ships, in which the Sailors' Union argued that " 'the system' . . . originated and is maintained upon the theory that brutal ships' officers can by threats and violence compel a small crew to do the work of the larger number of men required under a just system," thus permitting economies in wage payments.

In a sense, the story of the fight against the bucko system belongs further along in the Sailors' Union of the Pacific story, for it was only at the end of the 19th century, years after the Union's foundation and in the period when the Union was testing its growing strength, that the full horror of the Yankee "hell ships" was brought to the attention of the American people.

Legal Servitude

Undoubtedly, the most outrageous aspect of the brutal past oppression of American seamen was the complete lack of any means for redress of grievances. Basing themselves in traditional maritime custom, as it then existed worldwide, the U.S. shipowners, to emphasize, maintained the seafarer in a state of barely-disguised servitude. As Paul S. Taylor, author of the first major history of the Sailors' Union of the Pacific (published in 1923), wrote, "the revolutions and emancipating decrees of Europe, and the thirteenth amendment in the United States (which abolished Black slavery) passed the sailor by. The passage of time . . . not only failed to remove his bondage to the vessel but statutory enactment further stamped his status as peculiar and unfree."[8]

As long ago as 1790, the new government of the United States legislated the arrest, imprisonment, and

[5]J. Ross Browne, *Etchings Of A Whaling Cruise*, Cambridge, Harvard University Press, 1968; also, Richard H. Dillon, *Shanghaiing Days*, New York, Coward McCann, 1961. [6]Herman Melville, *Typee*, available in numerous editions. [7]Material on early unions is almost entirely based on Ira B. Cross, "First Coast Seamen's Unions:" in *Coast Seamen's Journal* (San Francisco), July 8, 1908. In general, Cross is invaluable; however, a comparison of some of his statements with such primary sources as the Coast Seamen's Union Minutes, a handwritten record kept in the Sailors' Union of the Pacific's central Archive, reveals inaccuracies in Cross's scholarship. For example, Cross asserts that the Coast Seamen's Union was originally known as the "Coasting Sailors' Protective Association," although the title "Coast Seamen's Union" appears in the Minutes beginning with the meeting of March 14, 1885. [8]Paul S. Taylor, *The Sailors' Union Of The Pacific.* New York, Ronald Press Co., 1923.

return to their ship of "deserting" sailors. The 1872 Shipping Commissioner's Act reinforced this degrading rule. Taylor states that "in recognition of the peculiar status of seamen, modern maritime nations . . . regarded them as 'wards of admiralty' incapable of making a freeman's contract, and deserving special care from their guardian, the state . . . with the exception of the rate of wages, the life of the sailor from the moment of signing articles to the time of paying off (had) always been regulated by law to the minutest detail. Only the power of self-help and self-protection has been denied. Workmen ashore have long been free to quit work, thereby incurring . . . no criminal liability, for that would smack of involuntary servitude. On the other hand, the very word 'deserter' applied to the sailor who quits his ship implies a different status."[9]

What means of protest were available to the seamen who suffered under the tyranny of the bucko system? It has become a commonplace of maritime and labor history that many, if not most, of the so-called "mutinies" that took place during the period of the "hell ships" were actually work stoppages or strikes, rather than true mutinies. A representative example of a seafaring rebellion of the time is that of the mutiny on the American schooner *Jefferson Borden* sailing in mid-Atlantic waters, from New Orleans to London, on April 20, 1875, during which two mates were killed. The *Jefferson Borden* has come down to us as one of the very worst of the "hell ships," and the subsequent trial of the rebel seamen stirred great sympathy among the shoreside public. Ephraim W. Clark and George Miller, two seamen who were sentenced to death in the matter, saw their sentences commuted to life imprisonment by President U. S. Grant, with the nation's chief executive responding to appeals from the prosecuting attorney, jurors, and prominent citizens.

Nearly 20 years after the *Borden* affair, Ephraim Clark dictated the story of the mutiny to a Boston writer, William E. Crockett. Clark said that as soon as the vessel had sailed from New Orleans the captain, William Patterson, ordered a general search of crew members, with "all articles that could be used in any way for defense . . . taken charge of by the officers." Patterson then explained that having just paid a $500 fine for whipping seamen, he intended to take it out on the new crew. Remembering the brutal usages of this officer, Clark agonizingly asked what means of defense the country's lawmakers had given seamen, adding "do you know, you dwellers on land, what it means to the seaman if he makes an offer to defend himself from abuse?" Clark avers that the *Jefferson Borden* was unseaworthy, requiring much work, but "hard work and poor grub made things go slow." When Miller displeased one of the mates by his handling of lines, the two mates, who were cousins, began beating and kicking the sailor while "his companions had to be silent witnesses of such abuse." Soon after, the days turned even more grim, with the mates showering pieces of wood and belaying pins on the men and with one of the officers throwing a hatchet at Clark's head. Once, Clark having fallen overboard, a line was heaved to him but as he attempted to come back on deck, Captain Patterson threw him back into the water. Luckily, he was successfully rescued a second time.

The rage of the sailors finally exploded and, in a midnight fight, the two mates were killed and cast over the side. Captain Patterson shot Miller six times, Clark four times, and crippled another man. The crew members were driven by gunfire back into the forecastle with hot water pumped inside to force them out again. Then, shackled and handcuffed, they were chained to the deck amid the wash of green seas, until the wounded Miller and Clark were removed and chained to the pump brake and ordered to pump with "little kindnesses, such as spitting tobacco juice in their faces, slapping and striking them (as) a daily, yes, hourly, visitation . . . Their torture by the captain came to a stop only when their wounds became so offensive as to make it unpleasant for him to go near them. Nor were they even allowed a normal sleeping period. One man was taken away to 'rest,' triced up to a stanchion to sleep as best he could, while the other continued pumping. As Clark declared during the trial "it makes no difference what the government does to me. If it could hang me a dozen times over, it would be as nothing compared to what I have suffered."[10]

"Crimps" and Boarding Masters

As previously noted, in addition to their legal servitude and the brutality of bucko officers, the seamen had to contend with "land sharks," the "crimps" and boarding masters, parasites feeding on "blood money," and experts in shanghaiing.

The crimp, a middle-man between the shipping employer and the seaman, extorted payment for arranging a job. The system was simple: in many cases, the crimp collected "blood money" from the master of the ship which was then deducted from the seaman's pay as a spurious allotment. Payments to crimps, who swindled seamen "on the beach" (ashore) into accumulating large debts, could virtually wipe out a seaman's pay. The crimps were assisted by runners who went aboard newly-arrived ships to hustle men into particular boarding houses; a common incident was the pulling of men off ships during a swarming attack on the vessel and its officers by crimps and runners. Once in the crimp's hands ashore, the sailor often found himself shanghaied onto a new vessel by the next day. The day aboard a vessel when the seaman celebrated the final working-off of an allotment to a crimp might feature an elaborate ceremony with the destruction of a dummy, the "dead horse," symbolizing the burden that had been imposed on the mariner's income, and the singing of a traditional chantey, *The Dead Horse.*

---

[9]Taylor, op. cit. [10]William E. Crockett, "Jefferson Borden Mutiny", *Coast Seamen's Journal*, April 12, 1893.

Writing in 1895, a union advocate noted the differences between the varieties of parasites that were the seamen's bane: "The shipping master makes his living as a go-between for the crimp or boarding-master and the properly constituted authorities in the matter of shipping seamen. While his business is in effect the same as that of the crimp it differs in the respect that, while the crimp may or may not include the keeping of a boarding-house in his scheme of fleecing the seaman, the shipping-master confines himself to the business of collecting fees from the crimps and others who desire to put seamen in vessels under the shipping-master's control."

Historian Paul Taylor noted that the crimps organized before the sailors: "the deepwater boarding masters in the early 1860s, and later the coasting boarding masters, organized into associations to control the sailor market." Taylor goes on to describe how "the law allowing holding of sailors' clothing for debt strengthened this power" of the crimp over the seaman, and "the payment of wages in advance (to boarding masters allegedly owed large debts) made the business profitable. And because a sailor in a deepwater vessel was entitled to two, three, or four months' 'advance' and was especially helpless, (the deepwater) boarding masters were the first to gain control of their sailor market and the last to give it up. The coasting boarding masters were never so powerful, nor was their reign so long. But during the decades in which the boarding masters were in control, no master could get a crew except from the crimps and then only after paying them the sailors' advance," in lieu of or in addition to blood money. Taylor summarizes the oppression of the 19th century sailor by saying that "it all meant virtual economic slavery for the sailor and perpetual poverty, as he was usually working to pay off a 'debt.' "[11]

Impact of the West Coast Lumber Trade

But the comparative weakness of those West Coast crimps that mainly preyed on coastal (rather than deepwater) vessels, as stated by Taylor, seems to have been among the factors that made it easier for the first permanent seamen's union in the world, the Coast Seamen's Union, to be organized. One element undermining the hold of crimps on the West Coast was the short duration of voyages; the coast seamen were in their home ports more often, where they built up friendships and other relationships lessening their dependence on crimps. Another factor was the tremendous expansion of the West Coast lumber trade between the close of the Civil War and the end of the century. With the spread of settlement throughout the coast region, the demand for construction materials boomed so that while California had around 300 small sawmills working in the redwoods in 1860, in 1885 the Humboldt Bay area alone had 400. Redwood lumber was especially prized because of its fire-and-insect-resistant qualities. The construction of line-haul railroads into the redwood country would wait until the very last decade of the 19th century, so that soon after 1865 a respectable fleet of two-masted lumber schooners had begun operating between the North Coast and San Francisco. They were later supplemented by three- and four-masters and then by the steam schooners, a few of which were still in service in the 1950s.

Several characteristics distinguished seafaring labor in the lumber trade from seamen in general. First, the ethnic background was almost exclusively Nordic, giving the ships the nickname 'the Scandinavian navy.' Secondly, on the lumber ships the sailors worked cargo, in contrast with deepwater ships which were increasingly loaded and unloaded by "men along the shore," or longshoremen. The small lumber ports of the California and Northwest coasts had no longshoremen; in addition, the lumber vessels' cargo was usually loaded not only in the hold but to a considerable height on deck as well, and required frequent attention to the deck load lashings during the voyage. A breed of seafarer emerged from 'the Scandinavian navy' with skills difficult to replace in case of dismissal or strike. These skilled men commanded higher wage rates than deepwater men. Most importantly, as previously indicated, they had brought with them from Europe the labor and progressive consciousness that drew them to unionism. Their struggle for dignity and the good things of life on the distant shores of America paralleled the rise of the labor and social movements in their original homelands. Around this time, some 3,000 men were employed in Pacific Coast sailing vessels. Of them, 40 percent were Scandinavian, 11 percent Finnish, 10 percent German, 8 percent American, and the remainder other European nationalities. Some 50 percent were under 30, 25 percent 30 to 40, and the rest over 40.

The cause of seamen's rights on the Pacific Coast was also inadvertently made easier by a loophole introduced into the Shipping Commissioners' Act in 1874, and remaining in force until 1890. To save them time and money, vessel operators in the coastwise short-run trades were exempted from the requirement that men be hired before a shipping commissioner. Since seamen not shipped before a commissioner were freed of punishment for "desertion" if they quit, this loophole came to be used as a legal guarantee for protests in the form of work stoppages just before a ship was set to sail, a practice known later as "the oracle" and even later as "job action."[12]

Following the failure of the 1866 seamen's union movement, the field lay open until 1878 when a second attempt was made in San Francisco, the so-called

[11]A classic exposition of the operations of crimps, boarding-masters, and shipping masters is the series titled "Sailor Talk," appearing in the *Coast Seamen's Journal* (San Francisco), the organ of the Coast Seamen's Union and Sailors' Union of the Pacific, beginning in July 1895. The excerpt on shipping masters here quoted is from the issue of July 31, 1895. Also see Taylor, op. cit., and Dillon, op. cit. [12]Jack McNairn and Jerry MacMullen, *Ships Of The Redwood Coast*, Stanford, Stanford University Press, 1945; Gill and Markholt, op. cit.; Taylor, ibid.

"Seaman's Protective Union," set up with the questionable help of a number of boarding masters. The 1878 "union" was, however, mostly concerned with anti-Chinese agitation and the threat of the deepwater sailors to the coasting men's high wages and it, too, soon collapsed.

In 1880, as noted by Ira Cross, a group of steamship sailors and firemen, mainly under the aegis of Frank Roney, an Irish revolutionary and socialist with close ties to the anti-Chinese labor movement in San Francisco, made a third try at unionizing sailors under the title of the "Seamen's Protective Association." However, most of the leaders of the group, including Roney, were not seafarers. This third effort also had fallen apart by November 1882.[13]

March 1885: Coast Seamen's Union Founded

By March 1885, under severe depression conditions, seamen's wages had fallen to $20 per month for deepwater and $25 on the coast. The morning of March 3, 1885, in San Francisco, according to a version of the story put forward by Cross in 1908, Ed Andersen, a Norwegian, and George Thompson, a Swede, two seamen who were members of a radical labor group, the San Francisco-based "International Workmen's Association" (I.W.A.), began discussing the possibility of a seamen's strike for higher wages. They were joined by John Reade, a fellow sailor, and resolved to publish a newspaper notice calling on the seamen to strike. By the next morning, crews had begun walking off ships and were congregating on the city waterfront, talking over the situation. On the evening of March 4, a meeting was held on the Howard Street Wharf with a second assembly scheduled for Garibaldi Hall the night of March 5. Thanks to Andersen, Thompson, and Rasmus Nielson, a young Dane and, says Cross, also a member of the enigmatic radical group, the International Workmen's Association, the leading personality in the I.W.A., Burnette G. Haskell, a socialist lawyer and journalist, and P. Ross Martin, another I.W.A. leader, addressed the Garibaldi Hall meeting. The next meeting was set for the evening of March 6, on the Folsom Street Wharf, to organize a union of coasting sailors.

A slightly contrasting account of the circumstances behind the March 6 meeting is provided by a *Constitution and History* of the Coast Seamen's Union published soon after the event, in 1885. This earlier version states that on March 5, around noon, Sigismund Danielewicz, the corresponding secretary in the Italian language for the International Workmen's Association, passed by a crowd of striking sailors on the waterfront. Danielewicz had just returned from Hawaii where "he had been vigorously engaged in the labor struggle." Aside from his revolutionary activities with the I.W.A. and, apparently, some time as a coasting sailor, Danielewicz also contributed to the founding of a San Francisco barbers' union. The 1885 history states that Danielewicz suggested the sailors meet on the Folsom Street Wharf the next day, and promised to obtain speakers from the I.W.A.[14]

The night of March 6 a crowd of around three hundred met on the Folsom Street Wharf. George Thompson was prevailed on to act as chairman. The speakers were B.B. Carter and Joseph Kelly of the Steamshipmen's Protective Association, along with P. Ross Martin of the I.W.A. and the Knights of Labor, I.W.A. member J.J. Martin, Martin Schneider (I.W.A. corresponding secretary for the German language), Danielewicz, and Burnette G. Haskell.[15]

The first entry in the Minute Book of the Coast Seamen's Union, signed by J.J. Martin, reads as follows:

"Folsom St. Wharf San Francisco
March 6th 1885

"By general desire of those interested and at the call of George Thompson, R. Ni(e)lson and others a mass meeting of about 300 of the Coasting Seamen on strike was held at Folsom Street Wharf at 7:30 p.m. to consider a raise of wages from $25 per month to $30 per month for inside ports and from $30 per month to $35 for outside ports and also to consider what steps should be taken towards forming a permanent protective union.

"George Thompson was called to the chair.

"An organizing committee from the International Workmen's Association was present, viz. B.G. Haskell, Jos. Kelly, S. Danielewicz, M. Schneider, (P.R.) Martin and J.J. Martin.

"The meeting was addressed by various speakers who advocated unity of action and resistance to oppression in any and every form. Great enthusiasm prevailed.

"It was determined at once to form a permanent organization and at the suggestion of B.G. Haskell of the I.W.A. Committee, those who had pencil and paper proceeded to take the names and subscriptions of those who wished to form a union. Two hundred and twenty-two (222) names were enrolled and thirty-four 60/00-$34.60 were collected.

"It was then decided that the meeting adjourn until (tomorrow) Saturday eve at 7:30 p.m. the place of meeting to be Irish American Hall.

"B.G. Haskell of the I.W.A. Committee was instructed to take charge of the funds, secure the hall, and insert

[13]Data on ethnic and age groups from Gill and Markholt, op. cit. Cross, op. cit. Also, Minute Book of the Seamen's Protective Assn., 1880-82, S.U.P. central Archive. The activities of the 1880 Seamen's Protective Association have been treated somewhat extensively in Alexander Saxton, *The Indispensable Enemy*, Berkeley, University of California Press, 1971. However, Saxton's book, although well-intentioned, is flawed in the depth of its research and at a number of points in its analyses. Saxton depends excessively on Cross's sources, particularly Frank Roney, edited by Ira B. Cross, *Frank Roney, An Autobiography*, Berkeley, University of California Press, 1931, which is not free of errors. [14]Cross, "First Coast Seamen's Unions;" Roney and Cross, op. cit.; Coast Seamen's Union, *Constitution And History*, San Francisco, I.W.A. edition, 1885; Unsigned, *What The I.W.A. Is*, undated, (copy in the Bancroft Library, University of California, Berkeley); Paul Scharrenberg, *The Sailors' Union Of The Pacific*, unpublished ms., (1957?) in the Bancroft Library, University of California, Berkeley; Saxton, op. cit.; Ira B. Cross, *History Of The Labor Movement In California*, Berkeley, University of California, 1935. Cross himself eventually accepted Danielewicz as the main organizer of the March 6 meeting. Both versions have their attractions. The 1908 Cross version seems borne out by the C.S.U. Minutes, which Cross did not consult. [15]Cross, "First Coast Seamen's Unions," op. cit.

the necessary advertisements in the daily papers giving notice of the meeting and pay for same, also for all other necessary expenses.

"Before dispersing Three Cheers were given for the 'International' which was responded to by the I.W.A. Committee."[16]

To these eloquent words we might only add the details described by Cross: that rain fell upon the assembled sailors during the meeting but was ignored, and that the fiery speeches were delivered without the light of torches or lanterns, but with only the feeble glow of a few candles, rapidly quenched.

International Workmen's Association — Burnette G. Haskell

Before going directly on with the history of the sailors' organization created in San Francisco that rainy night, it is worthwhile to examine the background of the curious International Workmen's Association and its charismatic, although flawed leader, Haskell. Cross declares that Haskell was "the one man who more than all others aroused the enthusiasm of the sailors and made possible the formation of the union," adding that "when the history of the present Sailors' Union is written in detail, the author will, of necessity, give to this young enthusiast in the cause of labor, the greatest credit for its organization."[17]

Burnette Gregor Haskell was born in 1857 in Sierra County, California. His parents were well enough off to obtain for him an education in the law, but the young man proved too eccentrically idealistic to gain success in that profession, although he frequently defended unions and related "causes" in court. By 1882 he had come into contact with the ideas of socialism and anarchism and had created *Truth*, a radical labor newspaper. The organization of the I.W.A. was inspired by the International Working Men's Association — or "First International" — founded in 1864 by labor radicals linked to Karl Marx, but which had split in the early 1870s, thanks to Marx's war on the anarchist followers of the Russian revolutionary Mikhail Bakunin. After expelling Bakunin's followers at its congress in 1872, the Marxian wing of the First International was transferred to the United States where it held its last convention in 1876, with American delegates only. The Bakuninist wing continued to function as a rival organization, gaining thousands of members, particularly in Spain and Italy. In July 1881, in London, the Bakuninist faction reorganized, with significant American representation. In October of the same year, a Bakuninist congress was held in Chicago, resulting in an unstable and transitory organization. October 1883 saw yet another congress in Pittsburgh, Pennsylvania, at which a new group was organized, the International Working People's Association.

It appears that Haskell's I.W.A. was founded in San Francisco in about 1883 although a clear determination of the group's origins is made difficult by the lack of dependable written records. Labor historians Henry David and Chester M. Destler suggest Haskell's I.W.A. was founded in July 1881, following correspondence between Haskell and H. M. Hyndman, a British socialist, while Ira Cross first wrote that it was created in 1883 and then changed the date to 1882. But while we may be certain of rather little in the organization's chronological details, we know comparatively much about its outlook and activities.[18]

Haskell's San Francisco I.W.A. was founded in emulation of the "Marxian" wing of the original International, which Haskell thought would be reconstituted in 1885. (It was, ostensibly, in 1889.) Haskell's I.W.A. declared itself in at least a partial opposition to the Bakuninist I.W.P.A., with Haskell styling his group the "Red" as opposed to the "Black" Bakunin international. However, Haskell's group seems to have maintained only the most tenuous links with "official" Marxists, and sought to lay the basis for a united effort by the competing Marx and Bakunin factions. Thus, a small pamphlet titled *What the I.W.A. Is* (published without a date), advertises the book *Letters to Young People* (better known as *An Appeal to the Young*) by Peter Kropotkin, a Russian anarchist, along with *The Historical Development of Socialism in England and America* by Haskell, H. M. Hyndman, and William Morris, the great designer, writer, and social theorist. Haskell had also written an introduction to a book titled *Socialism*, by two members of the 1880 Seamen's Protective Association, A. J. Starkweather and S. Robert Wilson. This latter volume was published in 1884, the same year Haskell first met with some friends to discuss the possible foundation of a utopian socialist colony, a project that would prove a heavy burden on the young idealist.[19]

As pointed out by Cross, the Haskell I.W.A., "although appropriating the name of the First International and, although patterned along the lines of the two international groups," remained a local phenomenon of the Western United States. Unlike the groups on which it was modelled, its fealty to one or another factional doctrine, either Marxian or Bakuninist, was never strict. It asserted, in the words of a credo printed on the back of its entry-membership cards, that "the proletarians have nothing to lose but their chains. They have a world to win. Let therefore the workingmen of all countries unite! . . . Karl Marx. To each according to his needs. From each

[16]Coast Seamen's Union, Minutes, 1885-86, unpublished, held in the Sailors' Union of the Pacific central Archive, San Francisco. [17]Cross, "First Coast Seamen's Unions," op. cit. [18]On Haskell, I wish to express my appreciation to John Gerring, an undergraduate at the University of California, Berkeley, for help in locating important materials. See Joseph R. Buchanan, *The Story of a Labor Agitator*, New York, The Outlook Co., 1903; Henry David, *The History Of The Haymarket Affair*, New York, Russell and Russell, 1958; Chester M. Destler, *American Radicalism, 1865-1901*, New York, Octagon, 1965; Oscar Berland, "Aborted Revolution," M.A. thesis, San Francisco State College, 1966. William O. Reichert, *Partisans Of Freedom*, Bowling Green, Bowling Green University Popular Press, 1976; Paul Avrich, *The Haymarket Tragedy*, Princeton, Princeton University Press, 1984. Cross, "First Coast Seamen's Unions," op. cit., says the I.W.A. was founded in 1882; also see Roney and Cross, op. cit. Saxton, op. cit., gives the date of 1883. [19]Robert V. Hine, *California's Utopian Colonies*, New York, Norton, 1973. Also see Paul Kagan, *New World Utopias*, New York, Penguin, 1975.

according to his ability. No duties without rights. Educate, Organize, Agitate, Unite. Our motto: War to the Palace; Peace to the Cottage; Death to Luxurious Idleness. Our object: The reorganization of Society independent of Priest, King, Capitalist, or Loafer. Our principles: Every man is entitled to the full product of his own labor and to his proportionate share of all of the natural advantages of the earth."[20]

In its organizational system, the Haskell I.W.A. resembled the secret revolutionary societies organized in Europe between the French Revolution and the 1850s, with a conspiratorial method developed by Filippo Michele Buonarroti and Louis Auguste Blanqui. The membership was divided into groups of nine, with each individual pledged to form another group of nine. An individual member would only know a maximum of 16 others. Three grades of membership existed, denoted by cards of red (ordinary members), white (agitators), and blue (officers).

The extent of the membership of the Haskell I.W.A. is a matter for debate. Haskell tried to forge a unity pact with the other extremist labor groups in the United States in the early 1880s and his group seems to have attracted widespread interest and adherents. I.W.A. branches spread through Northern California, Oregon, and Washington, also penetrating the Rocky Mountain region where the Association was headed by Joseph R. Buchanan, an outstanding labor leader in Denver, Colorado. "The I.W.A. was more successful (than the competing 'Black' International group, the I.W.P.A.) in winning converts from labor ranks," says Henry David.[21]

The 1880s were marked by a level of labor radicalism in the United States that in most respects would never again be equalled. The first mass union movement, the Knights of Labor, shook the entire nation. Much of the skilled industrial working class in the United States was still German-speaking and, like the Nordics among the seamen, they had carried their political culture with them to the new world. The 'Black' I.W.P.A. and other groups actively encouraged workers to train in shooting and marching, in social clubs based on marksmanship, the *Schutz-Vereine* or *Lehr-und-Wehr Vereine*, a concept borrowed from Germany, and to adopt uniforms in preparation for class war.

But like the groups, often based on recent Central European immigrants, that appeared in the East, and which had at first urged immediate social revolution, the more "American" I.W.A. on the Pacific Coast seems to have quickly concentrated on building up the rising union movement, particularly the Knights of Labor, in which many including Haskell and Buchanan were active. Haskell's movement declared its goal to be "to assist and aid the organization of the Knights of Labor, the various Trades Unions, Granges, Farmers Alliances, and all other forms of organization in which the producers have organized, or may organize themselves, and after assisting such organization to aid in directing their future action on scientific, educational lines. In addition it is the object of the I.W.A. to print and circulate proper literature, to hold educational meetings and discussions; to systematize agitation; to maintain the labor press; to protect members from wrongs; to aid and assist all other toilers; to aid the establishment of unity and the maintenance of fraternity between all labor organizations upon the common ground of Truth; to aid an alliance between the industrial and the agricultural producers; to encourage the spirit of brotherhood and interdependence among all toilers in every state and land; to ascertain, segregate, classify, and study the enemies of the people, their motives, habits, and acts; to secure information of wrongs perpetrated against us, and to record and circulate the same; to arouse and maintain a spirit of hostility to, and social warfare against, and ostracism of, that portion of the capitalistic press which is in any way inimical to the labor movement; to obliterate sectional and racial prejudices, with a view to the International Unification of the producers of all lands."[22]

It was in the spirit of these ambitious claims that Haskell and the I.W.A. contributed generously to the foundation of the Coast Seamen's Union. Cross states that Haskell's I.W.A. reached the height of its popularity in the period just after the Union's formation, although soon declining. Haskell eventually turned from the public scene to a utopian community in Tulare County, the Kaweah Cooperative Commonwealth. What seems unarguable is that, in Cross's words, "these radicals . . . aided greatly in laying the foundations of the . . . California labor movement."

In some respects, Haskell's conception of revolutionary politics through union participation parallels the so-called "Chicago idea" described by social historian Paul Avrich in his recent *The Haymarket Tragedy*. Avrich traces the "Chicago idea" to the 1883 Pittsburgh convention that founded the I.W.P.A., at which a group of Chicago-based social revolutionaries put forward the concept of unions that would "shun political action, distrust all central authority, and guard against betrayals by self-important leaders. All . . . faith was to rest in the direct action of the rank and file." Avrich goes on to point out that the "Chicago idea" anticipated the emergence of "anarchosyndicalism" as a trend in labor politics a decade later. The Coast Seamen's Union arguably represented one of the most developed examples of this "idea," which was anything but limited to Chicago. In reality, the social convulsion that brought forward the "Chicago idea" was worldwide: a great global upsurge of working class protest had been in progress since, at least,

---

[20]Data on the I.W.A. are from the I.W.A. and Haskell family collections, Bancroft Library, University of California, Berkeley, and Cross, *History Of The Labor Movement In California*, op. cit. Also see David Selvin, *Sky Full Of Storm*, San Francisco, California Historical Society, 1975; Bruce Dancis, "Social Mobility and Class Consciousness: San Francisco's International Workmen's Association of the 1880s," in *Journal of Social History*, Fall 1977. [21]David, op. cit. On Haskell and Buchanan, also see Avrich, op. cit. [22]I.W.A. collection, Bancroft Library, and Cross, *History Of The Labor Movement In California.*

the Paris Commune of 1871, and the tide did not ebb until the mid-1890s. Trade unions had existed in the U.S. for decades, but the concept of a union that went far beyond the immediate economic needs of its members, and sought to become the vehicle for overall improvement of labor's role in society, seemed new. The fundamentals of this highly-conscious form of unionism would find, in the Coast Seamen's Union and its successor, the Sailors' Union of the Pacific, a continuing affirmation extending over a century, to the present. In this, the experience of the C.S.U. and S.U.P. in the American labor context is unique.[23]

Sigismund Danielewicz, the I.W.A. member whose name has always been associated with Haskell's in the foundation of the Coast Seamen's Union was, as we shall see, in some respects a more positive figure than Haskell himself, although much less is known about the bearded Pole. As a European, Danielewicz was, of course, closer than Haskell to old-world doctrinal socialism; but for all that, like Haskell, he contributed greatly to the Coast Seamen's Union. We should also take special note of the names of other I.W.A. figures among the leading Coast Seamen's Union pioneers, particularly James John Martin, Martin Schneider, William C. Owen, and Joseph R. Buchanan.

C.S.U. Continues Its Work

For some time after the March 6 meeting, the members of the new Coast Seaman's Union held meetings almost daily. The exhilaration of the moment, based on a determination to win the strike for higher wages, kept the sailors and their I.W.A. comrades constantly active. On the night of March 7th, the men once again met at Irish-American Hall. Haskell called for a committee to be formed that would visit all the coasting vessels in port to find out the number of their crews and their wage rates and to recruit for the Union. The motion was unanimously carried. Haskell then announced that an I.W.A. committee had already collected the names of all the coastwise ships in the harbor; further, he notified the members that he had some printed forms made up for the use of the committee. A large number of men volunteered to serve and appointments were duly made.

Haskell also suggested that a list of boarding houses be prepared and another committee appointed to visit them. Members were cautioned not to speak to outsiders about the business transacted in Union meetings. An offer by the I.W.A. committee to let the Union temporarily use an office rented by the radicals was accepted. At this second formal meeting 102 new members were enrolled.

A third meeting took place two days later in the same hall and, on a motion by Haskell, it was agreed that any boarding house or shipping office that shipped anyone not a Union member would be boycotted, with "hearty approval" for a complementary proposal to establish a Union shipping office. This was the beginning of the institution that would prove to be the cornerstone of the Sailors' Union of the Pacific: the hiring hall. A constitution written by Haskell was adopted after a reading and discussion. Speakers from the Longshore Lumbermen's Union, which claimed 300 members and a treasury of $7-8,000, addressed the meeting, with a reply by Haskell.

Haskell and J. J. Martin, his I.W.A. associate, had acted as, respectively, temporary treasurer and secretary beginning with the second meeting, on March 7th. At the fourth meeting, permanent officers were elected. George Thompson became the first president with Rasmus Nielson as secretary and Haskell continuing as treasurer. In accord with the constitution drawn up by Haskell, an advisory committee to the Union made up of I.W.A. members was also elected, consisting of Haskell, J. J. Martin, P. R. Martin, Martin Schneider, and Sigismund Danielewicz. It was also decided to divide up the San Francisco waterfront into six sections and to appoint patrolmen for each section. The patrolmen were authorized to procure boats for their work.[24]

Meanwhile, the strike continued. With the assignment of the six patrolmen, the Union soon was able to secure a raise to $30 per month from most of the ship operators. The Union's minutes reveal that by March 14 vessels were already departing San Francisco with full Union crews. Haskell was supported in a motion calling on the Union to accept all sailors, whether deepwater or not, but also told the membership that he had written to the principal European ports notifying sailors bound for the California ports that the coasting trade was now in Union hands. At the seventh meeting, on March 26th, a motion was passed to return to the boarding master, Fred Moller, a flag he had presented to the organization.[25]

The Coast Seamen's Union was on its way. In the weeks to come the high enthusiasm of the pioneering members kept meetings going at a rapid tempo. By the end of March, the Union reportedly had over 1,000 seamen enrolled. On April 1, at the eighth meeting, the members invited all "colored" seamen on the coast to join the organization. Plans for the establishment of the Union shipping office went forward under the direction of Haskell, Nielson, Edward Crangle, and D. C. Murray. Representatives of other nascent unions, including fishermen and steamship sailors, communicated with the Coast Seamen's Union requesting advice and assistance. On April 10th, the Union resolved to impose a $20 initiation fee on deepwater sailors who wished to join, adding that they must be proposed by two current members. On the 17th, it was agreed that the Union shipping master would send men to vessels in order of their time on the beach, with the oldest men "on the book" entitled to the first jobs. However, men were given the right to decline a berth without losing their place on the list. It was also

[23]Cross, ibid.; Avrich, op. cit. [24]Coast Seamen's Union Minutes, 1885-86, record cited. [25]Ibid.

noted, during the same meeting, that two Union members had been arrested in San Francisco and that an attorney had been retained to defend them.

Mention in the Union's *Minutes* of the two arrests is the first sign of the response from the entrenched interests on the San Francisco waterfront to the sailors' efforts at self-help. According to the 1885 *Constitution and History,* April saw a spell of harassment by the police, beginning around the 10th of the month, directed at Union sailors visiting ships to demand the removal of non-union men. The shipowners, the crimps, and the bucko officers recognized that a new spirit was alive on the coast and sensed that their dominion was threatened. The Union replied to the police attacks by calmly continuing its organizational business. Following the establishment of the basic shipping rules at the meeting of the 17th, the Union shipping office was opened at 7 Spear Street on April 20th. On April 21st, secretary Nielson recorded that with reports of further harassment and difficulties on the front, the members had agreed "that we would rather die in our tracks than retreat one inch."

With the Union less than two months old, lines of conflict were drawn. At the meeting of April 26th, the Union resolved to petition the Mayor and Board of Supervisors to withdraw a large contingent of extra police that had been posted on the waterfront. In concert with other union organizers in the city, including Frank Roney, the Union agreed to call a mass meeting to protest the police maneuvers. The May 12th meeting included a report of increasing non-union shipping. At that meeting Danielewicz spoke on the importance of opening a Coast Seamen's Union boarding house.

In May, the Union also moved to expand its influence by acquiring a Whitehall boat, a type of small, swift craft widely used on the Bay, for its officials to visit the ships as they entered the Golden Gate. Dubbed *The Union*, the boat was christened on May 31st and the Union boasted that it was the biggest Whitehall in service.[26] That month, the initiation fee for deepwater men was reduced from $20 to $17 in reaction to shipping of deepwater sailors by coasting captains. The deepwater men were presumed by the employers to be less susceptible to the Union's appeal, and the organization hoped that reduced dues would eliminate a potential pool of non-union "scabs."

In June, Union members in San Francisco learned that two San Pedro members had been arrested, tried, and sentenced to 90 days in jail for encouraging seamen to leave the schooner *Lillibone*. It was resolved that the officers of the Union should appoint agents in each of the coast ports where necessary. That month, however, the *Minutes* also show that Haskell had begun introducing what could be interpreted as elitist considerations into the Union's activities. In the meeting of June 15th, he proposed that a red card be issued to each member who had "showed themselves most prominent in the Union." Apparently, this demand for special recognition of a "vanguard" elicited no immediate support.

By July, the Union had established its first link with a fellow-organization in a foreign land: a regular correspondence was set up with the Federated Seamen's Union in New South Wales, Australia. At the same time the office of president was replaced by a board of six vice-presidents. The following month saw an event that although minor in its immediate effect was a herald of the future for the waterfront labor movement: "steps had been taken to federate all the waterfront unions," with each union to send three delegates to a San Francisco meeting early in September. The Coast Seamen's Union also called for a city-wide union convention to meet October 14th. Ferment in labor was matched at the time by increasing agitation on the so-called "coolie" issue, involving the importation of Asian laborers. In the meeting of September 28th, Haskell warned the Coast Seamen's Union of the danger that the "anti-coolie excitement" might promote unscrupulous demagogues. "He explained how one man could use his influence over a great body of men to ride himself into power," stated Rasmus Nielson's minutes.[27]

At the meeting of October 5th, Haskell and Nielson reported on a project that would, sadly, soon prove disappointing to some members of the Coast Seamen's Union. The two men had gone "to the country to secure some land which would give employment for a good many seamen who would otherwise be idle during the winter."[28] This was a first concrete step toward the hoped-for but elusive realization of a utopian scheme, the Kaweah Cooperative Commonwealth, which would bring disillusion and defeat for Haskell.

In outlining the creation of the Coast Seamen's Union, this weapon for the improvement of the sailors' conditions, we must emphasize three elements: the political awareness of the Scandinavian immigrants, the specialized character of coastal shipping work, and the support of the radical I.W.A. To these might be added a fourth: the nature of San Francisco as a crucible for new political and social developments. A group comparable to the Haskell branch of the I.W.A. probably could not have flourished anywhere else in the United States. There was a distinctive feeling of freedom in the city; it combined with the will of the seamen and the tension of the 1880s to produce an organization ready to set a new course: the Coast Seamen's Union, which would come to be called "the lookout of the labor movement" by another labor pioneer, Colorado's Joseph Buchanan.

Burnette Haskell and his I.W.A. comrades were to prove difficult partners at times, for the Coast Seamen's Union. But nearly all historians of the organization agree on the positive contributions of the

---

[26]Coast Seamen's Union *Constitution And History*, op. cit. [27]Coast Seamen's Union, Minutes, 1885-86, record cited. [28]Ibid. Also see Unsigned, "Has the S.U.P. Been a Credit to Organized Labor," series in *West Coast Sailors* (San Francisco), beginning September 17, 1937.

socialist "advisors". Perhaps significantly, one element of the original I.W.A.-C.S.U. project would survive the successive changes in the Union constitution, namely, the "obligation" or members' oath written into Haskell's 1885 *Constitution and History* and still almost entirely retained a century later: "I pledge my honor as a man, that I will be faithful to this Union until death. That I will work for its interests, and will look upon every other member as my brother. That I will not work for less than Union wages, and that I will obey all orders of the Union. I promise that I will never reveal the proceedings of the Union to its injury and to people who have no right to know the same. And if I break this promise, I ask every brother here to treat me as a rascal, unworthy of friendship or acquaintance. So help me God."

CHAPTER II
New Horizons
(1885-1900)

As described in the preceding chapter, the 1880s, the decade in which the Coast Seamen's Union was born, was marked by a wide-ranging labor upheaval in the United States. Workers were radicalized by depressed economic conditions, as well as by the visible concentration of wealth in the hands of the rich and the accompanying extension of the power of corporations.

In an unstable and anxious situation, the working class was swept by currents of fear directed at enemies both real and imagined. On the West Coast of the United States, the labor movement was seized in the late '70s and early '80s by agitation against the immigration of Chinese and other Asian laborers.

Anti-Chinese Agitation

The history of the anti-Chinese labor movement in California has been outlined by Alexander Saxton, in his book *The Indispensable Enemy*,[1] which gives significant attention to Burnette Haskell, Sigismund Danielewicz, and others active in the International Workmen's Association and the Coast Seamen's Union. Most importantly, as Saxton points out, it was from the ranks of these two groups, in the person of Danielewicz, that the anti-Chinese hysteria was met by a principled stand for the unification of all workers — white, Asian, and all others. But, as we shall see, this call for multi-racial labor solidarity was to go unsupported.

It may be argued that the "Chinese question" on the Pacific Coast was only secondarily a matter of race, and was primarily economic. Simply put, the Chinese could be compelled to work longer hours and for a lower wage than the majority of non-Asians. Such advantages for the employer were often supported by the hiring of Chinese in large work-groups that were housed together and might eat together. The most famous example of the large-scale importation of Chinese laborers came with the construction of the transcontinental railway, during the 1860s, in which Asians were used (and abused) in great numbers for the building of the sections between Pacific tidewater and Utah.

The anti-Chinese issue intruded into the business of the Coast Seamen's Union in late 1885. Ethnic relationships within the Pacific Coast labor environment had long been irritated, but other influences also drew the Union into the anti-Chinese camp. A belief in white superiority was by no means absent from the ideology of many labor agitators and socialists of the time, Karl Marx included.[2] Similarly, before the Civil War, some anti-slavery elements on the American scene based their position on a call for an end to the flow of Blacks into the United States; they opposed slavery for racist reasons.[3] Much anti-Asian sentiment on the Pacific Coast seems to have been motivated by anger at the corporate power that seemed eager to utilize "coolie labor armies," apart from the issue of the racial composition of the latter, although the difference in ethnicity naturally exacerbated resentment. What seems unarguable, once one reviews the anti-Asian literature of the time, was that the movement was often aimed mainly against the *employers* for whom the Asians acted as apparently-willing servants and strikebreakers.

The Coast Seamen's Union began a discussion of the "Chinese question" at an October 27, 1885 emergency meeting. Within the socialist I.W.A., debate on the issue had already gone on for some time, and seems to have been a particular point of conflict between Haskell and Danielewicz. The I.W.A., unlike the C.S.U., had been continually disrupted by personal disputes, and Haskell encountered difficulties in maintaining control. According to the I.W.A. *Minutes*, Danielewicz, the organization's "corresponding secretary for the Italian language," and, as we have seen, a

---

[1]Saxton, op. cit. [2]See Karl Marx and Frederick Engels, *Selected Correspondence*, New York, International Publishers, 1942. [3]See George Olshausen, *American Slavery and After*, San Francisco, Olema Press, 1983 and 1985, a major work of legal scholarship on slavery, by a friend of the Sailors' Union of the Pacific.

figure in the C.S.U., had resigned from I.W.A. office in mid-1885 after going to Stockton, California, for a propaganda tour. On the other hand, the Chicago labor newspaper, *The Alarm*, (which we will encounter again, in more dramatic circumstances), for October 17, 1885, listed Danielewicz as a traveling organizer for the I.W.A. and, in November, he was chosen for the Association's only salaried position as general corresponding secretary.[4]

On November 22, 1885, Danielewicz rose in a meeting of the I.W.A. held in the C.S.U. headquarters on East Street (after 1909, officially San Francisco's Embarcadero), to argue *against* participation in the anti-Chinese agitation. Rather than align themselves with a movement whose aims were, at the very best, of minor interest, according to Danielewicz, the I.W.A. should go to a coming anti-Chinese convention with a socialist proposal for class solidarity of all races, afterward withdrawing from the meeting.

Saxton, author of *The Indispensable Enemy*, has described how, gaining the agreement of the I.W.A., Danielewicz was allowed to present this minority position at the anti-Chinese convocation in December 1885. Danielewicz argued eloquently that, as a Jew, he could not support the further persecution of the Asian minority, and he called upon the Irish and German delegates in the audience to consider the situation of the Chinese in light of their own people's experience with oppression. However, the majority of the organized labor movement on the Coast was, then, still "white;" and its prejudices had yet to be seriously challenged. Danielewicz found his appeal met with jeers and rejection. During the convention the rest of the I.W.A. delegates, led by Haskell, attempted to emphasize that (in Saxton's words) "the Chinese were not to blame; the main thrust must be against the real culprits — capitalists, land monopolists, and those governmental agencies which did their bidding." But the tide was too strong; anti-Asian hatred continued to dominate the Pacific Coast labor movement, including the C.S.U., for years to come.[5]

New Faces: Anders Furuseth, W. C. Owen

Within the Coast Seamen's Union, the role of the I.W.A. was beginning to diminish as non-socialist rank-and-filers began to come to the fore. Among these latter stood Anders Furuseth, a young Norwegian destined to play a greater role in the history of the Union, and of maritime labor, than any of the I.W.A. partisans. When, in December 1885, Alfred Fuhrman reported to the C.S.U. that its treasury was troubled by considerable losses of funds, a committee made up of Fuhrman, Xaver Leder, Hugo Westling and "Fourcet" (whom we presume was Furuseth) reorganized the financial situation of the Union to the satisfaction of the membership.

The Coast Seamen's Union and Haskell were active early in 1886 in setting up the San Francisco Federated Trades Council, the forerunner of the present-day San Francisco Labor Council. In the meeting of the C.S.U. for February 1 of that year, Haskell discussed a "coming strike," indicating that the Union was preparing for a major showdown with the waterfront employers. At the March 1 meeting, wage demands were formulated: San Francisco to Puget Sound, $35 per month; to the "outside" or unprotected lumber ports, $40 per month; to the Hawaiian Islands, $30 per month. In the intervening weeks, the Union had adopted the procedure of electing a chair at each meeting, where before the position had been occupied by a vice-president; the practice was maintained until 1921. At the end of March, Anders Furuseth was elected secretary of the Union; but early in April, Furuseth reported he could not secure bond, and the position went to John Haist.

On April 26, 1886, a further link in the chain of maritime union history was forged with the organization of the Steamship Sailors' Protective Union, again with the help of Burnette Haskell. Unfortunately, relations between the C.S.U. and the steamship union were to prove uneven until 1891, when the two organizations fused to form the Sailors' Union of the Pacific. "Coasting" seamen, who worked on sailing vessels, often discounted the skill and fidelity to unionism of the steamship crews.[6]

During May 1886, Sigismund Danielewicz was dropped from the C.S.U. advisory committee and, after that, this man whose protest against anti-Asian racism was well within the noble tradition summed up by the Polish motto "For Your Freedom and Ours," disappears from the Union's history. (Danielewicz later edited a revolutionary newspaper, the *Beacon*, in San Diego.) Danielewicz's seat on the committee was taken by William C. Owen, a labor and reform agitator whose life is also of some interest. Born in India in 1854 and described as Haskell's political teacher, Owen would later become a leading editorial crusader for penal reform in California before taking over the English-language section of the journal *Regeneración*, published in the U.S. by the brothers Ricardo and Enrique Flores Magón, leaders of the social revolutionary Mexican Liberal Party. Following a U.S. government campaign to suppress *Regeneración*, Owen returned to Britain in 1916, and died in 1929, forgotten by the California labor movement in which, as Cross notes, he was a major figure.[7] But a moment was approaching when individuals, no matter how courageous or principled, would nearly all fall into the background, and when the Union as an institution existing above all individual personalities, would face its first major test. For the Pacific Coast waterfront

---

[4]I.W.A. Collection and Haskell Family Papers, Bancroft Library. [5]Saxton, op. cit. [6]Coast Seamen's Union, Minutes, 1885-86; also Taylor, op. cit. [7]On Haskell and Owen, see J. A. Lawrence, "Behind the Palaces," Ph. D. dissertation, University of California, Berkeley, 1977. Also see Ricardo Flores Magón, W. C. Owen, and others: *Land and Liberty*, Sanday, Orkneys, Cienfuegos Press, 1977; unsigned, "Passing of W. C. Owen," *The Road to Freedom*, (New York), September, 1929; T. H. Bell, "Recollections of Librado Rivera," *The Road to Freedom*, June 1932; Roney and Cross, op. cit. Lowell L. Blaisdell, *The Desert Revolution*, Madison, University of Wisconsin Press, 1962.

employers had prepared the first of many attempts to crush the Union in an organized, calculated manner.

1886 Strike

Dissatisfied with the failure of attempts to destroy the Union through direct intimidation, through the crimps, and through the police, in June 1886 the employers set up the Shipowners' Association of the Pacific Coast. A strike of all unlicensed seafaring personnel, led by a group of firemen, had begun on the Spreckels line. The Shipowners' Association announced that its members would only employ seamen contracted through an association shipping office, and would require workers to keep "grade books" listing qualifications and employment history. To obtain a grade book each crew member would be required to surrender his union book.

On August 25, 1886, the Union declared a strike on the entire coast against the grade book. This strike is chronicled by Pete Gill, a sailor born in Norway in 1863, who joined the C.S.U. (book number 43) on May 3, 1886. Pete Gill would become the Union's agent in the Port of Seattle, and would later write, with labor historian Ottilie Markholt, an encyclopedic history of the Union from 1885 to 1929 — truly an invaluable document although still, today, unpublished (Gill died in 1945; typescripts are held at the Bancroft Library, University of California, and the library of the University of Washington.) In their narrative, Gill and Markholt state that "to understand the reasons for the 'great strike' of 1886, one must look to the revolutionary character of the labor movement. The preceding two years saw the development of the Knights of Labor into a frankly revolutionary body, declaring that 'the attitude of our Order to the existing industrial system is necessarily one of war.' Its slogan, 'An injury to one is the concern of all,' was being literally demonstrated in widespread successful boycotts, with their implications of sympathetic action. It had challenged Jay Gould successfully in his Southwestern railroad system and subsequently on other roads . . . so infectious was the philosophy of mass action that the Federation of Organized Trade and Labor Unions [later the American Federation of Labor] in 1884 named May 1, 1886 as day for a general strike for the eight-hour day in all trades. San Francisco shared the spirit of the times."[8]

During the 1886 seamen's strike, the C.S.U. issued strike duty cards with the following message printed on the back:

"Carry this Strike Card on your person with your Union Card and show when demanded, and while you have it on you go to no place where you would not show it with pride, and do nothing to put on the Stain of Dishonor. When the strike is over the Secretary will endorse upon this card the fact (if true) that you have assisted in saving the Union. And then when sailors are free enough to [word illegible] to marry and have children this will be your certificate of honor to them.

"This strike was ordered to SAVE THE UNION, to enforce your rights as free men, as Americans, as haters of slavery. Never give it up until ordered by the Union. Never yield a single inch. Remember that BUCHANAN of Colorado called you the 'Lookout of the American Labor Movement,' the backbone of Organized Labor on the Pacific Coast. Remember your glorious history and die in the streets of San Francisco of starvation before you think of yielding.

"And remember that if we have to beg the public of San Francisco for food, then I will be the first man to go from house to house for dry bread to keep life in our bodies while we are fighting for the right of the sailor to resist the blood-monied infamies of San Francisco.

"Burnette G. Haskell

"Chairman, Advisory Committee"[9]

In launching the strike, the Union demanded either the complete abolition of the Shipowners' Association hiring office, or, as alternatives, joint control of hiring by the employers and the Union, or full Union control. The employers conceded nothing. Strikebreakers were obtained from deepwater vessels — hundreds of deepwater square-riggers were in port to carry away the San Joaquin Valley grain harvest, and their crews, for the most part recruited in ports of Britain and the continent, had no loyalties to sailor conditions on the Pacific Coast. Early in September striker Charles Norgreen, killed by a scab, was buried by the Union. Twenty C.S.U. members were arrested in Eureka and charged with inciting a riot.

The Union lost the strike of '86. Notwithstanding their fighting spirit and the idealism of Haskell and their other socialist allies, the C.S.U. could not yet prevail over the might of the employers. The Union *Minutes* show that by September 30, 1886, although the strike was not officially called off, the Union's members were authorized to find work wherever they could, with Haskell later reporting some opportunities on the railroads.

Furuseth Replaces Nielson

Early in January 1887, Anders Furuseth was elected to replace Rasmus Nielson, who, occasionally alternating with other members, had previously served as the Union's secretary. Burnette Haskell briefly departed San Francisco for Denver, Colorado, to take over the editorship of the *Labor Enquirer*, an important newspaper published by his collaborator, Joseph Buchanan. At Haskell's suggestion, a new C.S.U. advisory committee was set up, consisting of R. A. Gilbride, P. R. Martin, E. W. Thurman, Arthur Vinette, William Christie, W. C. Owen, and Buchanan, along with Haskell, under the chairmanship of Volmer Hoffmeyer.

The name of Haskell's friend Buchanan appears at many places in the early history of the Coast Seamen's

[8] Gill and Markholt, op. cit.; on Markholt, see Stephen Schwartz, "Ottilie Markholt — Labor Activist & Labor Historian," *Industrial Worker* (Chicago), July 1984.
[9] The "strike card" text, taken from that issued to Pete Gill, was first published in the *West Coast Sailors*, December 21, 1945. It is not included in Gill and Markholt, ibid.

Union, although Buchanan's main base of operations, Denver, was nearly two thousand miles inland. Writing some twenty years after these events, Buchanan would declare, in his magnificent book of memoirs, *The Story of a Labor Agitator*, his pride in having been associated with the C.S.U., even then "one of the best organized and strongest labor unions in the country." Buchanan's memoir further describes the Union's custom at the time of marching publicly with rifles, and his wish that certain "Denver lynchers might have witnessed the sight."

Buchanan's *Story* is something of a "lost classic" of American literature, and not simply an important work in the genre of labor history. Like Pete Gill, he brings to life the truly revolutionary hopes that gripped the working class movement of the 1880s, and shows the remarkable extent to which the I.W.A. created by Haskell and himself was able to penetrate the ranks of the many-membered Knights of Labor. To the general public, the I.W.A. and its "red card" became notorious for a time, thanks to anti-radical columns in the national press.

Unlike Haskell's I.W.A. branch in San Francisco, which in itself, and apart from its union allies like the C.S.U., never grew beyond an extremist circle dominated by a single individual, the Buchanan wing of the I.W.A. in Denver became a mass labor phenomenon. The contrast between Burnette Haskell and Joseph Buchanan illumines aspects of the special role of local psychology (San Francisco versus Denver) in the development of labor and socialist culture in the great American West, from the 1880s to the present. In addition, however, Haskell and Buchanan symbolize the character tendencies that have traditionally formed the two poles of labor and socialist politics around the world: the flamboyant literary promoter of sectarian polemics, Haskell, and Buchanan, the sober, cautious, but no less idealistic man of action from labor's own ranks. It is little short of amazing that Haskell and Buchanan worked together as well as they did; each represented, in the end, an utterly different outlook. To their great credit, and unlike so many of the radical figures of a later era, they were able to keep the flame of their mutual esteem and respect alive long after the I.W.A. had faded from memory everywhere save in the halls of the Sailors' Union and in the memories of Colorado's union militants.

Closer to home, Volmer Hoffmeyer, like Haskell before him, was to play a major role as an outside ally for the Union in San Francisco. According to Ira Cross, Hoffmeyer, a Dane, was a professional musician and music teacher, active in the Knights of Labor, and had been involved in an unsuccessful attempt to set up a Knights of Labor Neptune Assembly made up of seamen.[10]

But Furuseth was by now the most important of the "new men" of the C.S.U. According to his main English-language biographer, Hyman Weintraub, this man who was to play so great a part in the eventual emancipation of the world's seamen, was born in Norway, on March 12, 1854, the son of Andreas Nielsen and Marthe Jensdatter. Anders Furuseth, the fifth in a family of ten children, grew up in exceptionally hard circumstances. His father earned a slender living, once as a lock tender at a dam, and the family diet was often reduced to potatoes and rough bread, supplemented by wild game and fish. Anders was sent to work on a farm at the age of eight. There he stayed for eight years until he went to the city of Christiania (now Oslo) where he clerked, unsuccessfully sought entrance into a maritime school, and taught himself several languages. Finally, in 1873, he sailed in the crew of the bark *Marie* from the port of Draman. After shipping in Norwegian, Swedish, British, French, and U.S. vessels, and possibly fishing on the Grand Bank of Newfoundland, Anders Furuseth landed in California in August 1880.[11] Soon after the March 6 "lumber pile" meeting, he joined the Coast Seamen's Union.

Haskell and Kaweah

Burnette Haskell, as we have noted, had left for Colorado to join Buchanan in January 1887. But Haskell soon returned to San Francisco, and at the end of the year resumed his sporadic law practice. From then on, his role in the affairs of the C.S.U. remained that of a sympathetic observer. Although he spoke at March 6 celebrations in 1888 and 1889, and, as an attorney, defended the Union against terrorism charges in 1893, his time was increasingly occupied by his utopian colony near Visalia, California, the Kaweah Cooperative Commonwealth.

Haskell's utopian experiment was set in the slopes of the Sierras, surrounded by fine stands of timber. The intention was to utilize the forests to create a strong foundation for a system of alternative economic enterprises: a lumber export operation, carrying its products in Kaweah-owned ships manned by C.S.U. members. To enter the colony, a new member was required to put up $500, with $100 down and the rest payable in assets or through work. Membership averaged some 65 men and women.

At the beginning, canvas tents provided the colonists' only housing. A tent-village grandly titled Advance was occupied until 1889, and tents continued in use while a logging road was built. The tents eventually gave way to clapboard cabins at Kaweah, six miles from Advance. Once the lumber operations began in earnest, in 1890, a community center appeared, with dining and meeting halls, a store, printing and blacksmithing facilities, a barn, and sheds. However, bachelor members continued to sleep in the barn or to board with families.[12]

The Kaweah colony included a number of the founders of the C.S.U., including J. J. Martin, and the

---

[10]Buchanan, op. cit.; Cross, *History Of The Labor Movement In California*; V. Hoffmeyer, "Letters — 1887," in the S.U.P. central Archive. Also see Stephen Schwartz, "Waygood & James Donates Gift to Sailors' Union," *Pacific Shipper* (San Francisco), March 26, 1984. [11]Hyman Weintraub, *Andrew Furuseth*, Berkeley, University of California Press, 1959. [12]Hine, op. cit., and Kagan, op. cit; Haskell Family Papers.

Kaweah pioneers originally presented the colony as a "snug harbor" for unemployed and retired Union seamen. It has been asserted that many members of the Union contributed financially to the effort. Unfortunately, the Kaweah participants ostensibly failed to adequately observe the norms of capitalist society in filing their land claims, and the federal government began an investigation for supposed timber fraud almost as soon as the claims were entered. The basis of the fraud charge was, it seems, that too many signers of the land claim were transients who gave the C.S.U. boarding house in San Francisco as their address. The colony also found itself amid a scandal over the scope of its intended logging operations.

Kaweah may inevitably have failed for the same reason most such efforts have failed: the differences in personality among the members could not be reconciled simply by appealing to higher principles. Virtually the only meaningful task accomplished by the colonists proved to be the 18-mile logging road built between 1886 and 1890. Even with the installation of the road, however, the Kaweah logging operation turned out to be unproductive. But worst of all, early charges of despoiling of the redwoods by the colonists were taken up in the San Francisco daily press and increased in shrillness until the hue-and-cry against Haskell and Kaweah became a major topic of the day. Haskell himself had long been a target for journalistic abuse, earning insults from the distinguished wielder of the poison pen, Ambrose Bierce.

The press hysteria grew to an incredible extent, with California dailies competing for more lurid tales from Kaweah, although the local Tulare County *Times* defended the colonists. In 1890, the U.S. authorities established Sequoia National Park, including land occupied by the commune, and the historian Paul Kagan notes, in his book *New World Utopias*, that "when federal troops were sent in to administer the new park . . . the local press had labelled it 'Cossack terrorism,' and residents of the nearby towns had booed the soldiers in the streets and shot at them in the forests."[13]

In 1891 the ultimate blow fell when the colonists were charged by the federal government with lumber poaching on U.S. property. The colony disbanded in January 1892 after the trustees were indicted for mail fraud. The colonists had begun their worthy venture by naming the tallest tree within their redwood groves the "Karl Marx Tree." It was renamed the "General Sherman Tree" by park administrators, and so remains today. In its brief life, the Kaweah commune had sparked the enthusiasm of socialists and reformers throughout the U.S., with support from such national figures as Laurence Gronlund, author of the widely-read *Co-operative Commonwealth.* Work within the colony had been accounted for and remunerated through an innovative but difficult system of coupons and coins based on time measurement. Kaweah attracted a number of writers, musicians, and artists, and maintained a notable intellectual atmosphere.[14]

Meanwhile, the Coast Seamen's Union had fought to recover after the defeat of 1886. The Union reopened its shipping office in San Francisco but with small success. Still, the Union was able to survive by recruiting members who had acted as strikebreakers in the 1886 conflict, and by mid-1887, membership stood at 1,436. The C.S.U. adopted the tactic of boosting wage scales on individual vessels by "working the oracle," a practice later known as "job action." This consisted of quitting or threatening to quit the ship, between the time of signing articles and of letting go the lines, unless wages were raised. This was possible because, since 1874, coasting sailors had been exempted from the laws against "desertion" — thanks to a congressional amendment to the 1872 Shipping Commissioners' Act. The same "oracle" was used to get rid of the grade books.[15]

1887 Hearings: Role of Hoffmeyer

In June 1887, the California state labor commissioner's office invited representatives of the C.S.U. to participate in hearings on the condition of the coast sailors. The Union accepted enthusiastically, with its presentation coordinated by the Danish ex-musician and Knights of Labor organizer Hoffmeyer as chairman of the Union's advisory committee. Notable testimony was delivered by Furuseth and by Ed Andersen. In a pamphlet titled *The Sailors' Cause*, summarizing the inquiry, Hoffmeyer eloquently and concisely outlined the grievances that had brought the Union into being and for which resolution the organization had pledged itself to combat.

"It is common talk on the waterfront that the coast sailor is no longer what he used to be," Hoffmeyer wrote. "Why? Simply because a shortsighted policy among the shipowners has made them drive off the coast so many men whom they accused of having taken part in the disturbances during the past year and has replaced them with others who were willing to be used as tools wherewith to compel the former to submit. What the seaman wants, just like any other human being, is recognition — not to be considered a mere machine, a drudge, a something to be an abject ball for the caprices or brutality of anyone whom fate may have placed over him. Recognition he asks for, recognition as a human being endowed with the same gifts, strength, privileges, and rights as any other man . . . The recognition of sailors' rights will come here as it has come in other places," he added, pointing to contemporary organizing activities on the Great Lakes and in Australia. He went on to demand that "the shipowners . . . recognize the Union by giving the shipping office into their hands," and to argue that "the demand is not new. It has already been granted to one class of sailors. The steamship sailors conduct their own shipping and, therefore, we find the members of that Union, which was started by the aid and

[13]Kagan, ibid. [14]Kagan, ibid. [15]Gill and Markholt, op. cit.

assistance of the Coast Seamen's Union, free from the pestilence and scourge which is constantly blasting the hopes of the coast sailors — namely, the boardinghouse system."

The Union's representatives graphically supported Hoffmeyer's angry statements in their testimony. They described how the boardinghouse crimps kept their hold over the seamen by developing usurious bills for lodging, food, liquor, and provisions, enabling the crimps to steal the sailor's wages through the payment of advances. Boardinghouse masters, clothing merchants, and others who appeared before the investigation admitted, in so many words, to the existence of a conspiracy between them and the masters of vessels for payment of "blood money" to obtain seamen. Other abuses that called forth the protest of the Union at the inquiry included short wages, the operation of the crimping "Sailors' Home," and the blacklisting of union men. The Union also strongly attacked the attempt of the Shipowners' Association to break the Union through the employers' shipping hall and grade books.

Hoffmeyer's pamphlet stressed that "the Union recognized that reform in the shape of legislation must mainly refer to the deepwater sailor. It is the advance system which is at the bottom of all the trouble. By means of this system, it becomes possible for the boardinghouse master to fasten himself, like a leech, upon the sailors. Were the advance system abolished, the boardinghouses would disappear in the course of a few years. The blood-money system (by blood-money is understood any money paid BY the captain to secure the services of a sailor, or TO the captain to secure a berth in a ship) is of far smaller consequence." Concluding with a review of legal innovations in the maritime labor field, Hoffmeyer noted that "in 1872 the Shipping Commissioners' Act was passed, containing a complete system for the shipping and paying off of all sailors. This act was amended in 1874 to apply only to deepwater sailors. In 1884 another amendment was passed — commonly known as the Dingley Act — the principal features of which were that the seamen could be discharged in any port without three months' extra pay for foreign ports, (which) the Shipping Commissioners' Act provided; that a slop chest should be kept by the Captain on board . . .; that no more hospital money should be deducted from the sailor's wages and that no advance money should be paid to him when he shipped. The Dingley Act was later amended by allowing a certain amount of advance money, in accordance with a given schedule . . . The benefit which the amendment of 1884 was intended to give the sailor has been entirely neutralized by the later amendment, and the only effect of that act, beyond the abolition of the hospital money, is that the sailor can now be discharged in foreign ports without the former three months' extra pay."

The Union, through Hoffmeyer, asked for a prohibition on boarding masters' being present in the Shipping Commissioner's office when men were hired, so that the sailors could arrange their conditions of hire with captains on their own; a ban on payment of advances; a rule against appointment of boarding masters as shipping commissioners; full payment of wages in any port of discharge; and trial and disposition of any case on recovery of seamen's wages before a court within 48 hours of filing, all to be included within a national law.[16]

Coast Seamen's Journal — Haymarket

The progress of the Union toward these aims was soon to be significantly aided by the foundation of a newspaper, the *Coast Seamen's Journal*, a project first conceived during a steamer trip to San Diego by Andrew Furuseth (as he now began to sign himself) and Xaver H. Leder, a member of the I.W.A., as well as the C.S.U.; together they had been delegated to the southern port to handle Union affairs. But before the journal could be founded, the Union was called to action by a sequence of events of national and international significance: the aftermath of the Chicago Haymarket bombing of May 4, 1886, with condemnation of seven prominent labor leaders in that city to capital punishment, and one of their associates given a long prison sentence.

The Haymarket affair had taken place against the backdrop of a national struggle for the eight-hour working day with, as we have seen, May 1, 1886, declared a national strike day by leaders of what would become the American Federation of Labor. Three days later, at a demonstration against Chicago police brutality during a strike at the McCormick farm equipment works, a bomb had been thrown. Almost immediately eight labor agitators associated with the anarchist International Working People's Association, some of whom had been present as speakers when the bomb exploded, were charged with the outrage. The main figure in the group, Albert Parsons, was editor of the I.W.P.A. newspaper, *The Alarm* (which reported on the far western I.W.A. in detail, and had been sympathetic to a possible national unification of the I.W.P.A. and I.W.A.) Parsons had long been the target of hatred by the business circles in Chicago. The other defendants were nearly all foreign born, consisting of British immigrant Samuel Fielden, and the German-speaking Adolph Fischer, George Engel, Louis Lingg, Michael Schwab, August Spies, and Oscar Neebe. Parsons, Fischer, Engel, Lingg, Spies, Fielden, and Schwab were sentenced to hang.

Aside from the links between the anarchist and labor movement in Chicago and the I.W.A., the C.S.U. was further associated with the Haymarket case through its relationship with Joe Buchanan. Haskell's counterpart as leader of the I.W.A. in the Rocky Mountain region, lately included in the C.S.U.'s advisory

[16] V. Hoffmeyer, *The Sailors' Cause*. San Francisco, People Publishing Co., 1887.

committee, became one of the organizers of a national amnesty movement for the Haymarket prisoners, which grew as the hour of execution approached. Carolyn Ashbaugh, a biographer of Albert Parsons' widow Lucy Parsons, has outlined the gambit by which Haskell and Buchanan, working through Denver District Assembly 89 of the Knights of Labor, which they controlled, sought to challenge the order's current chieftain, Terence V. Powderly, on his refusal of support to the Haymarket accused, as well as over his timidity during strikes. When faced with Haskell in Chicago, Powderly claimed that he "had from the brother of A. R. Parsons evidence enough to convict the men of Chicago for murder." Haskell shouted with indignation, *"Then Sir, why do you not denounce them at once!"* Powderly could not seriously reply, and was branded a liar by Buchanan, who befriended Lucy Parsons in the years after her husband's execution.

The primary motive for the amnesty movement, rather than sympathy with the Haymarket group's aims, was anger at the clear denial of justice during their trial. In September 1887, a national appeal to the working class, signed by fourteen moderate labor leaders headed by Samuel Gompers, declared that "the execution of this sentence would be a disgrace to the honor of our nation," and called for public demonstrations against the decision.[17]

The execution of the seven condemned was set for November 11, 1887. On the evening of October 3, the C.S.U. met in San Francisco to consider the case. In Andrew Furuseth's handwriting, the Union recorded a resolution calling for a new trial and specifying that "we have always been ready to espouse the cause of justice against the attacks of anarchism seated in the cushioned chairs on the judicial benches." The meeting went on to recommend the then-considerable sum of $300 be sent to the defendants' attorneys. The Union's solidarity actions were reconfirmed in the meeting of October 17, following an emotional speech by Haskell.

Journal's First Issue

The October 17 meeting also took up in detail the proposal for publication of the *Coast Seamen's Journal*, which had been further developed by a committee consisting of Hoffmeyer, Furuseth, Leder, Alfred Fuhrman, and John Haist. The first issue appeared on November 2, 1887 with Leder as its editor. Its opening message, or salutatory, asserted "With a feeling of natural pride, we venture to present to the public this opening issue of the *Coast Seamen's Journal* — beyond a doubt the first newspaper that has ever been published exclusively in behalf of the myriads who live upon the watery part of this globe of ours, the seafaring class.

"In taking this step, we do not lend ourselves to any delusion; we fully conceive the immensity of our task. Descendants, as we are, of the House of Want, and the pupils of such grim teachers as extreme hardship and continuous toil, we have even now a woeful apprehension of the scolding, cuffing and general ill-treatment which this offspring of ours is to receive, especially at the hands of that class of parasites who have grown corpulent and lazy on the hard earnings, the ignorance, and the proverbial generosity of the sailors. How they will hate its voice; how they will endeavor to stifle it; how they will employ each conceivable soothing charm to rock it to sleep again — for its voice, tiny and insignificant as it may seem, is a menace to their objects, a death message to their very existence. . . .

"The stories told in these columns will surely lack the fantastic sound of sea novels. They are not published to tickle your imagination but to arrest the thought of such men and women who are in search of Truth, and for the establishment of Justice, and who agree with us that Sailors have a right to aspire to as high a moral and mental standard as any other craft or class. Although published by the Coasting Sailors of the Pacific Coast, their *Journal* shall voice the appeals of our brethren — those upon deep water as well as upon the various coasts of the globe. The Sailors' cause is one which admits of no division. As long as the moral condition of the deep water sailor is such as to render him a wretched slave, morally, mentally, and physically, who bows in silent submission to the caprices and brutalities of unprincipled captains and greedy landsharks; so long as he may be overworked, underfed, beaten, swindled, and driven out of their vessels and forced upon our coast to enter into the most bitter competition for bread with ourselves, just so long will our struggle be worse than futile.

"Let us have a craft of intelligent men. We here, upon our coast, who have more advantages — we should see to it that a glimpse of light fall upon the mid-ocean. Let us read, let us discuss, let us educate ourselves; let the results of our education be sent broadcast across the ocean. This is the task of our union — surely one worthy of all the energy and goodwill within us."[18]

It has been observed that the reception of the *Journal* "was varied — 'the seamen were proud and enthusiastic; the seamen's friends were amused and skeptical; the seamen's enemies were openly contemptuous.' " But Gill and Markholt note that "in succeeding years the proud boast of the first editorial was fulfilled. The *Journal* became a powerful weapon in the seamen's hands for preservation of the Union and advancement of their battles for freedom. It was in fact a 'death message' to sea slavery."[19]

Decline of Radicalism

On November 10, 1887, Governor Oglesby of Illinois commuted the sentences of two of the condemned Haymarket prisoners, Fielden and Schwab. That afternoon, Lingg had committed suicide in his cell, his lower jaw blown off by explosives. The next day, Spies,

[17]David, op. cit.; also see I.W.A. Collection, Bancroft Library, and Carolyn Ashbaugh, *Lucy Parsons, American Revolutionary*, Chicago, Kerr, 1976. [18]*Coast Seamen's Journal*, November 2, 1887. [19]Gill and Markholt, op. cit.

Fischer, Engel, and Parsons were hanged. In 1893, Governor John Peter Altgeld of Illinois pardoned Fielden, Schwab, and Neebe, finding the trial unfair. The memory of the "Haymarket martyrs" was taken up by the labor movement throughout the world and in countries as distant from Chicago as Spain and Uruguay they are remembered today.

The 1887 execution of the five Haymarket leaders may have marked the beginning of the end for the radical labor movement of the 1880s in the U.S. From then on, a decline in social revolutionary agitation is visible, as labor attempted to establish itself as a reforming, rather than a subversive, element within the existing society. The later attitude of the Coast Seamen to the anarchists and other revolutionaries is well put by Gill and Markholt who comment that "although they defended the right of the Chicago anarchists to parade through the streets celebrating May Day with as many red flags as they desired, the sailors roundly condemned anarchists." Still, they add, "however much the Sailors' Union might dislike socialists and anarchists, it anticipated a future time when the labor movement would bring about a new social order through gradual peaceful reform." A statement in a contemporary issue of the *Coast Seamen's Journal* called for "a government of the actual producers of wealth in which the condition of labor shall be the first consideration," and specified that "the employers had better realize the fact that they hold what they call their own business only as long as the toilers, who are in the majority, please to let them."[20]

The early *Coast Seamen's Journal* under Leder was fairly typical of the radical labor press of its time, interspersing union news, maritime affairs, features and poetry, along with such documents as the Knights of Labor declaration of principles. The newspaper published, in full, the testimony delivered before the California state labor commissioner by Hoffmeyer, Furuseth, Andersen, and other C.S.U. members in 1887. A radical tinge did remain visible for some time, with the *Journal* publishing essays by Karl Marx on wages and on the working day, in 1888.

Already fighting anti-labor currents in society, the Union had begun, as the '80s wore on, to emerge from its somewhat chancy origins, in which dissatisfied sailors on a lumber wharf had received instruction from committed San Francisco radicals, with a distinct program for alleviation of the seamen's grievances. The Hoffmeyer presentation in 1887 had indicated the option of legislative action which was taken up and expanded under the encouragement of Furuseth. The Union's enemies were powerful and widespread. Gill and Markholt quote a newspaper editorial from the *San Diego Sun* charging that the Sailors' Union "stands between the American sailor (who is usually too self-respecting to submit to its un-American methods) and a livelihood; and, yet, lays claim in its broken English to the honor of having kept up the standard of American wages."[21]

But even as it began to concentrate on the limited issues of maritime law reform, the Coast Seamen's Union continued to extend its hand in aid to the rest of labor. By 1888 the annual celebration of March 6th, "Sailors' Independence Day," had become a major event for the Union and the city of San Francisco, and at the festivities that year, Burnette Haskell hailed the emergence of a working women's movement on the coast. In April and May the Union acted to help set up the first formal organization of the waterfront unions, the Federated Council of Wharf and Wave Unions, with Xaver Leder as its recording secretary. The council brought together the C.S.U., the Marine Firemen's Union of the Pacific Coast, the Steamship Stevedores Union, the Stevedores Protective Union, the Independent Longshoremen, the Riggers Protective Union, the Stevedore Engineers, the Brickhandlers, Shipwrights, Wharf Builders, Longshore Lumbermen, and Ship Calkers. However, the council did not last.

Campaigns Against 'Buckoism'

For the next three years, the Union's members applied themselves to the strengthening of their internal organization, betterment of the *Journal*, and campaigns for improvement of wages and conditions. In January 1889, Furuseth was temporarily replaced as secretary by W. T. Burke but the Union was strong enough in spirit to keep up the fight regardless of any individual leader. In March, the *Journal* publicized the dreadful conditions aboard the bark *Aquidneck*, commanded by Captain Joshua Slocum, later known for his navigational achievements, including the first single-handed round-the-world sailing voyage, in the sloop *Spray*.

In April, the *Journal* was taken over by two excellent writers, W. J. B. Mackay and Walter Macarthur. We should here note that, among the circle of men who became leaders of the Union in this period, Macarthur stands out as one of the best and most dedicated. Macarthur was born in Glasgow, Scotland, in 1862, and joined the Coast Seamen's Union in 1889. According to Paul Scharrenberg, who later replaced him as editor of the *Journal*, "Macarthur participated in virtually every forward move by the labor movement." Almost immediately, the tone of the paper changed perceptibly, as it began to concentrate its fire on the horrors of "buckoism," along with the bad food and cramped quarters offered the seamen. Furuseth returned to office in San Francisco and began serving as C.S.U. representative to the San Francisco Federated Trades Council, a position previously occupied by Haskell, Hoffmeyer, and others.

The situation on board the deep water ships at that time is exemplified by the case of the vessel *Reuce*, under Captain Adams, which arrived in San Francisco in November 1889 after 154 days at sea, with 17 men suffering scurvy and one already dead. The sailors' diet consisted of a small tin of coffee sweetened with one teaspoon of black molasses, two slices of beef and

[20]Gill and Markholt, ibid. [21]Gill and Markholt, ibid.

two slices of bread, for breakfast; for lunch, the same with tea; for dinner on Sunday, two pounds of soup and a hash of rice and water for 20 men; on Monday, Wednesday, and Friday, three tablespoons of pea soup, one slice of beef and one of bread; on Tuesday and Thursday, two tablespoons of baked beans, two pieces of pork and two slices of bread; on Saturday, rice boiled in salt water. The water supply was restricted to a pint per day. The first scurvy had appeared 75 days out. Only six of the crew were sailors, but all had suffered the typical brutality of a "hell ship" or "blood boat." The C.S.U. obtained legal aid for the men and, in May 1890, $3,600 in damages was awarded to the crew. During the *Reuce* campaign, the Union and the Federated Trades also organized a protest against Captain Healy of the U.S. revenue cutter *Bear*, a drunken bucko of the worst kind. Public attention began to focus on the tortures and indignities suffered by seamen.[22]

The month of November 1889 saw the foundation of the Atlantic Coast Seamen's Union through the joint efforts of the C.S.U. and Samuel Gompers, leader of the American Federation of Labor. This was the beginning of a long and fruitful relationship between the C.S.U. and its successors, on the one hand, and the A.F.L. on the other, reflected today in the affiliation of the Sailors' Union of the Pacific with the AFL-CIO. Labor ferment was also visible among the sailors on the Great Lakes, who had organized under the aegis of the Knights of Labor.[23] The following year saw the forces of the C.S.U. attempt to bolster their international contacts with the visit of a Union delegation consisting of Furuseth, Ed Crangle, and Frank Waterhouse, to the International Seamen's Convention in Glasgow, Scotland. On his return from this meeting, which was largely unproductive from the point of view of the C.S.U., Furuseth for the first time met personally with Gompers. Gompers himself later recalled that in response to suggestions that Furuseth be coopted into the national leadership of the American Federation of Labor, he had argued the Norwegian crusader should remain at his post in San Francisco while the Union gained economic strength.[24]

The C.S.U. delegates to Glasgow conducted a tour through the Atlantic, Gulf, and Lake ports, reporting on the deliberations and, on their return to San Francisco the delegates began working on a call to seamen's unions throughout the nation, proposing a national organization. This trend was actively supported by Gompers.

Among its links beyond the U.S. West Coast, the C.S.U. had come to place special value on its relations with the Seamen's Union of Australia. Labor news from the Antipodes began to occupy a considerable space in the *Coast Seamen's Journal.* The early bond between the two organizations had many sources. Both countries faced each other, distantly, on the Pacific, and maritime commerce between them had grown to a respectable level. In addition, the Australian labor movement was then one of the most aggressive and forward-looking in the world, and its progress was closely followed in all the English-speaking lands. Like Scandinavia, Australia stood forth as a guiding example for labor and reform politics. The Australian seamen had established their first union organization in Melbourne in 1872 and, by 1880, had brought in the New Zealand seamen as well, setting up the Federated Seamen's Union of Australasia. As contacts between it and the C.S.U. flourished, the unions adopted the practice of honoring each other's membership cards.[25]

Unfortunately, the year 1890 saw the passage of legislation with a sinister meaning for sailors. By law, arrest and imprisonment for "desertion" was restored by a further amendment to the 1872 Shipping Commissioners' Act. The new law, according to Paul Taylor, "applied the penal clauses of the . . . Act to seamen in the coasting trade shipped before a U.S. Shipping Commissioner without granting them the protection and privileges of that act."[26]

Events of early 1891 included a visit by Gompers to San Francisco with a notable address by the A.F.L. leader at the annual March 6th celebration. A brief internal "scandal" involved misappropriation of funds by one Henry Ark. In July 1891, the Union arrived at the end of one phase in its history and the commencement of another with the amalgamation of the C.S.U. and the Steamship Sailors' Protective Union.

Sailors' Union of the Pacific Founded

Although the Steamship Sailors had organized in 1886 with the help of Burnette Haskell and the C.S.U., relations between the two unions had not always been good. The Steamship Sailors did not have to contend with the crimps and boarding masters since they shipped through their own hall or "off the dock". The Steamship Sailors had managed to improve their wages and conditions since organizing, but a serious jurisdictional dispute had emerged between them and the C.S.U. almost immediately, centering on the steam schooners. The first steam schooner had been built at the foot of San Francisco's Mason Street, later Fisherman's Wharf, in the early 1880s, and a couple of dozen were launched there and at the head of navigation on Mission Creek at Seventh Street, before the decade ended. These early specimens of the type, as their name implied, encompassed both steam and sail propulsion — principally steam. They originally ran to the "dog-hole" ports (unprotected coves) of the Sonoma and Mendocino coasts. In time, they grew in size and were numerous from Puget Sound to San Diego. Late in 1887, the Steamship Sailors were expelled from the regional Federated Trades at the instance of the C.S.U., which charged the steamship organization with jurisdictional poaching and other

[22]Scharrenberg, op. cit.; Gill and Markholt, ibid. [23]Weintraub, op. cit. [24]Samuel Gompers, *Seventy Years Of Life And Labor*, New York, Dutton, 1925 and 1957. [25]Brian Fitzpatrick and Rowan J. Cahill, *The Seamen's Union Of Australia, 1872-1972*, Sydney, Seamen's Union of Australia, 1981. Before the 1930's the histories of the two Unions have a great many points in common, including the involvement with failed Utopian colonies. [26]Taylor, op. cit.

anti-C.S.U. activities. The Steamship Sailors were re-admitted to the trades body in 1889 but relations between the two seagoing unions remained tense. The Steamship Sailors' representatives argued against an exchange of union cards, claiming that the hold of the crimps over coast shipping put the coasting sailors at a disadvantage with which the steamer sailors did not want to contend. Finally, after extended negotiations, the Steamship union, now led by the Norwegian-born Nicholas Jortall, fused with the C.S.U. to form the organization that continues today: the SAILORS' UNION OF THE PACIFIC.[27]

The declining power of the crimps in the face of the Union's will to battle had contributed to pro-merger sentiment among the Steamship union's members. The new S.U.P. counted a membership of around 4,000 and a treasury totalling $50,000 and was "probably the strongest labor union local in the country at that time as it now began final preparations for a great effort . . . to wrest control of shipping from the Shipowners' and Coasting Boarding Masters' Associations and to abolish finally the abuses which had pursued the sailor wherever he went," according to Paul Taylor. The former Steamship Sailors moved into the Union's headquarters at Mission and East Streets (The Embarcadero), in a structure known as the Audiffred Building, the only building now surviving on the old San Francisco waterfront from that period. Later in 1891, the Union passed a further landmark with the foundation of the first Canadian branch at Victoria, British Columbia.

The following year, the stronger S.U.P. launched its biggest legislative effort yet. In January, the Union's Committee on Maritime Law was set up, including Ed Crangle, Nick Jortall, Frank Waterhouse, George M. Lynch and George Bolton. The immediate targets of the committee were the following grievances:

- Involuntary servitude (penal punishment for violation of civil contract), as embodied in laws on 'desertion.'
- Corporal punishment (subject to being beaten by, or by order of, the master).
- Small and badly ventilated forecastles.
- Insufficient and unwholesome food.
- Insecurity of wages contracted for, caused first by the system of advances or allotments; secondly by dilatory proceedings in suits to recover wages when such are in dispute.
- No provisions for survey of sailing vessels, no regulation manning of vessels, and no standard of efficiency for such men as were actually shipped.
- Retention through contracts of wages already earned until the contract time was served, except at the option of the master.

The recommendations for legal redress of these points were presented in an "Appeal to Congress." Late in 1892, the S.U.P. endorsed James G. Maguire, a former Superior Court judge, for Congress, representing San Francisco, with the understanding that Maguire would fight to obtain congressional approval for a seamen's act securing the seven goals noted above. Judge Maguire was an eloquent speaker and a respected judicial official, retired since 1888. Born in Boston, on February 22, 1853, he had come to California with his parents in May, 1854. He was educated in Watsonville, graduating from a private academy there, and then followed, in succession, the calling of blacksmith, schoolteacher, and lawyer. In 1875, he was elected to the California State Assembly, and then elected San Francisco Superior Court Judge, in 1882, serving for six years. Maguire was duly elected to the national Congress and began working toward passage of the bill.[28]

At a meeting in Chicago in April 1892, representatives of the S.U.P., the Lake Seamen's Union, and the Gulf Sailors' and Firemen's Union met and formed the National Seamen's Union, affiliated with the American Federation of Labor. The national union's first elected officers were Charles Hagen of New Orleans, president; Frank Waterhouse, S.U.P., vice-president; and former Knights of Labor local master workman T. J. Elderkin, of the Lake Seamen's Union, Chicago, as secretary-treasurer. The N.S.U. began its work with an ambitious project for unionization of Atlantic coast sailors as well as support for the S.U.P. legislative program. The N.S.U. constitution was ratified by the S.U.P. in June 1892, and the *Coast Seamen's Journal* became the N.S.U.'s official publication.

Employers' Association Set Up

The Pacific Coast shipowners were preparing another anti-union campaign, this time operating with yet more sophisticated methods. An Employers' Association had been set up with the declared goal of smashing the strong San Francisco unions. Gill and Markholt point out that "industry had passed the peak of good times in 1891 and was beginning to coast down to the panic of 1893-94. Unemployment was increasing. Thus . . . the employers attacked."

In summer 1890, before the establishment of the Employers' Association, the San Francisco Iron Molders' Union had been broken after a strike, and its leaders blacklisted. The Boot and Shoe workers' organization was similarly smashed. In March 1891, the Longshore Lumbermen's Union was broken by the Pacific Pine Lumber Company. Blacklisting spread as union after union began to feel the blows of the employers' concerted action.

November 1891 saw the first foray by the association against the Sailors' Union. An attempt to lower wages was repulsed but the Sailors realized that "the employers had only begun." Deepwater men who were stranded on the coast by the declining maritime commerce that marked the advancing depression became willing scabs in the "guerrilla war" against the Sailors' Union. The employers also utilized the police. In

---

[27]Gill and Markholt, op. cit. [28]*Coast Seamen's Journal*, November 16, 1892; Gill and Markholt, ibid.

March 1892, eleven men were arrested in San Pedro and charged with assaulting scabs. After eight months in jail, the men were tried and the charges dismissed. June 1892 saw the fatal stabbing of Otto Anderson, a Union member, by a scab from the bark *S. C. Allen.* Anderson's funeral became an occasion for participation by the entire Bay Area labor movement. His assailant never stood trial.

Through scabherding, the shipowners slowly began to effect wage cuts. The scabs were protected by the police and the forces of order joined with the press to loudly accuse the Sailors' Union of assorted crimes of violence. The main blow came in January 1893 when a new Shipowners' Association opened a scab shipping hall in San Francisco which the men were required to use to obtain work. Gill and Markholt state that "ostensibly, the shipping office was established to reduce wages. Actually, it was to crush the Union by compelling seamen to sign before a shipping commissioner and thus render them liable for imprisonment for refusal to work or desertion and permit the shipowner to keep their wages from them under the (law of) 1890, which made it optional for seamen in the coastwise trades to sign before a shipping commissioner but made them subject to the penalties of the Shipping Commissioners' Act of 1872 if they did so. Thus the shipowners planned to deprive the seamen of their newfound independence through union control of shipping and return them to the crimps' power."

The strategy of the Shipowners' Association was developed by one Walthew, alias G. C. Williams, who had been hired by the association for this purpose alone. Walthew had come to San Francisco and, working as a journalist, first "studied" the labor movement and then went to work attempting to destroy it. Walthew acted through the press as well as through the business organizations. During the period, he successfully disguised his identity. "Walking delegate Williams," as the *Coast Seamen's Journal* called him, became the very incarnation of anti-union intrigues on the West Coast waterfront.

The newspapers began the attack on the Union with a series of stories charging members with attempts to stop scab shipping through sabotage. The Union was alleged to have organized the sawing of anchor chains, the cutting of lines, and planting of explosive devices in ship bottoms. The Sailors' Union were branded as anarchist bomb-throwers, seeking to overturn all civilized society. Such propaganda was naturally intertwined with and supposedly justified by the slanders on the sailors' "un-American" ethnicity. The "insolent" fight of the seafarers for dignity and respect was met with contrived hysteria and with brutality.

As his main weapon against the Union, Walthew revived the grade book, modelled this time on the British Shipping Federation's "continuous discharge book." This credential was, in effect, identical to that introduced in the 1886 strike, listing physical description and qualifications with spaces for comments on conduct and other blacklisting remarks. Further, in his campaign to coordinate the employers' offensive, Walthew "courted the favor of deepwater shipowners and ship masters who protested against payment of blood money to deepwater crimps, by inviting them to join the Shipowners' Association and promising to supply sailors without blood money. In fighting the crimps, Walthew's purpose was to demonstrate to the shipowners still outside the Association its strength and value and punish deepwater boarding masters for standing in with the Sailors' Union by not voluntarily cooperating with the Association."[29]

As the Union fought scabs and police, the "sabotage" hysteria rose to a higher pitch. In mid-1893, as the country was dragged further downward into business depression, the Union held fast, but the employers' aggression combined with the economic collapse began to be felt. Late in the year, the Union voluntarily reduced its wage scale to cope with the situation.

Curtin Bomb

On Sunday, September 24, 1893, an area of Main Street four blocks south of Market Street in San Francisco was shaken by an explosion. Six non-union seamen had been on their way back to the boarding house of the notorious crimp, John Curtin, at 334 Main Street, when they had found a valise lying in the doorway of Curtin's establishment. Curtin's son, Johnny, who happened to be on the scene, was reported to have looked into the valise and shouted "Boys, it's dynamite" before dropping it and fleeing. The sailors were examining it themselves when it blew up. Four men were killed outright and a fifth died later. Curtin's son recovered from injuries. The front of Curtin's boardinghouse was destroyed and the sidewalk and adjacent buildings were severely damaged.

The Curtin bomb was used as an excuse for the worst press campaign yet against the Sailors' Union. Walthew declared in the *San Francisco Examiner* that "from British Columbia to San Diego there have been mutterings and threats from the army of nearly 4,000 sailors who are abjectly under the command of the Union." The Union responded to the Curtin outrage by voting a $1,000 reward for the arrest and conviction of the bombers.

Soon after the incident, a non-union deepwater sailor, Terrence Tracy, and two former S.U.P. members, John Tyrrell and James Wood, who had been removed from the Union's rolls for non-payment of dues, were charged with the blast on the strength of a claim by Curtin's wife that they had spoken threateningly to her. Police searched the lodgings of S.U.P. men, including Furuseth. Curiously, the bombing of Curtin's boarding house was followed within days by the revelation that "Williams" was actually Walthew and that under his original name he had been charged with various

[29]On Elderkin, see Hoffmeyer, letters cited; otherwise, Gill and Markholt, ibid.

crimes in the state of Michigan, from whence he fled to California to avoid prosecution. The *Coast Seamen's Journal* ceased referring to him by the nickname "Walking Delegate Williams" and adopted that of "Criminal Walthew," repeatedly pointing out that in swearing under the name Williams in various proceedings, Walthew had committed perjury. But although Walthew's past should have made him a candidate for an interview by the San Francisco police for possible involvement in the Curtin affair, such an investigation never took place. The forces of the law were, in 1893, firmly arrayed on the side of privilege. The legislation depriving the seamen of the right to quit a ship, the persecution of the Union by employer groups like the Shipowners' Association, and police violence against working people were all features of a nationwide offensive by the powerful "interests" opposed to the labor movement.

A coroner's jury declared that the Curtin blast was the work of "persons unknown," eliciting condemnation from the police who insisted on the guilt of Tyrrell, Wood, and Tracy. Finally, Tyrrell was charged. The S.U.P. helped set up a Tyrrell defense fund and hired Burnette Haskell and an Easterner, Guilfoyle, for the defense. Haskell, inactive in labor affairs since the virtual suppression of the Kaweah colony, handled the Tyrrell case masterfully and, on March 20, 1894, after six minutes' deliberation, the jury voted for acquittal. This was, perhaps, Haskell's greatest moment. The Union extended its thanks to its eccentric old friend, stating that he "had a good case but his skillful handling of it deserves commendation and appreciation."[30]

Simultaneous with the Curtin affair, the Union had to defend itself in the trial of James P. Hansen, first patrolman, on a charge of placing dynamite aboard the tug *Ethel and Marion*. Fortunately, the testimony produced by the main state witness, one "Hoodlum Harry" Hendrickson, a crimps' runner, so discredited the prosecution that, following a hung jury and a second trial, Hansen was acquitted just before Tyrrell.

The true character of Walthew was simultaneously exposed to the public. In February 1894, the *San Francisco Examiner* published a letter of his to the Seattle representative of the Shipowners' Association, in which Walthew wrote the following: "A dose of cold lead has a wonderful effect. Create the impression upon both the union men and the community in general that your greatest desire is to preserve peace; that you will do anything to avoid a conflict; that you will submit to any indignity without retaliation; but when it becomes necessary to guard the property of the association you will not hesitate to kill. Once you obtain that reputation, you will discover that you will have far less trouble."[31]

Walthew's unspeakably brutal suggestions turned sentiment in the city back toward the Union and away from the employers.

'The Red Record'

By the time the Curtin bomb trial ended, the Sailors' Union had already set its course in a determined way toward a full reform of maritime labor laws. With the issue of the *Coast Seamen's Journal* dated February 14, 1894, a new "feature" was introduced, headed by an engraving, printed in bright red ink, of a hand gripping a blood-covered belaying pin: "The Red Record," a chronicle of some of the more notable cases of abuse suffered by U.S. sailors since November 1887. The first listed case was that of the whaler *Hidalgo*, on which the captain had succeeded in enforcing a spurious claim of seamen's debts owed to the vessel by securing their arrest and delivery on board another vessel in Eureka — a case of "official shanghaiing."

The "Red Record" ran through several issues of the *Coast Seamen's Journal* and was revised and published as a pamphlet by the National Seamen's Union at the end of 1895. This chronicle of oppression was sent to every periodical in the land and presented to legislators and other public figures. In pamphlet form, *The Red Record* enumerated 64 cases dealing only with actual violence, originating in ports throughout the globe, all of which had occurred within seven years, "proving that cruelty to seamen has not ceased with the notorious cases which happened at an earlier date," as N.S.U. president Elderkin noted in a prefatory statement. Of the 64 cases, 40 were reported in San Francisco. The roster included 14 deaths "under circumstances which justify the charge of murder." Only three convictions for brutality by marine officers were secured. The rest were "either 'exonerated' or dismissed on the ground of 'lack of evidence,' 'justifiable discipline,' or, in the case of the seaman's death, because no 'official' charge had been made."

Elderkin's preface went on to point out "the frequency of the accused officers' 'disappearance' upon arrival in port . . . as a feature of the system by which these men evade arrest," adding that "the frequent recurrence of names of particular ships and officers, and the boasts openly made in contempt of the courts, show the effects of immunity from punishment". The cases listed in the pamphlet were undeniably horrible and produced great outrage. Through "The Red Record," the Union was to focus national attention on the continuing terrorism of "bucko" officers.[32]

The following excerpts convey the flavor of "The Red Record:"

"*Tam O'Shanter*, Captain Peabody, arrived in San Francisco, September 6, 1888. First-Mate Swain arrested on three charges of cruelty preferred by Seamen Fraser, Williams and Wilson. Captain defended his mate on the ground of incompetent crew; did not say how he came to sail with incompetent men. Mate released on $450 bond. Case still in the courts.

"*Hecla*, Captain Snow, arrived in Tacoma, November 1, 1888. Sixteen seamen, being all-hands forward, entered complaint of cruelty in the District Court.

[30]Gill and Markholt, ibid., and *Coast Seamen's Journal*, March 28, 1894. [31]Gill and Markholt, ibid. [32]*The Red Record*, San Francisco, Coast Seamen's Journal, 1895.

Near Cape Horn captain attacked the carpenter; struck him with a heavy instrument, breaking his jaw and knocking out several teeth. Captain nearly killed another man, and, with the aid of the first-mate, beat several of the crew. Crew were put in the hold for forty-eight hours and secured in such a manner that they could neither stand erect, sit nor lie down. One man was tied to a stanchion four days and kept without food. The latter was placed within sight, but out of reach. In Acapulco the crew were imprisoned ashore until the ship was ready to sail. Application was made to the Consul for assistance, but the latter refused, saying the only thing to be done was to "rough it." Captain Snow boasted that he had never been beaten in a difficulty with seamen ashore, and refused to pay his crew the wages due them ($600 in all) for the passage from Cardiff.

"*Solitaire*, Captain Sewall (son of the Bath ship-builder and owner of that ilk), arrived in Dunkirk, France, about January, 1889. In the Channel the mate called a seaman from aloft, knocked him down, jumped on his breast and inflicted wounds from which he died next day. The body was kept in the afterhatch for four days. When the corpse was so black that the bruises could not be distinguished the story was given out to the Deal authorities that the man died of consumption. Captain beat two men for talking while at work; first-mate also set upon them and broke one man's nose. Second-mate beat one of the boatswains with knuckle-dusters because the latter omitted the usual 'sir' from his address. A sick seaman was hauled out of his bunk and made to go aloft. Another seaman accidentally spat on the deck; was made to go down on his knees and lick it up. Boatswains were beaten for refusing, or being unable, to beat the seamen. An old seaman was given liquor and then plied to tell tales about the crew. With the cues thus received the officers made occasion to beat the seamen. At Dunkirk the second-mate fled to England, and remained in hiding until the *Solitaire* was ready to proceed to sea again.

"*John F. Kearns*, Captain McDonald. Complaints of general abuse. Some of the crew determined to desert the vessel while still lying in New York harbor, about February 4, 1889. L. Kaldron and three others launched a roughly made raft and endeavored to make the shore. A storm of wind, sleet and snow came on and drove them to sea. Two of the seamen were washed from the raft and drowned. The steamer *Old Colony* picked up the remaining two, covered with ice and nearly frozen to death. One of these subsequently died in the hospital.

"*Lewellyn J. Morse*, Captain Lavary, arrived in San Francisco, February, 1889. First-Mate Watski, charged by Seaman Arthur Connors with striking him on the head with a pair of handcuffs, imprisonment in the lazarette and gagging because the complainant was singing. Captain was present during these inflictions, but refused to interfere. Watski released on $500 bonds. Case still pending.

"*St. Andrew*, Captain Heckster, arrived in New York, March 31, 1889. Captain, First-Mate Beveridge and Second-Mate Campbell were arraigned before the United States Commissioner, charged by six seamen with having caused the death of a half-witted Norwegian named Elias Neilson. Soon after leaving London, the seamen charge, the captain and mates commenced to illtreat Neilson most brutally, knocking him down with marlinespikes on the slightest pretext. As a result of this treatment the man died on March 20th. Commissioner Shields remanded the prisoners for further information.

"*Solitaire 2* [i.e., second entry], Captain Sewall, arrived in Philadelphia, April 18, 1889. Warrants were sworn out for the arrest of the captain, First-Mate F. Ryan and Second-Mate J. W. Robbins, on complaint of brutality on the passage from Dunkirk, France. One man was hit aloft by the second-mate and fell eighty feet into the buntlines, and was thus saved. Another man was also struck off the yard and fell to the deck. He was killed outright. When the seamen made complaint to the officials at Philadelphia they bore upon them the marks of their sufferings. The mates deserted the ship while towing up the Delaware; Captain Sewall also disappeared for a time. It is reported that Captain Sewall "healed the wounds of all complainants" with $440 in cash and proceeded on his way.

"*Commodore T. H. Allen*, Captain Merriam, arrived in San Francisco April, 1889. A seaman, McDonald, reported that while expostulating against the vile language of the third-mate he was struck several times by that officer and thrown against the rail with such violence that his shoulder was dislocated. Captain remarked, when appealed to: 'Serves you damned well right,' and ordered the mate to confine McDonald in the carpenter's shop. As treatment for his wounds he was given a dose of salts. Another seaman fell sick and was confined with McDonald in the carpenter's shop — a combination of hospital and prison. There being only one bunk in the place, the weakest man had to sleep on the deck. Diet for the sick man, common ship's fare; medicine, salts. For four days he ate nothing. Finally he died. Interviewed about the matter, the third-mate acknowledged McDonald was a good seaman, but that he (the third-mate) was "down" on him.

"*Bear*, United States revenue steamer, Captain Healy. Three seamen — Holben, Daweritz and Frandsen — of the American bark *Estrella* charged that while discharging coal into the *Bear* in the harbor of Oonalaska, in June, 1889. Captain Healy, without provocation, ordered them placed in irons and confined in the forepeak of the *Bear*. Then they were triced up, with their hands behind them and their toes barely touching the deck. The punishment lasted fifteen minutes, and the pain was most excruciating. They were then tied with their backs to the stanchions and their arms around them for forty-two hours. They were then put ashore (on the island) and made to shift for themselves. The seamen accused both Captain

Healy and Captain Avery of the *Estrella* of drunkenness and gross incapacity. Healy exonerated by Navy Department.

"*Bear 2*, United States revenue steamer, Captain Healy. Crew of whaling bark *Northern Light* refused duty in Port Clarence, June 8, 1889, on account of cruelty from the officers. Captain Healy ordered them all in irons. First-Lieutenant of the *Bear* was sent aboard the *Northern Light* to execute the order. Crew triced up to the skids with arms behind their backs and toes just touching the deck. One man's hands were lashed with hambroline (small cord), as the irons were too small for his wrists; line cut into the flesh three-eighths of an inch. One man fainted from pain, and the *Bear's* doctor had to bring him to. Men were triced up fifteen minutes, suffering untold pain."

Maguire Act Passed

The "Red Record" campaign was developed simultaneously with the introduction of the Maguire bills into the U.S. Congress. The original Maguire package called for, among other points, abolition of punishment for desertion, a practice which had been reestablished in 1890; the improvement of seamen's forecastle quarters; a ban on violence by officers; a two-watch (four hours on, four off) system, with legal holidays; prohibition of advances, allotments, wage attachment; publication of a handy directory of maritime laws along with a standardized identification and discharge form; regulation of vessel surveys, and civil penalties rather than imprisonment for refusal to ship on unsafe vessels.

Absurdly enough, the sea-slavery then prevalent in the U.S. maritime industry was considered so "natural" and necessary a feature of economic life that the provisions of the Maguire bills were viciously attacked in Washington as "communistic." In 1895, however, the Maguire Act was finally passed. But the fight for legal abolition of seamen's involuntary servitude was not easily concluded. During 1894 while the country was shaken by a massive railroad strike led by Eugene Victor Debs and the American Railway Union, Furuseth used the pages of the *Coast Seamen's Journal* now under the full editorship of the brilliant Walter Macarthur, to warn railroad workers and others that if the legal chains applied to the seamen were not soon struck off, they would be extended by the courts to other sections of labor. The *Journal* added that among those opposing the bill, some, "instead of favoring the abolition of involuntary servitude in the case of the seamen . . . favored its extension to the railroad worker."[33]

It was therefore a difficult and contradictory time for the Union. Pete Gill later recounted how "the morale of the Union was severely tried during the dark winter of 1893-94. A small nucleus of loyal union men worked heroically to control the wavering mass of the organization. But even while the Union was forced to give ground under the attack of shipowners and police, it gained strength in another direction. The same situation that prompted sailors to join the Union prior to the attack, and force wages and conditions up to the place they had been in 1892, reappeared when the Union's control over them was broken. Many of the scabs on the ships were deep-water men; the landsmen who remained aboard for any length of time were becoming sailors. Thus the victory of the shipowners and the ensuing miserable conditions *drove their own scabs* [emphasis added] toward isolated revolts against low wages, abusive treatment and intolerable working conditions, and beyond the individual revolts toward the increasing realization that the Sailors' Union was their only protection . . . Three months after the Curtin bomb, headquarters reported non-union men wanted to join."[34]

Abuses continued; masters of vessels still paid "blood money" for men and then "worked them off" through brutality or overwork in order to forego paying wages. The slop chest was a center of corruption, with officers making steep deductions from the final payoff, ostensibly for provisions. Shanghaiing remained a common custom. Food was still often inedible, and at least unhealthy. The U.S. merchant marine, with less than 10 percent of world commerce, reported over half as many cases of scurvy and beriberi as the British merchant fleet, with 67 percent of world shipping. (As a remedy against scurvy, a daily portion of citrus juice was issued to all men aboard British Ships — hence the nickname "limejuicer" or "limey" ships.)

But passage of the Maguire Act was an encouraging step. It prevented the crimps, at long last, from holding men's clothes, did away with the worst abuses of the "advance" system, and freed the sailor from imprisonment for "desertion." These reforms aided the Union in raising wages through a strike in April 1895.

Arago Case

The powerful interests opposed to seamen's emancipation were not prepared to concede without a struggle. In May 1895, the scandalous case of the barkentine *Arago* erupted. Four seamen who shipped on the vessel in San Francisco for a voyage to the Columbia River and thence to Chile attempted to quit the vessel at Knapton, Washington. They were arrested and imprisoned until the *Arago*'s sailing, when they were carried on board in irons. They refused to turn to and were removed from the ship in San Francisco, where they were arrested on a charge of "refusing duty." It was the first major test of the Maguire Act. The seamen's case was carried to the U.S. Supreme Court and Congressman Maguire himself argued in their favor. But when the decision was finally handed down in January 1897, the Supreme Court justices shockingly upheld imprisonment for desertion, holding that the "surrender of personal liberty" involved in the seamen's contract was valid, and was not nullified

[33]*Coast Seamen's Journal*, August 22, 1894. [34]Gill and Markholt, op. cit.

by the Thirteenth Amendment, which had purportedly abolished involuntary servitude. The court supported its judgment by citing precedents derived from medieval maritime law, including the Catalan compilation known as the *Consolat de Mar*, which evolved as an authority for Mediterranean shipping between the years 1200 and 1400 A.D., and the Visby rules, a Baltic maritime code, some of whose insurance provisions remain in effect today. They further appealed to the archaic status of the seaman as a "ward of the nation." The message of the high court was unmistakable: so far as the sea was concerned, the laws regulating the freedom of the laboring class would not recognize the abolition of feudalism; further, the rulers of the nation were intent on crushing unions and would balk at no measure in this quest.

The only member of the Court to dissent from the case was Justice John Harlan, who stated that "we may now look for advertisements, not for runaway servants as in the days of slavery, but for runaway seamen." The decision was immediately labelled the "Dred Scott Decision Number II", and the response of the Union was understandably bitter. A petition for a rehearing of the matter was presented to the Court. The Sailors' Union, asked to join in festivities for July 4, 1897, in San Francisco, replied by stating that it, "being mindful of our status . . . that of involuntary servitude . . . felt it would be an imposition on our part to . . . inflict our presence . . . the presence of bondsmen . . . upon the freemen who will on the Fourth of July celebrate their freedom." In January 1898, the Supreme Court refused a new hearing on the matter and the Union that year again declined to celebrate Independence Day, declaring that "the spectacle of a slave worshipping his chains would be less ludicrous than that of the American seamen celebrating Independence Day." The *Coast Seamen's Journal* soon noted the effects of the *Arago* decision on the legal inviolability of a laborer's contract in the shoreside unionized trades, with a contract signed by the Pittsburgh Plate Glass Company at two plants in Indiana "filed in the county court (with) a violation of it . . . considered as contempt of court. That is to say, either party is liable to imprisonment without trial by jury. This is a practical reversion to the statutory wage system of the 16th and 17th centuries," the *Journal* commented.

White Act

A number of the early clauses of the Maguire Act had been dropped during the congressional fight for its passage and soon the seamen's organization, which in 1896 changed its title from the National Seamen's Union to the International Seamen's Union, sought to introduce them anew. In March 1897, Senator Stephen White of California proposed a Senate version of the original 1896 Maguire bills with Maguire himself handling the battle in the lower house. The White Act was confirmed in the Senate in July 1898, although subcommittee amendments struck out clauses requiring watch-and-watch (four hours on and off) and enlarged forecastles, and included a one month's pay allotment in the foreign trade and one month's imprisonment for desertion outside the U.S. The White Act passed the House in December 1898 with further amendments including a transfer of liability from the owner to the master for incidents of brutality and a reduction of the prescribed water ration. The main thrust of this legislative victory, following on the Maguire Act, was to cut down the power of the crimps, with a fine for payment of advances and for charging of a shipping fee.[35]

At century's end, the seamen had gained significantly in their fight for recognition. The fortunes of the Union may have yet seemed mixed: each legislative victory was balanced by the maintenance of "escape clauses" for the shipowners. But the crimping system had been dealt a severe blow. The Union had withstood the attacks of a venal press, and those who sought to defeat the seamen's movement through the tactics of libel and slander, smearing the Union as "un-American" and "radical," had discovered that their efforts only strengthened the sailors' will to resist oppression.

The Sailors' Union had reached a position of eminence within the ranks of labor on the West Coast, nationally and internationally. The year 1900 saw the beginning of a major campaign to organize seamen on the Great Lakes and, in 1901, the Union joined in the organization of a new City Front Federation of San Francisco "wharf and wave" unions. But the enemies of labor were prepared for another, even better organized, attack. Walthew had eventually been abandoned by the employers as a liability but his ruthlessness was to be revived and applied anew in the mighty battle of the 1901 San Francisco transportation strike.

[35]Gill and Markholt, ibid.

CHAPTER III
Storm Birds
(1900-1915)

With a new century beginning, the Sailors' Union of the Pacific found itself in a contradictory position. A historian of San Francisco Bay Area labor relations in the period, Robert Knight, has noted that "the Sailors' Union was unusually influential in the San Francisco labor movement. The *Coast Seamen's Journal* (was) the only union paper existing in San Francisco. The Sailors' Union donated large sums to support strikes by other unions, and by 1900 many of its members had been active in organizing onshore workers and in serving as outstanding leaders of various San Francisco unions and labor councils."[1]

But while the previous 15 years had shown improvement in the situation of union labor in general and of the Sailors in particular, underlying social conflicts remained unresolved and, in many cases, became more aggravated. Pete Gill, just then beginning his long tenure as agent for the Union in the Port of Seattle, has described the threatening aspect of the time in eloquent terms: "Employers nationally were . . . organizing both industrially in the first huge monopolies and trusts, and defensively against labor in national trade associations . . . Labor and capital were consolidating for battle. Shorn of revolutionary phrases, it was nevertheless a very real and bitter class struggle that was born out of the old century."[2]

The end of the nineties had seen a new increase in labor organization. The weakened economy of the 19th century's final decade gave way, at last, to a recovery that made the improvement of labor's fortunes possible. The stronger labor movement generated yet stronger militancy, and was answered by the employers with yet another attempt at destruction of labor's rights, perhaps the most serious ever seen in the United States. In San Francisco, the battle between the unions and business culminated in the dramatic, bloody 1901 transportation strike, one of the paramount class war incidents in U.S. history.

Internal Dispute

In 1900, the year before that conflict, a brief internal struggle broke out in the S.U.P., about which we unfortunately can say little today. We do know that Furuseth, increasingly preoccupied with his legislative agitation on seamen's rights, found himself opposed by a group of the Union's pioneers, headed by the two Jortall brothers, Nick and Chris, founding member Ed Andersen, and John Kean. According to Furuseth's biographer, Hyman Weintraub, this dissident group gained the support of the majority of the organization's members, and began to direct fire against Walter Macarthur, Furuseth's stand-in as editor of the *Coast Seamen's Journal,* and Ed Rosenberg, who functioned as temporary secretary in Furuseth's absence. Early in 1900, Macarthur and Rosenberg resigned their posts in anger at the growing dissident constituency. Rosenberg attacked the anti-Furuseth group in exceptionally strong terms, asserting, "I did not want to play to the dungaree sailor element by pretending that I was one of them. Their filthy language, their beastly carousing, their dirt, I despise, and I shall always say so. It is evil and it should be fought against." Rosenberg described Nick Jortall, a man who had ably distinguished himself in the service of the seamen's cause, as a "demagogue among the white shirt sailors who for lust of power or for personal gain play to the dungaree sailors."

Furuseth responded to the criticism of the opposition first by arguing that it played into the employers' hands. He then carried out a successful campaign against John Vance Thompson, who had taken over the position of *Journal* editor following Macarthur's resignation. This was not the last instance in which Furuseth and Thompson, a dedicated labor journalist, would come into conflict. By mid-1901, Macarthur was back in the top editorial slot on the paper. The internal struggle faded with the coming of the big strike of that year.[3]

---

[1]R.E.L. Knight, *Industrial Relations in the San Francisco Bay Area, 1900-1918,* Berkeley, University of California Press, 1960. [2]Gill and Markholt, op. cit. [3]Weintraub, op. cit. Furuseth's biographer bases his account of these events on documents formerly held in the S.U.P. archives but not currently locable.

It is difficult to ascertain, today, the real character of this quarrel. Most unfortunately, the original records consulted by Hyman Weintraub are now lost. What seems to have developed was a political competition between two factions of the so-called "white shirt sailors," meaning, apparently, those who, in seeking community respectability, consciously set themselves apart from their fellow seamen. It would seem that the catalyst of this split was the tendency of one side, that of the Jortalls, Andersen, and Kean, to criticize the other for what might, in the context of the times, have appeared as opportunistic place-seeking.

The events are important, however, for a number of reasons. First, they show that such accusations of demagogy, which continue in the labor movement — and in the Sailors' Union of the Pacific at the time of this writing — are anything but new. Second, they establish the precedent of conflict between John Vance Thompson and Furuseth, which would flare again two decades later (see chapter IV). Of one thing we may be sure: neither the Jortall brothers, nor Andersen, nor Macarthur, nor Furuseth can be doubted, in retrospect, as to their loyalty and enthusiasm in the Sailors' fight for freedom. What we may hope is that, at some future time, the records will be retrieved from their present oblivion, and the matter seriously evaluated by historians.

The Union had by then, in addition to improvements in legal status, attained a number of minor goals in protecting its members' working conditions. The half-hour dinner period observed on steam schooners had been extended to a full hour. A nine-hour day in port was adopted in the larger ports. The Union's first set of working rules had been developed, calling for both the full dinner hour and the nine-hour day, as well as overtime for moving ship in San Francisco Bay. The Union had expanded its geographical influence with the establishment of the Honolulu branch on July 1, 1900.

City Front Federation

A most significant public action by the Union in the period leading up to the 1901 strike was the foundation, in January of that year, of the City Front Federation, linking the Sailors with the longshoremen, teamsters, mates, engineers, marine firemen, freight-handlers, and lumbermen. Altogether, 44 delegates represented nine unions. John Kean, Chris Jortall, and F. Johnson were elected from the S.U.P. In May 1901, a new member of the maritime labor family was born: the marine cooks and stewards established their first stable organization.[4]

The anti-union business elements were also organizing. In April 1901, fifty San Francisco employers revived the Employers' Association on a secret basis and pledged the eradication of the unions. San Francisco had, in many respects, led the way for the national labor movement as the first important city in which unions won full recognition. The Employers' Association was now preparing an attempt, in reply, to make the city the standard bearer for the "open shop." The Association operated through sub-associations in each industry, all directed by M. F. Michael, an attorney, and the only individual publicly identified with the secret group.

With the coming of spring, the new employers' campaign began. A strike by culinary workers was followed by secret actions by the Employers' Association to block the delivery of oysters, bread, and meat to restaurants that recognized the union. Wholesalers to the wagon-delivery industry declined to supply materials to unionized firms. During the summer, beer bottlers fired their union workers and announced adherence to a rigid "open shop" policy. Ironworkers and machinists were already on strike. The test was approaching.

1901: Teamsters Locked Out

The clash between the employers and the mighty ranks of San Francisco labor began in earnest in July when a group of teamsters were locked out for refusing to haul non-union baggage. At mid-month the Employers' Association, acting through its constituent draymen's group, informed the teamsters that they must all leave the unions or quit their jobs; 6,400 teamsters walked off the job, in protest.

The City Front Federation, led by Furuseth, attempted to arbitrate the growing crisis, but soon learned that the employers' side was definitively controlled by the secret Michael group, which refused even to meet with union representatives. The San Francisco Labor Council described the secret group as a "menace to the peace and prosperity of the community," while the Sailors' Union referred to the employers' conspiratorial group as an "order of industrial assassins."

The war on the unions was supported by the courts, the police, and the city administration. Against a backdrop of national labor unrest, the San Francisco workers found themselves in a genuine life-and-death struggle for their rights. A similar determination to wipe out unionism was also becoming visible in other major cities around the world.

At the end of July the City Front Federation, in protest against the terroristic secrecy of the Employers' Association, unanimously declared its willingness to fight. The *Coast Seamen's Journal* declared that "San Francisco has now entered upon the greatest epoch in her career, and the issue will decide, for a long time at least, whether she will continue to grow as a free, sovereign commonwealth, peopled by free and self-respecting manhood and womanhood, or fall into a state of rot and decay, breeding nothing but industrial parasites and the stuff they prey on." The *Journal* went on to assert that "the City Front Federation of San Francisco now holds in its hands the fortunes of the entire labor movement on the Pacific

[4]Gill and Markholt, op. cit.

Coast and, to a considerable extent, of the labor movement throughout the country. The result of the present struggle in San Francisco will either strengthen or weaken the forces of labor now aligned to meet the onslaught of concentrated capital against the liberties and the common manhood of the American people. The result lies with ourselves. The workers, united and firm in the demand for decent conditions of employment, are supreme and invincible . . . no employers' association or other array of opposing forces can subjugate them."[5] In an accompanying statement over the signature of acting President John Kean, the City Front Federation warned that "we are satisfied that we have done everything we could to avert this crisis, but arrogant and designing capital will it otherwise. Those individuals in society who would use their industrial power to rob us of our right of organization granted to us by society as a whole must bear responsibility for whatever may now take place."

The ranks of the striking teamsters were increased by 20,000 with the declaration of a walkout of the City Front Federation. The open-shop forces also swelled, with the importation of strikebreakers. Neither side was prepared to surrender. Strikers were assaulted by police as well as by strikebreakers, nearly all of whom were armed. Special detective services provided "guards" to protect scab deliveries. The Sailors' Union patrolled the waterfront, issuing passes to union men. The pro-employer San Francisco *Argonaut* slashed at the Union for this practice, slandering Furuseth as "this Scandinavian dictator of ours (who) wants his Scandinavian scum to be permitted to beat American citizens into a bloody pulp."[6] Along with the Teamsters' Michael Casey, Furuseth, the seamen's champion, became one of the main labor spokesmen during the dramatic contest, thanks to his skill as a speaker and the determination of the Sailors' Union membership.

Account of Strike

Pete Gill and Ottilie Markholt's eloquent account of the strike deserves excerpting here:

"July 29th the City Front Federation met. After heated discussion the meeting declared: 'The full membership of the City Front Federation refuses to work at the docks of San Francisco, Oakland, Port Costa and Mission Rock. The steamers *Bonita* and *Walla Walla*, with mail and passengers, now in the stream, will be allowed to go to sea.' Delegates from 14 unions voted unanimously for the resolution: sailors, four locals of longshoremen, Marine Firemen, Brotherhood of Teamsters, Ship and Steamboat Joiners, Porters, Packers and Warehousemen, Ship Clerks, Pile Drivers and Bridge Builders, Hoisting Engineers, Steam and Hot Water Fitters and Coal Teamsters.

"At 11:45 P.M. the delegates from the City Front Federation brought the news to the sailors' meeting. With a roar the 350 members endorsed the action unanimously. Two thousand teamsters at the San Francisco Athletic Club, when they received the news, 'leaped to their feet, men fell over each other in their excitement, and when a minute later the doors were opened it was a torrent of shouting humanity which poured out into Sixth St.,' according to a press report. At the meetings of longshoremen and porters, packers and warehousemen, waiting for the decision, the cheering continued after the men were out on the street. The City Front Federation said officially:

" 'After having waited four days for a definite reply to our request for a conference, the Employers' Association steadily refused to do anything to adjust the difficulty; they refused to meet us; they refused to continue to employ the men now in their employment, except upon the condition that they are to quit their union and cut themselves loose from all affiliation with their fellow-workmen.

" 'The Federation has exhausted all honorable means to have the difficulty adjusted, but has failed in its efforts, and finds that there is nothing left but to appeal to its membership to be true to the cause for which organized labor stands . . .'

"The morning of July 30th 20,000 men struck. All shipping companies were affected except Pacific Coast Steamship, whose firemen remained at work under an agreement similar to one reached with the sailors before the strike. Three coasting steamers, a ship and a schooner sailed. Steamship owners cooperated with the Shipowners' Association. Work that had been delayed by the teamsters' lockout ceased entirely along the front. It was reported that as a retaliatory measure wholesale houses would close, but this was denied by the Employers' Association, who were confident of victory. San Francisco awaited developments expectantly. The press reported minor disturbances among the strikers. Twenty five more scab teams were sent out under police protection.

"That night Theodore Wesselink, a seaman, was clubbed about the head and seriously injured on the Broadway dock while actually moving on. He was arrested, charged with disturbing the peace, but the charge was dismissed. (S.F.P.D.) Captain Wittman defended the police: 'If innocent people are in the crowd and are hurt it will be their own fault. I will stand by my men when they are doing their duty and obeying orders. Several times people have taken the numbers of policemen who were using force to disperse crowds, but as the policemen were acting under orders I will stand by them and fully endorse their action.'

"The next day a few scab longshoremen worked at Oceanic and Pacific Coast Steamship Company docks; five steamers were loading and many more waiting. Two sailed, and two the following day. A Japanese labor union instructed its members to support the strikers.

[5]*Coast Seamen's Journal*, July 31, 1901 [6]Knight, op. cit.

"July 29th the Employers' Association rejected the City Front Federation's proposal through Mayor Phelan, demanded the open shop and renunciation of sympathetic strikes and boycotts. The following day Mayor Phelan submitted the terms to the City Front Federation, recommending acceptance. The Federation 'rejected without debate' the propositions. July 31st Phelan reported on a conference with the Directors of the Employers' Association in which they reiterated their previous proposals, but agreed to recommend reemployment of strikers, except 10 or 12 teamsters. He urged capitulation. The same day the City Front Federation proposed through Phelan that the Association should not discriminate against union shops or union employees, reemploy strikers, and endeavor to adjust disputes peaceably. August 2nd Michael replied through Phelan recommending employment of teamsters regardless of union affiliation, the open shop, and a pledge that employees would not support sympathetic strikes or boycotts. Phelan asked the employers to modify their stand against sympathetic strikes and boycotts, to which the Federation objected. The employers refused. Phelan delivered the letter to Furuseth and Michael Casey of the teamsters, urging settlement. The evening of August 3rd the Executive Committee of the City Front Federation resolved that there was no basis for settlement; the negotiations ended. Furuseth declared:

" 'The letter is grossly insulting to labor, and would deprive us of all our rights. The provision that employees must neither directly nor indirectly support or engage in any sympathetic strike would prevent us from even contributing to the support of striking workers. The assertion that the Employers' Association has never discriminated against firms employing union labor is a barefaced lie. It has repeatedly so discriminated in the past. It stopped the supply of meat to compel butcher shops to employ non-union men. It compelled the draymen to discharge their union employees on pain of losing business. The letter is an arrogant refusal to recognize the rights of the men.'

"The teamsters paid out $4,000 in benefits. Pacific Coast Steamship Company announced it would never again recognize the union, but take strikers back individually without firing scabs. Colored longshoremen scabbed; scabs at Oceanic dock struck successfully when the company tried to reduce wages from 50 to 40 cents an hour. August 7th 500 sand teamsters struck, and the Pacific Coast Marine Firemen struck Pacific Coast Steamship Company vessels; the company threatened to sue the firemen, an incorporated union with a large treasury. Two days later the Marine Cooks and Stewards walked out, and the strikers threatened to extend the strike along the Coast if no settlement was reached.

"The Sailors' Union elected an Executive Committee of seven to carry on the strike and instructed all members to report regularly for duty. The *Journal* declared: 'The long drawn out 'peace conference' talk is played out, and everybody is glad of it. We now know where we are at, and can set about the work before us in a businesslike manner. Let's do it!'

"August 8th the strikers held a huge rally at the Metropolitan Temple. Reverend Frank K. Baker of the Methodist Episcopal Church spoke first for a peaceful settlement through arbitration. When Andrew Furuseth rose to speak he was greeted with cheers.

" '. . . They said there would be riots on the waterfront. There have not been any, have there? (A voice, 'No!') It was a time to exercise self restraint. We know that he is thrice armed who hath his quarrel just. We can afford to wait and keep the peace. We know we are right. We should take the same course tomorrow were we confronted by the same identical conditions. (Applause) We were forbidden to remain union men. What could we do? We could quit work until we could gain recognition. We cannot renounce the right to support each other, to quit work in unison and we would not if we could. We throw our all in the balance. We take the chances of going months without employment, of lacking food and being met on going home by hungry wives and children. We know the cost. But if we can not take these chances we are not the true sons of men who gained us the liberty we have. (Applause)"

'A Strike Is War'

"Father (Peter C.) Yorke, a Catholic priest whose influence among seamen and especially longshoremen was great, spoke for the strikers. 'A strike is war. It is the last recourse . . . while you desire peace you cannot afford to accept any peace but peace with honor.' He spoke for the right of the worker to a living wage and the necessity for unions.

" 'And I say that it is a crying shame that, while the workmen have been orderly, and whatever shooting has been done has been from those who have been trying to take your place, it is a crying shame, I say, under such circumstances that the police force of this city, paid for by your taxes, should be turned into guardian angels of the draymen. (Great applause) If when this strike began the government of this city had held even justice between employer and employed, and had not thrown the whole force of the city's prestige and power into the hands of the employers, I believe the strike would have been ended before this time. (Great applause).'

"The next meeting of the Sailors' Union adopted resolutions thanking Father Yorke for his support and the San Francisco *Examiner* for its fair treatment of strike news.

"August 10th the Chamber of Commerce over the signature of George A. Newhall, president, demanded additional police protection for scabs or state troops from Mayor Phelan, charging violence and intimidation by strikers. The Executive Council of the Labor Council replied to Phelan, criticizing Newhall, a police commissioner appointed by the Mayor, for taking sides, and denying violence by the strikers.

" 'Whatever exceptional violence has occurred has been initiated by and is to be laid at the door of the

At the fore braces, bark Star of Finland, *an Alaska Packers vessel crewed by the S.U.P. (1918).*
(National Maritime Museum)

Sigismund Danielewicz
(Bancroft Library)

Loading lumber
(S.U.P. Archive)

Burnette Gregor Haskell

(Bancroft Library)

Some members of the C.S.U. and I.W.A.

(Bancroft Library)

Andrew Furuseth

(National Maritime Museum)

Early nameplate (1888)

AUSTRALASIAN FEDERATED SEAMEN'S UNION.

(WELLINGTON SECTION.)

QUEEN'S CHAMBERS. POST OFFICE SQUARE

Links with unions "down under" were important

(S.U.P. Archive)

An early headquarters for the S.U.P., on the San Francisco waterfront

(S.U.P. Archive)

S.U.P. and I.S.U. symbol

(S.U.P. Archive)

Union men gather in front of S.U.P. headquarters during the 1901 transport strike

(National Maritime Museum)

ORGANIZED FEBRUARY 2, 1901 MEETS EVERY WEDNESDAY EVENING

City Front Federation

Of the Port of San Francisco, California

R CO No. 93 STUART STREET

(S.U.P. Archive)

The Alaska Packers fleet, manned by the S.U.P., tied up in Alameda in the early 20th century

(National Maritime Museum)

The I.W.W. represented a radical challenge

(S.U.P. Archive)

The coast lumber trade: ships wait for loading in Port Blakeley, Washington, winter of 1905

(National Maritime Museum)

Internationale Transportarbeiter-Federation

Adresse: H. Jochade, **Berlin S. O. 16**
Engel-Ufer 18 II.

Telegramm-Adresse
Telegraphic-Address } **Intransfe-Berlin**
Telegrammes

The S.U.P. and I.S.U. were active in the I.T.F.

(S.U.P. Archive)

The S.U.P. maintained contact with seamen's unions from all over the world

(S.U.P. Archive)

THE NATIONAL SAILORS' & FIREMEN'S UNION

OF GREAT BRITAIN AND IRELAND. *(Registered T.U. No. 1493).*

Telegraphic Address
"SEAROVING, POP. LONDON."

(Approved under the National Insurance Act, Certificate No. 128).

Telephone No.
EAST 905

Registered Office:

MARITIME HALL,

WEST INDIA DOCK ROAD,

LONDON, E.

Affiliated with the National and International Transport Workers' Federations.

Furuseth forged a bond with England's maritime union leader, J. Havelock Wilson

(S.U.P. Archive)

Marine Transport Workers

Organize into ONE BIG UNION

AND BRING THE BOSSES TO THEIR KNEES!

Addressed to all marine transport workers on the Atlantic and Pacific coasts, the Gulf ports and the Great Lakes; to seamen and deckhands; firemen, oilers, watertenders, coal passers and wipers; marine stewards, cooks, bakers, butchers, messboys and waiters; engineers, pilots, mates and masters; checkers and longshoremen.

You have been on strike since May 1, 1921.

On that day the U. S. Shipping Board and the American Steamship Owners' Association locked out all men carrying membership cards in the three unions that make up the International Seamen's Union of America, refusing to have anything more to do with your unions.

And you lost the strike. You are beaten to a standstill. Your unions are as dead as a doornail. **Why?**

Because you lacked solidarity in your ranks. The shipowners are united in **One Organization**—they know the value of scientific efficiency—while you are **split up** in a half dozen organizations: Eastern and Gulf Sailors' Association, Marine Firemen, Oilers & Watertenders' Union, Marine Cooks and Stewards' Association, Sailors' Union of the Pacific, National Marine Engineers' Beneficial Association, International Longshoremen's Association. Craft unionism was allright in its day, but it is now unable to

I.W.W. literature during the 1921 strike

(S.U.P. Archive)

I.W.W. art

(S.U.P. Archive)

THE MARINE WORKER

"AN INJURY TO ONE IS AN INJURY TO ALL"

No. 3 August 1st, 1921 New York, N. Y.

PACIFIC COAST SEAMEN MOVING TOWARD O. B. U.

Seek Unity With All Transport Workers. Vote Down Union Wage Cut Plan.

WASHINGTON.—Returns from the referendum vote of the sailors, the marine firemen and oilers, the marine cooks and stewards of the Pacific coast, on the union agreement negotiated with the association of steam schooner owners, show that the agreement was rejected by the sailors by about 15½ to 1, rejected by the firemen and oilers by 4 to 1, and accepted by the cooks and stewards.

SWEDISH CRAFT UNIONS DEFEAT THEMSELVES

The sailors, firemen and longshoremen here in Sweden are getting their mouths full of craft union dry rot. We will give you a short resume of the mess that the craft unions have made for the workers here in the marine industry.

The leaders for the sailors and firmen's unions started the new year by bargaining with the shipowners for the prolongation of their agreement. The shipowners agreed so far that they would retain it, but inserted the clause that they could heave it overboard with two months' warning. The shipping was then practically at a stand-

ITALIAN SEAMEN OWN BIG COMPANY

Six Ships Operated and Controlled by Their Union.

BALTIMORE. — Captain Brigneti, of the Italian steamship Pietro Cori, which arrived to-day from Trieste, is in the employ of the seamen aboard that ship and enjoys the distinction of being able to tell his employers what to do instead of taking orders from them. Every sailor aboard the

I.W.W. literature after 1921 defeat

(S.U.P. Archive)

S.S. "WEST MAHWAH" JUNE 17th 1924.

NOTICE TO MEMBERS OF CREW

EFFECTIVE FROM THIS DATE, ANY MEMBER OF THE CREW THAT DOES NOT DO A FAIR DAYS WORK DURING THE EIGHT HOURS IN ANY ONE DAY, WILL BE ORDERED TO WORK NINE HOURS A DAY. AND FAILING TO PERFORM A FAIR DAYS WORK DURING THE NINE HOURS IN EACH DAY. THEN, A REDUCTION FROM A.B. TO O.S. OR WORKAWAY WILL FOLLOW, WHAT EVER THE CASE MAY WARRANT.

TRUSTING ALL OF YOU WILL ACT AS MEN, AND THEN YOU WILL ALL RECIEVE A FAIR DEAL THROUGHOUT.

MASTER S.S. "WEST MAHWAH"

(S.U.P. Archive)

The Olson steam-schooners were among the few unionized ships during the bleak period 1921-1934. The steam-schooner Oliver Olson.

(S.U.P. Archive)

The Cynthia Olson *under load*

(S.U.P. Archive)

UNITY OF SEAMEN, LONGSHOREMEN AND HARBOR WORKERS

For an Industrial Union Based on Ship, Dock and Fleet Committees

LONGSHOREMEN AND HARBOR WORKERS OF GRAYS HARBOR!

FELLOW WORKERS:

For 20 years the longshoremen and harbor workers of Grays Harbor have been unorganized.

Communist literature. (See account of Grays Harbor & Aberdeen incident, p. 74).

(S.U.P. Archive)

A steam schooner at work

(S.U.P. Archive)

Calm before the storm: San Francisco's Embarcadero, early 1934
(National Maritime Museum)

Aftermath of July 5, 1934: A National Guard machine gun nest.
(S.U.P. Archive)

STRIKE-SEAMEN-STRIKE

International Seamen's Union of America

PACIFIC DISTRICT

The Sailors' Union of the Pacific, the Pacific Coast Marine Firemen, Oilers, Watertenders and Wipers' Association, and the Marine Cooks and Stewards' Association of the Pacific Coast are on strike for enforcement of the wages and working conditions submitted at the Shipping Code hearing held at Washington, D. C., November 10, 1933.

These demands provide for $75.00 per month for Sailors and Firemen, and 75 cents per hour overtime, abolition of the scab shipping offices, for union recognition and full union conditions.

Now is the time to fight for better conditions and remedy long standing grievances.

ALL SEAMEN UNITE! PULL TOGETHER!

Strike call, 1934

(S.U.P. Archive)

Action in Seattle: minutes before the police charge strikers, June 21, 1934

(S.U.P. Archive)

"Opening the port of San Francisco": retreating strikers, July 3, 1934

(Associated Press — S.U.P. Archive)

Police action against strikers

(S.U.P. Archive)

Strikers on Rincon Hill

(S.U.P. Archive)

View of Rincon Hill, scene of fighting in July 1934, from the westernmost tower of the San Francisco–Oakland Bay Bridge, then under construction. White markings indicate locations for bridge structures

(Hugh Crandall Collection)

employers, of those they are using to hurt us and of the police themselves . . .'

" '. . . In the first place, that the police are acting as teamsters for the employers; that they direct those men who have been imported to take our places and who are unfamiliar with the city, and that they even help in the management of the vehicles and goods. We have protested in the second place that the police have shown bias and have used unnecessary violence in dealing with peaceable and orderly crowds of American citizens who have as much right to line the sidewalks on the 4th of August as they have on the 4th of July . . .'

" '. . . The police cannot be impartial when the head of the commission, to which they look for orders and promotion, is rabidly opposed to one side of the community.' The Labor Council demanded Newhall's removal from the Police Commission because he was unfit for the position.

"The following day the San Francisco Board of Trade repeated the sentiments of the Chamber of Commerce in another letter to Phelan asking additional police protection. Phelan replied to the Labor Council August 13th, whitewashing Newhall by claiming that it was not his letter, but the Board of Directors', and Newhall merely signed it as an officer. 'I am of the opinion that he will act fairly and impartially as a member of the Board of Police Commissioners.'

"The Labor Council replied the next day that Phelan's excuse was 'puerile beyond conception,' and reiterated its charges against Newhall and the Police Commission. The police were put on scab wagons and assisted scab teamsters 'to show sympathy for employers, to dishearten workers, to give the appearance of riots.' They used unnecessary violence against strikers, 'address us as dogs and drive us as cattle.'

" 'Is it against the law for a non-union man to speak to us? If not, why, then, are they worked in pens like cattle before the stock yards? Why are they housed in floating bastilles? Why are they led out under the shotgun?' Because the employers had deceived these men and feared to have them learn their rights, the Council replied, warning the Mayor that the citizens, who were with the strikers with the exception of the small clique of employers, 'would not permit the government to be used to injure their interests.'

"It was announced that the regular policemen would be taken off the trucks and assigned to the streets to preserve order. The draymen then declared they would hire special deputies to guard their trucks, at their own expense, and asked that the specials be deputized. The Police Commission obliged, claiming that they would thus be controlled by and responsible to public authorities. . .

"August 19th the Labor Council protested to the meeting of the Board of Supervisors against: retaining Newhall, using police on the wagons, and employing special deputies from everywhere without inquiry into their character or fitness. August 22nd the Board of Supervisors met and referred the Labor Council's protest to the Police Commission, with a resolution condemning Newhall's letter calling for militia and special deputies:

" 'Resolved: That the Board of Supervisors of the city and county of San Francisco condemns the intemperate language of President Newhall of the Police Commission and declares that the conduct of the striking wage earners has been, in the main highly creditable to their citizenship; that with nearly 20,000 men on strike it is not to be expected that some disturbances of the peace should not occur; but that no occasion exists for a proclamation by the mayor, or for the calling out of the military by the governor; and be it further

" 'Resolved: That the character and qualifications of special police officers should be scrupulously inquired into before appointment; that they should be required to wear uniforms and should be under the special and continuous supervision of the regular police; and be it further

" 'Resolved: That the Police Department should preserve absolute impartiality between the parties to the present labor controversy; that the wage earner and employers are equally entitled to the service of the police and that the functions of the police should be strictly confined to maintaining the peace, and they should not directly or indirectly give aid or assistance to either of the parties to the labor controversy.' "

"August 23rd 9,000 strikers marched in a huge parade led by Mike Casey, business agent of the Teamsters; Andrew Furuseth; and Rosenberg, Secretary of the San Francisco Labor Council; and two bands. The police platoon were absent. In San José the same day a torchlight parade and mass meeting was held for the strikers, at which a resolution condemning the Employers' Association and supporting the strikers was passed.

"The *Journal* summarized the status of the strike August 23rd: 12,000 City Front Federation members were out; 800 scabs working on the front; and 300 scab teamsters working. The employers did about 35 per cent business at such an expense that it cost a consignee for lumber or coal double or triple what it was worth. Two hundred vessels were tied up along the front; no men had gone back to work; and during the previous week 200 additional men had been induced to quit work. The work on the front was merely a bluff to break the morale of the unions. Morally and financially the employers were ready to break at any moment. Public opinion was turning more openly toward the strikers, rising throughout the entire west. Large and small unions were doing their part. Vessels that got away used deepwater men taken from British ships. August 26th Casey addressed a four-hour meeting at (S.U.P.) headquarters, attended by 550 members.

"Reports reached the strikers that students of the University of California were scabbing on the longshoremen at San Francisco and Oakland, and President Wheeler of the University defended their actions. A letter protested: 'It is one of the marks of a liberal education that those who receive it gratuitously should do what even uneducated men consider vile and infamous?' Headquarters meeting September 2nd submitted a resolution to the Coast, assessing each working member $5 (passed) and resolved:

" 'Whereas, some vessels that have been in the bay of San Francisco during the strike have tried to get away manned by officers and non-union crews with the purpose of proceeding up the coast and there getting union crews, and as this will have a tendency to spread the strike, therefore be it

" 'Resolved: That any vessel that has been in the bay of San Francisco during the strike be refused a crew of union men.' "

Labor Day 1901

"Labor Day, 1901, over 20,000 unionists marched in a four mile parade that took two hours to pass in close formation; 150 carriages for women, eight floats and twelve bands marked the parade. The City Front Federation, 9,400 strong, led the parade. 'Labor must be respected.' 'A Union in every port.' 'Hands off; we demand fair play,' read the placards. Delegations from Port Costa, Crockett and Vallejo unions joined the parade. Walter Macarthur of the Sailors was president of the day.

"Andrew Furuseth addressed the strikers:

" 'We have won because the employers couldn't in fifteen weeks find anybody to take the places of steel workers; because in six weeks they couldn't find anybody to take the place of the teamsters.

" 'They think they can starve us out. If they looked at our line today and looked at our thousands of sympathizers all along the streets they can understand that the starving process won't go . . .

" 'There are several ways by which strikes are broken. One way is to bring in other men. That has been tried and failed. Another way is to get one side of the labor force arrayed against the other. That, too, has failed. Another way is that which was used at Haymarket. They have schemed to break the strike through rioting. The soldiers cannot load and unload the vessels if they come but they can discourage the men who are on strike . . .

" 'For weeks we have had 20,000 men on strike and there has been less trouble than there was when 7,000 soldiers were let out on a holiday.

" 'Six hundred men have been picked up by Curtin from God knows where and have been sworn in as special policemen. But do not oppose these men.

" 'Turn yourselves into martyrs. Suffer any indignity. But don't permit them to draw you into any violence. I was told three months ago that we would all be forced into a strike, incited to violence, and then the soldiers would be called in. This was to break up the organization of labor.

" 'If you don't know what to do, find out what your enemies want you to do, and then — don't do it.

" 'There is no telling how long this is going to last — whether a week or a month. But if you have any regard for your children, stay with it.

" '. . . Prosperity came, in some degree, at least, but who got the benefit? Have they given any of the prosperity to the workingman? Now they are trying to make our conditions worse than ever, and we must resist. They are trying to incite us to resentment, but they will not succeed. We will stay away from work and ask for the sympathy of all the people, but we will not be led into violence.' "

Gill and Markholt's account continues, "At the meeting of the Board of Supervisors August 19th, at which the Labor Council's protest was considered, a committee was appointed to investigate the strike and make recommendations for settlement. September 2nd the committee requested the Directors of the Employers' Association to meet representatives of the unions, pointing out that public opinion was turning against the Association. Several more letters were exchanged, and September 7th the Employers' Association rejected proposals for conference. They repeated that the draymen were handling it; the Employers' Association was not directly involved; and 'they have nothing to compromise and nothing to arbitrate.'

"The teamsters under signature of M'Laughlin and Casey charged the Employers' Association with being an irresponsible, secret society, organized to destroy labor, and injecting itself into the affair between the teamsters and draymen to prevent settlement. September 9th headquarters minutes reported the tie up the same or more complete. A few steam schooners were sailing without any crews, the officers doing the work. A talk of Chief of Police Sullivan came into possession of the strikers:

" 'I am dissatisfied with the conduct of you men toward the strikers. I have gone about the city and seen my police chatting with strikers. You have neglected your duty by being too lenient with the strikers.

" 'The strikers must be driven off the streets.

" 'You must see that this is done. Drive them to their homes and see that they are kept there. The strikers must not be allowed on the streets.

" 'I will not permit my men to speak with or be on friendly terms with any of the strikers.

" 'Drive the union men to their homes and make them stay there.

" 'Keep the streets clear of union men.

" 'If any of you men do not feel disposed to carry out these orders you will probably have a chance to join the labor unions and the ranks of the strikers.

" 'I don't want you men to speak to any one of what I have said.' "

Stalemate

The strike continued at a stalemate, with days and weeks turning into months. Finally, on October 2, California governor Henry T. Gage announced a settlement consisting of nothing more than a declaration that the transport strikes and lockouts then in effect were ended. No details of any agreement were ever revealed, and the Battle of 1901 was widely conceded to have ended in a draw. Gill described the conflict as "the most remarkable (strike) in the history of the city;" during the two-month period, 5 men were killed with 336 recorded assaults, 250 requiring medical attention.

However, the Sailors, and the general labor movement had gained certain further advantages. Although the S.U.P. obtained nothing for itself, the unions had clearly won recognition. Strikers were to be rehired without discrimination. The secret Michael group had failed in its bid to extirpate unionism, and the Employers' Association returned to a less-belligerent course. According to historian Robert Knight, "in the crucial struggle of 1901, only the alliance forged by the members of the City Front Federation enabled San Francisco labor to halt the open-shop drive."[7]

Aftermath of 1901

Soon after the conclusion of the strike, the Sailors' Union won a new victory when federal judge Edward J. Bradford held that the provisions of the White Act barring the payment of advances applied to foreign seamen when in American ports.[8] The Union scored another triumph in the aftermath of the 1901 strike by finally securing a written contract with the West Coast shipowners. As indicated by historian Paul Taylor, the contract signed in 1902 marked the first full recognition won by the Sailors, after 17 years of struggle. The agreement was set for six months' duration with extensions subject to 30 days' notice of cancellation by either party.

In the 1902 agreement, the Union declared itself (somewhat contradictorily to its past position) opposed to sympathetic strikes, and the shipowners were allowed to set up a non-union shipping office in San Francisco (although barring the use of crimps). On the other hand, union work rules including the nine-hour day (except in San Francisco) and overtime, were recognized, at last, in a legal, contractual form.

The agreement was duly renewed in 1903. Although in 1904 the question of the Union shipping office re-emerged within the organization, it was set aside for a year. The Union expanded its agitation for improved shipboard conditions, concentrating on the bad forecastles for which the coastwise steam schooners were notorious. In addition, steam schooner space more appropriately used as a messroom, was utilized for cargo and passengers, forcing the crew to eat on the deck or even on the lumber load.

In a 1963 interview with West Coast maritime historian Harold Huycke, steam schooner veteran Art Swanson graphically described how, in the first decade of this century, meals were taken on a small such vessel. The ship was tied up to a log buoy, under a wire-chute. With no messroom or place to eat at a table on the little ship, the crew went out on deck and sat on the lumber load during the noon hour. With both hands full of dinner, a plate and a mug, Swanson went back to get a piece of pie from the galley. Returning to the deck-load, he saw a seagull taking wing with Swanson's steak in his beak! It was only with the passage of the 1915 LaFollette Seaman's Act that proper messrooms were made mandatory.

Understandably, every winter the absence of messrooms brought complaint from steam schooner sailors. Moreover, the living quarters under the forecastle head, right "in the eyes" of the little vessels, gave rise to other complaints. John Kean pointed out that originally the entire topgallant forecastle had been intended for the crew, but lately had been also used to accommodate steerage passengers. (This arrangement prevailed on the steam schooner *Wapama* as long as she was engaged in the coastal trade; the starboard half of the forecastle was for steerage passengers — $5.00 a head to Los Angeles — until she was sold to the Alaska Transportation Company in 1937.)

Kean went on to say that when the whole forecastle was available to the sailors there had been some light and ventilation, but that was entirely cut off by the deckload (which butted right up to the forecastle door); the deckload also blocked any emergency exit. The sailors were living in the part of the ship most vulnerable to collision, but it was to be many years before their quarters were forbidden by law to be in the bow of the ship.

Steam and exhaust pipes, Kean pointed out, to power the anchor and hoisting winch on the deck above, led through the forecastle, bringing extreme heat and drops of scalding water — the pipes could have been led around the sailor quarters. When the vessel was heavily laden in bad weather, the sea itself made its way into the forecastle by way of the anchor chain pipes. These mechanical intrusions were largely absent in sailing forecastles. Some forecastles were actually shrinking in size.

Steam schooner conditions had been the object of special Union attention beginning in 1900. In a period when steam schooner owner profits reached 33 percent, steam schooner sailors, one out of five of all coasting sailors, worked 10 to 20 hours in port. Union sources asserted that steam schooner men were a majority of Marine Hospital cases.[9]

New Radicalism

The 1901 strike had been but one illustration of a potential for class war on a broad scale in the U.S. Although the brunt of the workers' defense against abuses of the employing class had come to be carried by the mainstream union movement, extremist voices were again, as in the time of Haskell, Buchanan, and Parsons, heard in Labor. A dissatisfaction with the slow rate of progress sank roots.

Thus, nationally-known railroad labor leader Eugene Victor Debs turned to a political socialism strongly influenced by Western European models, after attempting to organize industry-wide through

[7]Gill and Markholt, op. cit.; Knight, ibid. [8]*Coast Seamen's Journal*, October 16, 1901. [9]Taylor, op. cit., Gill and Markholt, op. cit. Harold Huycke, notes, 1984.

the American Railway Union of the early 1890s, Daniel De Leon, a more rigorous socialist thinker, warned the working class that false "labor leaders" could betray the ranks and end up as allies of the exploiters, if not exploiters themselves. In the inland U.S., unions like the Western Federation of Miners found themselves in an even more violent situation than the Sailors' Union of the Pacific: in the metal mines of Idaho, Colorado, and Montana the W.F.M. established itself after 1893 through its members' markmanship against company police and pro-employer government authorities. Some leaders of the W.F.M., which received considerable moral support from the S.U.P., went on to attack the American Federation of Labor as, in effect, an employers' agency working to suppress the proletarian revolt. Finally the W.F.M. dropped out of the A.F.L.

Within the A.F.L., some other unions were clearly as radical in their thinking and methods as the W.F.M. The United Brewery Workmen had long acted as a militantly revolutionary body within the national federation. Mostly German-speaking and faithfully reproducing the socialist culture they had left behind in "the old country," the Brewery Workmen had inscribed "Workingmen of All Countries, Unite," on their union label, and, even before Debs' railroad movement, had fought tenaciously for industry-wide organization, in opposition to A.F.L. head Samuel Gompers' craft organization conception. The Brewery union was also strongly supported by the S.U.P. along the Pacific Coast, where Brewery leadership had been taken by Alfred Fuhrman, a socialist and former member of the Coast Seamen's Union. By 1904, the Brewery Workmen were, like the W.F.M., considering an exit from the A.F.L.

In June 1905, an event in Chicago marked a new stage in the development of the American labor movement, and foretold a long, momentous, and complicated set of changes within the Sailors' Union of the Pacific, the traces of which may still be found at the time of this writing, some 80 years afterward. This was the foundation meeting of the Industrial Workers of the World, a revolutionary labor organization that was to begin its work by repeating the classic socialist motto, "the working class and the employing class have nothing in common."

This was, at minimum, a direct challenge to the increasing trend on the part of some union leaders to collaborate with the employers in such groups as the National Civic Federation, a business-labor collaborative group which numbered the S.U.P.'s Furuseth and Macarthur among its leading figures, a questionable posture in hindsight. At maximum, the I.W.W. represented a cry of defiance to a whole society.

The participants in the earliest organizational steps of the I.W.W. included William Dudley Haywood, a hero of the W.F.M., William Trautmann, former editor of the Brewery Workers' journal, the *Brauer-Zeitung*, deposed from his editorship for endorsing the meeting, and representatives of Debs' and De Leon's socialist groups. The "Preamble" issued at the founding meeting, insisted that "instead of the conservative motto, 'A Fair Day's Wage for a Fair Day's Work,' we must inscribe on our banner the revolutionary watchword, 'Abolition of the Wage System.' " In this, the I.W.W. echoed the words of the same Marx whose thoughts had percolated through the Coast Seamen's Union in the late 1880s.[10]

1906: San Francisco Earthquake and Fire

The following year saw San Francisco rocked by the disastrous April 18, 1906 earthquake and fire. With the city in ruins, the Union's headquarters in the Audiffred Building at the southwest corner of Mission and East Streets (Embarcadero), was among the few surviving structures, reputedly because the proprietor of the famous Bulkhead saloon, the main first floor tenant, plied the firemen with firewater to convince them not to dynamite the building, which remained the site of the Union's central office. All surrounding buildings were destroyed. The *Coast Seamen's Journal* was transferred out of town, temporarily, but managed to publish its regular issue on April 25, although with only four pages in place of the usual sixteen. The paper reported that some Union members had been careless in their attitudes toward the soldiers and Navy personnel imported into the quake-struck city to enforce martial law, and had been shot, although none was apparently killed. In the following weeks the Union actively joined in the work of rebuilding the great city. The reconstruction boom led to increased lumber traffic and a rapid recovery in shipping. However, the improved economic situation stirred the Pacific Coast maritime employers to yet another attack on the Union. In June, 1906, steam schooner operators locked out longshoremen on certain docks, along with sailors, firemen, and cooks. The steam schooners were diverted to Oakland to pick up strikebreakers.

The City Front Federation attempted to settle the dispute, which ostensibly centered on wages but fundamentally reflected the desire of the steam schooner employers to dispense with labor representation. Employer intransigence spurred the Sailors to strike Pacific Coast Steamship Company, a leading scabherder. Striking sailor Andrew Kellner was killed in an incident on June 17, allegedly by a gunman who was later tried but found not guilty. The sailors, firemen, and cooks withdrew from the Federation in an attempt to end the lockout of the longshoremen; the sailors continued striking, but the longshoremen returned to work. The local press called for military action, and, ever generous to the Sailors in matters of slander, attacked "czar" Furuseth, accusing him of professing peace in San Francisco and murder in other ports. The strike wore on, and ended in November with the employers' surrender. Although the Sailors

[10]On the I.W.W., see Fred W. Thompson and Patrick Murfin, *The I.W.W.: Its First Seventy Years*, Chicago, I.W.W., 1976.

did not reaffiliate with the City Front Federation, they considered the outcome a major victory won by a combination of intelligent tactics and the favorable situation in shipping.[11]

From the end of the 1906 strike until 1921, the Union engaged in no further industrial action of this type. In this regard, it is clear that Furuseth gave ammunition to dissidents who now began accusing the S.U.P. leadership of excessive diplomacy toward the employers, and who found the radical perspectives of the I.W.W. more appealing. The discontent of militants with an increasingly-conservative "standard trade unionism" was spreading.

"Syndicalism"

In Western Europe, at first in the Latin nations of France, Spain, and Italy, the trend known as "syndicalism" had come to influence the labor movement in the period beginning around 1895. Syndicalism was to be defined by the anarchist Emma Goldman, one of its most spirited defenders, as "the revolutionary philosophy of labor conceived and born in the actual struggle and experience of the workers themselves."

Goldman stated that syndicalism was predicated on a rejection of political activity in the pursuit of union demands, with an emphasis on radical economic measures, especially direct action and the general strike. The syndicalists insisted that "economic emancipation of the workers must be the principal aim . . . to which everything else is to be subordinated." Goldman had seen the effect of the doctrine on the workers of France, whom it inspired with strength, enthusiasm, and hope. Still, its premises were not immediately optimistic; according to Goldman, "while the old trade unions, without exception, move within the wage system and capitalism . . . Syndicalism repudiates and condemns present industrial arrangements as unjust and criminal, and holds out no hope to the worker for lasting results from this system.

"On the other hand," Goldman affirmed, "syndicalism, like the old trade union fights for immediate gains but it is not stupid enough to pretend that labor can expect humane conditions from an inhuman economic arrangement." The partisans of the new outlook rejected labor contracts, since they did not "consider labor and capital equals." Syndicalists also denounced negotiation in labor disputes "because such a procedure serves only to give the enemy time to prepare his end of the fight, thus defeating the very object the workers set out to accomplish."

A convinced advocate for the new program, Goldman underscored the commitment to "spontaneity, both as a preserver of the fighting strength of labor and also because it takes the enemy unawares, hence compels him to a speedy settlement or causes him great loss." The new movement attacked the accumulation of large union strike fund treasuries as a source of corruption and false pride. It strongly supported a system of self-help welfare organizations in France, the Mutualités, which aided the unemployed in finding jobs. In words that would have found a deep echo in many sailors, Emma Goldman reserved specially harsh condemnation in her exposition of syndicalist doctrine, for the "vicious role of employment agencies as leeches upon the jobless worker and nurseries of scabbery."[12] The Coast Seamen's Union, in its original fight against the crimps and for the Union hiring hall, had pioneered in the struggle for reform of hiring procedures. Some concepts hailed by Goldman and other syndicalists as a new revelation were long-established in the S.U.P. ranks; direct action in the form of "the oracle," was an old tradition on the West Coast.

A World Trend

The syndicalist trend first came to world-wide attention following the 1906 Amiens Congress of the French General Confederation of Labor (CGT). Syndicalism made its way from the Mediterranean countries to Scandinavia, where it was destined to win the support of major sections of the labor movement. And the impact of this was to be felt throughout the Scandinavian diaspora in the U.S., not only in the "old country," and thus in the S.U.P. Significant elements within the Sailors' Union were strongly sympathetic to syndicalism, and to understand this, it is necessary to observe a digression into Nordic history.

The established trade-union organizations in Scandinavia grew as follows in the period from 1900 to 1910:

Year	Denmark	Norway	Sweden
1900	77,000	5,000	44,000
1905	69,000	16,000	87,000
1910	102,000	46,000	85,000[13]

Throughout Scandinavia, the labor movement produced strong socialist parties. While the Danish socialists remained generally conservative and gradualistic, the Swedes, strongly influenced by German Marxist socialism, leaned somewhat more to the left. The leading force for labor extremism in the region was to be found in Norway, where labor became markedly syndicalist. In contrast to Denmark and Sweden, Norway saw, according to the eminent labor historian, Walter Galenson, "explosive industrialization of the country, and recruitment of industrial workers from small farms . . . The poor working and living conditions they found in the hastily constructed industrial towns . . . contributed to the formation of an extreme, radical ideology, matched by few others in Europe." An official history of the Norwegian central labor organization, the Arbeidernes Faglige Landsorganisasjon, eloquently describes how "the young farm boys . . . came from the quiet of the great plateaus and the endless woods, from broad valleys and steep mountains, from the rugged coast and the sheltered fjords.

[11]Gill and Markholt, op. cit. [12]Emma Goldman, *Syndicalism*, New York, Mother Earth Publishing Co., 1913; also see Peter Stearns, *Revolutionary Syndicalism and French Labor*, New Brunswick, Rutgers University Press, 1971. [13]Walter Galenson, *The Scandinavian Labor Movement*, Berkeley, University of California, 1952 (reprint).

They knew hunger and poverty from childhood. But they did not know the rhythm of industry. And the industry they encountered! These boys met the trade unions . . . they met the 'rollers' first, traveling construction workers . . . When revolutionary agitation swept over the construction projects and the new factories, inspired from Sweden and the syndicalist union that was established there in 1910 (Sveriges Arbetares Centrale, linked to the I.W.W.), it was small wonder that these boys listened to the appeal. The Landsorganisasjon was too heedful of the Employers Association and the capitalists. The leaders bargained and bargained . . . Direct action, that was the way."

Within only a few years, more than 100,000 workers had joined the Norwegian labor force. The main leader of the young generation was a dynamic but ascetic man, Martin Tranmael — a mixture of a Furuseth (in his strong morality) and a W. D. Haywood (in his combativeness). Tranmael had worked in the U.S., like so many more of his peer group, and had come under I.W.W. influence; his spirit would later influence the history of the S.U.P. through the personality of one Harry Lundeberg. Like the Mediterranean syndicalists, Tranmael rejected contracts and large union treasuries, and called for industry-wide unions with their chief weapon the strike.

Tranmael was later described by Franz Borkenau, the outstanding historian of the European left-wing, as "a man of quite unusual gifts . . . A man of extraordinary purity of mind and habits, a passionate teetotaller and moralist . . . at the same time, a brillant speaker, a supremely able journalist, and a great organizer." Tranmael gained fame in 1912, in an incident underscoring the split between reform-minded socialists and the syndicalists within the Norwegian Labor Party, the political arm of the union movement. At a meeting to support a mine strike, Tranmael asserted that the strikers should leave the mines at the scheduled time, without worrying if some dynamite remained in the mines, since the presence of explosives might discourage the entry of strikebreakers. The reference to "dynamite in the bore-holes," as noted by Galenson, brought condemnation of Tranmael as an "advocate of assassination."[14]

The cross-fertilization between American radical unionism and the new Scandinavian syndicalism in the S.U.P. also took place between the American and Spanish labor movements, centering on a section of the International Seamen's Union, the Atlantic Coast Marine Firemen. The Atlantic firemen, 85 percent of whom were Spanish, were brought into the I.S.U. in 1909-10, with the enthusiastic approval of Furuseth, under the leadership of Jaime Vidal, José Berenguer, Juan Martinez, and Secundino Bruge. The I.S.U. even contributed funds to two Spanish syndicalist newspapers in the U.S., *Cultura Obrera* and *Cultura Proletaria*. The latter had been established in New York by Spanish cigarmakers, and when the newspaper found itself, in 1910, in difficult straits, it was rescued by the I.S.U. It continued publishing until after the second world war.[15]

Unfortunately, a dispute between Furuseth and Gulf Coast I.S.U. agent George C. Bodine, disrupted the firemen's movement. Ed Andersen and others in the S.U.P., upholding Bodine, strongly criticized Furuseth's supporters for their supposedly insensitive attitude toward the radical Spanish firemen. Furuseth also came under attack from the Bodine group for his attachment to legislative rather than activist means of redress.

Developments in Spain may have strongly influenced Vidal and the rest of the leaders of the Spanish firemen on the Atlantic Coast, for in 1913, the entire Marine Firemen's organization on the East Coast would be reported by the I.S.U. to have left the organization and to have affiliated with the Industrial Workers of the World. Spain had long been a center of labor militancy, and its unions were predominantly syndicalist. In contrast with the Norwegians, the Spanish syndicalists built their movement on the basis of the country's strong anarchist tradition, decades old, and originating with the Iberian regional organization that adhered to Bakunin, against Marx, in the break-up of the original International Workingmen's Association. In 1910, stimulated by the growth of the movement in France, the Spanish rebel workers organized a peninsula-wide revolutionary labor organization, the National Confederation of Labor (Confederación Nacional del Trabajo — C.N.T.).[16]

Furuseth and the other dominant figures in the S.U.P. reacted with vehement condemnation to the activities of the I.W.W., castigating them as freaks and parasites, unfit to participate in the labor movement. But events would demonstrate that no matter how extensive the efforts of the 'traditional' labor leaders to counter-act the syndicalist threat, the support of the rank and file increasingly lay with the rebels.

Not long thereafter, Furuseth himself, when questioned by a newspaperman as to "the I.W.W. getting a hold upon our Union," would answer "it (is) true . . . they are holding public meetings on the street outside of our office and . . . they have hired our old office and set up a headquarters." He would further quote a communication from Pete Gill declaring that the "I.W.W. element in our Union is growing rapidly." Furuseth agreed that "I can well understand this to be so. Hope deferred maketh the heart sick, and waiting is wearing down the greatest patience on earth." He added that trouble between the seamen and the

[14]Gunnar Ousland, *Fagorganisationen I Norge*, Oslo, Tiden Norsk Forlag, 1949, cited in Galenson, ibid.; Franz Borkenau, *World Communism*, second edition, Ann Arbor, University of Michigan Press, 1962; Walter Galenson, *Labor in Norway*, Cambridge, Harvard University Press, 1949. [15]*Proceedings of The 15th Annual Convention of The I.S.U., 1910; Coast Seamen's Journal*, January 3, 1912. [16]*Coast Seamen's Journal*, May 21, 1913; and Weintraub, op. cit. The I.W.W. historian, Thompson, in Thompson and Murfin, op. cit., claims the Spanish Firemen never actually joined. An important document on Vidal and the so-called "Latin Branch" of the I.S.U. consists of the "Minutes and Decisions, Committee on Rodriguez and Carlson, 1910," held in the S.U.P. central Archive.

employers "might be forced through the agitation carried on . . . and the failure of the owners to grant some slight things that would allay the difficulty."[17]

A glimpse of this period comes from Fred Klebingat, a veteran West Coast seaman interviewed by Karl Kortum:

"We were three weeks in the five mast schooner *Crescent* from Makaweli to Portland. I paid off and Dutch Harry, the second mate, took me around. He pointed out the crimps: there's Sullivan, the son of a bitch, and right there is Grant. Stay away from both of them — they're a couple of bastards. 'Come on up and join the Union — I'll take you up.'

"If you didn't have any money you were at the mercy of fellows like Sullivan and Grant; I always managed to keep part of my pay and so stayed out of their hands. Union (monthly) pay for an offshore voyage was $30 in 1908: non-union men got $25. (Seaman's pay in Australia was two pounds ten, or not quite $22 American.) When I landed in Portland the Union orders were to ship for $25 to keep the boarding masters out of it, although the going Union wage on the coast was $30.

"The *Annie E. Smale* had preceded us to Portland and Captain Colstrup — Four-Foot Nothing, also called Double Face Fritz — shipped his men through Sullivan and Grant. Why go to the boarding house masters if you could get your crew for $25 from the Sailors' Union? The Union supplied men free, no charge — call for as many as you want *and at the same price*. If you went to a boarding house master, you had to pay blood money. So why not use the Sailors' Union? The answer is that Colstrup got a piece of change out of the transaction; he split the blood money with Sullivan and Grant."

In November, 1907, the *Coast Seamen's Journal* announced the death of Burnette Haskell. Recognizing the socialist leader's contributions to its foundation, the Union took charge of Haskell's funeral arrangements, with the interment ceremony held under its auspices in the Union's plot at the old Mount Olivet Cemetery in San Francisco.

On the Pacific Coast, the Canadian province of British Columbia had long remained an open-shop bastion. In January, 1908, the S.U.P. reopened its agency in Vancouver, B. C., inaugurating a new campaign for union recognition on Canadian vessels. The Canadian seamen complained about their working conditions, under which life more resembled that of deepwater sailors than of coastwise crews, with cargo worked on Sundays and holidays but with no overtime paid. In 1911, the Union fought the lockout of steamship crews by the feudalistic Canadian Pacific Railway, largely on the overtime issue, and, after court intervention, the Union won. However, British Columbia remained "the weak spot on the coast in organization, and conditions remained substantially below those of the rest of the Coast," Gill and Markholt note.[18]

The year 1913 saw the resignation of Walter Macarthur from the editorship of the *Journal*. Macarthur accepted a position as U.S. Shipping Commissioner, which he fulfilled until his retirement in 1932. He authored a number of important works on marine law and in 1929, published a useful handbook for historians, *Last Days of Sail on The West Coast*, which showed his love for ships. This book notes that, in 1928, San Francisco was the last great repository of American square-rig. Of 76 such vessels under the Stars and Stripes, 52 were registered in San Francisco; of 31 barkentines, 20 were registered in the city. Macarthur was also a talented painter.

Macarthur was replaced by Paul Scharrenberg, who had been the paper's manager. Scharrenberg, born in Germany in 1877, had joined the S.U.P. in 1899. He landed in San Francisco rather curiously. He had begun shipping out in his teens, and, after some time, located on the East Coast. He then signed aboard the hell-ship *T.F. Oakes*, whose name had been changed to the *New York*, for a ten months' trip from New York to San Francisco, via Shanghai and Hong Kong. The vessel fell into bad weather in the approach to the Golden Gate, and ended up aground at Half Moon Bay; the young German swam ashore, realizing the ship was wrecked. Later, on applying for membership in the S.U.P., he presented his discharge from the ill-reputed and ill-fated ship to Furuseth, who asked him "our standard question for applicants: 'how do you take down a royal yard?' " Scharrenberg replied that the New York not only had royal yards but was a three skysail yard full-rigged ship, and Furuseth answered, "Well then, how do you take down a skysail yard?" Scharrenberg later called this the beginning of a friendship that would last until Furuseth's death in 1938.

Legal Improvement

The first decade of the century showed unquestionable further improvement in the legal position of the seafarer. Through court action to enforce the Maguire and White acts, the sailors largely wiped out the abuses of the allotment system, shanghaiing, and buckoism. A Supreme Court decision in the *Osceola* case established the principle that vessel operators must provide for maintenance and cure of sick seamen, including full payment of wages for the duration of a voyage, and further made the shipowners liable for injuries caused by unseaworthy or otherwise defective equipment. Other legal petitions secured the requirement that a ship put into the nearest port for aid to injured crew members. One of the most important legal victories came with a Supreme Court decision holding that foreign seamen on foreign vessels in American harbors were subject to U.S. laws, although later judicial action provided foreign consular officials with legal support in their enforcement of their own countries' laws on "desertion."

---

[17]Andrew Furuseth, typed letter, July 20, 1913, in S.U.P. central Archive, "I.S.U. Correspondence." [18]Fred Klebingat, interviewed by Karl Kortum, 1963, National Maritime Museum; on the death of Haskell, *Coast Seamen's Journal*, November 20, 1907; on British Columbia, Gill and Markholt, op. cit.

Furuseth's strategy was based on the belief that improvement of legal status was the key to seamen's welfare. Pete Gill, responsible for the Union's affairs in the Seattle area, pointed out, however, "if conditions had been improved somewhat in matters affected by seamen's legislation, they had become infinitely worse in all things left to the discretion of the shipowners. The most glaring example of this was the disregard for safety."

Ships and lives were lost in an increasingly terrible hecatomb; by 1916, life insurers stated that the accident rate among seamen stood at 17 percent, compared with 10.5 percent for the general population. Government safety inspectors seemed to play the role of happy courtesan to the shipowners. In 1914, the *Coast Seamen's Journal* published figures showing that lives lost at sea worldwide had risen dramatically over the previous half-century from 1,018 between 1860-64 to 5,445 in the four years and five months covered between 1909 and 1914.[19]

Another unresolved grievance involved conflicting federal and state authorities. The White Act had abolished penalities for "desertion" in U.S. ports, but the states of California, Washington, Oregon, and Massachusetts maintained imprisonment through fugitive sailor laws. In 1904, the Massachusetts law was used for strikebreaking purposes. The year before, the S.U.P. had sought repeal of the California law but a partial reform was achieved only in 1907, when regulations against "harboring deserted seamen" were abolished, but penalties for "enticing seamen to desert" were allowed to remain in force. The latter rule was strongly attacked by the S.U.P. as a shield for strikebreaking. The activities of the Union in patrolling the waters around struck ships in its own launch had been halted by this law. Finally, in 1911, California governor Hiram Johnson, then an authentic progressive and an opponent of the giant railroad and other "interests" in the state, had signed a bill completely eliminating fugitive sailor legislation. Repeal of the Washington state equivalent had come already in 1909, with the Massachusetts law struck from the books in 1910.

LaFollette

Projects for full emancipation of the sailor had been introduced into the national Congress in the period from 1900 to 1911 but there was no substantial legislative success after the Maguire Act. However, the Maguire Act had failed to provide seamen with the right to sue for return of clothing held unlawfully; a successful 1904 bill shepherded by Furuseth at least stiffened penalties for such seizure.

An ambitious 1910 seamen's bill, authored by U.S. Senator Robert M. LaFollette, a progressive from Wisconsin, included broad requirements on safety, manning, and other improvements, including abrogation of any foreign treaties calling for arrest of foreign 'deserters.' But this effort, guided by Furuseth acting jointly with LaFollette, failed at first.

In June, 1911, LaFollette had tried again, introducing his Senate bill simultaneously with the submission of a House of Representatives version by Pennsylvania congressman William B. Wilson. When hearings of the House Merchant Marine and Fisheries Committee began in December, a large body of I.S.U. officials offered favorable commentary. Pete Gill testified that allotments were still paid to crimps in the deepwater trade, whether or not a sailor actually owed a debt. Payment of advances was still particularly prevalent on British-registered ships.

The LaFollette bill called for safeguards against crimping and abuse of allotment and advances, reduction of 'desertion' penalties to loss of wages and effects, protection of foreign seamen's rights in American harbors, and a guarantee for payment of a "draw" in any port of half wages earned. The proposd law also specified that forecastles must include at least 108 cubic feet of space per crew member, well-heated, with separate messrooms, and hot and cold showers. British, French, German, and Norwegian laws called for 120 cubic feet of forecastle space for each sailor.

Looking to safety, the LaFollette bill supported the right of seamen to demand a survey of vessels, and the banning of the "Kalashi" watch system, under which men worked through the full day and slept through the night, with the vessel handled by the watch officer, the man at the wheel, and (perhaps) a deck lookout. The Kalashi watch system permitted shipowners to hire unskilled men except for two steersmen and two lookouts. The seamen proposed a watch-and-watch system (two fully manned watches of 12 hours each) for the deck department, with three watches in the engine department, and the nine-hour day in port. They also advocated a manning scale under which 75 percent of the deck crew must be able seamen with three years' sea time.

Most of the clauses in the LaFollette bill were supported by precedent in Britain, Norway, and other leading maritime nations, but this did not prevent the shipowners from fighting them down to the last comma and period. On the other hand, elements within the I.S.U. also criticized the bill as inadequate. Severe criticism came in 1912 from James Vidal, Bodine, and others among the Atlantic Coast Marine Firemen, whose organization had yet to leave the I.S.U., over the establishment of standards for efficiency, which Bodine contended were too restrictive, and over a clause requiring that 75 percent of crews speak English. The latter clearly victimized the Spanish-speaking firemen, although the arguments in its favor advanced by Furuseth and others were primarily directed at imported Asian labor.

The House had passed the bill in 1912 but a substitute bill favorably reported by the Senate significantly

[19]Walter Macarthur, *Last Days of Sail on the West Coast*, San Francisco, Walter Macarthur, 1929; on Scharrenberg, Paul Scharrenberg, "My Association with Furuseth," in *A Symposium on Andrew Furuseth*, New Bedford, The Darwin Press, n.d., and Urban D. Mackins, "Masons I Have Known: Paul A. Scharrenberg," *Bulletin* of Amity Lodge No. 370 (San Francisco), March 1985. On marine casualties, *Coast Seamen's Journal*, August 26, 1914.

altered the document in the shipowners' interest. Imprisonment was to be prescribed for "refusal or wilful neglect in boat drill" in port, which the Union viewed as a reestablishment of penalties for desertion. The safety standards originally developed with two able seamen for each lifeboat, were replaced by a rule calling for "a sufficient number of efficient lifeboat hands," to come from engine and steward personnel, as well as the deck department. The A.B. efficiency requirement was reduced from three years' service at sea to one year with passage of an examination. Vessels under 300 tons were exempted from the greater part of the law. In place of the English language minimum, the new version called for employment of enough men capable of interpreting for officers and unlicensed men, although the disorganization and disorder inherent in emergency situations would obviously prejudice such an arrangement. The Union was unenthusiastic about the Senate version of the bill which, in any case, was vetoed by President William Howard Taft, in an action to which the Sailors did not strongly object.

The fight resumed in 1913, again under stewardship of Senator La Follette. The shipowners arranged for the introduction of an alternate bill. The La Follette document passed the Senate but seemed destined for defeat in the other house by the shipowners' proposed bill. Congress delayed action on the competing measures until 1915 but finally approved LaFollette's bill. On March 4, President Woodrow Wilson signed the Seamen's Act into law.

The 1915 Seamen's Act established:

- That masters must fill vacancies in a crew during a voyage with men of the same or higher rating. Previous law called for men of the same rating "if available".
- Two watches on deck and three in the "black gang" at sea with nine hours' maximum work in port, and a ban on unnecessary Sunday and holiday work.
- Two days' pay for each day's delay in paying off seamen, doubling the previous penalty.
- A draw of half wages earned in any port of discharge with provision for full pay if the request for a draw was refused. Previously, the master enjoyed the option of abrogation of half-pay.
- The right of a majority of crew members to demand inspections for seaworthiness.
- 120 cubic feet and 16 square feet of forecastle space per individual, bunks a maximum of two high, washrooms for sailors and firemen, a hospital aboard each vessel, fumigation and at least two exits in forecastles.
- Abolition of imprisonment for desertion in foreign ports.
- Removal of U.S. consuls from the duty of arresting "deserters."
- Equal liability for damages between masters and owners, with the master liable for failure to surrender an officer charged with brutality, thus providing means to eliminate corporal punishment.
- A doubled butter allowance and 25 percent increase in water.
- Prohibition of allotment except to dependent relatives.
- Inclusion of fishermen in prohibition of garnishment of seamen's wages except for attachment by a court for support of a spouse or minor children.
- Except for inland waters, all vessels over 100 gross tons to carry 40 percent A.B. seamen in the first year, to be eventually raised to 65 percent, with a 75 percent English-language requirement.
- Efficiency standards for able seamen and lifeboatmen.
- Yearly reports to Congress on men lost while working on barges.
- Protection of foreign seamen's right to quit in U.S. ports.
- The right of seamen to collect damages for officers' negligence.

Subversion of the LaFollette Act

The shipowners and their henchmen in government responded to the passage of the Act by attempting to subvert its enforcement. The Justice Department held that A.B. and lifeboat efficiency standards only applied on foreign ships when passengers were carried. The government also called for rigorous physical examinations for A.B.'s which resulted in an 11 percent failure rate on the Pacific Coast striking hard at the "old-timers." The Commerce Department asserted that forecastle requirements were restricted to vessels built after passage of the Act.

Court tests found that seamen asking for half wages still could be deemed "deserters" and their claims denied, and also reestablished advance payments by masters of U.S. vessels in foreign ports. This last ruling was upheld by the U.S. Supreme Court.

The Seamen's Act was rightly viewed by Furuseth and his lieutenants as a vindication of their long legislative campaign. Unfortunately, within the rank and file, rumblings of dissatisfaction increased as the "old man" and his group were seen to be too wedded to their congressional lobbying roles, to the detriment of the economic struggle faced by the seafarers themselves "at the point of production." Some viewed his legal triumphs as enthusiastically as he did himself, while others felt he belonged more in San Francisco and less in Washington.

Another source of discontent was the increasing adherence of Furuseth to a very restricted version of the craft-union theory, which called for sailors not to mix their ranks *too* closely with their brother marine workers on land, the longshoremen. The period between 1900 and 1920, in the annals of the I.S.U., was disfigured by a series of jurisdictional battles between the Union's officialdom and its rivals in the longshore field, who attempted to organize seamen, too. Furuseth stoked the conflict by constantly denigrating the dock workers as employees and as men, arguing, in effect, that sailors' special skills set them apart from longshoremen, who were hired only to move cargo, often on a day-to-day basis, at that. Furuseth's education in sail forever marked him with a strong sense of pride in seamanship. A true sailor might find himself on a bad ship with brutal officers, but never failed to perform to the best of his considerable ability. This was dictated by the dangers of the profession, but also by this special attitude about seamanship, an important element in history since the time of the Phoenicians. A phenomenon to be noted at this point is that no man — and, recently woman — with the slightest nautical abilities, is anything but unvariably proud of them. But since the I.W.W. emphasized the need for unity of all the marine workers, organizing sailors and longshoremen alike into its Marine Transport Workers Industrial Union, Furuseth's onslaughts against the dockworkers often, and even when directed against the A.F.L. International Longshoremen's Association, only increased support for the "Wobblies," as the I.W.W. members began to be known.

The struggle between A.F.L. union leaders such as Furuseth and the I.W.W. has therefore been interpreted by some labor historians *mainly* as a conflict between the craft and industrial organization programs. But this is only partially true, even for Furuseth. The clash was not merely over methods of organization, but over primary aims. Furuseth and his circle saw the Union as an institution that would improve the situation of its members through more gradual methods, although a "commonwealth of labor" might be the eventual goal. The I.W.W. saw labor organization as the basis for an immediate social revolution.

The passage of the Seamen's Act propelled Furuseth into the national limelight, making him an important public figure, a leading representative for labor's aspirations throughout the U.S. and around the world. What the Wobblies and other anti-Furuseth radicals of the time could not understand — and probably could not have been expected to understand — was that, in taking responsibility for the enormous project involved in the emancipation of seamen *throughout the globe*, Furuseth's I.S.U. had made itself a labor organization unlike any other in America. In contrast with the other A.F.L. afiliates, the I.S.U. was alone in that it did not merely seek to represent its members, but to be *truly* "international" and "of the world" in a way other Unions, including many grandly styled "international," and even the I.W.W., could not conceive. This was implicit in its struggle against the application of foreign desertion laws within the U.S.

A major part of Furuseth's and the Union's international impact came with participation in the International Transportworkers' Federation, in which the I.S.U. and the British maritime unions sat alongside socialist union activists from Germany and French revolutionary syndicalists. (The Russian-Italian socialist leader Angelica Balabanova served as translator at the I.T.F.'s international meetings.) The I.T.F. brought European sailors and dockers together, and attempted to heal the division between the two crafts in America.

The I.T.F. had come into existence during a period of European labor history parallel, in many respects, to the American upheaval of the 1880s, beginning in 1889 with the great London dock strike led by Tom Mann and Ben Tillett. Mann, Tillett, and J. Havelock Wilson, the founder of the National Amalgamated Sailors' and Firemen's Union in Sunderland, England in 1887, took the first steps toward the federation's formation in 1896, following Wilson's intervention in a dock strike in Rotterdam, bringing the solidarity of the British workers to the aid of the Dutch. An early addition to the group was the Swedish seamen's and dockers' organizer Charles Lindley (born Karl Gustaf Lindgren) who had worked with Wilson at Sunderland, and went on to organize marine unions in his native Sweden, including the powerful Swedish Transport Workers' Union.

During that period, strikes by the European waterfront labor movement showed an idealism and daring, comparable to that evidenced in the American seamen's movement at the same time. High points include the Antwerp dock strike of 1900, a Danish national shipping strike in 1902, and the massive Dutch transport rebellion of 1903, involving the Amsterdam dockers and the nationwide railway workers. Soon, the I.T.F. moved to Germany, home of the biggest labor and socialist movement in Europe. As we will see in Chapter IV, through Furuseth's association with Wilson and relations with various I.T.F. tendencies, European labor activities would again, as with the influence of socialism and syndicalism, come to affect the S.U.P., an ocean and a continent away.[20]

Two features of "old Andy's" personality were revealed many times during this epoch and both showed a special courage. The first was in his fight against the court injunction as a "law and order" weapon against strikers. This chapter of Furuseth's life properly belongs to all of labor, and not simply to the seamen, for the old Norwegian's resistance to injunctions provided a magnificent example for the rest of the union movement.

It was in the context of his fight against use of injunctions that "old Andy" first used a phrase that would contribute to his fame and, eventually, stand as his epitaph. These words have been made into legend by historians of the Union and of Furuseth himself but perhaps the most convincing account of their origin is that offered by Judge William Denman, reminiscing in 1947: "My first contact with him, in 1904 or 1905, was in a hall near South Park, San Francisco. There in a

[20]Information on the La Follette Act in this chapter is largely derived from Gill and Markholt, op. cit. Also, see Senate Commerce Committee, *Seaman's Bill* (Comparative Print), Washington, Government Printing Office, 1915, Taylor, op. cit., Weintraub, op. cit., and Joseph P. Goldberg, *The Maritime Story*, Cambridge, Harvard University Press, 1958. On the International Transportworkers Federation, see S.U.P. central Archive, and K.A. Golding, "In the Forefront of Trade Union History, 1896-1971," London, International Transportworkers' Federation, 1971.

discussion of the use of 'inyunction,' as he pronounced it, in labor disputes, in response to a question of 'What would you do if an anti-labor injunction were served on you,' he replied: "I would put the inyunction in my pocket and go to yail and in yail my bed would be no narrower, my food no worse, nor I more lonely than in the forecastle."[21]

The second aspect of the man, the "unknown Furuseth" who remains virtually uncommented-on in the literature of I.S.U. history, is in his anti-imperialism. At a time when many clamored for the "big stick" and gunboat diplomacy to carry the U.S. flag as the banner of domination throughout the world, Furuseth and the S.U.P. stood in opposition to imperialist adventures. The Union defended the people of the Philippines against U.S. intervention there; recognized the rights of the Chinese in their effort to remove the stigma of foreign meddling; opposed U.S. colonial impositions in Mexico and Central America. Ironically, men who long supported the exclusion of Asian labor, from the U.S. firmly supported the right of Asian nations to exclude U.S. exploiters.[22]

Furuseth and the Union also indicated their unease at the growth of the war menace in Europe. In 1914 the first of the world wars finally began. The U.S. did not become involved until 1917; American entry would create, at first, some apparent benefits for the seamen, before bringing forth disaster.

[21]See *A Symposium on Andrew Furuseth*, op. cit. [22]See *Coast Seamen's Journal* for the period; also, Weintraub, op. cit.

CHAPTER IV
Twilight of Freedom
(1916-1933)

Even with passage of the Seaman's Act, the S.U.P. had found itself on a battle course, fighting for full enforcement of the law. It was quickly apparent that the continuing struggle would require even greater vigilance and sacrifice on the part of the seafaring workers. For American labor as a whole, the period just before U.S. entry into the first world war saw a rising trend toward violence in industrial conflicts. The Sailors' Union greeted the arrival of New Year 1916 by supporting a call for congressional action to stop the interstate shipment of "strike-breakers, armed guards, and machine guns" for use by employers. Arguing for such a ban, President John White of the United Mine Workers cited the most infamous example of industrial repression in 20th century U.S. history: the killing of 13 women and children and six men, with the wounding of many more, by the gunmen of the Rockefeller-owned Colorado Fuel and Iron Company, at Ludlow, during the 1913-14 Colorado coal strike.[1]

Approach of World War

Amid the flames of what seemed to be a spreading class confrontation, the U.S. slowly found itself drawn toward active involvement in the conflict taking place in Europe. The labor movement in the San Francisco region expressed opposition to the growing propaganda for U.S. participation, with Paul Scharrenberg of the S.U.P. and a group of labor figures ranging from socialists to conservatives, including a mercurial, Norwegian-born agitator from the construction trades, Olaf Tveitmoe, calling for a boycott of such events as the "Preparedness Day" parade scheduled for San Francisco on July 22, 1916. "Do not march . . . Do not let your employers coerce you . . ." the unionists argued; the San Francisco Labor Council joined the Tveitmoe-led Building Trades Council in a resolution declaring that "labor is opposed to the fostering of the war spirit by 'preparedness parades,' " and warning that "an attempt may be made by the enemies of labor to cause a violent disturbance."[2]

Scharrenberg spoke at a mass peace meeting on July 20 at Dreamland (later Winterland) Arena in San Francisco, voicing the line of the *Coast Seamen's Journal*, which scored "the preparedness hysteria which has swept the country and found expression in conscript parades." Scharrenberg stated that he welcomed "this opportunity to voice my earnest protest against the popularizing of militarism . . . This great Republic may have foes abroad but some of its most deadly enemies are to be found right at home . . . They are the industrial vampires who undermine the Nation's vitality by cruel, merciless exploitation . . . Special privilege, monopoly, and greed are rampant . . . The babies of the poor die three times as fast as those of the rich. Yet they have the nerve to ask Organized Labor to take part in military preparedness parades designed to intimidate some unknown foreign foe when the known foes of the Nation, who live among us, are brazenly taking the lead in these demonstrations."

The *Journal* editor took aim, in passing, at the shipowners, noting that "these mercenary gentlemen dearly love and honor our flag. They actually shed tears over its beauty when the sailor who hoists it is brown or yellow and works for $7.00 per month." But he went on to point out that "the shipowner is not a bit worse than the other war profiteers . . . Some shipowners actually take a risk in their business but the captains of preparedness industries ashore take no chances whatever. The manufacturers of shot and shells usually insist upon payment in advance." He concluded by asking "shall we teach our children military ideals, blind obedience, and an unquestioning 'patriotism' in the schools?" He answered, "a thousand times, No. Let us protest tonight and continue to

[1]*Coast Seamen's Journal*, January 12, 1916. [2]See Knight, op cit. Tveitmoe became one of the leading radical labor advocates in the U.S. as editor of the San Francisco construction trades paper *Organized Labor*, and was sent to prison in the McNamara brothers case, involving two prominent figures in the A.F.L. Structural Iron Workers, charged with bombing the *Los Angeles Times* Building in 1910. On Tveitmoe, see Saxton, op. cit., who is laudably fair, and Louis Adamic, *Dynamite*, New York, Harper and Row, second edition, 1960, which must be read with great caution, as Adamic's lively imagination caused him to read a great deal into matters he studied only superficially.

protest with all our might against an incipient militarism, falsely labeled preparedness."[3]

Two days later, during the "Preparedness" parade, a bomb exploded at the corner of Steuart and Market Streets, killing six and wounding some 40 more. Within a week five labor radicals had been arrested and charged with the outrage: Tom Mooney, an active member of the Molders' Union, a left-wing Socialist, and associate of the anarchist Alexander Berkman; Mooney's wife Rena; Warren K. Billings, an I.W.W.-minded radical; Israel Weinberg, of the jitney-bus operators' union, and Edward D. Nolan of the Machinists' organization. Mooney and Billings had been involved in a number of strikes, including a major struggle against the Pacific Gas & Electric Co. in which the strikers were defended, by Paul Scharrenberg, against the majority of the A.F.L. San Francisco authorities attempted to implicate Berkman in the affair, but he was out of their reach.

San Francisco labor refused to accept the supposed complicity of Mooney and his associates in the bombing, and a struggle of more than twenty years, to prove their innocence, began. Of the defendants, Mooney was at first sentenced to die, with Billings sent to prison for life. During the trial, proof of a frame-up by the district attorney's office was revealed, but the increasing attacks on labor radicalism throughout the country prevented Mooney from obtaining a change in his sentence, to life imprisonment, until years had passed. During this period the I.W.W., which stood for an undisguised revolutionary opposition to the war, came under especially severe pressure from the forces of the government, with assaults on Wobbly members and halls. Scharrenberg combined his principled opposition to militarism with a defense of the Wobblies' rights to free speech, and led the campaign for the exoneration of Mooney and Billings.[4] Throughout this time Scharrenberg's line within the Sailors' Union, as revealed by the *Journal*, was one of near-socialism, with a great deal more in common with the Wobblies and other radicals than has been generally noted.

By Spring of 1917 it was obvious that the U.S. was about to enter the war. Interviewed by the *San Francisco Bulletin* Furuseth declared that "the sentiment of the working people of the U.S. is overwhelmingly in favor of peace and against war . . . If war comes, and even now with vessels armed, it is the seamen who will bear the brunt for some time to come. Each man will have to decide for himself whether he will go to war. Each man's life is his own and he will ultimately be guided by the sentiment that is in him."[5] On April 4, as U.S. entry was being consummated, the Union endorsed and approved President Woodrow Wilson's "utterances in defense of human rights, but deeply regret(ted) that our great Republic should enter the war as the ally of several kings and a mikado." The *Journal* promised that "American seamen will do their full duty," but warned that "they will never willingly shed a drop of blood for the tottering thrones of Europe and Asia!"

U.S. Involvement

U.S. involvement in the conflict decisively altered the character of the U.S. maritime industry. The war-reorganized economy required a tremendous expansion of the U.S. steamship fleet. Almost overnight, sail shipping fell to a small minority of bottoms. The sailors' craft, and, therefore, the sailors' conditions of existence and of self-perception, was transformed.

Respect for the special windship crafts of the traditional seaman had been a cardinal principle for Furuseth and his colleagues in S.U.P. leadership. The old-style windship seaman who knew a special and difficult system of work techniques was replaced by a crew member whose work plainly demanded much less.

At first, effects of the war on seamen were not clearly perceptible. The full significance of the change, and its disastrous impact, would not be felt until 1921, three years after war's end. However, that was in the future. With the U.S. declaration of war against Germany, the government and the employers, spurred by the colossal needs of the war machine, sought industrial peace by securing an agreement that effectively legitimized unions.

In May, 1917, the I.S.U. joined the U.S. Shipping Board, a federal agency, and the Committee on Shipping of the Council of National Defense, in signing an Atlantic War Agreement calling for payment of union wages, war bonuses, liberal manning, and recognition of the union as the workers' representative. At the end of the year the I.S.U. national convention issued Furuseth's *A Message To Seamen: A Call To The Sea And To Seamanship*, beginning: "Men of the Sea: The nation that proclaimed your freedom now needs your services. America is at war. Our troops are being transported over the seas. Munitions and supplies are being shipped in ever increasing quantities to our armies in Europe . . . Thousands of skilled seamen, seafaring men of all capacities who left the sea in years gone by as a protest against serfdom from which no flag then offered relief, have now an opportunity to return to their former calling, sail as free men and serve our country."[6]

Although Furuseth and the I.S.U. leaders, once the U.S. joined in the war, sought to maintain an image of patriotism and reliability, powerful voices within the government opposed the wartime agreement with the unions, and demanded that the merchant marine be brought under Navy control. This attempt at militarization of the seamen was unsuccessful.

The government quickly moved to establish Sea Service Bureaus or government hiring halls, to regulate employment, a setback for unions, although accepted without major protest at the time. Under the

[3]*Coast Seamen's Journal*, July 26, 1916. [4]Knight, op, cit. It is a matter of great sadness that Paul Scharrenberg, in his manuscript history of the S.U.P., op. cit., completely ignored these experiences. [5]Gill and Markholt, op. cit. [6]Andrew Furuseth, *A Message to Seamen*, International Seamen's Union, n.p., n.d. Also Gill and Markholt, ibid.

Atlantic agreement, preference on 60 percent of jobs was provided to the union, with the non-union Sea Service Bureaus required to call the union first for the remainder, before taking on men obtained through a federal recruitment service. By 1918, the S.U.P. held closed-shop control over 97 percent of West Coast shipping.[7] At first seemingly innocuous, the Sea Service Bureau would, in the postwar years, acquire a specially evil repute as the government "fink hall."

U.S. entry into the war brought other events destined to have major impact on West Coast sailors. The most prominent leaders of the I.W.W. were arrested and convicted for espionage, on the claim of the authorities that the militant movement was actually a secret agency of the Imperial German government used to undermine the U.S. war effort. The persecution of Wobblies over opposition to the war created an exceptional climate of hatred and revenge in the West Coast areas where the radical and syndicalist tendencies were strongest. Attacks on the I.W.W., in which Furuseth was to join, at first did little to stem the radical upsurge. For some five years, between 1917 and 1923, the I.W.W. greatly expanded its influence among the "wage slaves" of the West, particularly maritime and lumber workers.

A Changed World

Indeed, the whole world was changed utterly by the war, and the S.U.P. was not exempt from the process of social transformation. Limited, local concerns of seamen on the West Coast of the U.S. would fall into the background, to a greater extent than in previous periods of radical political influence, as events in Europe began to profoundly alter the politics of the entire international labor movement. For this reason, the period in our narrative beginning at this time and extending until 1934, the year when the S.U.P. was, in effect, reborn, must at many points take us far away from the Pacific Coast. If some of what we here examine might seem digressive, it should be kept in mind that the seamen could no longer address themselves, in the main, to concerns that often had reflected a benign isolation from the affairs of the outer world.

A most important event of 1917, bearing inexorably on the later history of the S.U.P., took place thousands of miles from the U.S. West Coast, in the then-capital of Russia, Petrograd. On November 7, a minority party of self-styled revolutionary socialists, the Bolsheviks, directed by Vladimir Lenin and Leon Trotsky, seized power, six months after the tsar's fall, through an alternative governing apparatus, the "soviets" or "councils." Thus was born the Russian Bolshevik state which, in the name of communism, was to become a major world power and, over some 70 years, play a disruptive role in the history of all labor movements, not least the American seafaring unions.

Sailors, in the form of *naval* personnel, had played a crucial role in the Bolshevik coup; the revolutionary spirit of the fleet, organized in committees, had been considered a major asset by Lenin's conspirators.

At the beginning of the Bolshevik experience, the concept of "councils" as a form of public or labor administration received support from within the Sailors' Union, with Scharrenberg's *Journal* noting in its issue of August 8, 1917 that a "People's Council for Democracy and Terms of Peace," had been set up in the U.S., modelled on "the Russian Workmen's Councils, and . . . the British People's Council movement of which Robert Sm(i)llie, head of the British Miners' Federation, is the head." The U.S. council called for peace in Europe, along lines suggested by the pre-Bolshevik Russian government, put in power by a democratic revolution in March, 1917: no forcible annexations by the European powers, no indemnities, and free development of all nationalities. In addition, the council aimed at a safeguarding of labor's rights and of democracy throughout the U.S.

The *Journal* indicated that A.F.L. leaders under Samuel Gompers disapproved such activities. Scharrenberg and others dissented from their condemnation, pointing out that "the A.F. of L. Executive Council is, fortunately, not the final authority in matters of this kind." The most recent annual convention of the federation had "minced no words on war and militarism," and the *Journal* expected that the next would offer "a more enthusiastic reception" to the council's principles. The *Journal* spoke favorably of a controversial meeting proposed for September, 1917, in Switzerland, by the Dutch, Danish, Norwegian, Swedish, Finnish, German, Austrian, Hungarian, and Bulgarian unions, to discuss peace demands.[8]

"The Rebel Sailor": A Digression

The Bolshevik coup was a product of a massive war-weariness in Russia. Anger, disgust, and the discrediting of the established order swept Europe as a consequence of the war. The German Navy at the same time underwent a proletarian rebellion that harked back to naval revolts that had taken place during the Russian revolutionary rehearsal in 1905. The fleet committee agitation by the Bolsheviks in 1917 carried to the outside world a stirring political myth: "the rebel sailor." Although radical naval revolts had little or nothing to do directly with the problems of merchant seamen, *the glamor of mutiny* was to "rub off" on the seafarers in a curious way that, as we shall see, was to have its effect. For this reason, these revolts bear examination here.

The German sailors' movement is believed to have begun in September 1916, with a protest over poor food on the battleship *Helgoland*, moored with the High Seas Fleet in North Sea waters. Small revolutionary groups had begun working in the ranks of the sailors. During the winter, food demonstrations also took place in the port of Kiel, at the same time as a wave of strikes in Berlin excited the anti-war left with

---

[7]Goldberg, op. cit. Gill and Markholt, ibid. [8]*Coast Seamen's Journal*, August 8, 1918.

the possibility of a workers' revolt against the Imperial regime. In January, 1917, peace slogans were set up on the vessels *Oldenburg* and *Posen*, with at least three sailors imprisoned. News of the democratic March revolution in Russia (which made possible the later Bolshevik takeover) further stimulated the radicals in the German fleet. By June, sailors made contact with the Independent Social Democratic Party, a mass organization that had split off from the giant Social Democratic Party in disagreement with the latter's pro-war stance.

The naval commander at Kiel banned left-wing newspapers from the ships; the support of the officers for various right-wing journals and organizations further alienated the ranks. As the summer wore on, crew members on the battleship *Prinzregent Luitpold* refused to load coal, and halted the vessel in mid-passage during a trip from Kiel to Wilhelmshaven through the Kiel Canal. Protests spread, centering on food. The *Luitpold* "black gang" refused to eat dried vegetables known as "barbed wire," and sailors on the *Helgoland* would not load flour which they said was unfit for human consumption. A bread strike took place on the *Friedrich der Grosse*, followed by a protest on the *Luitpold* against "wormy" soup. On July 20, 1917, 137 men walked off the cruiser *Pillau* at Wilhelmshaven, over the reluctance of the high command to grant leaves, and fraternized with port workers. They were punished by three hours of drill. But on August 1-2, 49 firemen went ashore from the *Luitpold* to hold a meeting, and on their return 11 were arrested and placed in the brig. The next day, 400 men left the *Luitpold*, marched into the Wilhelmshaven dockyards, and visited another vessel.

The German naval authorities first sought to quiet the rebellion by moving the *Luitpold* away from Wilhelmshaven, but demonstrations were also taking place on the *Friedrich der Grosse* and the *Kaiserin*. By the end of August, 1917, this wave of disturbances had diminished. Some 5,000 sailors had taken part in "acts of insubordination, mass desertion, hunger strikes and acts of sabotage," according to a German naval historian. Most importantly, the sailors had, it seems, organized a Union, which apparently took control of the protests aboard the *Friedrich der Grosse*, transferred away from Wilhelmshaven to join the *Luitpold*.

The eventual reaction of the German high command to the actions of the (to some mythical) Sailors' Union was predictable: 200 sailors were arrested and 150 were demoted on the *Luitpold* alone, out of a crew of around 1,000. Courts martial resulted in 77 men judged guilty, with nine sentenced to death. Of the capital punishment sentences, only two were carried out: Max Reichpietsch, the sailor from the *Friedrich der Grosse* who had contacted the Independent Social Democrats, and Albin Kobis, reportedly an anarchist, from the *Luitpold*, were shot. Reichpietsch had, it is averred, sought the introduction of dissident sailors' petitions to the previously mentioned international peace meeting, scheduled for September, 1917, by the central and northern European labor movements. This meeting was supported across continents and oceans by the S.U.P. in San Francisco.

By October, 1918, it was clear to the world that Germany and its allies had lost the war, but it was precisely at this time that rumors began to run through Wilhelmshaven that Admiral Franz Hipper, commander of the High Seas Fleet, was preparing to move the fleet into a major battle with the British navy.

With one of the cruisers from a scout group ordered to depart from Wilhelmshaven for possible battle, 45 members of the engine department fled into the dockyards, but were hunted down and dragged back. Within two days, sailors on a command vessel, the *Regensburg*, refused to turn to, and were supported by the "black gang." Some 300 men from the battle cruisers *Derfflinger* and *Von der Tann* went ashore, and were apprehended.

Lord Jellicoe, the British naval commander, had commented that he was the only man "who could have lost the war in an afternoon" — Hipper may have had in mind winning it in the same length of time. As it became increasingly obvious that the fleet was preparing for battle, incidents proliferated. On the afternoon of October 29, sailors gathered in the forecastle of the *Markgraf* and gave three cheers for U.S. President Wilson. Officers intervened and one was attacked. The demonstration was broken up with the imprisonment of a group of supposed ringleaders. New mutinies occurred on the *Helgoland* and the *Thuringen*, with sailors refusing to operate deck equipment and allowing pressure in the boilers to fall. Within hours, in rain and fog, the remainder of the bigger vessels had sailed, leaving these two mutinous ships behind. A destroyer signalled its intention to fire on the rebellious *Thuringen*, and then turned away. The mutineers were convinced to surrender, and were locked up with others inside the dockyards.

However, the revolt of the naval personnel had struck fire ashore, and on November 3, a crowd of some 20,000, including shipyard workers and women, fought a pitched battle at Kiel in an attempt to gain the release of the imprisoned sailors, resulting in eight dead and 21 wounded. Naval officers were attacked on the streets and their epaulets and cap insignia torn off. The movement grew as bands of sailors circulated through the town. By November 5 the red flag of socialism had been raised on all the vessels and shore facilities at Kiel, except for the battleship *König*. A battle over that vessel's flagstaff produced five dead. In Wilhelmshaven a Sailors' Council took control on November 6, the same day the disturbances spread to Bremen when a train full of convicted rebels from the *Thuringen* and *Helgoland* stopped there and the men escaped. A Workers and Soldiers' Council at Cuxhaven declared that it would "reject the idea of national defense and would therefore hoist the white flag if the English were to come."

Rebellion of the North Sea sailors had contributed strongly to a burgeoning political crisis throughout Germany, and by November 6 the Kaiser's government fell, replaced by a republican government under the control of the Social Democrats. But it was primarily the action of the sailors that made the German Revolution a reality. If our examination of their rebellion seems overly extended, it should be recalled that the hold of this kind of outbreak on the minds of radicals around the world was to influence the politics of the worldwide maritime labor movement for decades to come. As we shall see this mythical symbol of proletarian revolt, the "rebel sailor," was to assume remarkable dimensions in the imagination of political thinkers and, even of artists. For those bent on subversion, the most important aspect of the German naval revolt was probably its proof of the potential effectiveness of small, conspiratorial revolutionary groupings working within a large rank-and-file. *The all-powerful High Command of a great Navy was reduced to helplessness by the determined action of a conscious minority, organized through secret committees.*[9]

Nordic Echoes

Wartime radicalization deeply affected Norway, birthplace of many S.U.P. members, although the Scandinavian countries managed to stay out of the conflict. At the 1918 Congress of the Norwegian Labor Party, the syndicalist opposition under Martin Tranmael took over the party. A new statement of principle was adopted by the Norwegian Labor Party; where in the past the party program renounced "any dictatorship by force," the opposition resolution stated that "as a revolutionary class warfare party, social democracy cannot recognize the right of the ruling class to exploit and suppress the working class, even if such exploitation and suppression are supported by a parliamentary majority. The Norwegian Labor Party must therefore reserve the right to employ revolutionary mass action in the struggle for the economic liberation of the working class." The congress reflected great enthusiasm over the Russian and German events, and workers and soldiers' councils were formed throughout the country, although they apparently achieved little.

Another distant event that unquestionably molded the outlook of the Scandinavian backbone membership of the S.U.P. was the short-lived attempt at proletarian revolution in Finland in 1918. With the Bolshevik takeover, Finland had been freed from Russian control. The resulting struggle for power between Finnish White conservatives and Red socialists was, writes Franz Borkenau, a "frightful catastrophe." In April 1918, after a landing of German troops on Finnish soil, the socialist movement attempted evacuation of the entire Finnish working class to Russia, for as Borkenau points out, at that time the Finnish population stood at only three million. But the effort broke down, and the ensuing white terror led by General Karl Mannerheim with the support of Swedish rightists, "avenged the few hundred victims of the propertied classes in the blood of tens of thousands of the poor." Within months the S.U.P. passed on to its members the report of Carl Sandburg, the American poet, working in Europe as correspondent for a U.S. news service, that "the workers of Finland owned some 800 labor temples and people's houses, practically all of which have been taken over as drill halls and arsenals. Upwards of 27,000 persons are held in convict camps, 10,000 have been butchered in mass executions, 12,000 starved to death, one colony of 10,000 moved to Russia . . . all labor and Socialist newspapers have been suppressed and censorship is rigid."

The Finnish Reds were closer in their outlook to the moderate German socialists than to the ruthless Russian Bolsheviks, and this may have been their downfall. Their martyrdom was to have wide, though little-known effects, for it made thousands of Finns, at home, in Russia, and in the U.S., where a large Finnish diaspora had settled, fanatically pro-Moscow. When the U.S. Communist Party was stabilized in the early '20s, the largest single ethnic group was Finnish, derived from the Finnish Federation of the American Socialist Party, which had been the largest and most prosperous section of that party. For many years the Finnish Communists in the U.S. maintained a daily press. So, indeed, did the Finnish Wobblies, whose daily newspaper, *Industrialisti*, in Duluth, Minnesota continued publishing until the mid-1970s. (It is also perhaps significant that at the time of this writing the American head of the U.S. Communist Party, Gus Hall, is a Finnish American from Minnesota.)

While the Bolshevik Revolution had captured the attention of socialists throughout the world, events in Norway and Finland cannot help but have molded the outlook of the many Norwegian, Swedish-Finnish, or Finnish members of the S.U.P. Because of the high educational standards in the Nordic lands a voluminous correspondence had continued, back and forth, between the Pacific Coast and Scandinavia. The S.U.P. Archives are filled with letters in Danish, Norwegian, Swedish, and, occasionally, Finnish and German.[10]

The fall of the Imperial German government in November 1918, brought an armistice, and the U.S. shipowners and government began preparations for conversion of the expanded wartime fleet to peacetime activities. Shipbuilding continued at a good pace until at least 1920. Meanwhile, the I.S.U. leaders showed their desire to broaden the interests of the union by

---

[9]A thorough account of the German naval revolt is David Woodward, *The Collapse of Power*, London, Arthur Barker, 1973. A limited but useful memoir is Icarus (Ernst Schneider), *The Wilhelmshaven Revolt*, London, Simian, 1975, by a participant who provides information on the political background. Also see Paul Schubert and Langhorne Gibson, *Death of a Fleet*, New York, Coward, 1932, excerpted in Edmund Fuller, editor, *Mutiny!*, New York, Crown Publishers, 1953. [10]Finn Moe, "Does Norwegian Labor Seek the Middle Way," *New Frontiers* (New York), April, 1937; Galenson, *Labor in Norway*; Borkenau, op. cit., on both Norway and Finland; O.W. Kuusinen, *The Finnish Revolution: A Self-Criticism*, London, Workers' Socialist Federation, 1919 (in S.U.P. archive); *Coast Seamen's Journal*, March 12, 1919; Victor Serge, *Year One of the Russian Revolution*, New York, Holt, Rinehart & Wilson, 1972. On Finns in the U.S. Communist Party, see *Fourth National Convention of the Workers (Communist) Party of America*, Chicago, Daily Worker Publishing Co., 1925; Aino Kuusinen, *The Rings of Destiny*, New York, William Morrow, 1974; Lowell K. Dyson, *Red Harvest*, Lincoln, University of Nebraska Press, 1982.

changing the name of the *Coast Seamen's Journal* to, simply, *The Seamen's Journal*, in April 1918.

Many eyes in the world's labor movements, the S.U.P. included, remained on Russia. On January 1, 1919, *The Seamen's Journal* published an ecstatic account by Albert Rhys Williams, a writer for *The Nation*, of a visit to the Baltic Red Fleet. Rhys Williams quoted from a message of the Russian sailors to the German naval mutineers, stating that the former tsar's yacht, the *Polar Star*, had been taken over by the sailors for the use of the revolutionary fleet committee. He cited Leon Trotsky's praise of the 6,000 sailors at the Kronstadt naval base, guarding the approaches of Petrograd, as the "flower and pride of the revolutionary forces." However, Rhys Williams also noted that even after the revolution, with the appointment of officers now ostensibly in the hands of fleet committees elected by the sailors, the officers received superior food to that served to the ranks. While the Bolshevik officers ate steak, the revolutionary sailors ate potatoes. When questioned about the difference, the sailor members of the fleet committee asserted that having gained the right to liberalized shore leave and to wear civilian clothes off duty, they did not "demand that the revolution give us everything." Nevertheless, Rhys Williams confidently ascribed to the sailors "a deep feeling of communal ownership."

Furuseth in Europe

The formerly belligerent nations' diplomatic representatives had begun conferring in Paris as 1918 came to a close, and Andrew Furuseth departed the U.S. in an effort to participate in what was universally viewed as the reorganization of "the world order." He sought the extension of the Seamen's Act to the entire globe, through the Paris Peace Conference. Furuseth particularly sought help from J. Havelock Wilson, head of the National Seamen's and Firemen's Union of Great Britain, founder, as previously described, of the International Transportworkers' Federation [I.T.F.], and a Labour member of Parliament. Wilson had come to represent the extreme conservative wing of British labor, and his leadership and journal, *The Seamen*, were the object of much rank-and-file discontent. During the war, he had reacted to the situation of the British sailors, facing German submarines, with an extensive anti-German hatred campaign, even barring European anti-war labor figures from travelling to England on British ships, as they were considered "the Kaiser's allies."[11] Wilson's anti-Germanism was so violent that Furuseth, whose own stance had become faultlessly patriotic once the U.S. entered the war, reproved him, opposing a Wilson call for condemnation of German seamen for serving on their country's ships.

Furuseth had argued "our chief concern ought to be directed to prevent any hatred of seamen by seamen. Seamen have no choice but to obey. By hating he will become morally responsible. Hatred once developed does not cease with the war and it will then be used by shipowners to pit seamen against seamen in the economic struggle."[12] Wilson promised Furuseth his backing in the fight for world recognition of seamen's rights, but we will see how faithfully this pledge was kept.

The Paris Peace Conference forged numerous international accords, laying the basis for such institutions as an International Commission on Labor Legislation and the International Labor Organization, as well as the better-known League of Nations. Furuseth viewed the latter structure with great suspicion and feared that "the world order" would be used to undermine the status of the expanded U.S. fleet created by the war, and to destroy the Seamen's Act even as it existed in the U.S.[13]

Early in 1919, another dramatic naval revolt began among the French forces stationed in the Black Sea for operations against the Bolshevik regime, launched in concert with other Western powers then intervening in Russia. In this instance, the revolt drew in, as summer progressed, groups of French soldiers in the southern Ukraine and Crimea, and sailors in French harbors as well as French naval vessels in other waters. Some claimed the Black Sea revolt was a product of bad conditions similar to those suffered by the German sailors in 1917, but André Marty, supposedly chief engineer of the destroyer *Protet* and leader of the action, would later assert that the main grievance was that the war had not yet ended for those obliged to fight in Russia alongside the anti-Bolshevik White forces. In addition, France itself was convulsed by strikes and demonstrations "for bread and progress, against Clemenceau's military dictatorship and against the military intervention in Russia," according to Marty's account. "The workers of Germany, Austria and Hungary were fighting an armed struggle, and revolutionary strikes were raging in Italy, Spain, Switzerland, all over Europe, and in faraway Argentina . . . (In Russia) the French soldiers and sailors saw before them the revolution which was rousing the masses of the people in France." Rebellion in the French infantry, which had been moved into the Ukraine to replace the former German occupiers, aided the Bolshevik Red army to gain the Ukrainian city of Kherson, while "a company of the 7th Engineers, influenced by the militant trade union members connected with the Bolsheviks, drove away their officers and handed over their material to the workers." Marty wrote that "the French Army had turned into a disorganized throng with every trace of military discipline gone. It became necessary to send it back to France."

The French sailors observed the retreat of the troops through the port of Odessa, carried out in "frightful disorder." On April 19, 1919, within a few days of the removal and shortly after the arrest of Marty and three other rebels, revolt began on the battleship *France*, moored in Sevastopol. The next day its sister

[11]Borkenau, ibid. [12]Taylor, op. cit. [13]Weintraub, op. cit.

ship the *Jean-Bart* joined the protest, raising the red flag. By the end of the month the fleet had departed the Black Sea, with the *Jean-Bart* headed for Istanbul and the rest of the ships returning to France. Marty, held prisoner on the heavy cruiser *Waldeck Rousseau*, later took credit for the mutiny of its crew and the raising of the red flag on April 27. Ships in France, in the Toulon navy yard and the Atlantic port of Brest were paralyzed by demonstrations against their proposed replacement of the Black Sea squadron, and sailors on the battleship *Voltaire*, in Bizerte, North Africa, refused to sail for Russia. Thus, Marty emphasized years afterward, "*French imperialism was compelled to relinquish its stranglehold on the October Revolution*" (emphasis in original).

As these events were taking place, *The Seamen's Journal* published a declaration by the French General Confederation of Labor (C.G.T.) known for its syndicalist sympathies, in which the confederation vigorously condemned the expeditions against Russia and any other continuation of the war.[14]

"Criminal Syndicalism"

Back on the Pacific Coast, militant unionists, and radicals in the labor movement, faced a new problem in the form of legislation against "criminal syndicalism." Laws against "criminal syndicalism," which was defined with exceeding vagueness, had been passed in 1917 in Idaho and Minnesota, and in 1919, California followed suit. The Golden State was not, then, a haven of liberalism; agricultural interests sought to keep the state locked into a kind of feudal Midwestern conservatism, and Los Angeles was considered the national center of anti-union "open shop" activities, as much as San Francisco was the cynosure of labor radicalism. The I.W.W. had to fight for free speech by organizing mass civil disobedience in San Diego, Fresno, and other California cities. The California "criminal syndicalism" law was a constitutional horror, for it judged as unlawful a "doctrine," which was left undefined, rather than a specific action. Any overt acts committed in the furtherance of revolutionary goals or during an industrial conflict would fall under existing criminal law; the C.S. law was aimed at an intellectual trend, rather than specific crimes. It banned the production, possession, or circulation of printed matter supporting "criminal syndicalism," in a clear violation of the First Amendment guarantee of press freedom. The S.U.P.'s Scharrenberg strongly opposed the California C.S. law, in a range of legislative, journalistic, and union efforts.

In the states of Oregon and Washington, the end of the war brought a genuine reign of terror against radicals, centered on the I.W.W. lumber workers. Spokane had seen a major "free speech fight" of its own, but the smaller Washington town of Everett had been the scene of bloody fighting over free speech in which several people were killed, and Centralia, Washington was to become infamous for a series of events in 1918-19 that culminated in the brutal murder of Wesley Everest, a lumberjack, a world war veteran, and a dedicated Wobbly. After a desperate battle that had ended in the Skookumchuck River with Everest's surrender to the respectable citizens of Centralia, the Wobbly was taken from the town lockup, castrated, and lynched. As he was dragged from the jail, he asked his fellow-prisoners to wire the I.W.W. in Chicago and "tell them I died for my class!"

The killing of men like Everest, including the Swedish sailor and I.W.W. poet Joe Hill, executed in Utah in 1915, and I.W.W. organizer Frank Little, also lynched in Butte, Montana in 1917, only further inflamed the sentiments of those workers — and they were many — who supported radical unionism.

The I.W.W. had become the main organization of the Pacific Northwest "timber beast," and in a labor trend that was typical of that region, Wobbly influence grew among the seamen shipping out from Puget Sound and the Columbia River. Between February 6 and 11, 1919, Seattle was shut down by the first general strike in U.S. history, led by the A.F.L. labor radicals allied with I.W.W. "two-card men," so dubbed because they held full membership in both the I.W.W. and the A.F.L. But the stubborn Furuseth and the San Francisco leadership of the S.U.P., avowed enemies of the I.W.W. and other labor radicals, opposed Seattle by refusing to support the strike and declined to concur in the decisions of the Seattle Branch to strike and to elect five delegates to the "Soldiers', Sailors' and Workmen's Council," modelled on the Russian "soviets," during the strike.

Steam Schoonering, 1918-21

A lively view of West Coast sailor life at this time was provided by Paul Hensel, as interviewed by Karl Kortum, director of the National Maritime Museum, in his pioneering oral history cycle, to which we will return:

"If you went in a big steam schooner up to Puget Sound or Portland, that was three weeks — $90 a month and some overtime. But in an outside-porter like the *Helen P. Drew* or the *Westport* up to Greenwood [now Elk, California] you could make $250 for sure . . . even $300.

"I am speaking about just after the first world war. You were working all the time, it was on overtime, and the small steam schooners had quick turnaround. Of course everything went to pieces in 1921 with the strike — back to $65 a month.

"In the larger steam schooners that took a couple of days to load, you broke sea watches when you arrived. But we didn't do this in the ones that ran to Greenwood. We kept sea watches, but got paid overtime, too.

"Say you arrived late in the afternoon at Greenwood, or more likely in the early morning — at night a steam schooner tried to be at sea. On shore they were ready

[14]André Marty, *The Epic of the Black Sea Revolt*, New York, Workers' Library Publishers, 1941; *Coast Seamen's Journal*, June 11, 1919.

for you; they had the word from San Francisco that you were coming. The boatmen we put over to make our lines fast got high man's overtime. Then you started to load right away. Lumber — one inch, two inch stuff. Ties. You didn't stop except for dinner and supper — an hour each. You finished up at night if you arrived in the morning.

"Six men, three watches. Say you're on the 4-to-8 watch. You arrive in Greenwood at eight o'clock in the morning. Instead of going off, you work overtime until noon. Then dinner for an hour, and then straight time until five. Say you sail at five or six o'clock, the 4-to-8 watch takes her back down the coast, but they're on overtime.

"Small vessels . . . it takes only nine or ten hours to load. Sometimes 200,000 feet, sometimes 180,000 if it's heavy. If the ties were green — sinkers — the ship would be loaded sooner. If she is down too low — they don't take any chances on that — you get out early. Sometimes in summer you take a little more — what they call a summer load. Another reason for taking less than the ship would carry was that the order might be for that amount.

"Also it depends on what kind of lumber you get. One inch stuff had to be handled by hand and it takes a long time before you get away with a load. Another thing that comes in to it are the tides. The ship is not so powerful, so they figured the tides that would be running in the Golden Gate when they arrived pretty close. Usually it takes you ten hours from Greenwood, but sometimes we loaded some butter and eggs at Point Arena on the way home.

"The different lumber orders had to be marked off. One stripe, two stripes . . . or you make a ring . . . an arrow . . . with chalk, otherwise you had to use paint. Down below you mostly used chalk because it wouldn't get washed off.

"When you got to San Francisco you went all over the bay — Sixteenth Street, the sea wall, sometimes to Oakland — Sunset (that belonged to Charlie Nelson Company), Hogans, any place . . . maybe three or four lumber yards in one day. Some of them took only 30,000 feet. Oakland Long Wharf . . . that was McCormick's . . . It depended on how much lumber you had to discharge. A little dab . . . just drop it any place. Depending on the room on the wharf.

"How we worked! You got a little rest crossing the bay . . . when it was eleven o'clock in the morning you could go to dinner; you eat early, in other words. (But you can't eat before eleven.) You eat while you travel.

"Sometimes you discharged on the bulkhead here between two piers, and they send long two wheeled trucks or dollies. We put a load down on one of these, they put a chain around it, and a horse pulls it out of the way. Another truck takes its place. Then a horse is hooked on to that one. And so on. In that way the dock was kept clear — no lumber pile.

"Breakfast was from 7 to 8 (while working), dinner from 12 to one o'clock, supper from 5 to 6. There were two ten minute coffee breaks. Any work before 8 and after 5 is overtime.

"You didn't break watches — next over to the oil docks to bunkers; the crew up at Sanguinetti's drinking . . . the mate comes to drag you back. Then you sail.

"But how long could you stand it? No sleep. You could live like that for a month. But it wasn't like that all the time, luckily. Say you had 1x4s — that slowed everything down. You could only pick up a few at a time.

"The *Unimak* was best — you could go to sleep on the wheel and she would stay on course for half an hour at a time. And she was speedy; she had a good little engine. Ten hours from Greenwood.

"Off watch you were nodding over the table you were so tired, but the captain or the engineer didn't care. He kept you awake, dealing cards. You'd get fired if you didn't gamble. That's the rule, them days. There was a lot of money floating around in those ships. A man who didn't gamble was resented because he was available to stand somebody's wheel watch at maybe the wrong time. It broke up the clique.

"They paid you off out at sea so you could gamble — they figured that out. You get paid when the lumber is out of the ship; you get paid for that whole day. That is the end of a trip. Going out the Golden Gate a new trip is starting.

"'Pay day! Come and get it,' they tell you.

"Mostly you eat first — five o'clock, or six o'clock if you had a little lumber left — that has to get out. So you eat when you're out at sea. They all leave at five o'clock or after, even the big steamers.

"You go up to the captain's cabin. One man at a time. The payroll is all made out. It doesn't take much time. One, two, three and you're done.

"On a long trip from Seattle or Portland down to San Pedro you would have a pretty good payday — maybe five days at sea. You got paid off outside when you leave San Pedro on the way back to 'Frisco. That's thirty-six hours, plenty of time to gamble. Once again, no sleep.

"It's easy to figure out, how it was supposed to work. A lot depended on the steward and how much booze he had on board. Or beer.

"They always got a bottle in the galley some place. Some needed a drink — they were nervous, like playing poker. Like the Finns, they've got to have a couple of drinks before they start. Gambling makes them nervous — they've been there a couple of trips. They know what is going to happen.

"The steward or the cook, they talk pinochle. Somebody else comes in . . . maybe you'll hear him tell the steward, 'Ah, let's get started! Get the game started . . .'

"Well, sure . . . everybody is waiting for it anyway. Get comfortable, have a drink. No charge. The steward or the cook starts it off free. But he gets his money back because later on it's: 'Gimme another drink!' You've got to pay for what you order after the first one. He just wets your whistle.

"Maybe a pinochle game to start things off. Then poker. Poker is money. But a poker player got broke sometimes — and then he was willing to make a dollar — he took somebody's wheel turn. Two dollars an hour.

"As I say, it was a different kind of life running up to the Columbia River. A McCormick ship always had freight going north; you left about midnight. At St. Helens, or — if you went to the Sound — Seattle, Tacoma, Port Angeles, it would take you a long time to load if there was no overtime. Six sailors, and the rest were longshoremen. When the ship was in a hurry or the market was good, you worked overtime — seven in the morning and up to midnight. A ship like the *Wapama* was pretty speedy when she first came out — full loaded it took about four days to get down the coast to San Francisco, five days to San Pedro. But the whole trip could take three weeks.

"Everybody was after money — you would quit a steam schooner that didn't work overtime. If there was no money in a ship, one trip was enough. You could go offshore in the big steamers, work eight hours and have nothing to do — I mean deepwater ships.

" 'Steam schooner life' they called it. Quit — go up — get your money.

"You ain't packin' much with you — pair of shoes, overalls, union card, hook.

"In 1917 we had only $55 and four bits overtime in the steam schooners; not only that but two watches. The United States got into the war in April and all the Germans had to get off the waterfront.* . . . When we came back after the Armistice, about December of 1918, we had three watches, $90 a month and a dollar for overtime!

"Another peculiar thing about the steam schooners . . . along about September you would hear 'the old men are coming back.' That meant you could be out of a job; the fishermen were coming back on the sailing ships from Alaska. We called them 'hungry'; they had a big pay day from the fishing in Bristol Bay but the mate always had a job for them. They met him in the Bulkhead or the Pilot Bar and maybe brought him a little barrel of salmon bellies.** They were considered the steady men. It happened in September every year . . . the old men coming back. You were never sure of your job. They stayed in the steam schooners all winter."

Furuseth Returns From Europe

Furuseth returned from Europe to argue before the national convention of the A.F.L. in June, 1919, against participation in the League of Nations and International Labor Office. He pointed out that Britain, through its colonies and dominions, controlled an oversized number of votes in the I.L.O., and that within the national delegations, union representatives were outnumbered by those of the employers and governments. The European shipping powers had expressed their frank hostility to the provisions of the Seaman's Act, which had been considered even by the leadership of the Socialist German merchant seamen's union to be outlandishly extreme and "anarchistic." The European transport worker — at sea or on the railroads — was considered the provider of an essential public service where the right to strike was inapplicable. Should the U.S. recognize the legal authority of the new international organizations, the Act was doomed, Furuseth argued. Although the A.F.L. endorsed the I.L.O. and the League, Furuseth's opposition was supported by a considerable number of delegates, including many who allied with him because they saw a British-dominated League as a barrier to the independence of Ireland.[15]

Furuseth that year published a *Second Message to Seamen*, in which he deplored the deterioration of craft standards in the maritime industry, while recalling the past abuses of "sea-slavery" and the crimping system. He went on to express once again, profound suspicion, if not contempt, for the longshore workers and their organizations, and to assail attempts at amalgamation of the seafaring and dock workers into a single union. To some, Furuseth's energy was being increasingly dissipated by inappropriate issues, for in the aftermath of the war the deadly threat to the union was represented by neither the longshoremen nor the League of Nations, but by the U.S. Shipping Board and the shipowners, who were preparing a plan to smash the sailors' movement thoroughly and definitively.

In 1920 Furuseth made a further attempt at a worldwide Seamen's Act, leading a delegation to a maritime law conference, again in Europe, supported by the International Seafarers' Federation. The I.S.F. had originally been set up within the ranks of the International Transportworkers' Federation, which was increasingly dominated by the continental European railroad, barge, and dock unions. But resentment of the I.T.F. leadership at the seafarers' desire for autonomy had apparently led the I.S.F. to break away. Furuseth participated in the I.S.F. along with Havelock Wilson's British union; but Wilson "honored" past promises by refusing, even within the I.S.F., to support Furuseth's proposal for a universal Seamen's Act. Wilson's forces declared at the 1920 conference that "the act had been beneficial to American seamen and foreign seamen visiting American ports," and should be maintained in its entire scope for the U.S., "but that extension of the Act at the present time to all countries may be detrimental to the best interests of the seamen of such countries . . . (and) should be left to the judgment and

* Hensel, like many other young Germans, came to the steam schooners by way of the dozen German square riggers caught by the outbreak of war in Santa Rosalia, Mexico. "I walked off the *Harvestehude* one Sunday mornng and forgot to go back . . ." Hensel made his way overland, by way of Nogales, to the United States and joined his first steam schooner, the *Tiverton*, at San Pedro in March or April of 1917: "I'll never forget breakfast aboard that first day. Ham and eggs, bacon and eggs, hotcakes — anything you want. I hadn't seen eggs for years. Then you go to work. Breakfast in the *Harvestehude* was hard tack and black coffee and what we called 'blau Heinrich', or blue Henry. That was mush. There was no milk or sugar unless you had some left from your weekly ration."

** The salmon bellies weren't canned in Alaska and the fishermen put them up for their own use in the small barrels that butter came in or in coal oil cans cleaned out or other containers. [15]On Scharrenberg and C.S. law, see E.F. Dowell, *History of Criminal Syndicalism Legislation in the U.S.*, Baltimore, John Hopkins Press, 1939. On Seattle general strike, S.U.P. Headquarters Minutes, 1919; Paul Hensel, interviewed by Karl Kortum, 1968, National Maritime Museum; on Furuseth in Europe, Taylor, op. cit., Weintraub, op. cit.

efforts of the organized seamen of each respective country."[16]

After this conference, Furuseth visited Norway and there contacted the marine unions, lobbying the government for repeal of laws against desertion that he feared would be reinforced by Norwegian support for the League of Nations. He did the same in Sweden and Denmark.[17]

In Norway, the Labor Party under Tranmael had by now broken with the moderates of the Socialist (second) International, and affiliated with the new, Communist (third) International that had been set up in Moscow. The Norwegian Labor Party was the only mass socialist party in Europe to fully join the Comintern, as the new international was to be known. With the split from the Socialist International, Tranmael declared that "the working class must today become aware that revolution and dictatorship are absolutely necessary." However, the Norwegian Labor Party's career within the Comintern's ranks would prove significantly brief. In Borkenau's words, it "was based upon a mutual misunderstanding."[18]

1921 Battles (I): Kronstadt

In January, 1921, *The Seamen's Journal* once again came under the editorship, after some twenty years, of John Vance Thompson (see Chapter III). This apparently-minor event was to have wide and lasting repercussions, giving rise to great misunderstanding on the part of labor historians as well as in the ranks of the Union. Thompson was an articulate and extremely militant sailor and editor, whose views in some respects paralleled those of the I.W.W. However, there is convincing evidence that he was never a member of the latter organization, although so branded by Furuseth. Thompson would stand at the helm of the paper during the most difficult period of the Union's history, for an immense and dramatic battle was about to take place.[19] However, before looking at the bitter — and failed — 1921 struggle for survival of the Sailors' Union, it is appropriate to examine the last of the major cycle of early 20th century naval revolts, that of the Russian sailors at Kronstadt in March of the fatal year.

The Sailors' Union, through its *Journal*, under both Scharrenberg and Thompson, was prominent among the many labor and liberal organizations in the U.S. that struggled to end the interventionist attacks of the capitalist powers on the Russian Bolshevik state. Implicit in that effort was a belief that the socialist doctrines to which Lenin and Trotsky paid homage were sincerely held. But as the Russian regime consolidated, under the rigid control of Lenin's party, it became increasingly doubtful, to the S.U.P. and other labor leaders, whether any of the promises of the Russians revolutionary dictators were good coin.

The 1921 Kronstadt naval revolt illuminated, clearly and undeniably, for all those with eyes to see, the true character of the Bolshevik order. The epic of the Kronstadt sailors has been discussed and written about much more extensively than either the German or French movements described in this chapter; an unarguably fair account is provided by Viktor Lvovich Kibalchich, a Belgian-born Russian, who wrote under the name Victor Serge. Serge, imprisoned in France before the war as an anarchist, had participated in a revolutionary labor uprising in Spain in mid-1917, then had gone to Russia and joined the Bolsheviks, and was present at Kronstadt.

Serge, although intellectually closer to the anarchists, had come into the Bolshevik ranks with a belief that the followers of Lenin represented the most advanced proletarian revolutionaries in history. In the last days of February 1921, the "frightful" news came that Kronstadt had been taken by the counter-revolutionary White army. The idea was terrifying, because if true it meant that Petrograd, the Red capital, could fall within literal minutes; Kronstadt was the naval base guarding the approach to Petrograd. Fortunately or unfortunately, according to one's point of view, it was a despicable lie.

The Kronstadt naval personnel, thousands strong, who had so recently been praised by Trotsky, had not joined the Whites. Rather, they had organized fleet committees on the Bolshevik, German, and French model, and had come out for the "soviets," that is, workers', soldiers', and sailors' councils, to be elected democratically, with competition by the various socialist tendencies, and without the dictatorial overlordship of the Bolsheviks.

Emma Goldman and Alexander Berkman, who had been deported to Russia from the U.S. as "dangerous radical aliens," supported by Serge and other anarchists on the scene in Petrograd, attempted mediation between the Bolsheviks and the Kronstadt rebels, and failed. Some of the Russian "mediators" were arrested.

The Bolsheviks had already chosen their method of dealing with Kronstadt. On March 5, the Bolsheviks delivered an ultimatum to the sailors, signed by Trotsky, as people's commissar for war, and three other military figures, saying "only those who surrender unconditionally can count on mercy . . . this is the last warning." The rebels had previously been declared outlaws. Martial law had been imposed in Petrograd. Led by S.M. Petrichenko, a sailor on the vessel *Petropavlovsk* and chairman of the revolutionary committee, the rebels, numbering some 15,000, and the remainder of Kronstadt's population of around 50,000, awaited the storm.

The Bolsheviks began their assault on Kronstadt on March 8. Crossing the ice, two parties made their way to the fortress, but this first attempt failed, for one section of the troops went over to the rebels, and a

[16]Andrew Furuseth, *A Second Message to Seamen*, San Francisco, 1919; also see Gill and Markholt, op. cit.; Taylor, ibid. [17]Gill and Markholt, ibid. [18]Galenson, *Labor in Norway*: Borkenau, op. cit.; also O. Piatnitsky, *The 21 Conditions of Admission into the Communist International*, New York Workers Library Publishers, 1934. [19]*Seamen's Journal*, throughout 1921; Gill and Markholt, op. cit.

group that broke through into the town was forced back. No further military action took place until the night of March 16, after an artillery bombardment. In the early morning of the next day, Red troops crossed the ice again, this time seizing the fortress. "The insurrectionists defended themselves with desperation and had to be dislodged building by building," an official Bolshevik source relates. The battleships *Petropavlovsk* and *Sevastopol* did not surrender until the complete occupation of the city by the Red Army, on the morning of March 18. Thousands of men, women, and children were shot *en masse* in the streets of the town.

The Bolsheviks had demonstrated to the world the reality of their socialist pretensions. Almost immediately, Goldman, Berkman, and other anarchists took up the example of Kronstadt to expose the Bolshevik danger. As we shall see, this anarchist minority, supported by the syndicalists in Spain and, later, in Norway, acted against the Bolsheviks decades before the broad community of liberal intellectuals were prepared to criticize even the most obvious horrors of the Soviet regime.

The incident at Kronstadt was to reappear again and again in the San Francisco publications of the S.U.P., as a cautionary tale, after the emergence of Harry Lundeberg as the Sailors' leader.[20]

1921 Battles (II): Crushing of I.S.U.

The capitalists of the democratic world were, in the end, no more willing to tolerate the emancipation of seafarers than the Bolshevik rulers of Russia.

Shipowners in the United States were backed up by the threat of weapons, in the hands not only of strikebreakers and police, but also of soldiers, as in Russia. The first sign of the coming clash came in January 1921, when the I.S.U. received communications from the U.S. Shipping Board asking for a reduction in wages. The Shipping Board, under Admiral William S. Benson, was supported by the American Steamship Owners' Association.

At a meeting in April, Union representatives were presented with proposals including the new, lowered wage scale, abolition of the three-watch system (i.e. the eight-hour day), and a non-union open shop. In response, the I.S.U. put forward a short list of demands, emphasizing enforcement of the Seamen's Act but also including shutting down of the government Sea Service Bureaus, the institution for recruiting and training of seamen, that threatened to become "fink halls," legal establishment of a Union shop, and Union determination of individuals' seamanship qualifications and efficiency.

Admiral Benson answered that the U.S. Shipping Board was willing to help enforce the law, but that the government hiring halls would remain in operation, and that the seamen must accept a 15 percent wage cut, along with a complete elimination of all overtime, replacement of three watches with two (a compulsory 12-hour day), and removal of Union officials' right to visit ships.

At this time, four major U.S. shipping firms averaged more than 230 percent return on their shares, with profits averaging $52 million each in the period from 1916 to 1920. Dividends were higher than in any other year since 1913.

Furuseth appealed to the shipowners to allow wages and conditions to remain in force pending arbitration by President Warren G. Harding, but this was turned down. On April 30, the union learned that the Shipping Board had ordered the imposition of new wages, conditions, and open-shop rules on board all vessels operating in the Atlantic trades: the Shipping Board and the Steamship Owners' Association had locked out the I.S.U., from coast to coast. Within days, John Vance Thompson was editorializing in the *Journal* on "A Need for Resistance."

Admiral Benson clearly indicated the intentions of his Board by a statement that "it will be unfortunate if the personnel of the merchant marine persists in refusing to do their part in the labor liquidation of the marine industry while still benefiting from the labor liquidation in other industrial fields;" this was his way of driving into line those employers who did not show sufficient speed in slashing wages by the prescribed 15 percent.

Naturally, wartime overbuilding, the postwar surplus in tonnage, and the economic depression of 1920-21 were utilized by the employers and government as an argument in their assault on union rights. "Shipping slackened toward the end of 1920, presaging hard times for the seamen, as the enormously-expanded shipping industry began to shrink, to normal and then depression proportions," Gill and Markholt noted. By the time the strike began, some 30,000 seamen were out of work.

During the war, the U.S. government and employers had needed masses of workers to keep the war industries going, and were willing to pay high wages; further, they needed the unions to assure orderly bargaining. Taking from a model originally developed by the Imperial German government, the U.S. had set up a kind of temporary "military socialism" or state capitalism. With the war over, President Warren G. Harding's government and the employers were unwilling to continue appeasing the workers and unions; more, they were eager to deliver a crushing blow, such as would not only return the industrial scene to prewar standards of exploitation, but would also dispel the threat of "Bolshevik" contagion, through varieties of repression.

The postwar offensive of the privileged class and its political servitors was felt throughout U.S. society. Racism exploded and the limited rights won by Blacks after the civil war were largely done away with; foreign-born workers and "radicals" of whatever citizenship were subject to deportation, imprisonment, and

[20]The literature of the Kronstadt Rebellion is large; apart from Victor Serge, *Memoirs of a Revolutionary*, Oxford, Oxford University Press, corrected edition, 1978, also see the most extensive treatment, Israel Getzler, *Kronstadt 1917-1921*, Cambridge, Cambridge University Press, 1983, and Paul Avrich, *Kronstadt 1921*, Princeton, Princeton University Press, 1970.

murder; and, most importantly, labor was, on many fronts, smashed. The outlook of the seamen's employers was eloquently expressed by a writer for the *Marine Register*, a San Francisco periodical, who asked, "What chance has an American boy in the forecastle?" He answered, "Nil. From the frozen North, whence most of our Pacific Coast sailors come, there is brought an innate mental Bolshevism, — an essence of 'I don't wash, it is true, but I am just as good as anybody on the bridge,' that disrupts ship discipline."

Strike Begins

The only response to the Shipping Board available to the Union was that of the strike, the first nationwide marine walkout in the country's history.

With imposition of the wage cut, where they were not already locked out by Admiral Benson's April 30 order, Union men walked off ships. Furuseth appealed to continue negotiations, but Benson refused. Shipowners began the massive recruitment of strikebreakers. One controversial source of recruits was the Berkeley campus of the University of California, which provoked a protest by the Union. In mid-June an injunction against all picketing was issued against the Union.

The Marine Engineers' Beneficial Association abandoned the strike at this point, dealing a major blow to those on the picket line. The I.W.W.s and other industrial unionists, active in the battle, pointed bitterly to the M.E.B.A. action as a "craft" betrayal. Under pressure from their enemies, the Sailors began reaching out to other natural allies, particularly the West Coast longshoremen, some of whom recently had sought to form a united Federation of Marine Transport Workers. The San Francisco longshoremen had been locked out since 1919 by the stevedoring employers, who established a "blue book" company union on the docks. The government and shipowners were hoping to apply the same medicine to the sailors, and a common front of labor resistance to these actions was obviously on the agenda.

In July, Senator La Follette called for a congressional investigation of the Shipping Board lockout, but his appeal was unsuccessful. That month saw the Pacific Coast shipowners reintroduce a non-government, employer-operated fink hall, along with the so-called continuous discharge book (fink book), the latest incarnation of the grade book of the past. At the end of the month, Furuseth admitted defeat, calling on the men to return to work.

In a message printed in the *Journal* for August 3, he declared "The battle is fought and lost. We have lost many battles before and this is only one more battle lost. To the real fighter for ideals a battle lost means nothing," he asserted. "You will not be able to make any money to speak of, but you never did except for a short time, and only a few of you," he added, "let us accept the real situation as men, who have higher thoughts than a few cents, more wages and a few minutes' less work per day. He that would earn money shall lose it; but he that is willing to lose money for principle's sake shall gain it — after awhile. Not now."

Strike Log

Under the heading *Strike Log — Pacific Coast*, Gill and Markholt describe the day-to-day course of events as follows:

"April 30th 42 vessels cleared San Francisco. May 1st seamen and engineers struck the Pacific Coast, refusing to sign on under the new wage scale. The Sailors' Union struck all vessels except those whose owners signed the 1920 agreement for a year, and Catalina boats, tugs or other vessels with which the Union had special agreements. Crews were to remain aboard to discharge vessels and complete the voyages. Three coastwise vessels sailed May 1st under the old agreement. Crews of 40 Shipping Board vessels quit, and scabs were sought.

"At the beginning of the strike many mates belonging to the Neptune Association joined the strikers, but the Association replaced those who quit in sympathy. The Masters, Mates and Pilots declared a sympathetic strike. Captain Wescott of the mates was president of the Seafarers' Council, seated as a joint strike committee. By May 5th 37 vessels were tied up in San Francisco, and the middle of the month the Sailors' minutes reported an almost complete tie up along the Coast. The Matson Line managed to get the *Matsonia* away with a crew of scabs, many of them students from the University of California. Passengers reported the trip a nightmare of bad food, filthy rooms and a total breakdown of service. The vessel burned excess fuel because of the scab firemen's inefficiency.

"May 12th *The New York Times* announced that the operators would ask Federal troops for San Francisco if 'further rioting' occurred there. Two days later they withdrew the request, implying that they were confident of breaking the strike without troops. May 17th W. Kincaid, operating manager for the Shipping Board at San Francisco, proposed that vessels be manned by naval reserves, declaring the strike could be broken in two weeks.

"The following day the operators admitted that San Francisco was the tightest port in the country, with 55 vessels tied up and 43 sailed, (conditions) under which they cleared unspecified. The press, printing shipowners' propaganda, appears to have included vessels that signed the old agreement and cleared fair to the strikers in the total sailings to give the impression that the strike was less effective than it was. The operators made no attempt to work the 125 steam schooners tied up along the Coast with scabs.

"June 22nd Justice Van Fleet of the United States District Court at San Francisco enjoined the Seafarers' Council, the six affiliates, 'and their officers, agents, members and employees, and all persons acting in concert with them, . . . From picketing the piers of vessels of the companies hereafter named, or operating the launch *Lillian* as a picket boat, in a manner tending to intimidate or threaten any passenger, employe, or prospective employe of such companies, and

From coercing, threatening or using violence toward any passenger, employe, or prospective employe, or trespassing on or injuring the vessels, piers or other property, or in any manner unlawfully interfering with the business of the following companies: . . .'

"Sixteen of the principal companies of the Pacific coastwise and deep water trade were listed. When picketing was continued union men were charged with contempt.

"Pacific Coast longshoremen declared no sympathetic strike, but many members helped on the picket lines, and others undoubtedly scabbed. While the longshoremen's support would have helped, it must be remembered that they were weakened by defeats in 1916 and 1919, and most ports remained open shop or only partially organized . . .

"Inefficiency and inexperience of scabs accounted for frequent accidents on the Pacific Coast during the strike. May 8th the *Governor*, belonging to Pacific Steamship Co., was wrecked because the scab at the wheel couldn't distinguish between shore and ship's light. May 20th the Alaska liner *Admiral Watson* was reported having engine trouble due to scab engineers, with 350 passengers aboard, and finally towed into Victoria, B.C. The *Alameda*, the *Eelbeck*, the *Schley*, the *Evans* and the *Harry Luckenbach* also had engine trouble because of their scabs, and the *Queen* was disabled.

"Two thousand seamen answered the strike call in Seattle. There, as in San Francisco, the Seafarers' Council constituted the Joint Strike Committee, under the leadership of Chairman P. B. Gill, agent of the Sailors' Union. The Seattle Council was composed of mates, engineers, sailors, firemen, cooks and wireless operators. The Seattle Sailors maintained a soup kitchen, but the strikers depended little on relief from the unions, relying instead on credit with their boarding places.

"Principal employers of the port were the Shipping Board, Pacific Steamship and Alaska Steamship Companies. This new Alaska scale cut wages 25 per cent, from $90 to $62.50, and no overtime. By May 5th nine vessels were tied up besides those trying to get scabs. Pacific Steamship and Alaska Steamship Companies cancelled their sailings. The following day the *Eelbeck*, operated by Williams Dimond, sailed for Grays Harbor with scabs taken off the streets, so inefficient that the officers had to take the wheel watches. The Admiral Line was reported combing the Coast for scabs for the *President*. The operators sought scabs from pool halls, speakeasies, the University of Washington, and employment agencies; it was feared that sailings to Alaska would be dangerous in vessels manned by such incompetents.

"May 8th the *President* sailed manned by port engineers and captains, women for waitresses and farmers on deck. May 12th 19 vessels tied up in Seattle, including eight Pacific Steamship Co. ships and five belonging to Alaska Steamship Co. In an attempt to turn public sympathy against the strikers by claiming that Alaska suffered from a food shortage due to the strike, the Seattle Chamber of Commerce appealed to the Navy Department to furnish engineers to man relief ships.

"In reply the Seafarers' Council May 12th offered to ship union crews without wages if the operators would send a free relief ship to Alaska, the proceeds to go to the Orthopedic hospital beyond the costs of fuel and food for the voyage. After some delay the owners refused May 16th on the ground that it was too 'cumbersome'. Similar proposals were made at Portland and San Francisco. The *Northwestern* sailed with Filipino and Negro scabs, whose strikebreaking was condemned by the Negro leaders of Seattle.

"The striking unions in Seattle were sued for $10,000 a day damages by the Shipping Board, which also asked an injunction restraining the unions from violence, picketing, and other interference. Ex-Senator George Turner was retained by the unions. The strikers testified at the injunction hearing June 8th that the picketing was orderly, contending that the injunction could not be issued because they were not a corporation. May 21st in Police Court strikers were fined $100 and given 30 day jail sentences, and armed scabs fined $25. Scabs on the *West Kappa*, with the aid of police, started a fight with the strikers, seriously stabbing one. June 11th the *Victoria*, owned by Alaska Steamship Co., sailed with scabs.

"Portland reported May 2nd that Shipping Board freighters were delayed, but privately owned vessels were sailing on schedule. May 9th the *Pawlet* sailed from Portland with scabs for the Orient. At the end of the second week the port remained practically closed. May 11th police were called out against strikers in a clash between strikers and scabs from the *President*. May 17th Portland police reserves were placed on the docks, following the beating of a scab. Numerous arrests were made after a pitched battle between strikers and scabs near the Broadway bridge. The unions charged that the Shipping Board was using force to hold engineers on the *West Nivaria* and compel them to go to sea.

"The middle of May San Pedro reported shipping at a standstill; oil tankers and lumber vessels were tied up, with a consequent slackening of lumber production.

"After the return of the Atlantic Coast to work (in late June), the shipowners, under the lead of the Shipping Board, attacked the Pacific Coast strikers with greater force. The strike remained on, partially effective on offshore vessels and almost totally effective in the coastwise lumber trade, where steam schooner operators made no attempt to operate with scabs.

Police Brutality

"In all ports police brutality increased. At San Francisco and San Pedro police were reported on twelve hour shifts. In the former port regular residents of the Dale-Tallac Hotel on Ellis street in the upper tenderloin district were thrown out of the hotel so it could be used to herd gunmen exclusively. Police were detailed to watch the place.

"In Seattle scabs were armed by the shipowners for trouble, and strikers were stabbed. June 23rd the *Union Record* reported armed thugs on the waterfront, including former Police Chief Wappenstein, who had served a jail term for participation in graft in 1906. Thugs were armed with guns, knives and razors. Police were concentrated on the waterfront aiding the scabs. June 25th police arrested 24 strikers on First Avenue for no offense, subsequently releasing seven. Clarence Kane, a union seaman, was fatally shot by a scab, and a scab arrested for gun firing. June 27th the papers reported strikers cut by Negro scabs.

"At Portland about the middle of June police and scabs clashed with strikers in a battle on the Linnton oil docks in which Nestor Dario, a striker, was killed. Six or seven seamen were arrested and later released.

"Damage to vessels continued. In June the *Queen* was disabled, and in August the *Alaska* was wrecked between San Francisco and Portland, with over 40 lost. Only five seamen were in the crew, the rest students. The vessel was going full speed ahead, 17 miles off the coast when the course was 33 miles off, to make time. The lifeboats were improperly equipped, and the crew couldn't man them.

"About July 1st the Shipowners' Association opened the Employment Service Bureau at San Pedro, in charge of Edwin Nichols, previously connected with the Training Service and Sea Service Bureau of the Shipping Board, to recruit scabs.

"Early in July the steam schooner operators, acting through the Shipowners' Association of the Pacific, offered the sailors an agreement providing wages at $77.50 a month, 60 cents an hour overtime, changes in working conditions, a pledge to work with non-union longshoremen, and the open shop. The majority of men in the Sailors' Union were employed on steam schooners.

"The Union was divided over accepting the offer. Furuseth wired from Washington urging acceptance as the best possible offer obtainable, since the engineers and the Atlantic seamen had returned to work and the strike was weakening on the Pacific Coast in spite of the seamen's efforts. Other officials favored acceptance. Those opposing the agreement objected to a provision that the master might set or break watches in any port at any time; a provision prohibiting a seaman from quitting a vessel until the cargo was discharged without furnishing a substitute; and the provision to work with non-union longshoremen. Sentiment was strong for a Marine Transport Federation, in which mutual support by seamen and longshoremen was essential, although in previous strikes seamen had worked with scab longshoremen.

"July 11th the Sailors' Union rejected the steam schooner offer 118 to 1,607. By ports the vote was: Seattle: For 8, Against 338; Aberdeen: For 44, Against 17; Portland: For 12, Against 87; San Pedro: For 14, Against 155; San Francisco: For 14, Against, 1,010. The *Shipping Register* of San Francisco charged the offer had been rejected because Vance Thompson, editor of the *Journal*, spoke against it.

"July 27th the damage suit and injunction were dismissed. Judge Neterer at Seattle said the unions had not countenanced violence, and that picketing the shipowners' property was not interfering with the Government. The Pacific district unions spent $23,600 defending members under injunction during the strike.

"Following rejection of the steam schooner offer, Nichols opened an Employment Service Bureau at 41 Drumm street, San Francisco, under the Shipowners' Association, to ship scabs for the steam schooners. He used the same forms and system as the Sea Service Bureau. According to Nichols, after 50 to 70 vessels had been moved the union men decided to go back. Furuseth returned to San Francisco from Washington, called a meeting at the Civic Auditorium, and announced the strike had failed.

"July 29th the Sailors' Union voted 1,272 to 481 to end the strike, after the cooks and firemen had taken similar action. The Seattle sailors voted against returning to work 111 to 184; the Seattle firemen for returning 738 to 183; and the Seattle cooks tied 50 to 50. August 10th the *Journal* reported shipping in steam schooners good at Aberdeen and shipping at Portland and San Pedro picking up. The members were gradually getting back on the ships as scabs were eliminated."

In the *Journal* for August 17, 1921, Charles Lesse, S.U.P. member number 1837, commented, "The battle is fought and lost. The hired brains of the shipping trust have been successful . . . They are marshalling all their forces to put the union out of business. They are fighting us with scabs, police, injunctions, courts and press, with other institutions held in reserve." Lesse concluded with a phrase that reflected the conviction of many members, calling for unification of "*all industrial unions into One Big Labor Alliance the world over*" (italics in original). The hour had struck for the I.W.W. and other radicals.

S.U.P. vs. I.W.W.

The I.W.W. ranks began to swell as sailors poured into "the M.T.W.," Marine Transport Workers Industrial Union No. 510, joining the many "two-card men" already there. In August, an I.W.W. periodical published in New York, the *Marine Worker*, saw "Pacific Coast Seamen Moving Toward O.B.U.," the initials a reference to One Big Union. This was a euphemism for the I.W.W. that was also used by an organization of radical former A.F.L. unionists mainly in Canada, distinct from but influenced by the I.W.W.[21] The *Marine Worker* noted with approval that the Pacific seamen had come out for unity with the longshoremen, and that militant action on the coast was "largely influenced by former I.W.W. members," the "two-card men," in the S.U.P. The paper declared that "sentiment for the I.W.W. among

[21]*Marine Worker* (New York), August 1, 1921, in S.U.P. central Archive. Also see Gill and Markholt, op. cit.

the seamen was never better than at the present time." The Wobblies pointed out that in Norway, where seamen had drawn shore workers into solidarity strikes against the shipowners, a threatened wage cut of 50 percent had been reduced to 12 percent. "That's what solidarity can accomplish," the I.W.W. counselled.

Shocked at the intransigence of the government and employers, Furuseth came back to them with a proposal that the I.S.U. do Benson & Co. the favor of denouncing, blacklisting, and otherwise eliminating I.W.W. members from ships, in return for restoration of the wartime agreement.

Within weeks, Furuseth's gambit had become public knowledge. His crusade against the radicals was broad, extending to *Seamen's Journal* editor Thompson, who was undoubtedly not an I.W.W. but whom Furuseth so labelled. Furuseth claimed that the I.W.W. had acted as agents of the shipowners, and were protected by them; he lumped together all dissident and industrial union elements with the I.W.W., including the International Transportworkers' Federation (I.T.F.) as well as the Canadian and Northwest O.B.U., which even Pete Gill, Seattle S.U.P. agent, described as a group seeking only a middle ground between the A.F.L. and I.W.W.

Furuseth began to concentrate fire on Thompson, in meetings of the S.U.P. to which the police had to be called to maintain order. But Thompson remained at his post, and the *Journal* in September condemned Furuseth for claiming that the S.U.P. had been taken over by the Wobblies.

Thwarted in his attempt to unseat Thompson, at least for the time being, Furuseth began publishing a separate journal, *The Seaman*, that became known chiefly for its anti-I.W.W. position. The I.W.W., in return, heaped scorn on Furuseth's claims to 100 percent Americanism, declaring "What you want are officials who are *100 percent working class*" (emphasis in original).[22]

Referring to the confusion of competing craft unions, which the I.W.W. saw as the main weakness of the sailors in their fight against the government and shipowners, the *Marine Worker* for September 15, 1921 printed a squib titled "On the Dog Watch," beginning "Say, buddy, do you belong to the International Sailors' Union of the Eastern and Gulf or to the International Sailors' Union of the Pacific? or perhaps you belong to the International Firemen's Union of the Eastern and Gulf or the International Firemen's Union of the Pacific? Or you may belong to the National Sailors' and Firemen's Union of Great Britain? or the National Sailors' Union of Switzerland (?) or the International Firemen's Union of Kalamazoo? Or perhaps you belong to the National Sailors' Union of — oh, hell! Say, let's dump all that junk overboard, and line up with the real thing, the MARINE TRANSPORT WORKERS INDUSTRIAL UNION: INTERNATIONAL AND WORLDWIDE."

In November, the stubborn Furuseth finally won out in the S.U.P., securing the expulsion of Thompson and 18 others. Selim Silver took over as *Journal* editor. Two members resigned, two more were expelled, and in December, 11 more were expelled, totalling 33 expelled or resigned for supposed I.W.W. membership, including second patrolman A.C. Wamser. Six more were expelled in 1922. The *Journal* carried an article by Furuseth, accompanied by a reprint of the California criminal syndicalism law, warning the members of the legal sanctions involved in I.W.W. activity.

A.C. Wamser, the expelled second patrolman, had been well known among the S.U.P. rank and file. Interviewed by Karl Kortum over 50 years later, Alwin Arlom described an incident involving Wamser during the 1921 conflict, as follows:

"They broke all the unions that time, one after the other. But the sailors fought back, as best they could. There were some young daredevils among them. They signed on the Matson boats as strikebreakers and brought their suitcases on board and turned to. But as the ship is leaving port, off Fisherman's Wharf (or Meiggs' Wharf as we called it in those days), they threw their suitcases over the rail and jumped overboard after them.The suitcases were empty — nothing in them but old newspapers. A launch was ready to pick up the sailors. And here was the Matson boat without a crew!

"One time crossing East Street [Embarcadero] during the strike I met a friend in front of the Ferry Building. He had been second mate of the steam schooner *Daisy* when I was there.

"'Where are you bound for?'

"'Oakland.'

"'So am I.'

"As we started to enter the building, there was a commotion. You know the front of the Ferry Building — it is a series of arches — square pillars with spaces in between. Well, ducking in and out among the arches and running full speed was a man with a package under his arm. He was being pursued — when I took a close look, here were some of my pals chasing one of the pursers from one of the Admiral boats that I was on when the strike broke out. He had this big bundle of new clothes.

"The purser wasn't out on strike and anybody who wasn't on strike was an enemy.

"The purser dropped the bundle and the strikers grabbed it and ran away with it. One I recognized was Charlie Wamser and another was Billy Riegel. Billy Riegel — everybody knew Billy Riegel! He was a young sailor like myself from the German sailing ships. I quit the four-mast bark *Egon* in Santa Rosalia, Mexico after hanging around a couple of years and came up to this coast on the steam schooner *Jim Butler*. There were a dozen square-riggers out of Hamburg and Bremen caught by the war down there. Many of these kids were from those ships and they were full of pep. You had to

[22]*Marine Transport Workers Organize into One Big Union And Bring the Bosses to Their Knees!* I.W.W. leaflet, n.d.n.p. in S.U.P. central Archive; also Gill and Markholt, ibid.

sail before the mast for a year in a square-rigged ship in order to sit for a German mate's license. A number of these fellows never returned to Germany, but stayed here on the Pacific Coast after the war. They didn't give a damn for anything . . . they were daredevils.

"Next thing I see is a young cop taking up the chase and hot on the heels of Billy Riegel. There was a streetcar parked in front of the Ferry Building — the cars stopped there until their schedule had them start up again. These Market Street car men were underpaid — very much underpaid. In fact there was a strike later on. The kids up on 24th Street would run after the streetcar when it started and pull the trolley and then the car was stuck. Then those Mission kids would bombard the strikebreakers with bricks. The streetcars had wire mesh outside the windows in those days.

"Anyway, when Billy Riegel and the cop came by, moving fast, the motorman on the streetcar put his leg out to stop Riegel. But Billy went over his leg just like a deer . . . hopped right over. And kept going.

"I thought to myself: what the hell is that guy doing? The Market Street Railway employees were underpaid; they were worse off than anybody. The other kids who had been chasing the purser among the arches didn't like the idea of streetcar people trying to stop strikers so that the cops could catch them. So when the streetcar started up Market a few minutes later, two of the striking sailors went along. Hard up as they were, they put a nickel in the box for the fare. They were going to work over the motorman when the car got out to the end of the line.

"I was very interested in the whole scene, you can imagine. When I saw all this commotion, when I saw the purser — I knew him — and when I saw this guy who was chasing him — I knew him, too — I got interested right away. And particularly when I saw Charlie Wamser, who was a Wobbly and a sailor, too, and who I knew the cops were looking for. It only took two minutes for a crowd to form at the Ferry Building in those days — there was a terrific foot traffic going and coming. I was running around, taking it all in. I didn't take any part, though . . . at that point. I just ran around to keep up and see what was going on.

"Billy Riegel is coming around the streetcar the second time. This is before the car started up Market Street. A guy in a grey suit comes dashing out of the main entrance of the Ferry Building and starts chasing Billy, too. I thought to myself — what the hell? Now even civilians are joining in. Why are they trying to stop these guys? (It never occurred to me that there were plainclothesmen on the scene.) I was a striker, too, so when the man in the gray suit made a dive for Billy, I tripped him. I put out my leg and — wh-o-o-om! — with all that speed he went sliding along the street.

"Somebody lifted him up by the seat of his pants.

"'What are you guys interfering for?' I asked him. I did not give it another thought — I walked away, following the crowd. I saw Wamser go one way and Billy Riegel go the other, shooting across East Street with the young cop in hot pursuit.

"There was a high curb in those days on the other side of the street, right at the corner, in front of the Ensign saloon. About a foot and a half high. Billy just hopped up there like a little bunny. But the cop was about played out; he had all this armor on him, gun, handcuffs, and so on, and he fell flat on the sidewalk.

"And what does Billy Riegel do? *He stops and helps the cop get on his feet again!*

"And then the footrace started once more.

"In the meantime, Charlie Wamser is after the purser. The purser got away when everybody's attention shifted to Billy Riegel. So now the police get after Wamser. Well, there used to be a little structure in front of the Ferry Building; it was there for years and years. A little shack. A traffic cop sat in there pushing the buttons that controlled the lights. He sat in there all the time; there really wasn't that much to do in controlling the traffic.

"Wamser is starting to put distance between him and his pursuers but this cop, a tiny little guy, comes out of the shack and throws his billy club. It was a clear forty five or fifty feet and it went right between Wamser's legs. Clear shot. Down went Wamser.

"The whole police department had been looking for Charlie Wamser and here they got him that easy right in front of the Ferry Building.

"Wamser was a radical, a real red-hot. He didn't fit in the Sailors' Union. He belonged to the Union, but the Sailors' Union wasn't radical by any means under Furuseth. All the office workers and the other patrolmen were of the same mold as Furuseth. A dedicated man. I knew some of these guys pretty well. One of them later was my partner driving winch on the Front. He had been an officer for years and years; he told me that there were no radicals at all in there.

"The reason that the cops were after Wamser was he had hit the captain of a police station with a brick. This was at the American-Hawaiian dock, Pier 26. They had strikebreakers aboard one of the ships, and a whole gang of sailors went through the gate and on board and cleaned up on those guys. While this was going on, someone lowered the steel gate at the entrance to the pier and called the cops. With the gate closed the sailors couldn't get out. The cops came in with their clubs. So Charlie Wamser reached for a brick and — bang! — he whacked him, slapped the captain of the station with a brick. Well, that cooked his goose. They were looking for Charlie Wamser — to get even with him. Wamser and the other sailors escaped from Pier 26 that time over a fence.

"So now the police had Wamser and they caught Billy Riegel, too. I didn't know how — maybe somebody intercepted him.

"That was the end of the performance. Now the big round-up started. Right in front of the Ferry Building . . . cops and plainclothesmen. We all stood around as if nothing had happened, but the plainclothesmen pointed us out: 'This one, and this one . . . this one.'

"All at once a big cop comes up behind me.

"'All right, me boy, y' go with me!'

"'I didn't do anything. I was on my way to Oakland.'

"'Never mind.'

"They had a substation on the right-hand side when you enter the entrance to the Ferry Building . . . that's where they took us until the wagon came. By this time the crowd is even larger; they didn't know what was going on. People are curious. When the patrol wagon came and we were marched out, the crowd opened up a little passageway for us to squeeze through. You would have thought it was the arrival of the Prince of Wales.

"A big bull had hold of my shoulder as if I was a criminal.

"'Gee, I'm not going to run away. Why don't you let go? What are people going to think of me?'

"Truth is, I was very ashamed to be seen in this situation.

"The wagon took us over to the Harbor Police Station. And we weren't there long before the two sailors who were heading up Market Street on the street car to teach the motorman some manners were brought in. It turned out that there were a couple of plainclothesmen on the streetcar too, which they didn't know. When the car got as far as Battery Street one of the plainclothesmen pulled the cord and the car stopped.

"'All right, boys — let's go.'

"'Let's go where? We're going home.'

"'Oh, yeah. You can go home later . . . maybe.'

"In the end there were about a dozen of us sitting on the bench in the Harbor Police Station. The captain came by. He would catch hell if there were riots at the Ferry Building — he said so himself:

"'If you bastards want to do something, go do it somewhere else. But not at the Ferry Building.'

"They booked us and wrote down our histories and then they took us in to lock us up. This big, tall, rawboned cop who drove the patrol wagon took Charlie Wamser in first, alone. There was an anteroom in front of the cell block. Another cop pushed me in — I was next. I saw the patrol wagon driver shoving Wamser along in front of him and he had a big iron key, almost a foot long, in his right hand. He unlocked a cell and said, 'Get in there, you son-of-a-bitch.'

"And as he said it that big guy gave Wamser an uppercut to the right jaw from behind with the hand that held the heavy key.

"Wamser began to spit blood. I wasn't supposed to see any of this. They had shoved me in a fraction too soon.

"I heard Charlie say, 'You coward, you hit me from behind . . .'

"'What are you talking about? I didn't hit you. You fell,' said the cop.

"Charlie's jaw was broken in four places.

"It was all made up. Wamser had hit the police captain on Pier 26. His goose was cooked from the time they got their hands on him.

"The patrolman from the Sailors' Union was there right away and bailed us out. $5 bail each. Wamser wound up in hospital.

"In the morning we appeared before the judge and the sergeant was there to testify. He was actually very nice.

"'Well, your honor, you know how it is. A strike . . . the boys get a little excited.' An Irish policeman, you know.

"Then my turn came. The judge asked what the charges were.

"'Well, we really have no charges against him. He just interfered a little bit.'

"'Case dismissed,' said the judge. I got the five bucks back.

"A couple of the others were fined.

"The captain at Harbor Police Station was sore that we got off easy. The one who didn't get off easy was Charlie Wamser. His jaw was broken so badly that they had to wire it back together. He was in awful shape. The Sailors' Union complained to the Mayor about it, but it didn't do any good."

Furuseth had, apparently, "cleaned house" with respect to the I.W.W. But the shipowners did not seem to appreciate the great favor he had done them. Walter J. Petersen, the chief scab-recruiter on the West Coast as head of the Marine Service Bureau of San Pedro, in a mid-1920s apologia entitled *Marine Labor Union Leadership*, indicated that the shipowners considered the old Scandinavian and his organization as dangerous labor radicals indistinguishable from the I.W.W. Furuseth perhaps believed that he could somehow maneuver with the government and the shipowners while splitting off his members from the I.W.W. and other rebels. The pro-shipowner Harding government saw much more clearly: it was a matter of class against class. The ruling powers were prepared to stand united against *all* labor organizations.

But Furuseth remained unwilling to unite with the radical wing of labor.

Smashing the S.U.P.

The determination of Admiral Benson to decimate the unions was clearly revealed by the attacks of the Shipping Board on those shipowners who demonstrated reluctance to either cut wages or lock out union members. The ruthlessness and thoroughness of the pro-employer forces had also been made manifest in the press and by actions of the police.

The Sailors' Union of the Pacific came out of 1921 ruined temporarily. The sailors were locked out, blacklisted, and forced to come to a fink hall, "fink book" in hand, to beg for work. The Union had been well and truly broken. A bitter segment of the membership held that this was not least because its leaders were more concerned with hunting heretics than with girding for war. It was the beginning of a dark time for the seamen, in which the S.U.P. would be reduced to almost nothing. It manned only those West Coast deepwater ships that called at Australia, where the dockers would not work scab shipping. The Olson Steamship Company (coastwise), Alaska operators, and many boatswains and mates on the steam schooners remembered past lessons and continued hiring union members for the dangerous skilled work needed to keep their vessels afloat. But as an effective union organization, the S.U.P. was on the rocks. In 1919, S.U.P. membership had stood at 8,781, with the I.S.U. at 113,000. By 1927, the S.U.P.'s ranks fell to an estimated 2,500, and eventually, during this period, to as few as 1,300; indeed, by 1927, more than 78 percent of West Coast shipping was handled through the "fink hall."[23]

Communist "Seamen's International"

But the seamen were not crushed. They continued turning to the I.W.W. Although the main national leadership of the I.W.W. had begun serving their sentences in the 1917 espionage cases, the revolutionary movement appeared to have gained strength. And new support seemed, momentarily, as if it might be coming from Russia. In July 1921, a Red International of Labor Unions (R.I.L.U.) also known as the Red Trade Union International and as the Profintern, after its Russian title, celebrated its first congress, in Moscow. An I.W.W. delegate, George Williams, rejected affiliation of the Wobbly movement with the Soviet-controlled "red international." On his return from Moscow, Williams published a lengthy report on the congress, describing the R.I.L.U. as an organization packed with "Communist minorities," tiny Moscow-line groups operating in the established unions, but, absent legitimate labor organizations, given the status of full organizations within the R.I.L.U. The I.W.W. delegate criticized this practice, first, for its use to suppress debate in the "red international," since the Communists could always create new "minorities" to stuff meetings with willing delegates. Secondly, he argued that this and other aspects of the congress showed the intention of the Communists was simply to use these minorities to take over the established organizations, rather than to build new industrial unions in their place.

In his report, Williams also gave details of an action by the Muscovites that was to have profound echoes in the decades that followed. "Besides bearing credentials for the Red International," Williams said, "I also bore credentials for a World's Congress of Seamen, which was scheduled to take place in Petrograd . . . This congress never materialized, but a so-called conference was arranged for and held in Moscow on August 12, 1921. According to the reasons advanced by (R.I.L.U. head) Lozovsky, the intended congress was annulled because in the light of the situation it was a wrong policy to organize a separate Seamen's International from the Red International. Together with this point of view there were few seamen's delegates present, and they represented but a small fraction of the workers in this industry. Delegates representing seamen were present only from four countries; Australia, Argentina, Germany and America . . . Nothing came out of the conference worth covering."

In time, as we shall see, the Russians would change their approach, fully adopting the strategy of a special "seamen's international."

Some Wobblies disagreed with Williams' assessment of Russian intentions, and the I.W.W. *Marine Worker* published statements in Spanish explicitly hailing "the red international, the Soviet of the workers, and industrial communism within maritime transport." An R.I.L.U. delegation from the Spanish National Labor Confederation (C.N.T.) consisting of Andreu Nín, Joaquím Maurín, Hilari Arlandis, and Jesus Ibañez, had gone to Moscow with the intention of sealing unity between the R.I.L.U. and the C.N.T., the largest anarchosyndicalist organization in the world. Angel Pestaña, a C.N.T. leader, had visited Moscow in 1920, but returned to Spain with an extremely hostile opinion, like Williams,' as to the validity of Bolshevik "workers' democracy." Although in October 1921 the C.N.T. approved a report by Maurín calling for R.I.L.U. affiliation, the C.N.T. broke with Moscow in June, 1922, choosing to join instead a new, world-wide anarchosyndicalist federation, founded in Berlin that year and titled the International Workingmen's Association in emulation of the original international to which both Bakunin and Marx had belonged. Significantly, the R.I.L.U. at first seems to have treated the new I.W.A. as a dissident brother, that might eventually return to the fold.[24]

Furuseth Continues Against Radicals

With the I.S.U. temporarily out of the picture as a major factor for the seamen's labor movement, the field was open to penetration by the Soviet-directed R.I.L.U., with or without the I.W.W. And in the years after 1921 Moscow indeed came to play a greater role in the lives of the U.S. seamen and their unions than many would have predicted.

The rampaging Furuseth for his part, at first neglected to attack the R.I.L.U., probably because it seemed to present no immediate threat. Instead, he continued the campaign against the I.W.W., as well as the allied One Big Union (O.B.U.) movement and the International Transportworkers' Federation (I.T.F.). The I.T.F., which had become part of the socialist-oriented International Federation of Trade Unions based in Amsterdam, was now led by Edo Fimmen, a tough Dutch unionist with a strongly radical line. Born around 1875 in Groningen, The Netherlands, Fimmen had been a longshoreman and socialist elected official. In the union field, he had become well-known as head of the Dutch union federation (N.V.V.). If anything,

[23]On the expulsions, see S.U.P. Headquarters Minutes, 1921, Gill and Markholt, op. cit. and file, "Members Expelled in 1921 for Advocating Principles Hostile to the Union," S.U.P. central Archive; Alwin Arlom, interviewed by Karl Kortum, 1976, National Maritime Museum; Walter J. Petersen, *Marine Labor Union Leadership*, San Francisco, Employment Service Bureau, 1925; membership statistics, Gill and Markholt. [24]George Williams, *The First Congress of the Red Trade Union International*, Chicago, I.W.W., n.d. (1922?); Theodore Draper, *The Roots of American Communism*, New York, Viking Press, 1957; *Marine Worker*, September 15, 1921, in S.U.P. archive; Wilebaldo Solano, *Andreu Nin: Assaig Biogràfic*, Barcelona, Edicions POUM, 1977, of which an abridged English translation was published under the title *The Spanish Revolution: The Life of Andres Nin*, Independent Labor Party, n.d.n.p.

Furuseth seemed to have hated independent "ambivalent" labor radicals like those of the O.B.U. or I.T.F., even more than he despised "committed" Wobblies themselves.

There is a tendency among historians, worthy of notice here, to confuse the Canadian One Big Union movement, or otherwise identify it wholesale, with the I.W.W. Created by A.F.L. dissidents as a separate movement in Canada, as we previously noted, but with strong influence in the U.S. Northwest, it seems to have attracted many who were *outside* the I.W.W. A later commentator has indicated that the O.B.U. emphasized broad proletarian rebellion throughout society, rather than concentrating on revolutionary "point of production" unionism as did the I.W.W. The O.B.U. called for the setting up of unitary workers' unions in each geographical region, while the I.W.W. remained attached to the concept of industry-wide federations.[25]

That Furuseth's main target, John Vance Thompson, the purged editor of the *Journal*, was not an I.W.W. himself, but only a radical A.F.L. unionist, is obvious to anyone who makes even a tentative examination of Thompson's editorial columns. The West Coast regional Marine Transport Workers' Federation, which Thompson supported, had restricted aims: for the seamen, recognition of the right to organize, respect for labor's legal rights, an eight hour day at sea and in port, a living wage and decent working conditions; for the dockers, abolition of the longshore shape-up, establishment of load limits in dock work, a short work day for dangerous cargoes. The Federation was to provide that "whatever agreements may be entered into between affiliated unions and their employers shall be put into operation and expire simultaneously, and they must be approved by the federation . . . A member of one union affiliated with the federation desiring to work under the jurisdiction of another union affiliated with the federation shall be entitled to transfer from one union to another without payment of initiation fee."[26] This last was Furuseth's sharpest point of protest, fearing as he did that the ranks of the sailors would be "diluted" by a wholesale invasion of dockers and others who lacked the skill of his profession — seamanship. The trends within the longshore labor movement toward maritime industry-wide organization along One Big Union lines had already drawn Furuseth's wrath in his *Second Message To Seamen.* Even during the period of the old City Front Federation, which Furuseth had once led, he had come to attack the longshoremen for their perceived threat to organize sailors, particularly steam schooner men. (The City Front Federation, with and without the S.U.P. had not survived the world war.)

Between the revolutionary program favored by the I.W.W. themselves and the radical unionism of Thompson, the longshoremen, and others, a gap clearly existed. Furuseth chose to overlook the gap. Unfortunately for the old Viking warrior, his fight against the militants only drove more members toward the I.W.W. Ironically, had Furuseth observed a greater tact and diplomacy, Thompson and his allies might have partially neutralized the Wobblies by raising the banner of industrial unionism while remaining within the A.F.L. But Furuseth was not proceeding along these lines, and that he unwittingly served the I.W.W. cause was widely felt.

Many I.W.W. members were, in reality, somewhat suspicious of the "one big union" trend as it existed within the ranks of the A.F.L. During this period, the Seattle I.W.W. weekly, the *Industrial Worker*, published a "Warning" that read: "Certain officials of the I.L.A. have withdrawn from the A.F. of L. and have formed independent organizations still retaining the craft form of organization for supposed unity, using the name of the Marine Transport Workers . . . the Marine Transport Workers have never authorized the use of their name and are not looking for unity with any craft unions . . . (we) warn all waterfront workers against this latest abortion which is nothing but the attempt of certain craft union leaders to hang on to their jobs and mislead the workers again." But in the same issue, the Wobbly organ reported "Docks Tied Up in Portland Wobs and I.L.A. On Strike."

During 1922, Furuseth expanded his campaign against the radicals. The *Congressional Record* for February 3 included a sequence of documents inserted by a friendly Washington State congressman who declared that they were "so patriotic that I think (they) should go in the *Record*." Furuseth charged therein that the movement for One Big Union had destroyed the hopes of the seamen in the Scandinavian countries just at the moment when they were attaining a freedom comparable to that secured in the U.S. He asserted the I.W.W. would permit a switchman, a warehouseman, a longshoreman or anybody within the same industrial union, to transfer into the sailors' organization and ship as an able seaman, as a fireman, or as a cook. Finally, he admitted that "a considerable number of seamen have been innocently flirting with the ideas and methods of the Industrial Workers of the World or the Marine Transport Workers Industrial Union No. 510, or the one big union, or the International Transport Workers Federation, or whatever name it may assume in furtherance of so-called revolutionary tactics." He then quoted the California state criminal syndicalism law, asserting that "it is not a question of whether such a law is really wise," and warning that "if you have such literature — as is prohibited in the law — in your possession, you will be sent to prison . . . While the law is morally wrong, it is also dangerous for you, because you may be punished by loss of liberty for years."

It should be noted, however, that, according to one criminal syndicalism imprisonment victim, Philip Mellman, conviction under the law came only where

---

[25]On the O.B.U., see Gill and Markholt, op. cit., Thompson and Murfin, op. cit., and Independent Labor Party, Britain, *The Changing Structure of Trade Unions*, n.d.n.p.; Edo Fimmen, see Solon de Leon, ed., *The American Labor Who's Who*, New York, Hanford Press, 1925, and Borkenau, op. cit. [26]Gill and Markholt, ibid.

membership was proven, with no guilty verdicts on possession of literature alone.

The I.W.W. responded to Furuseth's allegations with an extensive pamphlet, titled *Exposed* and signed by The Marine Transport Workers Industrial Union. Regarding the 1921 strike, the M.T.W. partisans argued that "the loss of the strike was due to: Corrupt leadership. Absence of solidarity. Lack of industrial union education and aims." They gleefully quoted Furuseth's testimony before a congressional committee warning that "*more than half the men manning American ships are members of the M.T.W.*" (emphasis in original), but appended a disclaimer that "the M.T.W. does not claim that more than half the men manning American ships are members of the organization. That is an exaggeration of Furuseth's."

Exposed included a standard statement on "Agreements" that shows that the I.W.W., far from being a strictly social-revolutionary organization, was prepared to take over the normal functions of a union. The Wobblies simply banned any contract in which a time period for its effect was specified, or which called for the workers to give notice before making demands affecting wages or conditions, or any agreement specifying that members must only work for employers belonging to an employers' association, or setting the selling price of a product. These rules would have been acceptable to most unionists.[27]

S.U.P In Crisis — I.W.W. Pursues Offensive

Furuseth's Union was beginning to show unmistakable signs of extreme crisis. In mid-1922, the proud masthead of *The Seamen's Journal* was removed from the tabloid weekly it had so long graced, and was affixed to a slender, small monthly, the only publication the Union could afford after Admiral Benson. By contrast, under the lash of the federal and state powers, the employers, and Furuseth, the Marine Transport Workers I.U. 510 of the I.W.W. stood "in the midst of the criminal syndicalism persecution with a strong, militant, and thriving maritime union," says Hyman Weintraub, Furuseth's main biographer, in his study of the I.W.W. in California. In January 1923, and again in April, "quickie" strikes, or "job actions," the I.W.W. equivalent of Furuseth's "oracle," were called by the West Coast M.T.W. for the three-watch system and for overtime pay. According to Weintraub, in San Pedro "rather than argue the point, shipowners granted the demands."

The I.W.W. General Executive Board, its national coordinating body, called on all members to stop work on May 1, 1923, with a demand for release of "class war prisoners," and action on economic grievances. I.W.W. historian Fred Thompson noted that "many were still in jail on wartime indictments; the number convicted under the criminal syndicalism laws particularly in California was growing; the Centralia victims were in jail, (with) a number, such as Mooney . . . out of labor trials not connected with I.W.W. Protest strikes occurred in northwest lumber, on many construction jobs and elsewhere, *but nowhere with such effectiveness as in the maritime industry* [emphasis added]. San Pedro, port of Los Angeles was tied up tight, as was Aberdeen (Washington), and on east coast, New York, Baltimore, Philadelphia, Mobile and Galveston. In most of these ports it was a short protest strike but won pay boosts of 15 percent. In San Pedro it developed into a lengthy free speech fight. It broke out again July 12 when 27 members, many of them seamen, were convicted of criminal syndicalism after a long trial in which they defended themselves to enjoy the freedom of saying what they wanted to. This was a five day protest strike in which all shipping in the port was tied up."

Gill and Markholt's manuscript on the S.U.P. cites reports that marine traffic in San Pedro was completely shut down, and that four intercoastal lines embargoed that port until the end of the Wobbly-led strike in May. Weintraub states that in San Pedro the M.T.W. brought both dockers and sailors out on strike, and the May stoppage tied up 90 ships. San Francisco's port was "seriously crippled," although the longshoremen remained on the job.

Along with the release of labor prisoners, the M.T.W. strike call, dated April 23, a week before the national strike date, demanded a universal wage scale for ships over 1000 tons, ranging from $300 per month for masters of vessels to $100 for carpenters, $90 for boatswains and A.B.s, and $80 for ordinary seamen, plus three watches, overtime at $1 per hour, the same menu for licensed and unlicensed personnel, clean bed sheets, free toilet articles, and related improvements. In addition, the Wobblies demanded that ships' committees be recognized by masters and that ships' stores include no California products until repeal of the criminal syndicalism law. They put forward ancillary demands for teamsters and other shoreside workers as well as the non-deck seafaring crafts.

Within a few days, the striking I.W.W. lumbermen in the Northwest had "transferred their general strike to the job," a euphemism employed to indicate a truce with the employer, and the marine workers seem to have followed suit, except in San Pedro where the strike was, at first, extended indefinitely. The San Pedro struggle, more a free speech fight than a strike, brought arrests of hundreds of sympathetic liberals and others, including Upton Sinclair, the well-known reformer and writer. The San Pedro strike was finally "transferred back to the job" on May 24, after three weeks at a meeting on the Pedro waterfront attended by 600 men, many of them non-I.W.W.s.

Within six weeks, however, the Pedro M.T.W. again called the workers out on strike. The five-day protest strike after the 27 criminal syndicalism defendants

---

[27]*Industrial Worker* (Seattle), October 21, 1922; *Congressional Record* (Washington), February 3, 1922, reprint in S.U.P. central Archive; Philip Mellman, personal interview, November 1983; *Marine Worker*, September 1, 1923, in Hoover Institution Library, Stanford, California; Marine Transport Workers Industrial Union No. 510, I.W.W., *Exposed*, Chicago, I.W.W., n.d. (1923?), in S.U.P. central Archive.

were found guilty in Los Angeles was apparently supported by unionists the length of the Pacific Coast.

This seems to have been the last major action by the Pedro I.W.W. organization. Still, the Wobblies had established some credibility in marine labor leadership; although they would never attain the status enjoyed by the S.U.P. in the pre-1921 period and after 1934, they remained a force as an alternative organization, small but combative. Some West Coast seamen would remain "two-card" S.U.P. and I.W.W. members and so until the 1950s.

Emmett Hoskins, a 1920s sailor interviewed by Karl Kortum, has described the I.W.W. at floodtide, in San Pedro in 1923, as follows:

"I attended a couple of meetings of the I.W.W. up on Vinegar Hill. I was surprised at the degree of organization that the local Marine Transport Workers #510 had achieved. They had rigged up a kind of a prize ring for a stage, about fifteen feet square, and shoulder high. In each corner was one of those gas lights that you pumped up. I was unacquainted with these devices at that time; they lit the stage brilliantly.

"I won't forget that first meeting. Although it was nighttime, I never saw a more beautiful view of San Pedro Channel, the Outer Harbor, and Terminal Island than from the top of Vinegar Hill. There was a big five topmast schooner that had just come in lying in the Outer Harbor. Her second mate was up on Vinegar Hill; he was one of the speakers. He gave a spiel on getting organized.

"There were half a dozen or more speakers and organizers on the stage and a crowd of two or three hundred people. The Wobblies always ended up their meeting with several songs. There were sometimes songs in between the speeches.

" 'Work and pray, live on hay
For you get pie in the sky when you die.'
(*The Preacher and the Slave,* by Joe Hill)

"Some of the songs were kind of beautiful. There was another:

" 'Raise the scarlet banner high,
For 'neath its folds we'll live or die.'
(The Red Flag)

"You heard these songs in the open meetings at San Pedro and other Pacific Coast ports, and even, at times, in the waterfront saloons. The Wobblies were strong enough in unlicensed crewmen to pull 100 percent quickie strikes, usually for higher wages or overtime pay. Usually they were fired on the spot. Yet they never asked for much, and I believe the master would sometimes have liked to grant their requests when he had an efficient crew on board. But the captain's hands were tied by company or Shipowners' Association agreements on the rate of pay and working conditions. Both the master and mates on one side and the seamen on the other showed courage in facing each other down during these quickie strikes.

"On the other hand, the Wobbly movement hurt the little fellows in the steamship business, those with one or two ships, steam schooners, say. The Wobblies had enough strength in a particular situation so that no man would ship in a vessel if they didn't want that vessel to go to sea.

"I can remember in Seattle. Here was a big schooner going deepwater. The master was 'Crazy' Killman (a notorious bucko). She was lying off Port Angeles fully loaded and ready for sea. The Wobblies and the other sailors get together along the waterfront and pass the word, 'Whatever you do, don't ship in that schooner.'

"That may not be the best example, what with Killman's reputation. But it shows you the way they worked. Although Wobbly ideas may have been good, I decided that the Sailors' Union of the Pacific was the best bet and I reinstated on my next to the last job, in 1925. . .

"Strangely, I never heard a Wobbly song used in doing any ship's work, say when hauling on lines. It's a wonder, too, because the Wobblies used songs on many occasions.[28]

Communists Again — "Seamen's Clubs"

The Moscow-based R.I.L.U. had greeted the West Coast I.W.W. seamen's strikes with a solidarity telegram, and that part of the international press controlled by the Kremlin began to pay considerable attention to the problems of marine workers. In May 1923, the Berlin Comintern bulletin *International Press Correspondence* (known as *Inprecorr*) published an article by one A.J. Smolan, on "Seamen in the International Labor Movement." Smolan noted that the International Transportworkers' Federation had organized a majority of seamen internationally before the first world war, but averred that the Edo Fimmen-led organization had fallen to only 40,000 marine members: 20,000 French seamen (compared with 46,000 before the war), 10,000 British (stewards only), and 6-7,000 German members of the "Transport Workers' Union."

Smolan further wrote that the International Seafarers' Federation led by Furuseth and Havelock Wilson accounted for the 6-7,000 members of the I.S.U., the British seamen and firemen at 90,000 members, some Swedes and Danes, and about 800 Dutch syndicalists. But this came to almost three times the I.T.F.'s numbers.

Smolan credited the pro-Soviet R.I.L.U. with the largest seafaring representation, consisting of the 55,000 members of the Soviet maritime union, 50-60,000 in the Chinese Seamen's Union, 20,000 in the German Maritime Union, which was the largest German seamen's organization and a bastion of pro-Moscow sentiment, and 11,000 in the Seamen's Union of Australia, reflecting a pro-Bolshevik tendency "down under" that long disfigured that organization, so spendidly built and so long associated with the S.U.P. The R.I.L.U. also counted in a "unitary" French

[28]Emmett Hoskins, interviewed by Karl Kortum, ca. 1980, National Maritime Museum; Hyman Weintraub, *The I.W.W. in California* (graduate thesis, 1937, unpublished, at Bancroft Library, Berkeley, California); *Marine Worker*, April 1, 1923, and April 15, 1923, in the Hoover Institution library.

sailors' faction, which had split away from the established national union organization, on orders of the French Communist Party; 4,000 Turkish maritime workers; 4,000 Dutch transport workers, of which 1,600 were seamen; and a Finnish seamen's organization with an unreported membership. Finally, Smolan tallied as "unaffiliated" the Norwegian Stokers and Sailors, the Greek Seamen and Dockworkers Union (of some 8,500), and the M.T.W.-I.W.W.[29]

At the end of June *Inprecorr* published an article titled "Lessons of the American Marine Strike," by George Hardy, a prominent I.W.W. Espionage Act defendant who had fled to Russia after serving his sentence in Leavenworth Penitentiary. Hardy stated that in the San Pedro strikes "the shipowners capitulated to the strikers because they feared . . . the M.T.W.", and he cited wage increases around 15 percent, reinstitution of the three-watch system, and the eight hour day in port, as gains won by the walkouts. However, he also argued that the rise in wages had come more because of changes in the structure of work ratings, and improved business conditions, than from the strike itself. Hardy is one of a group of figures who here enter the maritime picture under the auspices of the R.I.L.U., and who are representative of the fate of radicals who cleaved to the Moscow line. He had been in Leavenworth in the company of Harrison George, another I.W.W. espionage prisoner, and the two of them had grown close to a non-I.W.W. convict, a wartime conscientious objector and radical socialist (and R.I.L.U. founder), named Earl Browder. Hardy, George, and above all Browder were to become pillars of Russian-directed labor and political activities in the U.S., in the decades to come.

In July 1923, the R.I.L.U. announced to its acolytes the organizational form that would be used by Hardy, George, Browder, and their friends to steer the marine workers into the Kremlin camp: the "seamen's club." The seamen's club was to combine two institutions that had hitherto been held in disdain by radical sailors, at least in the U.S.: the church mission and the fink hall.

The church mission, exemplified by the Seamen's Friend Societies and the Seamen's Institutes, was a charitable institution that had existed since the early 19th century, through which religious denominations organized volunteers to work in missions in which seamen on the beach could obtain a meal and bed. However, while the price of the meal was usually only a sermon and prayers, that of the bed was normally fairly low, the missions were widely criticized as centers of corruption, intimidation, and blacklisting of union men. Many missions functioned as crimping establishments.

The S.U.P. had fought the missions on the West Coast, but the contempt in which most seafarers held them was weapon enough that the Union, historically, paid relatively little attention to the phenomenon. Unfortunately, after 1921, with the seamen pushed down the social ladder, missions and "coffee joints" began to play a greater role in the men's lives, since they often had nowhere else to go for shelter. Similar considerations might lead some seamen to the "revolutionary" R.I.L.U.'s brand of the "good news." The Communist "seamen's clubs" often provided cheap meals. The clubs were also designed to function as "hiring halls" for the Russian shipowners, to secure enthusiastic men, willing to work at a double pace for the greater glory of the Bolshevik "experiment," whenever Russian shipping might need to charter foreign-registered ships. This practice was widespread in Germany, and not completely unknown among U.S. seamen. The "socialist" Bolshevik government was a participant, both as a regular ship operator and as a charterer, in the Baltic and White Sea Maritime Conference, soon to be known as the Baltic and International Maritime Conference (BIMCO), the Copenhagen-based chartering cartel that is among the most powerful maritime business institutions in the world.

In October 1923 the R.I.L.U. declared, further outlining its plans for a network of "International Seamen's Clubs," known as "Interclubs," that "revolutionary propaganda among the seamen of the world, and their amalgamation within one organization, is one of the R.I.L.U.'s chief tasks." It should be noted that the clubs were originally a domestic Russian concept, set up by the authorities for the Russian sailors in a situation where, under the Bolsheviks, the independence of unions had been completely eliminated, with the "labor movement" attached to the central government in a structure controlled from above. The Russian government had no intention of allowing the seamen to improve their lot through autonomous action; the Bolshevik "egalitarian elite" would shepherd the sailor. In seeking to extend its influence among the world's seamen, the Russian government, practically more concerned with military intelligence needs than with ideals of international labor solidarity, simply decreed the extension of a local "sailor-catching" agency onto a worldwide basis.[30]

End of "Revolutionary Mirage"

Meanwhile, in Germany a political crisis emerged in 1923. But the "German Revolution" was not destined to mature. When the appointed day came, a planned workers' insurrection to set up a Communist state was suddenly postponed on the urging of the Russians on the scene; only Communist paramilitary groups on the Hamburg waterfront failed to receive the counter-

[29]"Telegram R.I.L.U. to I.W.W.," *International Press Correspondence Inprecorr* (Berlin), April 19, 1923; A.J. Smolan, "Seamen in the International Labor Movement," *Inprecorr*, May 24, 1923. [30]George Hardy, "Lessons of the American Marine Strike," *Inprecorr*, June 28, 1923. On Hardy, Harrison George, and Browder, see Ralph Chaplin, *Wobbly*, Chicago, University of Chicago Press, 1948, and Philip J. Jaffe, *The Rise and Fall of American Communism*, New York, Horizon Press, 1975. On the Interclubs, see Resolution of the 3rd Session of the R.I.L.U. Central Council, "The Harbor Bureaus and Work Among Seamen," *Inprecorr*, October 6, 1923. On BIMCO, see Baltic and International Maritime Conference, *BIMCO, 1905-1980*, Copenhagen, BIMCO, 1980.

order, and some hundreds of seamen and longshoremen went into action alone. The sad courage displayed in 1923 by the German "Red Marines" contributed further to the myth of "the rebel seaman." A young German sailor, Richard Krebs, who participated in the Hamburg uprising, was soon on the U.S. West Coast scouting out territory for the Communist seamen's clubs. (Through publication twenty years later, of his classic memoir, titled *Out of the Night*, he would provide the only really extensive look into Comintern maritime activities yet produced.)[31]

The Bolshevik failure in Germany in 1923 represented a turning point, however difficult it may have been for those who participated in the events to understand. Later, analyzing the reasons for this "loss of nerve," Leon Trotsky would argue that the "world revolution" had entered an ebb period. Certainly, the original enthusiasm of the international working class for the revolutionary mirage had diminished.

In Scandinavia, Tranmael's Norwegian Labor Party broke away from the Comintern, in November 1923. While the historians of Norwegian labor have preferred to see the main cause of the Tranmael-Moscow rupture in the insistence of the Russians on directing Norwegian political activities although they knew next to nothing of the country, historian Franz Borkenau, claims that "Tranmael consistently maintained that, after Kronstadt, the Bolsheviks had ceased to be a revolutionary party and that revolutionaries could no longer accept their lead."[32]

The departure of the Norwegian Labor Party from the Comintern was a confirmation of the decline of "the revolution." Similarly, although 1923 had shown the M.T.W.-I.W.W. at its highest point, for the I.W.W. as an organization, it turned out to be the "beginning of the end." The I.W.W.'s Fred Thompson ascribes a sudden weakening of the M.T.W. after '23 to criminal syndicalism imprisonments and to destructive disagreements within I.W.W. ranks after the release of the rest of the Leavenworth espionage prisoners.

The situation was more complex than that, particularly on the West Coast. The U.S. representatives of the Bolsheviks, the Communist Party, also helped weaken the I.W.W. by drawing away many of its members. "Big Bill" Haywood himself was induced to take refuge in Russia and although the old warrior seems to have done little there but grow depressed and lonely, the C.P. exploited his mere presence to manipulate the Wobblies back home. Still, although the I.W.W. became greatly weakened from an organizational perspective, undergoing damaging splits, thousands of sailors continued to consider themselves Wobblies in program and activity, if not in actual dues paid.

But the great wave of worker radicalism that seemed to have been touched off by the first world war had lost its momentum. With the I.S.U. shattered, the S.U.P. reduced to almost nothing, and the I.W.W. disorganized, militant seafarers understood that they must prepare for a long, cold watch.

And in 1924, the Russian-controlled seamen's clubs, which had already appeared in Europe, made their entry into the Pacific.[33]

---

[31]"Jan Valtin" (Richard Krebs), *Out of the Night*, New York, Alliance Book Corporation, 1941; Jac Wasserman, (Krebs' editor), personal interviews, 1976-77.
[32]Borkenau, op. cit. [33]Thompson and Murfin, op. cit.; Gill and Markholt, op. cit.; G. Voitinsky, "First Conference of the Transport Workers of the Pacific," *Inprecorr*, September 11, 1924.

CHAPTER V
Twilight of Freedom Part II
(1916-1933)

As the Nineteen-Twenties wore on, the condition of the West Coast sailors worsened. As but one eloquent example, on June 17, 1924, O. Manning, master of the steamship *West Mahwah,* posted a notice to his crew warning, "any member of the crew that does not do a fair day's work during the eight hours in any one day, will be ordered to work nine hours a day. And failing to perform a fair day's work during the nine hours in each day, then, a reduction from A.B. to O.S. or workaway will follow, whatever the case may warrant."[1] Once a sailor signed aboard a ship, he was again the captive of officers against whom there was almost no provision for recourse, and whose words were law.

Following Admiral Benson's first wage cut in 1921, wages continued to fall drastically, and conditions declined accordingly. Seamen were shoved back into the "glory hole" forecastle, with bunks crammed together, no space for gear, insufficient room for freedom of movement if more than one of the gang came below, inadequate sanitation, and wretched food.

Fink Hall and Fink Book

But the worst inequity was, by far, the "slave market" fink hall and its fink book. A sailor could fight demoralization, although not the physical health problems, caused by bad food and quarters, by keeping up the hope that the next ship would be better. But from the humiliation involved in crawling into the fink hall, book in hand, there was little immediate relief; and, in addition, the unity of the shipowners implied by the fink hall and the fink book stood as a warning that the bad treatment offered on the worst ships would become standard, should the shipowners wish it.

The Sailors had built their Union, sacrificing lives, talent, and energy, for an ideal of dignity and self-respect. The fink hall and the fink book were the unarguable repudiation of that ideal. To the committed unionists among the men the fink hall was an institution so degrading, so despicable, that should they be given the chance to destroy it, no power on Earth would be able to save it. Their chance came, and they smashed the fink halls, but not until years had passed. In the meantime, their only weapon was that pioneered by the early S.U.P. as "the oracle," and taken up again by the I.W.W. as "job action": the "quickie" or "wildcat" strike. In the mid-twenties, to offer the Sailors hope that the S.U.P. would regain its past liberty, Furuseth had come out for re-adoption of "the oracle."

In speaking of the fink hall and fink book, Harry Lundeberg, a young Norwegian-born sailor who had joined the Seamen's Union of Australia in 1919 and transferred into the S.U.P. in 1923, described "a dirty, filthy hall, with a big loudspeaker going. The fink hall was filled with all kinds of stiffs, hop heads, dope peddlers, floaters and these were in the majority. Sure you got a ship if you patronized the blind pig run by the clerks employed in the fink halls and how many of you had to PAY for the chance to go to sea — and many bonafide seamen stayed ashore anywhere from three to six months on the beach — and when you finally landed a rotten job after the half way decent ones had been SOLD in order to take said job you had to pack a FINK BOOK."[2]

The S.U.P. in the later 1920s carried out an extensive legal campaign for abolition of the fink halls, but without success. During court hearings on the issue, Union member Sam (Lloyd) Usinger stated that in his experience no work was available off the dock, by visiting vessels and inquiring for work. The answer was always the same: "We get our men out of Fink Hall." And because even the fink jobs were scarce, according to Usinger, the sailors were forced to engage in schemes to obtain multiple fink-hall registry cards, in the hope of juggling ships.

In the hearings, a shipowner representative declared that when enough men were not available from the main fink hall in San Francisco, the so-called Marine Service Bureau, he would obtain them from

---

[1]Document in S.U.P. Archives. [2]Gill and Markholt, op. cit. Also see Harry Lundeberg, testimony, House Merchant Marine & Fisheries Committee, *Hearings*, Washington, D.C., Government Printing Office, 1955.

the missions such as the Seamen's Church Institute or from the Scandinavian Sailors' Home. The usage of this latter organization as a crimping, fink hall auxiliary was a source of special anger among the Scandinavian-born unionists, as may well be imagined.

The beleaguered situation of the S.U.P. in this period has been vividly described by Emmett Hoskins. Describing the voyage home aboard the vessel *Wheatland Montana* during the late '20s, Hoskins recalled:

"We tied up alongside in Seattle . . . "There were a half dozen officials on the wharf ready to greet us, customs, immigration, Shipping Board people. In most ships we paid off in the captain's office. The shipping commissioner sits at the table. You were handed your discharge and your money at the same time. The captain, the commissioner, and yourself all sign the discharge — all three of you. The men are standing in line. It only takes a few minutes, because everything is arranged, the stacks of money, the pile of discharges. There is very little talking. Some of the men, waiting to get in line, are out on deck. The sailors were all together, as I remember, black gang came next, then the stewards, cooks and so on.

"After we had our money, those who were going to leave the ship went to the forecastle to pick up their suitcases and seabags. These would be in most cases already packed. The firemen had their forecastle on the port side, the sailors to starboard. Every one had on their best shore-going togs.

"At this point the patrolman for the Sailors' Union came on board. He was a good looking fellow, well-dressed. I had a few words with him; I told him I wanted reinstatement in the Sailors' Union. The voyage certainly needed improvement, better seamen, professionals, I told him.

"All the fellows ignored him, paid him no attention whatsoever. So I paid him eighteen months back dues and an advance of a few months at a dollar a month. A sailor needs friends, and the union is where to get it . . . so the mate won't use the deckhands as punching bags.

"The reason why I wasn't paid up was that in those years you couldn't ship from the Union hall; the owners had practically busted the unions in the strike four years before.

"Some of the runners for the foreign ships were kind of comical; they used to ship some of their 'pier head jumps' out of the jail on Kearny Street in San Francisco. That's not American style. We needed the Union, but it had fallen on hard times. It was almost broke. I was aboard a wooden steam schooner in the Southern Pacific slip in San Pedro during these years and the patrolman came aboard — he didn't collect a dime. It was a non-union crew, but more than that I was the only American in the forecastle.

"The Sailors' Union patrolman came aboard regularly in San Francisco. On the East Coast you never saw a union patrolman. What they had back there were shipping masters. You had to hustle for a berth back there. . ."[3]

The year 1924 saw Senator Robert M. LaFollette run for the U.S. presidency on the national Progressive and Socialist ticket, supported by the S.U.P. and Furuseth in gratitude for his work on behalf of the Seamen's Act. LaFollette received some 5 million votes but captured only one state, his native Wisconsin.

New Russian Activities

In 1925, the Russian government began accelerating its campaign for capture of the world's seamen. Richard Krebs, veteran of the Hamburg barricades, travelled along the U.S. West Coast and visited Hawaii, spying out the area for establishment of Interclubs. The Red International of Labor Unions (R.I.L.U.) created a network of International Propaganda and Action Committees to channel funds. The R.I.L.U. was then putting forward a two-pronged approach: where workers were already organized into unions, the local members of the Communist organization were to infiltrate and set up opposition groupings, aiming at an eventual takeover. Where no unions existed, or where they had been weakened or broken, the Communists were directed to organize Communist-controlled "Red unions." The Interclubs could be used for either purpose, in addition to their activities directed toward military spying, under the supervision of Red Army intelligence, and political surveillance and police action (controlled by the international network of the Soviet secret police, the G.P.U., later K.G.B.).[4]

An International Seamen's Club made its appearance in New York City in 1926. Its main feature was a so-called "lunch-counter" or "stewpot." The New York Interclub was described some years later as follows: "Oldtimers will recall the club in New York which was situated around the corner from the Seamen's Church Institute at 26 South Street. It was a dirty room upstairs where seamen could buy a greasy meal slightly cheaper than the neighborhood 'joints'." The stewpot was run as a private business by one George Mink, a sinister and controversial character. Mink was a former taxi-driver, who, according to some sources, became an I.W.W. on the Philadelphia waterfront, before, in 1926, joining the Communist Party.[5] It has been alleged that Mink murdered one Sam Orner, the head of the New York taxi-drivers' union.[6] He also was famous for his claim to be R.I.L.U. chief Lozovsky's brother-in-law.[7] Those who knew Mink well describe

[3]U.S. Ninth Circuit Court of Appeals, *Cornelius Anderson, et. al., vs. Shipowners Association of the Pacific Coast and Pacific American Steamship Association*, San Francisco, n.d., printed transcript in S.U.P. Archive; Emmett Hoskins, interviews cited. [4]Herbert Romerstein, U.S. Information Agency intelligence analyst, private communication, January 1985. [5]Jerry King, Ralph Emerson, Fred Renaud, Lawrence McRyn, *We Accuse (From the Record)*, New York, (1939?); Bert Cochran, *Labor and Communism*, Princeton, Princeton University Press, 1977; John S. Gambs, *Decline of the I.W.W.*, New York, Columbia University Press, 1932; William C. McCuistion, testimony, in House Special Committee on Un-American Activities, *Hearings*, vol. 11, Washington, D.C., Government Printing Office, 1939; Krebs, op. cit.; Pierre Broué, "Biographie: George Mink," in *Cahiers Leon Trotsky* (Grenoble), July-September 1979. [6]H.T., (further identification declined), conversation, December 1983. [7]McCuistion, testimony cited.

him as a gunman and an avid fan of prostitutes and pornography.[8] It soon became known that Mink was working for the Russian G.P.U. in the U.S., and his penchant for reporting to the secret police dissident feelings and other confidences bestowed on him by his stewpot comrades led to him being given the nickname "Mink the Fink."

The I.S.U. eventually responded to the appearance of the New York Interclub with a notable blast in *The Seamen's Journal*, titled "What is a Seaman's Club?" The *Journal* reported that Muscovite partisans had lately been active in disrupting the Seamen's Union of Australia, and warned that the club personnel's main goal was "to make use of the world's seamen as shock troops for communism." The I.S.U. argued that "in spite of all statements made to the contrary, Russia is building up along capitalist lines . . . the interests of Soviet Russia, from a national standpoint, do not always coincide with the interests of the working-class in the . . . capitalist countries. It is the attempt on the part of Russia to mold the labor movement in other countries along lines that will further her own national interests that causes the trouble. If we went to Russia and attempted to organize the Russian working class in a manner suitable to Canadian or British workers' interests, we should soon be made to quit. If we spent many thousands of dollars in an effort to secure control of Russian unions we should probably find ourselves in jail . . . The Third International . . . is simply the foreign office of Soviet Russia . . . the main purpose is to endeavor to get the workers of the western nations to sacrifice themselves upon the altar of Russian nationalism."

Victor Olander of the I.S.U. presented evidence that most of the members of the Interclubs were not seamen at all. "That this outfit are not seamen is proven by one of their demands — that sick seamen be returned to their home countries," Olander asserted. "Under the laws of every maritime nation the care and cure of sick seamen is an obligation of the owner, who must return the ill man to his home port. Under American laws he must pay his wages while ill on his way home. Were these 'red' propagandists seamen they would know that."

Communists vs. I.W.W.

The I.W.W. *Marine Worker*, similarly, dismissed the Interclubs' claim to status as a legitimate seamen's organization. In an article also titled "What is a Seamen's Club?" the Wobbly organ referred to "scratch-a-way-Inn," adding "any seamen who have been around South Street know who is running it. (T)he 'Commies' are, and they use one of their favorite tricks to lure penniless seamen, especially in the winter months, to come in and partake of watery stew and political propaganda. A few from the Bowery are the only ones attracted to the place."[9]

Mink the Fink was considered a member of the ex-I.W.W. "Hardy-George" group within the Communist ranks; that is Harrison George and George Hardy, to whom we have been introduced. Hardy turned up around the same time in London. He established an Interclub stewpot, which he turned into a personally profitable enterprise until, in the early 1930s, Richard Krebs scandalized the Comintern by denouncing Hardy's capitalist habits. Hardy's embezzlements had already elicited jocular warnings to the Comintern from both Havelock Wilson's British seamen's union and the I.S.U. Krebs eventually secured the reorganization of the London club, by shutting down its restaurant, and obtained Hardy's return to Russia in disgrace. Hardy was never heard from again.[10]

In addition to their stewpot businesses, the clubs which, as we noted before, held out the possibility that a member might obtain work on a Russian ship, were used to sell the seamen "Soviet Gold Bonds," touted as a safe investment in a period of capitalist chaos.[11] Soon the Interclubs were ordered to turn their attention to the Seaman's Church Institute. The Communists unleashed an extensive campaign of provocation and disorder inside and outside the missions.

Of course, what the seamen needed most was neither a stewpot, nor a fink hall, nor a church mission, nor especially a Russian-controlled political agency, but a real labor organization, ready for combat with the shipowners and government. The agenda for the fight, as in the past, need not be submitted to any authority but that of their fellow workers.

The I.W.W. Marine Transport Workers attempted to supply this needed militancy throughout the 1920s. Although it was unable to gain enough strength to lastingly establish itself as the seamen's sole representative, the I.W.W. remained the seamen's *leading* representative, particularly in the Pacific Northwest and on the Gulf until the rebirth of the S.U.P. in 1934. Gunnar Hexum, an S.U.P. militant during the post-1934 period, has stated that until 1934, the I.W.W. was the only union on many West Coast ships. "Everybody belonged . . . why, even mates would ask if you carried the red book."

In May 1926, the I.W.W. seamen announced a strike, claiming that 25,000 men were prepared to walk out for a $15-per-month wage hike (Shipping Board vessels were then paying the standard post-1921 rate of $62.50 per month for A.B.s). Other demands were for overtime, and the eight hour day. The I.W.W. claimed 2,000 men answered the strike call, but the rebels failed to win any concessions, according to Gill and Markholt.[12]

An I.W.W. leaflet from the period, addressed to all marine workers, pointed out, "life aboard ship is unbearable and is getting worse every day. Many seamen thought conditions would never become so bad. It is ridiculous to think that a union can be built as an

[8]Al Richmond, *A Long View From the Left*, Boston, Houghton Mifflin, 1973; Krebs, op. cit. [9]*Seamen's Journal*, September 1928; March, 1929, September, 1929. Also, *Marine Worker*, October 15, 1928, in the Hoover Institution Library. [10]Richmond, op. cit.; Krebs, op. cit.; *Seamen's Journal*, May 1928. [11]*Marine Workers Voice* (New York), March-April, 1932, in the Hoover Institution Library. [12]Gunnar Hexum, interview, January 26, 1986; Gill and Markholt, op. cit.

adjunct to a mission or social club. Those who offer such a type of union to the seamen either don't understand what real unionism is or are insincere in their arguments.

"Keep away from craft unionism," the leaflet went on, "Let us do away with the pessimistic slogan, which is common among seamen, 'it can't be done,' and get into (the) fight. JOIN THE MARINE TRANSPORT WORKERS INDUSTRIAL UNION NO. 510 OF THE I.W.W."

The leaflet listed the following immediate demands: the eight-hour day for all, abolition of cargo work in port, 75 cents per hour for overtime, higher wages on tankers than on freighters, because "tankers are potential bombs, they are liable to explode at any moment," better food and elimination of the difference between saloon and crew messrooms, a weekly change of bed linen, clean, dry and sanitary quarters and washrooms, the abolition of shipping masters and recognition of shipboard union delegates, and finally, shipping through the union hall only. The leaflet listed Wobbly halls in New York, Brooklyn, Buffalo, Baltimore, Philadelphia, New Orleans, Houston, Los Angeles, San Pedro, San Francisco, Seattle and Aberdeen, for the U.S.; Vancouver, Port Arthur, Canada; Stockholm, Sweden; Cuxhaven and Stettin in Germany, and Adelaide, Australia.

The large maritime group, the M.T.W., which also covered longshoremen in such ports as San Pedro, Portland, Oregon, New York, and Philadelphia, was not assimilated smoothly into the larger I.W.W. During the 1920s, the national organization's dues stood at 50 cents per month, except for members of the M.T.W., who paid a dollar. This was to help defray outstanding debts owed by the M.T.W. to the I.W.W. General Executive Board. The I.W.W. seamen seemed destined to repeat other of the organization's experiences, with such wage workers as the Western hard-rock miners or lumberjacks. Although the I.W.W functioned well as a general or "universal" organization of militant workers, it could not sustain regularly-operating "unions," industrial or not. Once numbers of workers in a particular trade attempted to actually join the cause, the day-to-day requirements of administration and negotiation — in essence, reality — proved too great a strain on a movement that was, above all, inspirational and rhetorical. The gap between inspiration and reality in I.W.W. activities was never bridged. By contrast, syndicalists in Norway and Spain, for example, were able to maintain their revolutionary temper while administering trade unions.

But the M.T.W. seamen were crucial to I.W.W. development internationally: they carried the message of the organization to Australia, Chile, South Africa, and other countries that saw the rise of I.W.W. sections. The history of the Wobbly movements in these countries has yet to be adequately studied; I.W.W. influence persisted Down Under for decades, while the Chilean movement, based on the maritime workforce in the ports, gained nearly 10,000 members. The Chilean ports of Valparaiso and San Antonio had struck in 1923, like San Pedro, under I.W.W. leadership.

The I.W.W. suffered continued internal pressure from the Communists, as revealed in an article, titled "Anarchy and Decentralization," published in the I.W.W. *Marine Worker* in 1926, under the signature of William Pettersson, M.T.W. secretary treasurer. Pettersson charged that Communists, led by a Wobbly renegade, Harrison George, were utilizing the I.W.W.'s organizational decentralization to promote internal chaos.

Quoting at length from Harrison George's correspondence, Pettersson demonstrated that the Communists were employing deceptive means to gain control of the organization, professing loyalty while conspiring to undermine. "Regardless of our friendliness for the Soviet revolution we must mete out to these rats the punishments they have earned," Pettersson declared. "If Moscow has ill-advisedly chosen its American representatives it must abide by the consequences." He concluded by asserting that Harrison George's slogan in the I.W.W. was "affiliation or annihilation;" and by characterizing George as having a "heart and soul, dried and warped, shrivelled, shrunken and soiled; his mind stunted and dwarfed by the ravages of the deadly political microbe."

In the I.W.W., Pettersson argued, "renegades have neither claim, title, or place. The political agent provocateur is equally as obnoxious and dangerous as any other, and does not belong amongst us. Let us clean house," he wrote.[13]

Communist Expansion

Under the Interclub banner, which showed an anchor and a red globe, the Communists set up halls in the U.S. cities of Philadelphia, Baltimore, New Orleans, Houston, San Pedro, San Francisco, and Seattle. Simultaneously, in 1927, the Russian government chose to answer the criticism of Western labor about the condition of workers in the "workers' state," by publishing a curious pamphlet by Mikhail Tomsky, head of the Russian trade union, titled *The Trade Unions, the Party and the State.* Tomsky stated flatly that should the Russian unions put forward a policy differing from that of the party and the state "we should then have to talk in the language of machine guns;" any assertion of trade union independence "would have to be settled by arms."[14]

The next year, 1928, the Interclubs in the U.S. became a front for a national organization, the Marine Workers' Progressive League, with a newspaper, the *Marine Workers' Voice.* A new trend became visible, in propaganda now strewn on the waterfronts by the

[13]*Solidarity of the Sea*, I.W.W. leaflet, n.d.n.p., I.W.W. boycott sticker, both in S.U.P. archive; Gill and Markholt, ibid; Gambs, op. cit.; Gordon Macnab and Signe Rasmussen, "A Bit 'Wobbly' — But Still on its Feet," *Oregon State Journal* (Portland), January 22, 1939; Paul Albert, "Chile: Anarchism and the Workers Movement," *Black Flag Quarterly* (London), Autumn 1983; *Marine Worker*, August 10, 1926, in Hoover Institution Library; Adamic, op. cit. [14]M. Tomsky, *The Trade Unions, The Party, and the State*, Moscow, Commission for Foreign Relations of the Central Council of Trade Unions, 1927.

M.W.P.L. In the past the U.S. Communists had attempted to disguise their infiltration into the larger labor movement, and even the I.W.W., by publicly posturing as the most consistent and conscientious supporters of the common cause. After the sixth world congress of the Comintern, in September 1928, things changed drastically. A new line emerged: the Communists were to deal with the bigger labor and radical movements, such as the A.F.L., the Socialist Parties throughout the world, and the I.W.W. and other anarchosyndicalists, on a platform of open hostility. Hereafter, they were ordered to emphasize slander, violence, and disruption. Parallel to the sixth Comintern congress, the fourth world congress of the Soviet international union body, the R.I.L.U., had met: maritime activities took up *four days* of the R.I.L.U.'s time. By early September 1928, the San Francisco branch of the M.W.P.L., in the first issue of its mimeographed bulletin, *The Lookout*, declared that Andrew Furuseth was "in league" with the "company unions, the fink halls, the blue books (the company union for the San Francisco longshoremen), and the rest of the trash."

The San Francisco *Lookout* was typical of the throwaways, grandly dubbed "shop papers," that would serve as a medium for Communist invasion of the maritime industry. The tone of the national M.W.P.L. press was hardly different. The first issue of the *Marine Workers' Voice* lyingly asserted that the I.W.W. had "literally turned its back on the masses of the seamen," that it consisted of "nothing but a little group of disappointed pessimists," and even (somewhat as an after-thought) that the Wobblies were stoolpigeons! The Communists declared that the I.S.U. "would never fight again," which would prove an exceptionally ironic statement in later years, as we shall see. The M.W.P.L. was organized with the stated aim of becoming an industrial union of marine workers, committed to the program of the Comintern. Its goals could only have been shared by a microscopic minority of U.S. workers; yet the Communists referred to the I.W.W. as "sectarian."[15]

In November 1928, the Lamport and Holt passenger vessel *Vestris,* flying the British flag, went down off the Virginia coast with the loss of 111 lives. Accusations of cowardice were directed against the crew. The Communist M.W.P.L. sprang into action, correctly pointing to the criminality visible in company and government policies that allowed the ship to sail "with a coal port that would not close" and "the rotten and insufficiently equipped lifeboats . . . as well as the captain's complete mismanagement of the abandonment of the ship." The captain was allegedly prevented from sending an S.O.S. in order to save salvage fees. However, a New York anarchist publication, the *Road to Freedom*, noted with disgust that "we do not . . . concur with the cruel inhuman attitude of the official Moscow spokesman in this country when it says . . . 'any worker who chose to save himself . . . rather than some idle parasite or sleek exploiter, did as he should have done . . . workers . . . will glory that the *Vestris* crew . . . refused to die that parasites might live . . . stand by the class struggle.' " The anarchist publication charged "this piece of infamy would seem to be just about the final word possible to be spoken out of the mouths of stupid, ignorant zealots bent upon visiting their fanaticism even upon the heads of innocent children . . . Communist viciousness can scarcely surpass such a ridiculous interpretation of the class struggle . . . Drunk with the quest for power, they reduce themselves below the level of the most detestable of beasts . . . social rebels cannot afford to condemn the innocent with the guilty."[16]

The Communist M.W.P.L., changing its name in 1929 to the Marine Workers' League (M.W.L.) continued its reckless attacks on the real seamen's organizations, the I.S.U. and the I.W.W. Neither logic nor truth nor integrity were obstacles to Communist mudslinging.[17] In view of the aid the S.U.P., *The Seamen's Journal*, and then editor Scharrenberg had given the young Bolshevik regime in the early '20s by fighting for a "hands off" policy on Russia, Communist attacks on Scharrenberg seem particularly obnoxious. In December 1929, the San Pedro *Lookout*, another "shop paper," began circulating the preposterous charge that because Scharrenberg served on the California State Board of Harbor Commissioners when this body had made two fink hall officials members of the state harbor police, "this is how the I.S.U. fights the fink halls. It's (sic) officialdom give police authority to the shipowner's finks and stool pigeons."

It was the state, not the I.S.U., that was qualified to bestow police authority, but the San Pedro leaders of the M.W.L., Lawrence Emery and Frank Waldron, (the latter, under the pseudonym Eugene Dennis, to briefly become top boss of the U.S. Communists two decades later), had other aims in mind than observance of journalistic ethics in the production of the *Lookout*.[18] During 1929, the Marine Workers' League declared itself a "union," and announced that its national leadership was in the hands of Mink the Fink, the stewpot king and Soviet secret police official. The League leaders also included one Harry Hynes, an Australian with experience in his native country's Seamen's Union. Hynes was remarkably devoted to the concept of "dock committees," as he described their functioning in Australia and New Zealand, and for a time the erection of assorted "committees" became a main M.W.L. slogan.

[15]On the Comintern, see the works of Leon Trotsky during this period, particularly *The Third International After Lenin*, New York, Pathfinder, 1970, and Draper, *American Communism and Soviet Russia.* On the R.I.L.U. congress, see House Special Committee to Investigate Communist Activities in the U.S., *Hearings*, Part 5; Vol. 4, Washington, Government Printing Office, 1930, documentation in testimony of William F. Hynes (hereinafter "W.F. Hynes documentation, 1930.") On the Communist "marine workers," *The Lookout* (San Francisco), September 1928; "Organize to Fight Shipowners," and "Phila. Club Sec'y Replies to M.T.W.," in *Marine Workers' Voice*, October, 1928, and "Foster Speaks to N.Y. Seamen," *Marine Workers' Voice*, December 1928, all unsigned, file in S.U.P. archive. [16]On the *Vestris* affair, extensive material is included in *Marine Workers' Voice*, December, 1928; *Road to Freedom*, December, 1928. [17]Unsigned, "Industrial Union, Ship, Dock and Fleet Committees' Call of Resolution on Organization," *Marine Workers' Voice*, September, 1929. [18]*The Lookout*, (San Pedro), December 2, 1929 (in S.U.P. central Archive)

Approach of Depression

1929 saw the first indication of the coming Great Depression, in the form of the massive collapse of stock trading. With the business downturn, millions of U.S. workers were to face unemployment or wage cuts, millions of farmers would suffer foreclosure, and the families of both would come to grips with terrible deprivations. Eventually, nearly a quarter of the nation's workers would enter the ranks of the unemployed. The crisis would create a social climate favorable to anti-capitalist sentiments, in which the radicals would once again find their audience dramatically enlarged. Almost overnight, the programs of socialists, Wobblies, and Communists faced a real test. As the year drew to a close, the Kremlin followers increased their propaganda on the West Coast. In San Pedro, a port considered important by the Communists because, among other things, it was a naval base, (as M.W.L. internal documents noted), an M.W.L. "lecture series" beginning on December 29, 1929, featured Leon Mabille, a Communist organizer, on "The Black Sea Mutiny." Publicity for the meeting declared, "The speaker was an active participant in this heroic revolt." The M.W.L. press was gleefully reporting that a new mutiny had taken place on the French cruiser *Waldeck Rousseau*, purportedly a violent protest against the strengthening of French naval forces in Chinese waters because of tension between Russia, Japan, and China in Manchuria.[19] The M.W.L. had begun a campaign to involve dockworkers as well as sailors in its activities, but issued further slanderous attacks on the established unions, claiming in its San Francisco sailors' and dockers' "shop paper," the *Bay Lookout*, that " 'COOPERATE WITH THE SHIPOWNER' has been (the I.S.U's) policy."

Relations between the Communists and the workers in this period seem to have assumed a character that fluctuated between the farcical and the tragic. For example, in the winter of 1929-30, Lawrence Emery, in San Pedro, hit on a new scheme for "making contact" with dockworkers: he purchased a city directory and began mailing Communist publications to those listed therein as longshoremen. He then proposed using this unique source of information to plan house-to-house visits. At first his disciples reported it was "impossible to visit longshoremen in their homes without making arrangements beforehand;" but these complainers had found it "impossible to talk to longshoremen" in general, and also claimed that M.W.L. meetings at the steam schooner docks had had only a negative effect. After a brief break, Emery's program of house-to-house visits was, for a while, in the forefront of League activity, but without any known results of significance.

A more sinister contact between the agitators and the workers had taken place in October 1929, in the Pacific Northwest. In this case the Seattle M.W.L. organizer, one R.H. McNeil, reported that he had gone to Aberdeen and Grays Harbor, the largest lumber-shipping port in the world, to try to head off an organizing drive by the International Longshoremen's Association, which had signed up some 600 members there. McNeil had leaflets printed up with the slogan "Smash the Corrupt I.L.A.!" — ignoring that there was as yet relatively little to "smash," apart from some newly-organized workers. Thus, at the commencement of the great West Coast longshore organization movement that would bear fruit in the 1934 maritime strike, the Communists played a role that can only be described as *scabby*. The delirious McNeil reported proudly on his (fortunately unsuccessful) efforts to his comrades, adding that the Sailors' Union of the Pacific, as well, was "stronger (in Seattle) than at other ports, but (we) hope to break it up!"[20]

Early in 1930 the Communists began proclaiming the transformation of the Marine Workers' League into the "Marine Workers Industrial Union." Naturally, the strong similarity between the Communist group's new title and that of the I.W.W. Marine Transport Workers Industrial Union was noticed by the latter. More than 50 years later, during the writing of this book, I had occasion to discuss the issue with old Wobblies in the S.U.P., one of whom was still moved to rage by the memory of this Communist propaganda maneuver. But although the Communists found it convenient to play on the name and reputation of the Wobbly militants, they did not cease their campaign of obloquy in that direction. In the March 1930, *Marine Workers' Voice*, when the call for the "new industrial union" was made public, it included the statement that the I.W.W. leaders "now openly advocate and practice fascist methods."

The Communists further asserted that the Wobbly organization was "practically out of existence. All that remains are a few degenerate, spittoon philosophers." But, of course, the most violent rhetoric was still reserved for the I.S.U., labelled in the same text as members of a "united front of the Shipowners with the American Legion." This issue of the *Voice* also included a fevered article on a recent mutiny in the German cruiser *Emden*, and a retelling of the 1905 Russian revolution and the mutiny of the naval vessel *Potemkin*. The latter incident had become the mythified subject of a classic Soviet film of the same name, directed by the gifted cinema artist Sergei Eisenstein. The film was an eloquent expression of the "rebel sailor" mystique, and it was widely shown, as a useful tool for stirring youthful revolutionary zeal.

The pearl in this issue of the *Voice*, a real anthology of Communist political smut, must be a blast at the I.S.U. headed "Sores Have Scabs and the I.S.U. has Scharenburg (sic)". The Communists referred to Scharrenberg as "the dry-land 'sailor' who unfortunately escaped from a shipwreck while making the Horn thirty years ago," conveniently ignoring that had Scharrenberg not done so he would have had no

[19]M.W.L. meeting announcement card, in S.U.P. archive; Unsigned, "Sailors Mutiny on French Cruiser," *Marine Workers' Voice*, October, 1929. [20]*Bay Lookout* (San Francisco), n.d. (in S.U.P. central Archive); W.F. Hynes, documentation cited.

opportunity to wage his campaign in favor of Bolshevik Russia's recognition in the years after 1917.

The Communists repeated the lie that Scharrenberg "gives police authority to the fink hall," and declared that "he is a scab and the son of a scab and the father of scabs. He is so scabby that he sweats pus. This scabherder doesn't dare get within a stone's throw of a bunch of real sailors without a full company of his (sic) policemen to guard him, as they would treat him like the Hamburg seamen's neat little slogan says: 'When you meet a Fascist beat him!' "[21]

The change from M.W.L. to M.W.I.U. had followed a plan set in motion by Soviet international trade union chief Lozovsky in February 1930, at a Moscow meeting of Communist marine operatives. The Red International of Labor Unions set up the "International of Seamen and Harbor Workers," demarcating Communist marine work from the functioning of the regular party and R.I.L.U. apparatus. The I.S.H. was headquartered in Hamburg, under the direction of a German, Albert Walter. The U.S. seamen's representatives at the gathering were (predictably) George Mink, and one Thomas Ray. Lozovsky assigned Mink the U.S. East Coast and Ray the Pacific.

But the creation of the M.W.I.U. was not an easy undertaking. Many M.W.L. supporters had begun to protest the lack of elections of rank-and-filers to office; all officials were appointed by the Communist Party. Dissidents resented Mink's stewpot business, his indulgence in rail travel, "union" dealings with Soviet vessels over wages and hours, and excessive publicity for the leaders, including repeated publication of photographs and names.[22]

The Communist propaganda machine still rolled on, spewing its filth and poison in all directions. In April the transformation of the M.W.L. into the M.W.I.U. was consummated; without, by the way, any vote or other democratic action to consult the ranks. (It should here be noted that although the Communists would, in the future, make incredible claims about the supposed membership figures of the M.W.I.U., there is no serious evidence to support them. One gullible admirer of the "comrades" in the academic community has recently claimed that the M.W.I.U. included at least 5,000 men. This is clearly preposterous, for such a large organization would have easily defeated the I.S.U. and I.W.W. for the dominant position among the seamen. It may be that 5,000 individuals at one time or another passed through the M.W.I.U., and it is more than probable that at least that many took membership cards in order to get a cheap meal from the stewpots. It should also be noted that initiation fees and dues were usually not charged for the "union's" membership books. New adherents were supposed to pay dues only after they went back to sea. We can say without hesitation that the Communist marine organization never drew in significant numbers of committed authentic seamen, and never became a genuine union or labor organization.)

Sometime in 1930 a certain N. Sparks, who had been editor of the *Marine Workers' Voice*, wrote a little booklet, published by the Communists under the title *The Struggle of the Marine Workers*. Here the Moscow line was well displayed: as for the I.S.U., "its whole activity for 25 years before the war was concentrated on discouraging strikes." (This included, presumably, 1901.) Sparks claimed that Furuseth "even practically *gave up the union* on the Pacific," a falsehood couched in a special kind of Communist vocabulary in which qualifiers like "even practically" could be used to make a statement mean virtually anything. (Many years later, an equally unscrupulous Communist writer, one Hugh Mulzac, would assert that the Interclubs "began to spring up almost spontaneously." That's a very big "almost.") Sparks declared the I.S.U. "a 100 percent company union." On the I.W.W., he was no more restrained: the M.T.W. was likewise "100 percent in the camp of the bosses, show(ing) not the slightest militancy." One wonders if Comrade Sparks himself had the courage to distribute his libels anywhere near an I.W.W. hall; indeed, one wonders how he or his successors would like the job of having to justify these statements today. Unfortunately, this is a task from which they have generally been excused, thanks to the bias of a later generation of "labor historians."[23]

Many further examples of Communist "scandal sheet" journalism in the service of marine union wrecking could be cited. Occasionally, drunk with words, the Communists let ugly truths be revealed. In June, 1930, the M.W.I.U. issued a "National Organizational Bulletin" in which a page was consecrated to "Activities in the Various Ports." The reports began, "The following excerpts culled from the minutes and reports of the various branches, are for the purpose of keeping all locals informed about the general activity of the union and to obviate the anarchistic practice, common in the 'Wobblies,' of interchange of minutes between locals, which had such a decentralizing effect." This "anarchistic practice" had also, of course, allowed anti-Mink dissidents to circulate their views around the country.[24] There then followed a series of reports of "big mass protests," endorsements "by longshoremen at mass meeting," etc.

In an explosion of bile that might have called forth ironic commentary, the San Francisco *Bay Lookout* for November 1930, charged in an attack on the Socialist Party that "the clubs of the Socialist police has (sic) in

---

[21]M.K. (further identification declined), conversation, July, 1983; George Mink, "National Convention, April 26-27," Unsigned, "Emden Mutiny," and "Sores Have Scabs and the I.S.U. Has Scharenburg (sic)," *Marine Workers' Voice*, March, 1930. On the false and real *Potemkin* events, the most important representation of the myth is, of course, the shooting script for the film: Sergei Eisenstein, *The Battleship Potemkin*, London, Lorrimer Publishing Ltd., 1968, which contains an essay by Andrew Sinclair indicating areas in which the script strays from the original events. An important original source is Kh. G. Rakovsky, "La Revolte du *Potemkine*," *Cahiers Leon Trotsky*, March 1984. [22]W.F. Hynes, documentation cited; King, et al, op. cit.; Krebs, op. cit. [23]W.F. Hynes, ibid; N. Sparks, *The Struggle of the Marine Workers*, New York, International Publishers, 1930, (in S.U.P. central Archive). Hugh Mulzac, *A Star to Steer By*, New York, International Publishers, 1963. [24]Marine Workers Industrial Union, *National Organizational Bulletin*, New York, June 1930 (in S.U.P. central Archive); W.F. Hynes, ibid.

no way differed from the others." Although the "subtext" of this statement may refer to a German context, it should perhaps be recalled that at that time Socialists still enjoyed some electoral support on the municipal level in the United States, so that indeed Socialist-administered police did exist even in this country. However, if there was no difference between the clubs wielded by policemen in, say, a Democrat-run New York and Socialist-run Milwaukee, whose Mayor, Dan Hoan, was a favorite Communist target for abuse, there was most assuredly a difference between the clubs of these forces and those of the Communist police in Moscow. In both New York and Milwaukee, strikers who fought with scabs on the picket line might run the risk of having their heads busted by the men in blue. But in Moscow, workers who even discussed going on strike faced the possibility of a Siberian exile, at the least, and should a walkout take place it would, in Tomsky's words, be settled in the language of machine guns. Tomsky aside, the *Bay Lookout* went on insisting that "the Communist Party . . . at all times represents the interests of the working class."[25]

Communist Failure

But regardless of its wild propaganda and the "prestige" of its Moscow backing, the M.W.I.U. was unable to stir many seamen or dockers to enlist. Further, dissident tendencies remained a problem. In September 1930, "sixteen members of the M.W.I.U., who were also members of the Party, were expelled for 'counter-revolutionary' activities and other assorted 'crimes.' " The sixteen formed the Marine Workers' Solidarity League in New York, which became the Marine Workers' Unity Council, and joined the M.T.W.-I.W.W. in August 1931. The Council "obtained approximately 450 dues-paying members and besides agitating for relief as one phase of their organizational activites, they also conducted a 'stewpot.' "

In a "resolution" appearing in the *Marine Workers' Voice* for March 1931, 12 loyal Communists who remained in the original group, currently residing in Leningrad, declared they were "categorically in accord with the action taken by the leadership of our union in liquidating the renegades who have attempted to smash our union" adding that "we demand that the fullest proletarian drastic action be taken to smash these splitters and if necessary to expel them from the union." Communist syntax again: if they were indeed "renegades," who had been "liquidated," why expel them only "if necessary?" Luckily for the dissidents, their residence in New York prevented the commissars from "liquidating" them in any but a figurative way. In an accompanying article, one of the signers of the loyal declaration, Benjamin Ambrody, described how he had attempted to work cargo on board ship on a Sunday, while the vessel, which was U.S. registered, was tied up in the Russian port of Novorossisk. But Ambrody ran up against U.S. union traditions: the ban on Sunday work, pioneered by the S.U.P., and against sailors working cargo, stressed by the I.W.W. These standard union demands were cheerfully "liquidated," naturally under justification of Mother Russia's needs. The M.W.I.U. and its predecessors were themselves no more than a company union for the Soviet employers.

The same issue of the *Voice* contained temporary statutes for the new I.S.H. that labeled the Dutch radical Edo Fimmen's International Transportworkers' Federation as "social fascist . . . the agency of the bourgeoisie in the ranks of the proletarians."[26]

September 1931, saw two events that marked the maturation of a new cycle of naval revolts. In the Chilean fleet, an uprising was followed by seizure of naval bases. A force of 80 government airplanes bombed and machine-gunned the mutineers, who apparently had been led into a trap by Communist prodding. Some 320 sailors were killed. An even more spectacular affair, in terms of worldwide attention, took place in the British North Sea Fleet, tied up in the Scottish harbor of Invergordon. Led by two soon-to-be Communists, Len Wincott and Fred Copeman, sailors on the battleships *Rodney* and *Nelson*, supported by a squadron of smaller ships, revolted against cuts in naval pay. In this case, the British admiralty acceded to the sailors' demands. The Invergordon mutiny had, perhaps, the greatest immediate impact of all naval rebellions. It told the world that even the British armed forces were not immune to disaffection.

A remarkable, if limited picture of the personal lives of the M.W.I.U. "activists" at this time has been given to us by Al Richmond, a former Communist leader, in his curious memoirs, *A Long View From the Left*. I say "curious" because, while the Communists have so often practiced reckless lying, Richmond has engaged in what might be called "reckless truthfulness." As a young Russian-born Communist, working in the U.S., Richmond was a part of the M.W.I.U. apparatus in Baltimore. Later, serving his apprenticeship under Harrison George, he would become editor of a San Francisco Communist sheet, the *People's World*, before being demoted from his editorship and hustled out of the Party ranks in 1969, as a "premature Eurocommunist," for truthfully reporting in the pages of his newspaper on the Russian invasion of Czechoslovakia.

At the time of this writing Richmond is a supporter of the Democratic Socialists of America, and in the author's experience has always been a warm, generous, and witty man. When he wrote his memoirs, which were published in 1972, he evoked an obvious nostalgia for his early days on the Baltimore waterfront, when the "truths" of Communism seemed simple and unstained. His conviction that his and his comrades' conduct throughout the years was basically defensible and positive has remained strong. And yet he "confessed" a number of disturbing facts

---

[25]*Bay Lookout*, November, 1930 (in S.U.P. central Archive). [26]12 signers, "Resolution by Crew Against Union Splitters;" Unsigned, "Voyage of 'Good Ship' *Hopatcong*;" "Temporary Statutes of Seamen and Harbor Workers' International," *Marine Workers Voice*, March, 1931; King, et al., op. cit.

about his co-workers in the M.W.I.U., who included Mink, Roy B. Hudson, who would replace Mink as the top Communist marine commissar in the U.S., Harry Hynes, Tommy Ray, and two others: Joe Bianca and William C. McCuistion.

Bianca, who was to enter the S.U.P. and then be made into a Communist hero with his death in the Spanish Civil War, is described in an extensive and unforgettable passage of Richmond's memoirs as nothing less than a thief and psychopathic sexual criminal, excited by the prospect of "cutting up broads;" the type of individual that would once have been called a "torso slasher," but today would be identified as an extreme case of "misogynistic sado-masochism." He enjoyed sticking needles through his cheeks for the amusement of young party comrades. William McCuistion, whom Richmond then admired, was probably the only "idealist" Communist among the older members of the group, most of whom were ten years Richmond's senior, including Bianca, Mink, and Hynes. But McCuistion, unlike Bianca, would turn against the Communists. McCuistion, eventually labelled a "stool pigeon" and "labor spy," held a sentimental attachment to the Communist movement that led him to compose an M.W.I.U. hymn, *The Red Union,* utilizing the British socialist anthem *The Red Flag,* sung to the German Christmas carol, *O Tannenbaum.* In McCuistion's version, the sailors would sing:

"We're through with Andy's I.S.U.;
The Wobblies don't know what to do;
Both they and every parasite,
With Mother Roper should unite."

(Mother Roper was the fabled head of the Seamen's Church Institute in New York.)

Richmond's memoirs show the emptiness of the M.W.I.U.'s pretensions as a "union." The organization was no more than a network of agitators paid by the commissars to hand out propaganda and administer stewpots. The real sailors never showed up. The M.W.I.U. would extend its control to nothing more than a tiny legion of Minks and Biancas, gunmen and abusers of women; of the young and naive like Richmond; and of the careerist functionaries, such as Hudson and Hynes, with an occasional McCuistion-type idealist.[27]

Communists Approach Longshoremen Again

In February 1930, the Communist marine organization, while viciously attacking the I.S.U. and I.L.A., suddenly instructed its cadre to form nuclei ("fractions") within the two A.F.L. unions. Late in 1932 a new "shop paper" appeared on the San Francisco waterfront, called the *Waterfront Worker*, edited by Harry Hynes. However, unlike previous examples of the genre, the new contribution did not, at first, even mention the M.W.I.U. It spoke non-committally of the general labor struggle, while attacking the International Longshoreman's Association leadership — but not the organization as a whole.

A new attitude had become visible among West Coast dockworkers. They were disgusted with the non-union hiring system that had been forced on them by the stevedoring employers after the first world war. The Depression had, by now, reduced their capacity for patience. But they had not come to the M.W.I.U. Rather, they had begun joining the International Longshoremen's Association. From its stronghold in Tacoma, the only port on the West Coast to retain the longshoremen's closed shop, the I.L.A. had retaken Everett and Grays Harbor in 1929, Portland in 1931, and Seattle in 1932–33.

Characteristically, the Communists carried out their decision to enter the I.L.A. in an underhanded manner. Rather than fight for a real united front *between* the forces of the M.W.I.U. and the I.L.A., as they claimed to have wished to do, they at first only vaguely mentioned the M.W.I.U. and then completely "submerged" themselves in the I.L.A., pretending as if their many previous attacks on that organization over the years had never taken place. Issues of the *Waterfront Worker* produced during spring and summer 1933 reprinted M.W.I.U. statements and acknowledged "help" from the Communist grouping; but by September of that year the M.W.I.U. was cast aside and the *Waterfront Worker* declared itself the voice of "a rank and file group within the I.L.A." The Communists were following, not leading, the workers.

The *Waterfront Worker* agitated for "unity" among the longshoremen, and as we shall soon see, its appeal was heard. The circle of Communist influence began to grow, and was particularly broadened by the action of an "independent" group of I.L.A. dock workers, led by Hynes' fellow-Australian, Harry Bridges, in allying their group with the Communists. Bridges had collaborated with Communists since the early 1920s. In the beginning, the new character of the *Waterfront Worker*'s activity seems to have disturbed some of the Communist bigwigs.[28]

At the beginning of 1933, the *Party Organizer*, an authoritative internal Communist publication, published statements in its "Shop Paper Editor" column condemning the *Waterfront Worker* for its "complete failure of even mentioning the M.W.I.U." In an unsigned contribution, an M.W.I.U. member complained that the "union" had been rejected by the longshoremen because it was mostly made up of seamen, although the stridency of its literature was undoubtedly a greater factor. What was undeniable was that longshoremen were joining the I.L.A. in great numbers.[29]

[27]On the Chilean revolt see Krebs, op. cit.; on Invergordon probably the most useful publication is Barry Duncan, *Invergordon '31*, London, Barry Duncan, 1976, written by a Communist-turned-anarchist. Richmond, op. cit. "The Red Union" appears in *Marine Workers' Voice*, March-April, 1932. [28]W.F. Hynes, documentation cited; the most complete file of the *Waterfront Worker* is held by the International Longshoremen's and Warehousemen's Union, Anne Rand Memorial Research Library, San Francisco, California. On Tacoma-based I.L.A. organizing drive, see Magden and Martinson, op. cit.; on Bridges, see Harry Bridges, interview, *Pacific Shipper*, February 24, 1986. Richmond, op. cit., McCuistion, testimony cited. [29]"Shop Paper Editor," *Party Organizer*, January, 1933, unsigned, "Our Work Among the Longshoremen," and "Shop Paper Editor," *Party Organizer*, February, 1933.

Roosevelt Elected — Unionism Encouraged

The most important effect of the Depression on U.S. politics came in late 1932, although without much comfort to the Communist Party. The people elected Franklin D. Roosevelt as their President. In 1933, one of the first actions of the new chief executive, the National Industrial Recovery Act, opened fresh opportunities for unions, since section 7A of the Act called for the federal government to recognize and protect unions as employee representatives, once they were certified by the "Blue Eagle," symbol of the National Recovery Administration. In addition, the Act called for development of "industrial codes" for minimum wages and hours in each industry, to be produced by the joint efforts of unions and employers. Both the I.S.U. and the M.W.I.U. began work on submissions to the N.R.A. code hearings.

The I.S.U. came to the hearings in a condition of extreme weakness. In the four-year period beginning in 1930, the sailor Union's activities had been limited to the issuing of charters to small local organizations (such as the Tillamook County Fishermen's Union, in Bay City, Oregon, and the Franklin County Boatmen's Union of Apalachicola, Florida), the publication of a reduced-size monthly *Journal*, increasingly occasional meetings, and limited legislative efforts. Its membership and its financial receipts were tiny.

The situation had long been similar for the national A.F.L., but a brief business upswing, and a rising demand for labor, in summer 1933, combined with the apparent Presidential endorsement of unionism, stimulated a number of more militant unions, including the United Mine Workers under John L. Lewis and the International Ladies' Garment Workers, led by socialists, to launch major organizing compaigns. Another aid to unionism was the Norris-LaGuardia anti-injunction law, passed in 1932. A national strike wave in 1933, in which the Communists played no role, included a successful walkout by 20,000 hosiery workers in July, which captured the formerly "openshop" mills in Reading, Pennsylvania. The shirt industry in New York and Pennsylvania, famous for sweatshop conditions, was victoriously organized by the Amalgamated Clothing Workers. Some 11,000 silk dyers and printers in New York and New Jersey struck in September, demanding speedy action on an N.R.A. code. The silk employers' code proposals, featuring low wages and long hours, brought expansion of the strike to include 50,000 employees. The most important single strike in 1933 shook the Pennsylvania soft coal industry, controlled by the steel companies through their "captive" mines, in which 30,000 workers stayed out for three months, ending in an election with a majority of votes for the United Mine Workers. In August, 60,000 New York dressmakers, of which only 20,000 were union members, struck. The "rag trade" employers gave up after two days. Between May and October 1933, the membership of the Ladies Garment Workers rose from 40,000 to 160,000. Many other important strikes took place, in the shoe industry, in steel, and in the automobile plants of Detroit, Flint, and Pontiac, Michigan, where 9,000 tool makers struck under the leadership of a radical union similar to the I.W.W., the Mechanics' Educational Society of America.

Unfortunately, as 1933 wore on it became apparent that the N.R.A. would not serve the workers without a prolonged legislative battle. Employer pressure had deformed the Act's codes in many industries. The strike wave had also provoked fear in the White House that working class militancy might disrupt the Roosevelt recovery. The administration began to study possible modifications of the N.R.A., including the creation of a National Labor Board to stop strikes in progress or, if possible, to prevent them altogether. The N.R.A. also came to grips with the problem of company unions, many of which sought "Blue Eagle" certification. And numerous employers simply ignored the new law.[30]

On the West Coast, militancy was visibly growing, among the sailors as well as the longshoremen. Beginning with a wage cut by American-Hawaiian Steamship Co. in 1931, pay rates had fallen, in two years, to 50 percent of 1921 levels, calling forth a bitter comment from *The Seamen's Journal* to the effect that "no other group of workers has been treated so shabbily and unfairly as the seamen." The organized longshoremen, according to the *Journal*, had suffered much less. President Roosevelt had held out the hope that after a decade the fink hall would finally come to an end; but then it became apparent that any improvements in labor's status would not be handed down by government, but would have to be fought for resolutely. The stage was set for the "big strike" of 1934, the first clash in labor's greatest epic in this nation's history, the great 1930s rebellion of the Pacific Coast maritime workers. The workers were preparing for battle; the Communists were preparing to battle for control of the workers. Late in 1933, the M.W.I.U. had between four and six functionaries working full time on the San Francisco waterfront. (Correspondence between Pete Gill, Seattle S.U.P. agent, and Union headquarters in San Francisco, for the last three months of 1933, includes continuing references to "marine Industrial" agitation in the Northwest; it is unclear whether this refers to the Communist M.W.I.U., which was insignificant in that region, or resurgent activism by the I.W.W. Marine Transport Workers.)[31]

Hitler

An ancillary, but significant event of 1933 should be mentioned. This is, of course, the Hitler takeover of

[30]Maurice Goldbloom, John Herling, Joel Seidman, Elizabeth Yard, *Strikes Under the New Deal*, New York, League for Industrial Democracy, n.d.; *Seamen's Journal*, April 1, 1936. [31]Robert James Lampman, "Collective Bargaining of West Coast Sailors," 1885-1947, graduate thesis, University of Wisconsin, 1950; *Seamen's Journal*, January, 1933; Sam Darcy, "Lessons of the Great West Coast Strike," in *Western Worker* (San Francisco), August 13, 1934; S.U.P. Seattle Branch correspondence with Headquarters, second half 1933, held at S.U.P. central Archive in San Francisco.

Germany at the end of January, an action that would never have taken place without the tacit support of the Communists, who, obsessed with their war on the Socialists, refused to cooperate in anti-fascist actions with the rest of the German working class.

It is instructive to examine the impact of the Hitler takeover on the Norwegian labor movement, whose history often parallels that of the S.U.P. Martin Tranmael's Norwegian Labor Party, immediately after the German disaster, warned that "in the interests of the working class of Norway the Labor Party must take power into its hands, to ward off in Norway the fate that had befallen Germany." Significantly, the tiny group of Norwegian Communists that had remained loyal to the Comintern after Tranmael's break from Moscow in 1923 reacted to the Labor Party's proposals by calling for a united front against fascism and by a resolution passed by the Oslo branch of the Metal Workers' Union, that said "the unity of the workers will be possible only when all parties throw aside their petty, party interests and enter into negotiations without consideration for their factional positions and without preliminary conditions." For this act of elementary sanity, the Norwegian Communists were upbraided and their leadership purged by the Comintern! Obviously, they had forgotten that according to Moscow, Tranmael, a "socialist fascist," was worse than the open fascists like Hitler!

In strong contrast to the divisive, sectarian tactics of the Communists, the Norwegian Labor Party acted for the strengthening of labor worldwide. In May 1932, the party acted with the British Independent Labor Party and left-wing Socialists in Holland and Germany, to form the International Labor Community, known as the I.A.G. from its German initials. At a conference in Paris in August 1933, they were joined by Dutch, German, Swedish, French, and Catalan (Spanish) independent Communists, Italian left Socialists, and the followers of Leon Trotsky, who were grouped under the name "International Left Opposition" (Trotsky had been exiled from Russia in 1929). Unlike the Communists, the Norwegian Labor partisans sought militant unity, rather than Soviet-dictated conformity, in the ranks of international labor.

1933 also saw another Communist-manipulated naval revolt: the mutiny of the Dutch East Indies fleet, centered on the cruiser *Zeven Provincien*, off Sumatra. Like Invergordon before it, the Dutch colonial navy mutiny projected the image of the rebel sailor on the screen of the world's consciousness. The mutineers operated the ship for several days, threatening to shell the city of Soerabaja. Finally, the ship was forced to surrender by bombing from the air. Fifteen Indonesian and three Dutch seamen were killed by the bombs, and 25 wounded. The mutiny had failed.[32]

But now we must turn to the year 1934.

---

[32]On Norway see O. Piatnitsky, *The Communist Parties and the Fight for the Masses*, Speech at the 13th Plenum of the Executive Committee of the Communist International, December 1933, New York, Workers' Library Publishers, 1934; on the Norwegian Labor Party and the International Labor Community (IAG), see Leon Trotsky, *Writings 1933-34*, New York, Pathfinder, 1971, and *Writings, Supplement 1929-33*, New York, Pathfinder, 1979, Robert J. Alexander, *The Right Opposition*, Westport, Greenwood Press, 1981. On the Dutch East Indies Fleet mutiny, see Irvin Anthony, *Revolt at Sea*, New York, G.P. Putnam's Sons, 1935, excerpted in Fuller, op. cit., also Krebs, op. cit.

CHAPTER VI
Year of Rebirth
(1934)

In the history of world labor, 1934 was the most significant single year of this century. The American working class burst out of the cocoon of the 1920s and early 1930s: a world of delusion based first on an intense post-war reaction against labor and then on the pain of the Depression. Three mass strikes in the United States, in Toledo, Minneapolis, and in the West Coast maritime industry, announced to the planet that the working class in the great bastion of capitalism had begun to take a new road.

Unlike the political convulsions of 1917-1923, the year 1934 was not the product of war, competing nationalisms, or the decadence of royal dreams. If the working class had played a major role in the Russian and German revolutions, it had done so almost without intention, whirling with the rest of the world in the maelstrom. By 1934, labor was different in its social composition and its outlook. And when it rose up, it did so with its own goals, with a truly organized, conscious, and self-disciplined unity of will.

The year 1934, as I shall try to demonstrate, saw events of world significance in France, Austria, Germany, Nicaragua, the U.S., Costa Rica, Spain, China, and Russia, but above all in the U.S. Fifty years later the echoes of the 1934 West Coast maritime strike, in which the Sailors' Union of the Pacific was virtually reborn, still resound. 1934 remains a symbolic date; a ray from a distant lighthouse, across history.

In this and the following chapter, against a backdrop of national and world events, I have attempted to reconstruct the day-to-day progress of events in the strike from the point of view of the S.U.P. alone, rather than of the labor movement as a whole or the general public. If this seems too narrow a focus, from which too much appears to be missing, some problems facing the historian must be kept in mind. Firstly, the S.U.P. is the only one of the striking unions to have preserved records detailed enough to make such a reconstruction even sketchily possible. Secondly, existing *printed* accounts, both journalistic and historical, are almost entirely valueless to one who seeks to arrive at an accurate chronicle, rather than a sentimentalized version. The historiography of 1934, on a serious and sustainable basis, has only just begun, and this reconstruction must therefore to taken as preliminary and tentative. The Battle of 1934 truly merits a study ample enough to reliably establish what really happened, from all vantage points, and to furnish the basis for a criticism of historians' errors.

Business Uncertainty

The year began, in West Coast shipping, with uncertainty over the seemingly-unstoppable Depression. Steamship companies showed arrears of $40 million in their debts to the federal authorities. The government indicated it might apply federal payments for carriage of ocean mail to the outstanding shipowners' debt. But a marine journal in San Francisco, *Pacific Shipper*, founded and edited by one George E. Martin, noted "persistent reports that the government would compel the holders of ocean mail contracts who are in default on construction or purchase loans to pay up or surrender their ships."[1]

In the labor field, *Pacific Shipper* and the shipowners to which it generally catered, anticipated success in the hammering-out of a federal maritime code, based on an employer-union partnership, under the National Recovery Administration. Depression realities had brought across-the-board changes in government policy through the administration of Franklin D. Roosevelt. In this country's new attitude toward world trade, direct government regulation if not control was now widely considered to be the guiding principle. Commerce between nations was strained by protectionist measures enacted by Depression governments. Threatening statements revealed new, competitive commercial tensions between the European powers, the U.S., and Japan.

[1]*Pacific Shipper*, February 19, 1934.

Unemployment continued to remain high, and business failures closely followed. Shiploadings stayed recessionary. Late in 1933, a mild upturn had been felt, but not enough to make a serious dent in the general economic distress. Smaller nations such as Cuba found themselves unable to manage their debts and threatened a moratorium on their obligations. In addition, Cuba and other less-stable countries witnessed growing political and social conflict.

Parallel with the new presidential administration in the United States, which seemed to promise a modernized and enlightened policy of social welfare, seemingly experimental governing methods were being tried in Germany, under the Hitler regime. But while in the U.S. the Roosevelt New Deal was accompanied by a typically American rhetoric stressing community fairness, in Germany the emphasis was on community discipline. (The means utilized stressed the club and pistol). In the interest of "national unity," Hitler had brutally suppressed the Socialist-led labor movement and had imprisoned or murdered countless labor and radical militants. The Communist Party, which had helped the Nazis to power by pursuing anti-democratic policies, was not spared. Even conservative dailies in the U.S. reported the gruesome details of political life in the Nazi state: concentration camps, torture, death, to the tune of a savage glorification of militarism. The Nazis' answer to the "New Deal" was imperial conquest for the welfare of the German "race," with an economic recovery based on massive rearmament.

In the Union's Ranks

In the ranks of the Sailors' Union of the Pacific, other uncertainties reigned. On January 1, member Harry T. Hollman wrote from San Pedro to George Larsen, Furuseth's stand-in as associate and acting S.U.P. secretary in San Francisco, attacking San Pedro agent Carl E. Carter as an incompetent and drunk. Hollman closed his letter by noting, bitterly, "hope they sign the (N.R.A.) Code soon and give us $40.00 per month or less." By contrast, Chris Aasted, a member of the S.U.P.'s Atlantic counterpart, the Eastern and Gulf Sailors' Association, also wrote to Larsen from San Pedro, in a more positive vein, "I am sure glad to see things are picking up a little again on this coast and people . . . seem to be more optimistic again."

Larsen replied to Aasted, "things are looking brighter than some time ago . . . A code for shipping, as you probably know, is now in the making, and should (be) about in the finishing stages by this time. However I don't expect anything like what we are asking for," he warned. He further wrote that "to make these codes really effective, strong organizations among the men affected by the code are essential. It's to be hoped the men will begin to see it that way."[2]

In the first week of January, Larsen wrote Pete Gill, S.U.P. agent in Seattle, that "we are suggesting to men in steam schooners, especially those paying above fifty (dollars) to wire protests . . . against a fifty dollar minimum wage for shipping code," but he admitted that "those spoken to here so far appear to assume a don't care attitude." "Things here are very poor," Gill replied. Later in the month, Gill reported that Thorndyke Shipping Company hoped to obtain vessels for trade with Russia and China and had indicated a cooperative attitude toward the Union.[3]

Certainly, little was smooth in the process of N.R.A. code approval. Larsen wrote to Gill toward the end of January that Paul Scharrenberg "has been appointed labor advisor" to the divisional code board but that this was "the only capacity in which the owners would consent to have him sit in on the deliberations." The gains to which the Union looked forward under the Code were extremely meager. A $50 per month minimum wage was no gain at all; but at least it seemed that the Code would establish an eight-hour day (three-watch system).[4]

In Portland, late January saw Communist demonstrations at the employers' fink hall, the Sea Service Bureau, as reported by J.A. Feidje, the Union's Portland agent. While the actual fink hall closed, a registration office continued to function. The "Communists" involved may not have been Communists but rather Wobblies. If they were indeed Communists, or proclaimed themselves members of the "Marine Workers' Industrial Union," a puppet organization of the Communist Party, they were likely not real seamen.

Larsen in San Francisco answered Feidje's worries by benignly remarking that the radicals "seem to be able to create enough to have attention called to them and, in some cases, to succeed in snarling things up in a way, as for instance, in the closing of the Sea Service Bureau in Portland. Which, incidentally, we have striven for, for some time, without any success. However, it does not do any harm to have these fellows around raising a little hell."[5] Feidje was then being replaced as Portland agent by Carl Carter.[6]

The Communist "Marine Workers' Industrial Union" had a high profile at that time in only one U.S. port, Baltimore. On January 25th, John Cooper, a Union ship's officer, wrote to Larsen from there, enclosing a clipping from a local newspaper. Thirty-two sailors and officers employed by the Munson Line had struck the *Munindies*, claiming that they were owed from two to six months' back pay. The press reported that the strikers "enlisted the aid of the Marine Workers' Industrial Union, which sent 300 of its members to picket

---

[2]Harry T. Hollman, autograph letter, January 1, 1934, Chris Aasted, autograph letter, January 3, 1934, George Larsen, typed letter [unsigned], January 8, 1934, all in "General Correspondence — 1934" file, S.U.P. central Archive, hereinafter abbreviated as GC-1934-HQ. [3]George Larsen, typed letter [unsigned], January 4, 1934, Pete Gill, typed letters, January 5, 1934 and January 15, 1934, in "Seattle — 1934" file, S.U.P. central Archive, hereinafter Seattle-1934-HQ. [4]George Larsen, typed letter [unsigned], January 25,1934, Seattle-1934-HQ. [5]John A. Feidje, typed letter, January 22, 1934, George Larsen, typed letter [unsigned], January 26, 1934, in "Portland — 1934" file S.U.P. central Archive, hereinafter Portland-1934-HQ. That the actual M.W.I.U. was inactive in the Portland area before the 1934 strike has been supported in conversation with me by Pele DeLappe, who visited Portland in the company of M.W.I.U. organizer Samuel C. Telford after the big strike, telephone interview, January 1984. [6]George Larsen, typed letter [unsigned], January 31,1934, Portland-1934-HQ.

. . . An effort to bring out the International Longshoremen's Association in sympathetic strike was unsuccessful." Cooper wrote that he had been approached by an M.W.I.U. representative but had turned him away.[7]

The Communists had encountered, as we have seen previously, little success in their organizing efforts among seamen, although this did not dissuade them from issuing continuous self-congratulatory sectarian propaganda. A "historical" pamphlet published by the M.W.I.U. at this time, titled *Four Fighting Years*, attacked the "once militant I.W.W." as "now to be found with strange bed fellows. Although they continue to mouth phrases about 'militant' action, about the general strike, their actions are in no way different from the leaders of the I.S.U. and I.L.A. They have led no struggles," the Communists declared. "They at first objectively supported the NRA but are now in 'opposition' to it by 'boycotting it' and failing to mobilize the masses for struggle against it." The use of the term "objectively" to mask a simple fabrication was a hallmark of Muscovite boilerplate. More, the C.P.-liners labelled the Wobblies as scabs, charging "they have . . . attempted to confuse and disrupt strikes," and claimed the I.W.W. was guilty of precisely what the Communists were known for: "trying to entice the workers into the I.W.W. by claiming credit for the struggle led by the M.W.I.U."[8] It will be recalled that the Communist group had deliberately stolen the name of the I.W.W. section, the Marine Transport Workers Industrial Union. M.W.I.U. commissar Roy Hudson, known as "Jerusalem Slim," "Horseface," and "The Archbishop," in the same pamphlet, blasted "the I.S.U., I.L.A., I.W.W., etc. . . . leaders (who) serve the shipowners by their policies of class peace and non-aggression, or by their pretended 'non-political' nature, which only hides boss politics by ignoring the central anti-working class functions of capitalist class government."[9]

"United Front"

At the same time, the Communists were maintaining a "united front" offensive toward the San Francisco longshoremen, who were increasingly joining the International Longshoremen's Association. Late in 1933, the newly-strengthened I.L.A. successfully struck the Matson dock in San Francisco, as noted by Larsen in a letter to Feidje in Portland. According to a later writer, Roger Buchanan, the Portland dockers at that time had been strongly impressed by I.L.A. success "in gaining wage increases in the North Atlantic ports in 1933." The Portland waterfront workers were not Communist-influenced; they were clearly more oriented toward the Wobblies, according to William W. Pilcher, a former Portland longshoreman who authored a major anthropological study of the community from which he came. On the other hand, the authoritative historian of Pacific Coast maritime unionism, Ottilie Markholt, has strongly questioned Pilcher's assessment, casting doubt on the "vanguard role" of *either* Communists or I.W.W. members. Markholt has established in her work the importance of the independent militant strain in the coastwide I.L.A., who rewon Portland in 1931, in continuation of tradition established during and after the first world war, (especially after the I.W.W. on the Portland waterfront had alienated the dockers by scabbing in 1922.)[10]

Communist inroads in San Francisco, however, were undeniable. The *Waterfront Worker*, the throwaway started by Harry Hynes, had become a major voice for the dock workers, with the support of the Communists' allies among the Albion Hall group of I.L.A. activists, headed in turn by Hynes' fellow- Australian, Harry Bridges. Bridges was perhaps *not*, himself, a dues-paying member of the Communist Party. However, he clearly accepted the post-1917 "Australian" principle of militant trade unionism aligned toward, although not controlled by, Russia, and had collaborated with Communist labor activists in San Francisco since the 1920s. The Seamen's Union of Australia, originally linked to the S.U.P., had repeatedly suffered the effects of Communist influence after the Bolshevik Revolution. But as with the S.U.P., the majority of the new West Coast I.L.A. members expected more relief from the N.R.A. code hearings than from the Kremlin.

The Communist-Bridges alliance in the San Francisco I.L.A. contended for leadership with three main rivals. These were, first, a large group of Irish Catholic dockers headed by one Lee Holman; second, a trend associated with William J. Lewis, a devoted militant from the I.L.A.; and third, a seeming "party of one" named Fred West. In confrontation with Holman and the Communist-Bridges group, Lewis and West apparently formed a coalition. Of these contestants for power within the dock union, West is perhaps the most interesting for later historians, although the least-known. In a book on Bridges that is very faulty and must be read with great caution, Charles P. Larrowe notes that West was San Francisco district organizer of the Proletarian Party, a group that originated in the Michigan state federation of the Socialist Party, and that had refused to follow the rest of the pro-Bolshevik forces in the United States into the "official" Communist Party. Apparently influenced by radical left-communist tendencies in Germany and Holland, the Proletarian Party criticized the Bolsheviks for their acceptance of bourgeois political methods. In the union field, the Proletarian Party rejected the alternating C.P. tactics of attempting to conspiratorially "take over" the established unions, or

[7]John Cooper, typed letter, January 25, 1934, with clip from unidentifiable Baltimore newspaper, January 25, 1934, GC-1934-HQ. [8]Unsigned, "A Short History of a Fighting Union," in Marine Workers' Industrial Union, *Four Fighting Years*, M.W.I.U., n.p., n.d., but almost certainly New York, late 1933 or early 1934. [9]Roy B. Hudson, "An Open Letter to Ships' Delegates," in M.W.I.U., ibid. [10]George Larsen, typed letter [unsigned], October 12,1933, Portland-1934-HQ; Roger Buchanan, *Dock Strike: History of the 1934 Waterfront Strike in Portland, Oregon*, Everett, Washington, Working Press, 1975; William W. Pilcher, "The Portland Longshoremen: A Dispersed Urban Community," in George and Louise Spindler, eds., *Urban Anthropology in the United States*, New York, Holt, Rinehart and Winston, 1978; Ottilie Markholt, letter, May 7, 1984.

bureaucratically impose "Red" unions in their stead. The Proletarians, more or less in the style of the Wobblies, clearly labelled the existing union leaderships as agents of the capitalists; but, like the I.W.W. and in contrast with the Communists, the Proletarians called on the working class to transform the union conception from the bottom up rather than to follow a "rule or ruin" party policy of top-down control. At around this time, some members of the Proletarians had broken away to form a new group, the United Workers' Party, along with former members of the I.W.W. They were led by a German left-communist scholar and agitator of great gifts, Paul Mattick. Unfortunately, West, who seems to have been a serious and honest revolutionary, was soon swept aside by the Communist-Bridges machine on the San Francisco docks.[11]

As the month of January drew to a close, the S.U.P.'s Pete Gill reported from Seattle that "a number of men on the steam schooners are joining the I.L.A." On February 2, Larsen described, in his reply to Gill, the situation of the San Francisco longshoremen. "The I.L.A. here is far from a harmonious body," Larsen wrote. "A so-called rank-and-file movement is particularly pronounced. Since they began organizing last summer, talk from some of them has been to the effect that cargo work in steam schooners should be handled by longshoremen, and not by the crew." This reflected a return by the longshore unionists to a policy, followed by the I.L.A. in the first decades of the century, of attempting to raid work away from the Sailors on "jurisdictional" pretexts. Larsen warned that the I.L.A. was arguing "one union book should be sufficient, and, of course, that should be the I.L.A. book. This seems quite a favorite argument among those who have been members of this union," i.e., past members of the S.U.P. who had been forced to work ashore by the bad conditions and miserable wages at sea.

A vivid description of an experience suffered by a seaman who temporarily took longshore work is given to us by Jack McGinty, interviewed by Karl Kortum:

"The fink hall in Pedro was a dirty place. Just to look at it left a bad taste in your mouth. And if you wanted to ship out, you had to slip the dispatcher $5.00 under the counter . . . it was a bad place, a really crumby place. These guys that were non-union hung around there. Matson used to hire through the fink hall. Dollar would take guys from anywhere; they were as bad as Standard Oil. I didn't want any part of it.

"And they were tough times. I am talking about the period of the '34 strike. I was sitting in the Union hall one day with Frank Pickard and a call came in for a couple of guys to work loading borax on a German ship. We took it; anything to make a few dollars, damn few. We didn't know what we were getting into.

"Work was non-existent . . . If we were older and wiser we would have known what kind of cargo we were getting mixed up with — just imagine, hundreds of longshoremen out of work and they are not responding to the call; it is necessary to call the Sailors' Union. They knew something we didn't know. But we were starving.

"The vessel's name was *Schwaben*. She was free for a union man to work on, being foreign. I never worked as hard in my life, unless it was as a scoop jockey levelling the sand ballast in the *Pacific Queen* that time, the scoop connected to the donkey engine by a lot of wires and snatch blocks. The borax sacks must have weighed two hundred pounds each, or close to it. You had a partner; mine was a guy about my own height. I couldn't pair off with Pickard because he was about six feet high. My partner had worked with borax before and he showed me how you worked your finger into the end of the sack until you got a little ear. Something to grab hold of.

"They were heavy . . . tremendously heavy. Particularly when you hadn't eaten for awhile and were not in the pink of condition. We stowed the sacks in tiers; you built up the tiers like steps and you climbed the steps with your sack, and your partner at the other end, and landed the sack in the highest tier.

"The German officers were very particular — every bag was where it was supposed to be. They wanted a tight stow for heavy weather. They strutted around watching things and giving orders. They were that kind of German — cold as an icy blade.

"There was an offensive kid on board, a member of the Hitler Youth. They put them on the merchant ships. He was all dressed up, cocky, associating with the officers. A supercilious bunch of buzzards.

"We went to work in late afternoon and got through at three in the morning. Not even a cup of coffee — God what I would have given for a cup of coffee. Frank and I did not know the system — we hadn't brought a lunch or anything.

"I crawled out of the hold. I was practically dead. Every rung of that iron ladder was agony. When I got on deck I collapsed. I couldn't get off. I was so beat up (I guess you would call me a guy of slight build) that I couldn't eat. Hungry as I was, I would have had to turn down a sirloin steak if anybody had offered it to me.

"But nobody did. We got a brass tag — Banning Stevedore Co. as I remember — with a number on it. You could turn it in for cash but that was later in the morning when the office opened for business.

"I pulled myself together and Frank and I got off the ship — still without the price of a cup of coffee in whatever dive might be open at that hour.

"I heard that the *Schwaben* — she was a well-kept ship, you can believe — got sunk during the war. I hope so."[12]

[11]Charles P. Larrowe, *Harry Bridges*, Westport, Lawrence Hill & Co., second edition revised, 1977. On the Proletarian Party, see Theodore Draper, *The Roots of American Communism*, New York, Viking Press, 1957, and Guy Aldred, *For Communism*, Glasgow, Guy A. Aldred, 1935. [12]Pete Gill, typed letter, January 27, 1934, and George Larsen, typed letter [unsigned], February 2, 1934, Seattle-1934-HQ; Jack McGinty, interviewed by Karl Kortum, 1985, National Maritime Museum.

World Events

February saw, outside the U.S., a series of dramatic political developments. On February 6, Communists in France, repeating an apparently suicidal strategy that had led their German counterparts to disaster, joined in rioting by fascist groups in Paris that were unsuccessfully attempting to overthrow democratic rule. The spectacle of the two extremist groups fighting side by side caused unease around the globe. William L. Shirer, the American newspaper correspondent, was an eyewitness to the Paris events, and noted, "The Communists fought on the same side of the barricades . . . as the fascists. I do not like that," he concluded.

A new epoch was obviously beginning; politics had become more than usually unpredictable. Following the long industrial downturn, in an atmosphere of profound anxiety, bordering, the higher one went in society, on panic, it seemed that anything could occur. It was a threatening time, made even more insecure by the violence and the verbal excesses of totalitarian movements. The vocabulary and public provocations in the day-to-day activities of fascist and Communist groups were new and ominous. Europe was a continent in flames.

But in repudiation of the de facto Nazi-Communist anti-democratic alliance, the month of February also saw a magnificent action by the Austrian labor movement, resisting fascism. Unlike Germany, Austria had brought forth Socialist unions that seemed immune to Communist influence, and the Austrian Social Democratic Party, in its willingness to defend itself actively and courageously, was closer to the "left extremist" Norwegian Labor Party, as described in the previous chapter, than to the very moderate German Social Democrats. On February 12, the Austrian workers rose in arms against an attempted right-wing coup. For nearly a week, the insurrectionary labor movement battled in the streets and houses against the army, police, and the Heimwehr, or Home Guard of fascist groups. The Austrian uprising electrified world opinion.

Labor throughout the world found in the Austrian events evidence that the new trends were not exclusively toward barbarism, although the most significant and sinister image, for that time, of the breakdown of the old order in Europe came during the Austrian struggle, when the fascist regime ordered artillery fire directed at Socialist-built public housing in Vienna. Cannon firing on residential dwellings had not been seen in Europe for nearly a century, and photographs of the damaged buildings were printed in dailies around the world, with a special and unforgettable impact, even in the U.S.

Of course, since their minuscule Austrian branch had played no role in the workers' heroic stand, the Communist Party utilized the occasion once again to defame the mainstream Socialist and labor movement. That the Austrian workers had learned firmness and daring in the ranks of the Social Democratic Party was unimportant to Moscow; the Social Democrats remained the "stepping stone to fascism," according to the Communist International.[13]

The preoccupation of Americans with the European drama is visible in an exchange between George Larsen and Carl Carter, now S.U.P. agent in Portland, at mid-month. Carter had written "I am having some time with the marine worker's organizers as we meet now and then in the same ship but the men don't seem to take much interest in their organization." The individuals referred to may have been I.W.W. Marine Transport Workers or the Communist M.W.I.U; Larsen responded, "I am of the opinion that the Marine Workers Industrial Union make very little impression on the men in the ships. The fact of the matter is they don't seem interested in any kind of organization. While it does not apply to all, it does to the majority. Sometime or the other in the not-too-distant future, perhaps, we will see them regret this. But then it may be too late. It will be, should we get into the same predicament which is now scourging almost all of Europe, Fascist, Naz(i), or what have you."[14]

While Larsen judged the seamen largely uninterested in unionism at this point, within weeks this passivity would, as we will see, be dramatically overcome — men would flock to the Union in the thousands.

Another foreign tragedy took place late in the month, in the Central American nation of Nicaragua; however, this event was without the immediate world impact of the French riots or the Vienna uprising. On February 19, late at night, outside the Nicaraguan capital city of Managua, a short, stocky, unassuming-looking man of Spanish and Indian descent, calmly sat down on a rock, with two of his comrades beside him, waiting for machine-gun-bearing soldiers to kill him. His name was Augusto César Sandino, and he died with one bullet through his brain and another through his left chest. Sandino, a Nicaraguan inspired by the Mexican Revolution of 1910-1920, had fought for a unification of the Central American states, and against U.S. intervention. He was a mystical dreamer, not a Bolshevik; in the period leading up to his assassination, Sandino had come under attack from Moscow's Central American representatives. Having spent a decade courting him, the Communists turned against Sandino for his refusal to accept their dictates, declaring him a traitor who had sold out to U.S. imperialism for $66,000.[15]

---

[13]On France, see William L. Shirer, *Berlin Diary*, New York, Knopf, 1942; Leon Trotsky, *On France*, New York, Monad, 1979; on Austria, see Bela Kun, *The February Struggle in Austria and its Lessons*, New York, Workers Library Publishers, 1934. An authoritative treatment of the C.P. line during this period is Harvey Klehr, *The Heyday of American Communism*, New York, Basic Books, 1984. Also see Walter B. Maass, *Assassination in Vienna*, New York, Scribners, 1972, on Austria. [14]Carl Carter, typed letter, February 15, 1934, and George Larsen, typed letter [unsigned], Portland-1934-HQ. [15]On the death of Sandino, see Gregorio Selser, *Sandino*, New York, Monthly Review Press, 1981. On Sandino and the Communists, see Rodolfo Cerdás Cruz, "Agustín Farabundo Martí: Testigo de Cargo," in *La Nación Internacional* (San José, Costa Rica), January 6-13, 1984.

I.L.A. Regional Convention

Against this worldwide background, in the last week of February and the first week of March, the West Coast I.L.A. organization held a regional convention, and voted to formulate demands for presentation to the stevedoring employers. Should the call for a closed I.L.A. shop, coastwide bargaining, a six-hour workday, and $1.00 per hour be rejected, the longshoremen were to take a strike vote on March 7.

"Strike fever" had emerged in various places around the country. In Pennsylvania, 30,000 independent anthracite miners struck for a month and won some of their demands. In New York, taxi drivers, laundry employees, and hotel workers joined "revolts," according to a contemporary account published by the League for Industrial Democracy, *Strikes Under the New Deal.* The study's authors pointed out that the taxi strike "which at its peak involved 30,000 drivers, would have ended fairly successfully had it not been for the disruptive tactics of the communists . . . They succeeded in having rejected an agreement which they had previously helped to negotiate. The strike lost strength, however, and within a short time the union was forced to beg for the terms previously rejected . . . the strike collapsed."[16]

During the coastwide longshore convention, the delegates learned the shipowners were not disposed to discuss wage demands or an I.L.A. closed shop. Further, the National Labor Board of the N.R.A. had indicated it would not order a union representation election until the shipping industry was covered by an N.R.A. code. The obstinate attitude of the employers was emphasized in a meeting held with I.L.A. representatives toward the end of the convention. Meanwhile, I.L.A. President Joseph P. Ryan asked the West Coast membership to hold off any action until March 22, when it was anticipated that an N.R.A. code would be signed by President Roosevelt. The convention therefore agreed to take the strike vote on March 7, if the employers continued in their resistance, and if a strike proposal was sustained, to set the walkout for March 23.

The March longshore strike vote showed 6,616 in favor of a withdrawal of labor and 699 against, the length of the Coast. The week of March 5, *Pacific Shipper* hopefully but wrongly reported that "the outlook for a stevedoring strike was considered less foreboding last week, after a meeting of the International Longshoremen's Association failed to issue its anticipated order for a lockout . . . The I.L.A. group is said to be divided," the pro-employer magazine asserted, "with the left-wing insisting on wages of $1.00 an hour against a present scale of 85 cents, and the 'right' wing seeking only recognition of the I.L.A."

The night of March 5, the Sailors' Union held its regular meeting in San Francisco but without recorded discussion of the possible I.L.A. walkout. Paul Scharrenberg had come back from Washington and, like the I.L.A.'s Ryan, expected an imminent approval of the N.R.A. shipping code. The Union had also received word from Andrew Furuseth in Washington, regarding the passage of immigration legislation considered favorable to the maritime unions.

With Scharrenberg's return from the East, Larsen wrote to Gill in Seattle "some representation on the Code Authority has been acceded to and the men on deck and in the engine room are not to be required to work more than 8 hours in port . . . (the) labor section on Pacific Coast Codes will be taken up locally, after all the other matters have been thrashed out in Washington." With reference to the bad state of Andrew Furuseth's health, Larsen added that "I suppose we might be called upon to send someone from here unless the old man's health is so as to permit him to take care of it."[17]

In Portland, the ferment in the I.L.A. had begun to have visible effects on the Sailors. With the end of February, Portland union agent Carl Carter, who had replaced Feidje, had written to Larsen warning that "the M.W.I.U. organizers are getting busy around here and I am having a lot of fighting to do." Larsen had commented in his answer on the Communist campaign, "With regard to members of the Marine Workers Industrial Union, it would seem they are getting increasingly active. However, that's well. The more they raise hell, the merrier, as long as we don't get too many of them within our own ranks . . . Incidentally, in the I.L.A. here, they have a considerable number of Communists, and they are creating considerable trouble and disturbance . . . Let them raise all the hell in and around the ships," he concluded benevolently.[18]

By the second week of March, the strike debate in the longshore union had begun to stir even greater interest in the S.U.P. On March 12, Gill in Seattle wrote to Larsen suggesting that "as for men jumping out (on strike) in case the Longshoremen go out, that will not happen in any large extent. In Alaska vessels, the crew does not work cargo on the Puget Sound and they will not work cargo if the walkout happens. In steam schooners it may happen to a considerable extent. However, there is little that we can do in the matter and, no matter what we do, we are condemned anyhow," he warned. By contrast, Carter in Portland wrote the same day, "the men at the present time are all talking about strike and I guess if the I.L.A. goes out on the 23rd of March the biggest part of our men will go with them."

The Sailors' Union meeting in San Francisco the evening of the 12th noted only that "there is talk of a walkout of the longshoremen but there is no definite information obtainable so far, it would appear. The so-called Marine Workers Industrial Union, however, are

[16]Larrowe, op. cit., reports the basic demands of the I.L.A. at this point as the closed shop, coastwide bargaining, and the six-hour day, but the $1 per hour figure is consistently reported in *Pacific Shipper*, March 12 and March 19, 1934. On national "strike fever," Maurice Goldbloom, John Herling, Joel Seidman, Elizabeth Yard, op. cit. Also see Klehr, op. cit. [17]Larrowe, ibid; *Pacific Shipper*, March 5, 1934; S.U.P. Headquarters Minutes, San Francisco, March 5, 1934, in the central Archive; George Larsen, typed letter [unsigned], March 2, 1934, Seattle-1934-HQ. [18]Carl Carter, typed letter, February 26, 1934, and George Larsen, typed letter [unsigned], March 1, 1934, Portland-1934-HQ.

becoming increasingly active in a move to project themselves into the situation." Several days later, Larsen replied to Gill and to Carter, writing to the Seattle agent that "the longshoremen will make a foolish move to walk out now to gain recognition. They have them all in the organization, or so they say, why don't they bide their time, nurse the organization along, and wait for a favorable opportunity. A wrong move now might upset the applecart. Probably that's what the owners want. But then, I suppose they are rearing to go, some of them, anyway."

Regarding Portland, Larsen declared, perhaps attempting to reconcile conflicting reports, that the dockworkers were "showing the right kind of spirit." The next day, March 16, he wrote to John Cooper, now in New York City, that "the longshoremen here according to all reports are getting prepared to pull off a walkout. I surely wish them luck. They will need it should they decide to go out. I expect a good many of the sailors will follow suit. Well, there is little we can do about it at this stage of the game."

On the 15th, Carter had written again to Larsen, stating that "things around here [are] very slow, the men do not want to part with their money as they are afraid of the I.L.A. strike and the sentiment amongst the men [is] that they want to go out at the same time and the biggest part of them will. They all want to know what the Sailors' Union is going to do so I like to have some information from you regarding this matter." On March 19, in his regular weekly report to headquarters, Carter emphasized that "the men seem to be all up in the air about the strike . . . and they are hanging onto their money."[19]

The March 19th San Francisco minutes record that discussion under Good and Welfare "centered around the reported walkout of the longshoremen and the position this union should take in the event the longshoremen walk out. It was agreed that headquarters advise our members as follows: that in vessels where our members are working under an agreement we continue to abide by our agreement; that our members in all other vessels, especially in the steam schooners, be advised to leave such vessels in case a strike is called by the longshoremen and that in doing so they are not merely doing so out of sympathy with the strikers but also because of the low wage and rotten conditions prevailing."

With this simple decision, the Sailors' Union joined the longshoremen at the center stage of the American labor epic of 1934. Although Larsen continued lacking confidence in the dock workers' ability to win a strike, the growing impatience of the rank-and-file was irresistible.[20]

Presidential Intervention

The curtain was about to rise, but was still to see a brief delay. On March 22, President Roosevelt intervened in the West Coast conflict, asking the I.L.A. to cancel the strike decision and to allow appointment of a mediation board. The I.L.A. concurred with the Chief Executive's request. On March 23, Carter wrote to Larsen, "I was kind of disappointed this morning when the I.L.A. did not go out on strike. Had all our men ready." *Pacific Shipper*'s owner, George Martin, gleefully editorialized "as so richly it deserved, the stevedoring strike at Pacific coast ports has been averted, at least temporarily and probably indefinitely." Mr. Martin's hasty enthusiasm would prove as baseless as S.U.P. agent Carter's discouragement. The 1934 rebirth of the West Coast maritime movement was to be painful but the infant, when it came into the world, would be strong, healthy, and loud.[21]

A marked change in the seamen's attitude continued to show itself through the month of April, in the reports of Carter and Gill. On April 6, Larsen wrote to Carter outlining the situation as he saw it. "The union represents but a minority of the men sailing," he noted. The defeat of 1921 had taken its toll; a hard core of loyalists had continued paying dues, although the Union was ignored by the employers when not repressed through the blacklist of activists maintained by the fink halls. The answer to the post-1921 decimation of the Union was coming, although still, as Larsen pointed out, "the majority, those who sail outside of the union, has done nothing and is doing nothing . . . If a majority of the men in the ships today was in the union we would not have to depend on codes for shipping to get decent wages and proper working conditions . . . Let the men understand that it is because of lack of organization among us that we are faced not only with delays but also have to sail for low wages, miserable working conditions, and intolerable employment conditions. Let them be reminded that in vessels where men are doing the hardest kind of physical labor, namely, in many steam schooners, no raise has taken place since they were reduced to the starvation point some two years ago . . ." He further stated that "whatever the longshoremen will finally get, they will get because they have sense enough to get into one organization. They get it through action which could not come otherwise than by concerted action. Their spokesmen speak for the majority group of longshoremen."[22]

Strike Begins

During April, *Pacific Shipper* reported a compromise had been worked out by the Federal Mediation Board, under which the I.L.A. would not gain a coastwide closed shop but would be recognized as the dockworkers' representative in the San Francisco Bay Area. Neither this nor various subsequent recommendations of the board found favor with the I.L.A. membership or with the employers.

[19]Pete Gill, typed letter, March 2, 1934, Seattle-1934-HQ; Carl Carter, typed letter, March 12, 1934, Portland-1934-HQ; Headquarters Minutes, March 12, 1934; George Larsen, typed letter [unsigned], March 15, 1934, in Seattle-1934- HQ, and typed letter [unsigned], March 15, 1934, in Portland-1934-HQ; Carl Carter, typed letters, March 15, 1934, and March 19, 1934 in Portland-1934-HQ. [20]Headquarters Minutes, March 19, 1934; George Larsen,typed letter [unsigned], March 22, 1934, Portland-1934-HQ. [21]Larrowe, op. cit.; Carl Carter, typed letter, March 23, 1934, in Portland- 1934-HQ; *Pacific Shipper*, April 2, 1934. [22]George Larsen, typed letter [unsigned], April 6, 1934, Portland-1934-HQ.

Nor were N.R.A. efforts in a similar direction to prove successful. On May 2, the daily newspapers reported that A.F. of L. head William Green had withdrawn all support from N.R.A. proposals for establishment of boards to settle industrial disputes, since N.R.A. officials demanded that company unions be represented on the boards along with A.F. of L. affiliates. A new longshore strike date was set for May 9 and, on that day, in the thousands, the West Coast longshoremen walked off the job. The daily newspapers on the West Coast, which had previously ignored the waterfront labor crisis, began paying attention. The second day, May 10, the *San Francisco Chronicle* headlined "Police Quell S.F. Riots As Strikebreakers Are Attacked by Dock Men."

The seamen in Portland joined the longshoremen on the picket line immediately. On May 10, Larsen wrote Gill in Seattle that the dockers had taken "a sudden notion" to strike but that "the longshoremen's union has not taken the trouble to notify any of the unions officially; nor, as far as I know, has the Labor Council been notified." Larsen advised the sailors should continue working on ships where a contract was in force and remain at their posts on other ships if the operators were prepared to sign a one-year agreement with the union providing for the conditions outlined in the union's N.R.A. code proposal to the federal government, namely $75 per month minimum wage, abolition of the fink halls, three watches at sea, and a six-hour day in port. Larsen added that "Harry Lundeberg has phoned here a couple of times requesting advice as to what they should do. Both times, he was advised to stay with the ship and take it back to Seattle." The ship on which Lundeberg was employed (as third mate), the steam schooner *James Griffith*, was a union vessel.[23]

It is here that Lundeberg, along with other previously-unknown members, stepped forward from obscurity and into the harsh light of public attention and, ultimately, of history. Harry Lundeberg decided not to take Larsen's advice. According to a later statement by Edward Coester, who would join Lundeberg as a major leader of the union in the period to come, "during the 1934 strike, Lundeberg walked off his ship in Frisco two days after the longshoremen's strike was called and was in Seattle during the entire strike as a member of the Strike Committee." It is fitting that we here examine the background of Lundeberg, this man who, as Coester went on to declare, "all but sacrificed his life in the interests of the seamen. No single individual during the 1934 strike took a more active, militant part than Brother Harry Lundeberg."[24]

Harry Lundeberg

Harald Olaf (Harry) Lundeberg was born in the city of Oslo, capital of a kingdom of Norway then still ruled by Sweden, on March 25, 1901. His father, Karl Vedel Torgerson Lundeberg, a worker in construction, the fabled industry of the syndicalist "rollers," (described in Chapter III), came from the town of Kvitseid, in the province of Telemark. Harry's father was married in Oslo to Alette Sofie Koffeld, from Ostfold, Thune, on December 5, 1893.

Harry was one of five children, all boys. Adolf, born in 1894, died in 1912, while working as a sailor on the British steamer *Charlton Hall*, on the east coast of South America. Henry, born in 1897, like Adolf, had the intention of making the sea his profession, and sailed for about two years; but on the death of Adolf, his parents prevailed on him to work instead in construction. A third brother, Kolbjørn, died at the age of 2. A fourth, given Kolbjørn's name, was born in 1905, the year Norway won its independence from Sweden. Kolbjørn also went to sea in his youth but, like Henry, "swallowed the anchor" and went to work in construction.

Harry's parents represented the best traditions of Norwegian labor. His father was an active syndicalist, with more interest in the practical side of union organization. His mother, Alette, was more politically active. Joining Martin Tranmael's Norwegian Labor Party in her youth, she soon became a leading figure in the movement. She fought for "women's right to vote and a more just social order," in the words of her youngest son, Kolbjørn. "Never one cent for postage and writing materials, elections and election agitation, strongly interested in schools and the students," she served for some 30 years on school committees in Oslo, from the least to the most important, fighting for free schoolbooks, free meals for pupils, and improved instruction. The day Norwegian women gained the vote was a great occasion for her. She sat as a chairwoman of the Labor Party women's organization in Oslo and, as recounted by Kolbjørn, "she had many duties and it is unbelievable that she could manage to do it all." She was also a supporter of the workers' movement for abstention from alcohol.

Above all, Alette dedicated herself to the liberation of the working women. She fought for vacation homes for housewives, a demand that most feminists, even today, would find highly advanced. "She was a speaker who was not afraid of expressing her opinions so for this reason she was feared by many opponents," according to Kolbjørn. All three sons, Harry in the U.S., Henry and Kolbjørn in Norway, were active in the labor movement and Kolbjørn wrote frankly, "Mother has surely influenced our views on the political line through her untiring fight."

Harry Lundeberg went to work when he was six, delivering milk to Oslo homes for a pittance. Later, he hauled firewood logs to the cellars of large apartment buildings. He still had time for fun. He was a good skater and able at running cross country and high

[23]*Pacific Shipper*, April 9, 1934; Larrowe, op. cit.; *San Francisco Chronicle* (San Francisco), May 2, 1934, May 8, 1934, May 9, 1934, May 10, 1934; Minutes, District Committee, International Seamen's Union, San Francisco, May 9, 1934, in "Strike — 1934" file, S.U.P. central Archive, Headquarters, San Francisco, hereinafter Strike-1934-HQ; George Larsen, typed letter [unsigned], May 10, 1934, in Seattle-1934-HQ; Paul Scharrenberg, *Statement on Behalf of the I.S.U. of A.*, N.R.A. Shipping Code Hearing, November 10, 1933, Chicago, I.S.U., 1933; Gunnar Lundeberg, interview, January, 1984. [24]Edward Coester, typed letter, November 17, 1935, Coester papers, Seattle S.U.P. Branch Archive.

jumping. "He was also fond of walking in the forests either alone or with friends," says Kolbjørn. "He often slept out for days in the forest during his trips."

Harry made his first trip to sea at 15, working as a deckhand on a pleasure yacht. When he graduated from high school at 17, his father sought a position for him in the municipal offices in Oslo. The boy had finished Kristiania High School with "fairly good" grades. He had not been a member of any of the political movements as a youth, although he belonged to sports clubs. But, at 14, he had already shown the direction his life would take. In Kolbjørn's eloquent words, "as a 14-year-old boy he was out fighting against the strikebreakers. He came home late at night with torn clothes from fighting with police and the strikebreakers."

Harry did not want an office job; he wanted to go to sea. The world war was on, maritime commerce was in chaos, and even in neutral Norway jobs were scarce. In the fall of 1918, a few months before the armistice, he signed on as a coal-passer in the Norwegian vessel *Rena*. The voyage took him to Africa, Australia, Java, India, and back to Norway. When they returned to the port of Bergen after nine months at sea, the engine crew, including Harry, were arrested, charged with mutiny in the Indian Ocean; they had complained about rotten food and "the steam had fallen." (Brother Kolbjørn's account, on which we must depend for these early years, does not specify the outcome of this premonitory incident.)

A liking for sailing ships soon threaded through Harry Lundeberg's seafaring career. After the steamer voyage in the *Rena*, in 1919, he signed on the full-rigged ship *Mafalda* of Dramen for three months, followed by a voyage in the bark *Oaklands* to Argentina and the South Atlantic, then to London. Next, he joined the big four-mast bark *Rewa*, ex *Alice A. Leigh*, in London, and made a voyage around the Cape of Good Hope and across the Southern Ocean to the coal port of Newcastle, New South Wales. He signed on with Captain P. Kennedy in the *Rewa* for a voyage to Auckland, New Zealand, and here followed Captain Kennedy to a new command, the bark *Rona*, when the mighty *Rewa* was laid up (eventually it was made into a breakwater).

The *Rona*, in which Harry Lundeberg voyaged across the Tasman Sea to Sydney, has been restored under her original name, *Polly Woodside*, and is now a proud feature of the Melbourne, Australia, waterfront.

Next he joined the ketch *Hawk*, apparently about the same time that maritime adventurer Alan Villiers was in her. Villiers later wrote: "She was a wretched little wooden thing over a half a century old, and even the Tasmanian deadbeats who had previously manned her could stand the parsimony of her skipper-owner no longer and fled.

All we know about Lundeberg's spell in the *Hawk* is that the captain's name was Sullivan and that Sullivan gave him a "Very Good" discharge. He was in her for five weeks. Probably, like Villiers, he found that long enough.

Lundeberg was issued his Certificate of Service as Able Seaman at San Francisco in August of 1923, and his Certificate of Efficiency as Lifeboat Man in December of the same year. The following year he paid off the splendid five-topmast American schooner, *K.V. Kruse* at Marshfield, Oregon in May and joined the four-mast schooner *Helene*, Captain Otto Lembke, in August. Apparently Harry thought well of the *Helene* and her captain because he made another trip to Honolulu in her in the winter of 1924-25. (Captain Lembke's son, Max, made seventeen voyages with his father in the *Helene*, the last in 1924. Lundeberg and young Lembke were to work in different ways toward the preservation of the *Balclutha* in San Francisco thirty years later, the latter as a member of the Ship Committee of the Maritime Museum.)

We next find Lundeberg making a voyage to Honolulu and return in the four-mast schooner *Alice Cooke*. Capt. Fred Klebingat has described this vessel:

"There were two Honolulu schooners I always was in love with; one of them was the *Alice Cooke*. She was a beauty when Captain Penhallow was skipper of her; his son is settled in Hawaii. I saw her first in Port Ludlow — the trucks of her masts were gilded; her nameboards were all picked out in gold leaf. The donkey engine glittered and glistened; if grease ran down, stop work and clean it up! It doesn't matter how long it takes to stow a piece of lumber, just stow it right. And if you used a pinch bar on the cargo, your time was up. Lewers & Cooke weren't in business to carry lumber; they were in business to sell lumber. They didn't want firewood; they wanted lumber . . .

"On Alice Cooke's birthday, if the schooner was in port, there was no work and a big spread. The Cooke family was a well-known one in the islands. My old barkentine, the S.N. *Castle*, was named for Samuel Castle, one of the two missionaries who founded the firm of Castle & Cooke.

"The other one I admired was the *Robert Lewers*, a beautifully kept up four-topmast schooner."

Next Lundeberg made a three-months voyage to the Hawaiian Islands in the four-topmast schooner *Minnie A. Caine*. The *Caine* was the setting for a best seller that swept the country at the end of the 1920s, *Cradle of the Deep*. It was written by Joan Lowell, daughter of Capt. Nick Wagner, who had salvaged the *Balclutha* after her shipwreck in Alaska in 1904. It is still a fine sea story although the captain's daughter took some liberties at the end of the book with a shipboard fire that supposedly destroyed the schooner, but in actuality caused less damage.

After a spell in the steam schooner *Norwood*, Lundeberg joined the five-masted barkentine *Forest Friend*, loading in Bellingham, Washington with a cargo of Douglas fir for New Caledonia (these Pacific Ocean voyages were all with lumber, almost invariably with a high deckload). The *Forest Friend* was one of three later day barkentines launched in 1919 in Grays Harbor, Washington. Capt. Zugeheur paid the 26-year old Lundeberg off in Newcastle, N.S.W.

The following year the Norwegian consulate in Sydney issued a Norwegian Seaman's Certificate of Identity. Lundeberg is described as having "Statue of Liberty on right arm, Girl on left arm." He plainly had ideas, but it would be six years before he obtained United States citizenship.

Lundeberg settled down on the famous old Oceanic liner *Sierra* for a number of trans-Pacific voyages in 1927. But he returned to sail in 1928 in the big modern four-mast schooner *Commodore*. The *Commodore*, only nine years old, was outfitted with steam schooner style double booms to facilitate the discharge of her lumber cargoes in Honolulu. She achieved a reputation as a racing vessel in her contests with the five-master *Vigilant* in the Honolulu trade in the 1930s. Her career was capped with a voyage around Cape Horn with lumber for South Africa in the Second World War.

A photograph in the possession of his son, Gunnar, shows the poop deck of the *Commodore*, the spanker eased off a bit on the port tack, and Harry Lundeberg at the wheel — a Viking come into his heritage.

Lundeberg, naturally, was an active unionist. He joined the Norwegian Seamen's Union in 1915 and the Seamen's Union of Australia in 1919 and also, according to some sources, the anarchosyndicalist Argentine equivalent of the I.W.W., the Federación Obrera Regional Argentina, or F.O.R.A. The latter was the strongest labor organization in Argentina and among the largest anarchosyndicalist organizations in the world. It was associated with the Spanish National Confederation of Labor, or C.N.T., which Lundeberg is said to have joined. The C.N.T. and F.O.R.A. stood as the main, recognized representatives of their countries' working classes, (unlike the large but diffuse anarcho-syndicalist organizations that also rose during the 1920s in Italy and Germany). Within the ranks of the F.O.R.A., the Federación Obrera Marítima or Maritime Workers Federation was a leading element, organizing dockworkers in the giant Buenos Aires port area as well as sailors. The F.O.M. frequently called strikes. Lundeberg may have participated.

In 1923, Harry Lundeberg came ashore in Seattle and transferred from the Australian union to the S.U.P. He then came into close contact with the I.W.W., and although it is not known whether he actually took out a red card, he later proudly alluded to his work in defense of the "Centralia boys," and the philosophy he had learned from his Norwegian Labor Party parents, as well as from comrades in the Norwegian, Australian, and Argentine unions, closely dovetailed with that of the Wobblies. In the years that followed, he became well-known and respected in the Seattle S.U.P. branch, so that during late 1933, when the branch set up a series of audit committees, he served on them.

The Seattle branch later that year saw agitation for reduction of S.U.P. dues to one dollar per month, with election of a local Seattle patrolman. The latter was a new concept for the Union. Larsen had commented early in 1934 to Carter in Portland that such a dues reduction would depend on enough men coming into the organization to lower administrative costs, but the issue of a Seattle patrolman had, it seems, been ignored by the leadership in San Francisco. In 1934, Lundeberg served on the Seattle strike committee alongside Mike Gallagher, William J. Doyle, Joe King, and Joe Hart.[25]

Effect of Walkout

On May 11, the district committee of the International Seamen's Union met in San Francisco. The S.U.P. was represented by Larsen and Selim Silver, with J. McGovern and Joseph Stanley as delegates for the Marine Firemen, and Eugene Burke and T. McGlenchey for the Marine Cooks and Stewards. The committee heard reports of the increasing participation in the strike of the West Coast sailors, most of them actually non-union; "many of the steam schooners are tied up because the crews have deserted them. Several riots have occurred along the front between the strikers, non-union men and police. A serious riot broke out this forenoon on Mission outside the Shipowners' Employment Bureau and, as a result, the fink hall has been closed up."

The Union held its regular meeting at headquarters on May 14, and received a communication from San Francisco I.L.A. Local 38-79, dated May 12. The letter from the dockworkers stated that "we undertook this action with great faith in our men and their ability to win." The meeting heard a resolution passed by the I.S.U. district committee, restating reliance on the N.R.A. code process: once again, contract ships should continue to be worked by the sailors, with non-contract employers asked to sign a one-year agreement including the Union's code proposals. A resolution of the members present at the meeting was then put and carried, calling for a $75 per month wage rate, with 75 cents per hour for overtime and full union conditions, and for Union members to walk off all non-contract ships; further, that strike votes on this resolution be carried out at headquarters and in the branches.

Because of the poor financial condition of the Union, the resolution also noted that no strike benefits would be paid. Finally, it was carried that a committee be elected to confer with I.L.A. Local 38-79, "to bring about an agreement whereby neither sailors nor longshoremen on strike shall return to work until demands of both have been satisfied." The strike vote

[25]Harry Lundeberg biographical information from S.U.P. membership records and Harry Lundeberg personal files, closed, at Headquarters, San Francisco, as well as Lundeberg family papers, and Karl Kortum, personal files; Kolbjørn A. Lundeberg, typed letter, February 11, 1960, Lundeberg family papers; on the F.O.R.A., see Sebastian Marotta, *El Movimiento Sindical Argentino*, 3 vols., Buenos Aires, Lacio, 1960-61, Calomino, 1970; also on Lundeberg, Irving Bernstein, *The Turbulent Years*, Boston, Houghton Mifflin, 1970, Pete Gill, typed letters, October 4, November 6, and November 13, 1933, Seattle-1934-HQ; Curtis Fields, Jr., "Able Seaman Lundeberg Speaks His Mind," *Seattle Post-Intelligencer* (Seattle), September 7, 1947; on the ketch *Hawk*, Alan Villiers, *The Set of The Sails*, London, Hodder and Stoughton, 1949. On the dues cut, George Larsen, letter cited, April 6, 1934; for strike committee roster, Seattle Strike Committee, typed letter, June 13, 1934, Seattle-1934-HQ.

was set for the next day, May 15, and Larsen, Scharrenberg, and Silver were elected to meet with the longshoremen.

The sailors' strike vote recorded on May 15 showed, in San Francisco, 55 in favor, 14 against, 1 disqualified; in Seattle, where the branch had agreed on May 14 to walk out, 54 in favor, none against or disqualified. In Portland, S.U.P. men were already being fed by the I.L.A.'s soup kitchen, and they voted 14 in favor, 1 against. Finally, in San Pedro, 8 cast their votes in favor with none against, and 1 disqualified, for a total of 131 supporting strike action, 15 against, and 2 disqualified coastwide.

The small numbers of voting members illustrate better than any other statement the weak condition of the Union after 1921. But the truly grim period in the organization's history had passed. The greatest challenge to the dependent status of seafaring workers in the history of this nation and the world, the West Coast maritime movement of the 1930s, had been born. Woe to those employers, government officials, "labor fakers," or agents of a foreign ideology, who would seek to stem this mighty force! Rank-and-file men who went to sea for a living, like Harry Lundeberg; men like George Larsen conscientious if limited in his vision; and their brothers on the docks and sympathizers in the rest of society, had begun to seize their destiny. Labor politics on the Pacific had changed forever.

On May 16, a continuation of the voting meeting agreed to strike the Dollar Steamship vessels, Oceanic & Oriental Freighters, and the Oceanic Company ships *Mariposa* and *Monterey*. On the other hand, the steel steam schooner *Lumberman* was exempted. Pickets were dispatched to the waterfront, the scab hall, "and other places where attempts might be made to hire non-union seamen." The San Francisco dailies, more concerned with violence and Communist involvement in the waterfront strike, reported the S.U.P. decision between headlines claiming plots to dynamite piers and other sensational stories of death and destruction. The Hearst-owned *San Francisco Examiner* stated that the strike had reached the inland port of Spokane, Washington.[26]

Pacific Shipper responded to the strike by warning of the presence of "professional agitators." And, indeed, the Communists had been active on the scene. The M.W.I.U. had declared itself "on strike" almost immediately after the I.L.A. had walked out; in years to come, the Communists would attempt to use this "fact" to prove the spurious claim that the M.W.I.U. was the leading militant force among the seamen. But the M.W.I.U. was not a union, but a tiny group of Communist functionaries who could do and say whatever they wanted without consulting any membership. It was not the same with the S.U.P., which had democratic traditions to which it firmly held, requiring a genuine strike poll of the members in good standing, no matter how few, during the course of a regular weekly meeting. For the S.U.P. leaders to unilaterally join the strike, without consultation of the ranks, would be to throw out the basic constitutional principles on which the Union had been founded.

For the M.W.I.U., the S.U.P. was the main enemy, rather than the shipowners. The issue of the Communist seamen's newspaper, the *Marine Workers' Voice*, for May 1934, repeated the Communist Party's past sectarian attacks: the I.S.U. was a "bulwark of capitalism," the I.W.W. and the Socialist Party were "wreckers of working-class unity," Edo Fimmen's radical International Transportworkers' Federation was "the Yellow (strikebreaking) Transport International."

Pacific Shipper was wrong in ascribing the entirety of the strike movement to the action of a few Muscovites. Neither the dockers nor the seamen needed the presence of Communist or even I.W.W. agitators to spark their movement. The grievances of the West Coast maritime workers were genuine, vividly-felt, and legitimate. The Communists, working through their group in the I.L.A. and with individuals in the S.U.P., as we shall see, attempted to seize control of the strike, but they never succeeded.

The Communists remained a parasitical group trying to climb aboard and dominate the unions' structures during the battle of 1934. Eventually, they convinced themselves, their followers, and later historians, who have worked largely with secondary sources, that they had indeed been the masters of this great movement. They were not. Even the I.L.A., in which they were active, maintained a strained relationship with them.[27]

From Washington, on May 16, Andrew Furuseth wrote to Larsen asking for "first-hand information. I do not know what to think," he commented. "Is the strike really under the leadership and management of the International Longshoremen's Union (sic) or is it ostensibly under their management but really under the management of the Communists? What seems to be the opinion of the teamsters . . . I have not the faintest idea of what we ought or what we can do so I have got no advice to give but, of course, I am hungry for information. I know that you fellows understand the situation there much better than anybody else, even better than the longshoremen themselves." Later, Furuseth again sought information from Larsen, wiring him on May 18, "Bewildered by newspaper squibs about Pacific strike Stop Wire facts by Western Union."

Larsen replied to the head of the International with a telegraphed statement that, although unknown to

[26]Minutes, District Committee, I.S.U., May 11, 1934,Seattle-1934-HQ; Headquarters Minutes, May 14, 1934; Pete Gill, typed letter, May 14, 1934, Seattle-1934-HQ; Carl Carter, typed letter, May 14, 1934 Portland-1934-HQ; Headquarters Minutes, May 15, 1934, and May 16, 1934; *San Francisco Chronicle*, May 15, 1934; *San Francisco Examiner* (San Francisco), May 15, 1934. [27]*Pacific Shipper*, May 14, 1934; Unsigned, "The Voice, Our Collective Organizer," and "ISH Leads Greek and Danish Seamen on General Strike," *Marine Workers' Voice*, May 1934; Minutes, San Francisco I.L.A. Strike Committee, May 13, 1934, in Anne Rand Memorial Research Library, International Longshoremen's and Warehousemen's Union Headquarters, San Francisco; for the classic Communist account of the movement, Mike Quin [Paul William Ryan], *The Big Strike*, Olema, Olema Publishing Co., 1949 [it would be difficult to imagine a more dishonest document—and one that had, in addition, gained so much unmerited credibility.]

the public until now, must stand as the single most eloquent statement of the background, motives, and sentiment of the movement: "Shipowners have sown the wind and are reaping the whirlwind Stop They defeated the maritime unions in 1921 with aid of Harding Administration Stop They stripped maritime personnel of wages and conditions until wage reductions reached 65 percent Stop Married seamen of all grades unable to support their families sought work as longshoremen, teamsters and other shore work suffering the hardships of newcomers Stop The shipowners after the defeat of seamen imposed harder and harder conditions on longshoremen Stop And shipowners kept on raiding the United States Treasury Stop This is common knowledge Stop Present strike flareup of trades wherever possible is not directed by labor union officials for they are swept along by this deep-seated resentment against the shipowners Stop The communists are loudmouthed but not in control Stop I am doing all I can to unite our side with the common cause Stop That is our only salvation Stop [undersecretary of labor] Edward McGrady I trust understands permanent peace in shipping callings can only be gained through a fair settlement for all branches."

On May 21, Furuseth answered "I have not the slightest doubt that the fight will be made as vigorous as circumstances will at all permit and this should bring back to the Union a lot of feeling that once belonged to it. You will understand I am glad of the action you have taken. I could not see any other thing to be done."

However, although one could hardly imagine a more humble and supportive approach to the West Coast members than that taken by Furuseth, the "old man" of the I.S.U., whose real outlook was little known outside the Union, had begun to serve as the target for an extended campaign of Communist defamation, in which the Muscovites sought to paint him as a strikebreaker, repeating that false charge day after day. The chief medium for this slander-mongering was to be the mimeographed throwaway published by the M.W.I.U. in San Francisco during the strike, titled the *Fo'c's'le Head*. Although in dealing with the I.L.A. dockers the Communists had adopted a more circumspect tactic, in their relations with the Sailors it was the uncautious M.W.I.U. that continued to set the tone.

Action in the Gulf

On May 18, a struggle much like that on the West Coast opened up in the Gulf of Mexico when seamen began walking off ships in Houston at the call of I.W.W. Marine Transport Workers Industrial Union 510. The Wobblies, who were remarkably well-established as the seamen's representatives in the Gulf, with active halls in the major regional ports, demanded "more men in the crew and standard shipping board wages," i.e., the 1921 scale of $62.50 per month, along with "1929 conditions:" eight A.B. seamen on deck with two ordinaries, a second cook and baker, watertenders on water tube jobs, another messman, three watches, no 'field days' (compulsory cleanup work aboard ship on days considered "off"), and time back for all overtime. "More Men in the Crew Means Less Men on the Beach!" the Wobblies counselled, reflecting Depression concerns over unemployment. The Sabine District longshoremen had been on strike since the beginning of May, and workers on the coastwise docks in Houston and Galveston now joined the walkout, along with the whole body of New Orleans longshoremen. On May 21, seamen in Galveston "walked out solid," the I.W.W. declared. It was later reported, as we will see, that the Communists scabbed on the Wobbly strike in the Gulf.[28]

The next regular S.U.P. weekly headquarters meeting took place on May 21 with 300(!) present, and saw election of a strike committee consisting of Carl Lynch, W.W. Caves, J. McLoughlin, Fred A. Kunce, and Nils Jensen, and appointment of a negotiating committee including Caves, Edward Schieler, and Herman Bach. Strike cards had been printed "to be issued to members and non- members alike as long as they have joined us in strike action for enforcement of our demands . . . It was an enthusiastic meeting, the men determined to carry out their duty and fight this struggle through to victory for recognition of the unions," the minutes stated.

It was reported that the I.L.A. had voted unanimously to support the demands of the Sailors. That same day, the Portland S.U.P. branch agent reported to his members that 150 pickets were on duty with two automobiles in use and that "the Sailors and the I.L.A. (are) pulling together 100%." Portland I.L.A. delegates sent to San Francisco had been instructed that no settlement should be approved until the sailors, firemen, and stewards obtained the closed shop. In Seattle, Pete Gill added as a postscript that the local Cereal Workers Federal Union had been locked out for refusing to act as strikebreakers against the dockworkers. The local I.L.A. had, with S.U.P. support, stated they would not end their walkout until the Cereal Workers were rehired.[29]

On the afternoon of May 21, the West Coast maritime movement buried its first martyr. Dick Parker, a 21-year-old I.L.A. picket who joined the union on May 13, had been killed on the night of May 14 in San Pedro. Other strikers had been shot in the legs and stomach. Harry Fisher, an I.L.A. mourner, wrote "all the wiles of the Merchants and Manufacturers and kindred anti-union combinations can never make me believe that such an upstanding, American, he-man lad could have had malice in his heart as he stood in the line of that murderous barrage of gas and bullets on the night of

[28]Andrew Furuseth, typed letter, May 16, 1934, telegram, May 18, 1934, George Larsen, draft of telegram, May 18, 1934, Andrew Furuseth, typed letter, May 21, 1934, all in Strike-1934-HQ; *Fo'c's'le Head* [San Francisco] file in the Graduate Social Science Library, University of California, Berkeley; I.W.W. strike calls, "San Francisco Waterfront Strikes, 1934; a Collection of Pamphlets, Broadsides, Etc., 2 Volumes," also in Graduate Social Sciences Library, University of California, Berkeley, hereinafter 1934-GSS-Berkeley. [29]Headquarters Minutes, May 21, 1934; Carl Carter, typed letter, May 21, 1934, Portland-1934-HQ; Pete Gill, typed letter May 21, 1934, Seattle-1934-HQ.

May 14." John Knudsen, an older, long-time member of the San Pedro I.L.A., later died of wounds suffered in the same incident.[30]

Minneapolis and Toledo

May 21 and 22 brought further stirring news from across the country. In San Francisco, the liberal *News* had reported NEW PEACE PLAN OFFERED IN DOCK STRIKE; but in Minneapolis, where members of the Teamsters Union had been on strike since May 15 for higher wages for truck drivers and unionization of newly-organized warehouse workers, a major clash came when employers attempted to move freight with scab drivers. Fighting began between the strikers, organized along virtual military lines, and scabs, deputies, and police, with numerous wounded and many arrests. On May 22, 5,000 strikers defeated hundreds of deputies in open combat. The deputies tore off their badges and fled. May 22 also saw dramatic developments in Toledo, Ohio. There, the Electric Auto-Lite Company had been struck since April 13, by the A.F.L. Auto Workers. The evening of the 22nd, mass picketing in open defiance of a federal court order led to hundreds of scabs refusing to leave the Auto-Lite plant in fear for their lives. Strikers began to battle company guards and tear gas bombs were thrown onto the picket lines from the factory.

Minneapolis and Toledo, 1934's two other "big strikes," shook the nation with headlines bigger, at that point, than those produced by the West Coast maritime walkout. Fighting in Toledo continued through May 23 and, next day, National Guard officers arrived at the struck plant.

The struggles in Minneapolis and Toledo, like that on the West Coast, were taking a new shape. But in contrast with the maritime movement, in which the Communists and even the Wobblies played a secondary role, following after the rank-and-file, in the Midwest left-wingers had genuinely taken the lead in organizing. However, the radical "vanguard" to be found there came not from the Communist Party but from tiny dissident socialist and communist groupings; in Minneapolis, the U.S. followers of Leon Trotsky, who belonged to the Communist League of America, and in Toledo, an independent organization, the American Workers' Party, led by a minister, A.J. Muste, operating through a "front" organization, the Lucas County Unemployed League.

In Toledo, with the arrival of the Guard officers, the struggle became semi-insurrectionary. At the onset of picketing on May 24, deputies and, apparently, the Guardsmen, again showered the strikers and their sympathizers with tear gas bombs while scabs inside the plant pelted the pickets with nuts and bolts. The radical leaders urged the picketers to remain peaceful while the sympathetic crowd reached 10,000. Several pickets were arrested; the turning point came when a deputized company guard beat an old man "in full sight of most of the ten thousand people," according to writer Louis Adamic. The crowd lunged into the deputies, police and Guard, throwing rocks and bricks and cutting off the plant's power supply. In Adamic's words, they then "rammed the factory doors with great timbers" (actually telephone poles). "Groups fought with the police and deputies through most of the night, while the scabs were prisoners in the lightless plant."

In 1984, the author of this history spoke with Ted Selander, a leader of the Toledo fight, who attested to the great drama and heroism of the struggle; Selander broke down crying while describing the scene.

The day afterward, Guard troops marched to the plant, touching off two more days of fighting with two dead reported among the strikers and many wounded on both sides. Another account points out that no Guardsmen had been called up from the Toledo area for duty at the plant since the sentiment of the community was so clearly with the strikers that even the police seemed to side with the angry crowds. Adamic commented "Toledo gave millions of workers all over the country . . . an important lesson, a clear suggestion — namely, that they physically and openly defy injunctions and face danger to their lives." The lesson was not to be lost on the West Coast.[31]

Back on the Coast

By the third week of May, after only 10 days, at least *8,000* sailors had joined the Pacific maritime strike. The shipowners had begun hiring longshore strikebreakers as soon as the work stoppage began, but *Pacific Shipper* noted with dissatisfaction in a survey of dock operations after only some 10 days, that "work accomplished by strikebreakers, many of them inexperienced and laboring under unfavorable circumstances, was by no means comparable to the numbers actually employed. In some cases, at the Northwest ports, the operators themselves ordered the workers to desist as a precaution against violence to them." The slow work by scabs had backed up foreign ships in the coastal ports; and, in addition, the Australian trades were threatened by the probability that dockworkers Down Under would refuse to touch scab-loaded bottoms.

The walkout had brought about "partial strangulation" of California business and a "blockade" in the Pacific Northwest, according to the *Shipper*. Much of the lumber industry was shut down, and California fruit and vegetable growers were loud in their complaints. *Pacific Shipper* was worried by the effects of the strike on the police; although it reported that in Los Angeles and San Francisco "good order" had been

---

[30]Harry Fisher, "On the Short Life and Death of Dick Parker," *Random Lengths* (San Pedro), August-September 1983; on John Knudsen, *Western Worker* (San Francisco) leaflet ["Baby Western"], number 2, n.d., 1934-GSS- Berkeley, where he appears as 'Tom Knudson,' and Markholt, letter cited. [31]*San Francisco News* (San Francisco), May 22, 1934. On Minneapolis and Toledo, Goldbloom et al., op. cit.; further on Toledo, Louis Adamic, op. cit. Adamic's account, which I have followed, differs slightly from that of Goldbloom et al. Also on Minneapolis and Toledo, Art Preis, *Labor's Giant Step*, New York, Pioneer Publishers, 1964; on Minneapolis, Farrell Dobbs, *Teamster Rebellion*, New York, Monad, 1972, and on Toledo, Ted Selander, public talk, San Francisco, February 19, 1984.

maintained, the effort in Portland and Seattle was "vastly less" successful, for there the police proved faint-hearted in confronting strikers who were, in many cases, their neighbors and relatives. On one ship in Seattle, "ships' officers held the rioters back at the points of their revolvers" during an attack by strikers on scabs; most of the latter chose to vacate the area. On the other hand, strikers in Puget Sound had responded to Alaska's supply problems by allowing sailing of one vessel, the schooner *C. S. Holmes*, northward. The Northwest unions were threatening a general strike if troops were brought in; although British Columbia dockers continued working, they were considering joining the movement. In contrast with the *Shipper*, whose reporting of the strike was anti-union but notably factual and realistic, the dailies kept up a steady barrage of sensational and often-false reports. In some cases, the misleading news purveyed by the dailies reflected a certain erroneous optimism: on Friday, May 25, for example, the *San Francisco News* again headlined DOCK STRIKE PEACE EXPECTED BY MONDAY.[32]

Pete Gill had written to headquarters that over 200 picketers, round the clock, including non-members as well as members, were showing the S.U.P. flag in Seattle. In San Francisco, W.W. Caves, freshly elected to the post of strike committee chairman, replied that an average of 3-4000 men were actively patrolling the waterfront with 610 signed up for picket duty and issued strike cards. At the regular San Francisco meeting of May 28, J. O'Brien, A. Palm, J. Swanson, H.J. "Blackie" Vincent, and S. Bayspool were added to the strike committee. A joint relief committee kitchen had been set up with the cooperation of the other striking unions, at 84 Embarcadero.[33]

The Communists, who had previously been active only within the I.L.A., had established some points of contact in the Sailors' ranks. On May 25, W.W. Caves appeared for the I.S.U. with Sam Telford from the M.W.I.U., to represent the seamen at an I.L.A. strike committee meeting in San Francisco. On May 26, Carter in Portland wrote to headquarters that he had met with a committee representing the "Red Element," who had "demanded the right to be allowed to be on the front and do some picketing. But he refused to grant them their demands telling them they were nothing else but a lot of finks and skunks." However, he had promised to discuss the matter with the I.L.A. local leaders, and "we came to a conclusion that as long as they don't stir up any trouble and do everything peacefully we could not refuse them to be on the front. We contacted the Reds the next morning and told what action (had been) taken the night before, giving them a clear understanding that we did not want any 'soap-box' talk. No literature of any description to be distributed on the waterfront. So at the present time, they have about five pickets on the front where we have in the neighborhood of three hundred and fifty men," he concluded.

On May 30, at noontime, the S.U.P.'s Maritime Hall at 59 Clay Street in San Francisco was the scene of a "special meeting" including delegations from the I.L.A., Sailors, Firemen, and the M.W.I.U. Carl Lynch, strike committee secretary, stated that an ultimatum had been delivered from the longshore union declaring that the S.U.P. must "either call a mass meeting of all rank and file seamen, regardless of union affiliation to formulate demands to be presented to the shipowners, or else the longshoremen will vote to return to work and leave the seamen holding the bag."

This was a gambit by the Communists to use control of mass meetings as a means to impose parity between the Communist M.W.I.U. and the S.U.P., or even better, the simple substitution of the former for the latter, as the seamen's representatives. Lynch reported that this demand that the S.U.P. call a mass meeting had been amended by John Schomaker, a member of the I.L.A. strike committee, who later admitted membership in the Communist Party. Schomaker declared that "if we could come to no agreement in regard to holding the mass meeting by five p.m. today . . . the longshoremen would call a mass meeting of all striking seamen for the same purpose." Credentials were additionally presented by one Harry F. Meyer, who belonged to no union, but supposedly represented 1,000 rank and file seamen in San Pedro. At three that afternoon, a full Sailors' strike committee meeting was held in the hall, chaired by Caves, with seven members in attendance. The proposal for a mass meeting of all striking seamen, as put forward by the M.W.I.U. and the I.L.A., was unanimously rejected.

A report submitted by the Sailors' strike committee covering the period from May 27 to June 4 emphasized the Union's rebuff to Communist overtures for fusion with the M.W.I.U., and proudly noted "the spirit of loyalty to the I.S.U. and to the A.F. of L." that marked a mass meeting of 1,800-2,000 seamen held on June 1. The success of the meeting had been noted by the I.L.A. strike committee which, on June 2, observed that federal labor undersecretary Edward F. McGrady had called for an election pitting the I.S.U. against the M.W.I.U.; the longshoremen's representatives agreed to back whichever organization gained a majority of votes. That day Larsen wrote to Carter: "we have the reds on the run."[34]

In the meantime, the Toledo struggle, which had gained considerable space in the national press, had ended. With the occupation of the Auto-Lite plant by

[32]*Pacific Shipper*, May 19, 1934; *San Francisco News*, May 25, 1934. Headquarters Minutes, May 28, 1934. [33]Pete Gill, typed letter, May 22, 1934, Seattle-1934-HQ; W.W. Caves, typed letter, May 24, 1934, Strike-1934-HQ; Headquarters Minutes, May 28, 1934, ibid. [34]Minutes, San Francisco I.L.A. Strike Committee, May 25,1934; Carl Carter, typed letter, May 26, 1934, Portland-1934-HQ; Minutes, San Francisco S.U.P. Strike Committee "Special Meeting," May 30, 1934, Regular Meeting, May 30, 1934, and Special Open Meeting, June 1, 1934, Carl Lynch, Synopsis of Work Accomplished by the Strike Committee, S.U.P., During the Week of May 27 to June 4, all in Strike-1934-HQ; on Schomaker's C.P. activity, Klehr, op. cit.; Minutes, San Francisco I.L.A. Strike Committee, June 2, 1934; George Larsen, typed letter [unsigned], June 2, 1934, Portland-1934-HQ.

troops, "the inevitable happened," according to the authors of *Strikes Under The New Deal*. "A volley was fired into the crowd and two men fell dead and six wounded. All night long ambulances and fire apparatus screamed into the fight zone." The Central Labor Union began organizing for a general strike. Tear gas continued to be used against the strikers and the total of wounded reached 200. Ninety of the 103 affiliates of the Central Labor Union were ready to walk out. On June 1, over 10,000 workers and radicals paraded through the city in anticipation of mass action. Announcement of acceptance of workers' demands by the management of the Edison Electric Company, where another strike was in preparation, blocked the general strike; the next day, the Auto-Lite Company also capitulated. Toledo had ended as a labor victory, thanks to the threat of a general strike.

In the Pacific Northwest

In the Pacific Northwest, the I.L.A., on a proposal of its Tacoma local, had set up a Joint Northwest Strike Committee representing dockworkers in the ports of Bellingham, Port Angeles, Everett, Seattle, Tacoma, Olympia, Aberdeen, Raymond, Longview, Port Townsend, Port Gamble, Anacortes, Port Ludlow, Vancouver (Washington), Astoria and Portland. As May came to an end, the Northwest committee had begun discussion of the most important achievement of the 1934 struggle; the idea of a Waterfront Federation embracing all the marine crafts. With the conclusion of the strike later in the year, the groundwork for such a federation would be seriously laid. Today it is difficult to establish in which geographical area the Pacific Coast longshoremen's traditional sentiment for a maritime federation first re-emerged; the San Francisco I.L.A., at a special meeting on May 24, had carried a motion calling for the Teamsters, marine officers, unlicensed seamen, radio operators, and shipyard workers to join the longshoremen in such a federation.

Historical accounts, both those sponsored by labor and those produced by academics, have traditionally identified San Francisco as the center of the 1934 coast waterfront rebellion; but the *highest level of militancy* came in the Northwest. Pilcher, the earlier-noted Portland docker-turned-anthropologist, aptly declares of the longshore union literature on the strike that "most of it is concerned with affairs only in San Francisco. Indeed one would receive the impression that there was almost no activity in any port except San Francisco, if the union literature were to be taken at face value." Pilcher intimates this reflects a bias toward the Communist Party, which was important only in San Francisco, and inactive or non-existent in the Northwest, the main arena of militant action. Although the present account focuses on San Francisco, as well, Pilcher's point is very well taken.

According to a recent history of the Tacoma longshoremen, *The Working Waterfront* by Ronald Magden and A.D. Martinson, "in the Pacific Northwest, strike activity took place mainly in Seattle, Portland, and Everett . . . Tacoma escaped most of the violence because Commencement Bay employers made few efforts to import scabs and force the docks open. Perhaps the reason for the reluctance of the employers to break the picket lines was the formation of a special unit of Tacoma longshoremen called the Flying Squad." In the first three days of the strike, some 600 Tacoma dockers and 200 from Everett had "stormed the Seattle waterfront" clearing out scabs, and the Tacoma Flying Squad "spent much time in Seattle and other Washington State ports strengthening the ranks of their co-workers whenever employers threatened to open a port with scabs." One of the leaders of the Tacoma dockers, T.A. "Tiny" Thronson, would later emerge as an ally of the S.U.P. in internecine fighting between the waterfront unions. Tacoma's labor movement was also the source for a threat that troops would be met by a Northwest general strike.

Pacific Shipper reported the strike in San Pedro was largely carried by the seamen rather than the longshoremen, who failed to successfully strike the port. The southland harbor was operating as a "comparatively 'open port' " as far as dock work was concerned, but could not fully function because of the actions of the ships' crews.

During this period, Joseph P. Ryan, top executive of the International Longshoremen's Association, was touring the Northwest promising an imminent settlement of the strike. Although Ryan's so-called "settlement," better referred to as a "surrender," was roundly condemned by the militants in Tacoma and elsewhere, a newly-organized joint I.S.U. strike committee in San Francisco, representing the Sailors, the Marine Firemen, and the Marine Cooks and Stewards, decided in the first week of June to send Caves to Seattle in the company of an I.L.A. representative "to attempt to counteract the propaganda being spread there by Mr. Ryan." Caves was replaced as strike committee chairman by Blackie Vincent.

With combativeness running high in the Northwest, Caves' presence was hardly necessary to counter Ryan; it is not impossible that he was sent northward to remove the presence in San Francisco of an apparent pro-M.W.I.U. individual. Conflict between the S.U.P. and the Communists was approaching the point of irresolvable crisis.[35]

[35]Goldbloom, et al., op. cit., and Adamic, op. cit. On the Northwest Joint Strike Committee, see Minutes, Anne Rand Memorial Research Library, I.L.W.U. On the Waterfront Federation, Minutes, I.L.A. Local 38-79, San Francisco, Special Meeting, May 24, 1934, held by S.U.P. in Strike-1934-HQ. On Portland, Pilcher, op. cit. On Tacoma, Ronald Magden and A.D. Martinson, *The Working Waterfront*, Tacoma, International Longshoremen's and Warehousemen's Union Local 23 and Port of Tacoma, A Municipal Corporation, 1982 [the importance of this work, which draws on the efforts of Tacoma I.W.W. and labor historian Ottilie Markholt, for general West Coast waterfront labor historiography as well as for that of the S.U.P., cannot be too highly emphasized.] On Caves' trip to the Northwest, Carl Lynch, Synopsis of Work Done by the Joint Strike Committee During the Week of June 4th to June 11th, 1934, and Minutes, San Francisco S.U.P. Strike Committee, June 7, 1934, both in Strike-1934-HQ; on the situation in San Pedro, *Pacific Shipper*, May 28, 1934.

CHAPTER VII
Year of Rebirth Part II
(1934)

The Communist problem had become acute by the first week of June, after only three weeks on strike. As we have seen, the daily press kept up a steady chorus identifying the maritime strike with the subversive aims of Moscow-controlled organizations. The Communists themselves had strongly contributed to this false front, erected by the local dailies to "explain" the strike to the public. One tool used by the Communists was a two-sided, printed leaflet with the heading *Western Worker*, under which was printed "This Bulletin is issued by the Western Worker for the striking Longshoremen, and its contents are authorized by the Publicity Committee of the Strikers." Known as the "Baby Western," this sheet was issued, it seems, to substitute during the strike for the *Waterfront Worker*, the mimeographed Communist dockside throwaway. The parent weekly *Western Worker* carried relatively little real news about the strike; most of its contents followed then-standard Communist journalistic practices, according to which it was sufficient to concentrate on "creative" (that is, invented) reports of Communist successes in demonstrations, strikes, etc., around the world, along with hysterical appeals to join. The "Baby Western", on the other hand, gave the strong impression that the Communists were in control of the strike, which they definitely were not.

These leaflets promoted the M.W.I.U., referring to "the Marine Workers Union leading the strike" in Seattle and claiming 1300 members signed up for the spurious "union." A typical "Baby Western" headline read "Many Labor Organizations Support Us." Whether the "us" referred to the strikers or the Communists was left unclear. The regular *Western Worker* from which the "baby's" nameplate had been borrowed was identified on its front page as the official organ of the Communist Party.

For its part, the San Francisco I.L.A. brought out responsible daily strike bulletins that avoided a hysterical tone.

To further confuse the situation, the M.W.I.U. had an additional publication, its mimeographed *Fo'c's'le Head*, which concentrated its fire not on the shipowners, but on Furuseth, Scharrenberg, and the other I.S.U. leaders, whom it falsely accused of attempting to sell out the strike. It is an unpleasant task to read through this periodical today; the insults directed at the I.S.U. leadership are so extreme, so unfair, and so low that one wonders how the M.W.I.U. partisans had the effrontery to distribute this divisive paper, during the strike. Their main attacks were on Furuseth, who was depicted as senile and, by hints, homosexual. Unfortunately, it had to be admitted that to an extent they were effective. Hyman Weintraub, Furuseth's biographer states that, "repeated often enough to men who scarcely knew the 'Old Man of the Sea' and who knew little of the union's history, the smear campaign was successful."

The Sailors began a series of organizational steps to isolate the M.W.I.U. An open meeting on June 6 allowed two rank-and-file members of the Communist "union" to attend, but as observers only. In response to the Communist paper offensive, the Sailors decided to produce a throwaway sheet of their own. The S.U.P. resolved to obtain a mimeograph "to issue a publication, to be thrown away on the waterfront. This is to counteract the poison publicity of the M.W.I.U."

The Communists had even encountered criticism within the I.L.A. ranks for their irresponsible activities. At a longshore strike committee meeting on June 9, after an I.L.A. report of an agreement with the Teamsters to monitor movement of scab freight, the M.W.I.U. was forced to state, almost apologetically, that it did not wish to break up any union. The splitting attacks on the S.U.P. pursued by the Communists were, from the beginning, seen by the strikers themselves as what they were: a form of strikebreaking in the interest of Communist control.

June 12 saw a meeting of the I.S.U. joint strike committee in which, once again, the "question of 'M.W.I.U.' (was) discussed at length." The day before, the strike committee had admitted a delegation from the M.W.I.U., consisting of Sam Telford and Q.A. Gorgan, who proposed a joint approach to the federal government to demand relief for strikers. The Sailors replied that they would handle their own relief, without going "begging" to federal authorities. At the June 12 meeting, a motion was carried that the M.W.I.U. be excluded from all future meetings.

W.W. Caves reported at that meeting, having returned from Seattle, that two agreements with Alaska shipping employers releasing vessels had been signed. The Alaska agreements, reflecting the isolation of the then-Territory and its need for supplies, included full recognition of the unions in both the longshore and seafaring crafts.

The Sailors then carried a motion that their San Francisco strike committee and the I.L.A. committee should meet jointly. This was a milestone in the history of the strike, and, indeed, of maritime labor: the waterfront workers were now truly united. The same day, this unity trend was reinforced when the S.U.P.'s H.L. Whiting was admitted to the I.L.A. Joint Northwest Strike Committee. On June 13, a mass meeting of the Sailors continued discussion of the Alaska issue, since the ranks were not convinced that the merciful gesture of releasing vessels was correct, and a balloting committee was set up to supervise a vote, including Bennie Barrena, Joe Voltero, and Morgan Rock. It was then "regularly moved and seconded and carried unanimously, that Brother W.W. Caves, be given a vote of confidence."

On June 14, at a meeting of the I.S.U. joint strike committee, from which Caves was absent, a resolution written by him was read, "which is intended as an answer to the accusations which have been publicly made that this strike is being run by a bunch of Communists." The resolution voiced "emphatic protest" at such "libelous statements made without a scintilla of truth," and went on to "absolutely repudiate any and all Communist organizations including the so-called Marine Workers Industrial Union."

The next day, in a meeting of the I.L.A. strike committee, the M.W.I.U. admitted that they had been labelled as strikebreakers. They had issued a notice that the strike had ended. The Communists at the meeting explained this by arguing that they believed it to be true. Harry Bridges appeared at a special mass meeting of the seamen that same evening to denounce the Sailors' anti-communist disclaimer of hours before, saying "that such resolutions were dangerous to the complete unity of strikers."

Rumors of War

The Sailors gave little immediate reaction. Much more important matters were at stake by this time; the State Belt Railroad, which served the San Francisco waterfront, had continued moving scab freight throughout the strike. Although owned, like the San Francisco docks themselves, by the state of California, the Belt Line was operated by the Santa Fe, Southern Pacific, and Western Pacific rail companies, none of which was well known for union sympathy, while Santa Fe was notorious for its anti-union conduct. The joint I.S.U. strike committee had appointed a committee to meet with an equivalent I.L.A. committee "for the purpose of laying plans for direct action against the Belt Line." Indeed, while the Sailors' leadership had been occupied with the attempts of the Communists to gain control of the movement, a series of major incidents had taken place away from the Union's internal conflicts.

Most notably, continuous attacks by police had swung a certain section of public opinion toward the strikers, especially in San Francisco. Further, rumors of possible strike action on the East Coast and Gulf were spreading. Bargemen on the lines serving the Bay and connecting rivers were prepared to join the movement. In Portland, the strikers had issued a public challenge to Mayor Joseph K. Carson, asking "why have you had nothing to say about the intolerable conditions which brought on the strike? You drag the red herring of communism across the trail. Has no one ever told you that the only agitator we need fear is injustice?"

Meanwhile, the I.L.A.'s international president Joseph P. Ryan was trumpeting the claim to the dailies that the strike was "settled." The Ryan "settlement" called for a joint union-employer hiring hall, preference for union members (without a closed shop), and arbitration of wages and conditions. But Ryan was out-of-step with the rank and file. The dockers sought victory, and nothing less. Further, Ryan's proposals offered the striking seamen nothing. On June 17, the I.L.A. met in San Francisco to vote on Ryan's proposals.

At a San Francisco longshore mass meeting with 3,000 present, the I.L.A. voted to reject the Ryan "settlement," mainly because of its betrayal of the seamen, and called for election of a joint marine strike committee composed of five delegates from each of the striking unions. An inter-union liaison committee had first met on June 14 but played no executive role; now, however, the new broad strike committee assumed leadership of the movement.

No member of the Sailors' Union was officially invited to the I.L.A. mass meeting, but Caves was admitted and spoke in his capacity as chairman of the Sailors' strike committee. He *repudiated* the anti-communist resolution of which he had been the author, claiming he was forced to sign it. That evening, Caves called a mass meeting of the striking seamen, on his own, without the knowledge of the rest of the S.U.P. strike committee. There he argued for recognition of the M.W.I.U. and permitted that organization's leader, Telford, to speak. A committee of five was elected to represent the S.U.P. on the new joint marine body, including Caves.

On Monday, June 18, Caves made a number of charges in the presence of a reporter from the San Francisco *Call-Bulletin*, a Hearst daily, repudiating the Sailors' strike demands and attacking the Union's official representatives. He strongly assailed George Larsen, using "strong and profane language" to affirm his support for the "United Front" rather than the "I.S.U." We need not emphasize that the I.S.U. had done nothing to damage the *real* united front that then existed with the striking longshoremen. "United

Front", to Caves meant "United with the M.W.I.U.," as he himself admitted.

The *Call-Bulletin*, an evening paper, seized on Caves' statements and that afternoon revealed them to the general public. Larsen then suspended Caves from the Union strike committee. Caves, in turn, provoked the storming of Larsen's office by an angry crowd of union rank-and-filers. Although Larsen showed them the Hearst sheet, they threatened and vilified him before leaving.

At the regular union meeting that night, Caves' suspension was repudiated by the membership, following his pleas of loyalty and his suggestion that if the members believed the Hearst press, they should expel him from the Union. Caves was reinstated to the S.U.P. strike committee and named officially to the Joint Marine Strike Committee (J.M.S.C.). The other S.U.P. delegates to the J.M.S.C. were Jack O'Brien, Justus Swanson, Herbert Mills, and Herman Bach.

The next morning (June 19) Mayor Angelo Rossi of San Francisco held a meeting in his office with Harry Bridges of the I.L.A. This followed, as it happened, on a session of the Joint Marine Strike Committee to which the M.W.I.U. was refused entry, even as observers without a vote. Bridges had chosen to develop negotiations through the Mayor's office, so long as protection against blacklisting of strikers and a joint settlement for all the unions could be secured. That night Caves spoke at a meeting of 10,000 people in Civic Auditorium, with Rossi in attendance, that was called to explain the talks. Caves reversed himself once more and expressed himself in favor of the M.W.I.U., publicly denouncing Larsen and violating the S.U.P. members' oath of obligation by revealing the proceedings of the previous night's Union meeting.

On the 20th, the Joint Marine Strike Committee sent five I.L.A. members, five seamen, and one representative for each of the other striking unions to a second meeting with the Mayor. At the joint marine meeting held that night, in the ships clerks' hall, the M.W.I.U. made another attempt at a seat, this time as ships' scalers rather than seamen. Early in the day the M.W.I.U. had reported to the I.L.A. that some 325 striking scalers were unrepresented on the joint committee, and the I.L.A. had recommended or demanded, unsuccessfully in any case, that the M.W.I.U. be seated as their delegates.

Later in the night, the Sailors' strike committee heard Caves defend his policies, plus the M.W.I.U., its representation on the joint marine committee and its demands. He claimed that any disagreements between him and other members of the Sailors' committee were motivated only by his opponents' personal jealousy. Jack O'Brien then lashed Caves for seeking to represent the M.W.I.U. rather than the S.U.P., and for thus breaking his oath of obligation as a Union member. O'Brien cited Caves' M.W.I.U. advocacy at the June 19th public event, where none of the other speakers had even mentioned the Communist group.

In reply to continuing criticism, Caves defended the M.W.I.U.'s slander campaign, saying "I have never seen anything in the *Fo'c's'le Head* that isn't true and I think the I.S.U. should be criticized." O'Brien finally demanded to know if Caves had even taken the member's oath of obligation to the Union, and on examining his union membership book it was found that he had not, and was therefore not a full member of the organization.

Caves' offensive collapsed at that point. Although he promised a "fight to the finish" he was allowed to withdraw from the meeting, and a motion to remove him from the office of strike committee chairman was carried unanimously. He was warned not to make any more statements in the name of the committee, and was replaced by Herbert Mills. A firm stand against seating of the M.W.I.U. was recommended, along with an investigation of the amount the M.W.I.U. was actually contributing to the joint strike relief kitchen. Caves was allowed to remain a member of the S.U.P. strike committee and the negotiating committee, but by June 24 he had been labelled a traitor by the Portland branch and was suspended from the strike committee, "because he has not been around for three days, and because his attitude and general disposition seems to inject a spirit of dissension in the Committee." His place was taken by J. Evans. On June 25, the regular weekly Union meeting voted not to accept the credentials of any so-called 'United Front' representatives, i.e. Communists.

The "Caves affair" was over; the reborn Sailors' Union had won its first major battle with Communist disruptors. It would not, of course, be the last. But at least, as Carl Lynch noted, it was now possible to "awaken both the strike committee, and the pickets, out of the stupor that has come over us in the past ten days."

It is tantalizing to speculate at Caves' motives. It may be that he was not, after all, a secret Communist or sympathizer, but simply an ambitious individual who, after serving on the strike committee, reading the daily newspaper reports of Communist domination in the strike, and falling under the influence of one or two of the more glib "comrades," decided that the party, not the unions, represented the wave of the future. However, given the precarious hold of the Communists on the coat-tails of the movement, in a situation where even their M.W.I.U. could not gain admission to the Joint Marine Strike Committee, the argument of strong overall Communist influence in the movement swaying the man seems unlikely. But what seems unlikely is unfortunately precisely the thesis that would be subscribed to by many historians: that Communist prestige and power in the movement were irresistible. The Communists played, in reality, as we are beginning to see, only a very restricted role. It may be that some person or persons on the Communist side reached Caves with a proposal that was simply too tempting to refuse. For Caves, or anybody else in the Sailors' Union, to have gone to such lengths on their behalf indicates some factor beyond the excitement of the moment: either a previous, but unadmitted, affiliation, or, again, a convincing proposal made to him personally.

Evidence that Caves was not simply a fledgling demagogue drawn into events is provided by M.W.I.U. literature distributed during this period on the East Coast. For example, in Philadelphia, the M.W.I.U. issued leaflets claiming that as of May 20, "I.S.U. Rank and File repudiates proposal of their leaders to split United Front and demand reinstatement of Chairman Caves of Strike Committee and UNITY with M.W.I.U. throughout present 'Strike' action." Knowledge of the "Caves problem" on the other side of the continent strongly suggests some kind of coordination if not control.[1]

Action in Seattle

Dramatic events were taking place in Seattle that would foretell the course of the movement in San Francisco. On the pretext of the Ryan "settlement," the Seattle employers prepared for a forcible "opening of the port." On June 18, it was reported that the city's police had been reorganized along military lines, with squads equipped with gas, smoke bombs, and shotguns, and a fleet of cars prepared for service day or night. A cavalry section of 20 men had been set up.

Seattle's "open port" was set to begin operations on June 20. In Portland on June 19, two men were arrested in a crowd that gathered at the home of a scab. The next day, Seattle turned out 450 police. Two hundred deputies were dispatched to dockside guard duty, with 150 in reserve to protect scabs. But 100 strikers blocked work on the wharves by sitting on the Great Northern railroad tracks and thus stopping switching at Pier 40. The pickets also turned back trucks with supplies for the police and scabs, and persuaded a city utility crew not to install police floodlights.

June 21 saw a battle at Pier 41 in which Sailors' Union member Ole Helland was wounded in the head by a gas grenade. Union representatives sought to prevent a massacre by warning the strikers not to sacrifice themselves to the machine guns of the police. Three strikers in all were injured when an attempt to stop a switch engine by another mass blocking of the tracks was answered by a mounted police charge, with clubs swinging. In response, the unions cancelled the agreement for movement of Alaska-bound ships.

"Opening the Ports": San Francisco

With the June 17 rejection by the rank-and-file of the Ryan "settlement," the strikers' enemies in San Francisco, including the Waterfront Employers Union represented by T.G. "Tear Gas" Plant, and the anti-union Industrial Association, an old enemy of the Sailors, declared a similar intention to "open the port" by force. The Industrial Association assumed responsibility for this coup, securing the needed warehouse space and vehicles and coordinating with police. The lines were unmistakably drawn and the decisive clash was approaching. After June 20 and its second meeting with Mayor Rossi, the Joint Marine Strike Committee repeatedly sent communications to the Mayor, but they were virtually unheeded.

The Joint Marine Strike Committee at its June 21 meeting reported word received by Bridges of looming Federal action. "Opening of the port" in the Bay Area was now set for June 24. A letter of protest to Rossi was ignored. On June 24, a "Special Strike Bulletin" issued by the S.U.P. strike committee warned "The next few days will tell the story. We feel that we are nearing the crisis, the most important time of the strike. Every man who is honestly fighting the shipowners, fighting for a decent living, will be on his toes! Now as never before, we are in need of good conscientious fighting pickets. Finks, rats, and yellow bellies may go home and sleep, if there are any such hanging around! Mr. John Shipowner, and our 'Industrial Association,' are planning to break the strike! They have a fleet of trucks all ready to go, and they have thugs, gunmen and scabs already to man them. They will attempt to open the docks in the very near future! . . . Are we going to lay down? Have we fought this thing for thirty eight days, only to be broken?"

Calling attention to members like Johnnie Lavoie, a prominent S.U.P. militant, and Bruce Pfeiffer, who were recuperating from wounds received in the battles with police and scabs, the union declared, "Strikers! Have you shed your blood in vain? Shall we tell the people of San Francisco that our brothers out in the Marine Hospital, were injured in a lost cause? Or shall we tell them that we will fight this thing to a finish! The answer rests with you! And make no mistake about it, you will be called upon to answer! And you must have your answer ready at a moment's notice!"

The committee went on to warn that "the employers have something up their sleeves." Turning to the daily press, they stated "Newspapers are notorious liars! No man with average intelligence believes everything he reads. Many smart people believe nothing they read. They wait for proof. Smart people think for themselves. There is a lot of poison publicity floating around these days. Most of it is directed against our union . . . Just remember to think for yourself." This latter point — *"think for yourself"* — was to be consistently emphasized by the S.U.P. leaders.

The committee also noted that "there are several 'mystery' cars reported, circulating around, . . . said to be filled with hired rats, and thugs, who specialize

---

[1]*Western Worker* leaflet ["Baby Western"], unnumbered [number 1?], I.L.A. official strike bulletins, both in 1934-GSS-Berkeley; *Fo'c's'le Head*, see note 28, Chapter VI; Hyman Weintraub, *Andrew Furuseth*, Berkeley, University of California Press, 1959; Carl Lynch, Secretary, Minutes of the Meetings of the [San Francisco S.U.P.] Strike Committee During the Month of June 1934, Synopsis of Work Done, Minutes of "Mass Meetings," Etc., Strike-1934- HQ; Ottilie Markholt, letter, cited in Note 10, on Alaska agreements; Minutes, San Francisco I.L.A. Strike Committee, June 9 and June 15, 1934; Minutes, I.L.A. Northwest Joint Strke Committee, June 12, 1934; Larrowe, op. cit., for the terms of Ryan's "settlement;" materials on the San Francisco Joint Marine Strike Committee are to be found in Strike-1934-HQ and "E.B. O'Grady — 1934" file in the central Archive; Portland S.U.P. Strike Committee, telegram, June 25, 1934, Portland-1934-HQ; Headquarters Minutes, June 25, 1934; "Open Letter to Mayor Joseph K. Carson," June 10, 1934, Portland-1934-HQ; Marine Workers' Industrial Union, Philadelphia, Pa., "Open Air Meeting" and "Open Air Meeting — Dock & Walnut," leaflets, n.d., Strike-1934-HQ.

in beating up single pickets. Don't be afraid to come down for picket duty at night, but always travel in groups if possible, and watch your step." It concluded with a dig at the Communists' largely-anonymous mimeographed handouts: "Watch for the strike bulletin. It will be issued regularly, and will contain all the dope. We are not afraid to sign our names to our news, either."

The effectiveness of the strike remained far from uniform up and down the coast. On June 25, after six weeks, *Pacific Shipper* described the strike as still almost non-existent in San Pedro, but stronger in San Francisco and Oakland, and virtually total in the Northwest, where few, if any, strikebreakers could be mustered giving further evidence of the higher degree of consciousness in the Northwest. Discussion of a proposed Pacific maritime labor federation again surfaced in the meetings of the San Francisco Joint Committee, with strong support for the concept from Portland. June 25 also saw an agreement by the San Francisco J.M.S.C. to submit four "basic principles" to labor undersecretary McGrady: recognition of all striking unions, union hiring halls, no discrimination against strikers, and immediate arbitration of hours, wages, and working conditions. George Nutting of the Portland S.U.P. branch and Whiting from Seattle now sat as delegates, along with the five local men, in the San Francisco Joint Marine Strike Committee.

On June 26, President Roosevelt officially intervened again in the conflict, appointing a National Longshoremen's Board consisting of Archbishop Edward J. Hanna, San Francisco lawyer O.K. Cushing, and undersecretary McGrady.

That day the first issue of the official Sailors' *Strike Bulletin* appeared, edited by Carl Lynch and Charles Quentin, a Marine Fireman. The publication lost no time in pointing out subversion of the strike, even to the point of strikebreaking, by the Communist M.W.I.U. Lynch and Quentin headlined their story "Truth is Stranger Than Fiction." They described how, in the Gulf, the I.W.W. "took the initiative in calling the seamen on strike, and it was progressing wonderfully, until a certain influence was felt by the seamen. There were a group of men who claimed affiliation with the M.W.I.U. These men adhered to a policy of dominate or ruin."

Although, the S.U.P. averred, the M.W.I.U. had only eight members in Houston, two in Galveston, and about twelve in New Orleans, "they started out with an appeal for a 'UNITED FRONT' of all seamen. The seamen were confused with the entry of a strange appeal, because they were already UNITED. Next came a series of rumors followed by leaflets issued by the M.W.I.U. These leaflets stated that there was NO STRIKE . . . Then came more whispers, and LIES, to the effect that the strike was over, that all men should try to ship out, and that the picket lines should be abandoned. After a few days of this *underhand* work THE DESIRED EFFECT WAS OBTAINED . . . it can be proven by affidavit that M.W.I.U. members took jobs and SCABBED on struck ships during the strike."

The seamen's strike in the Gulf was suspended after a mass meeting, at which a majority voted to "carry the strike back to the job." "BY A UNANIMOUS VOTE OF STRIKING SEAMEN, THE M.W.I.U. WAS BRANDED AS SCABS AND TRAITORS," the S.U.P. reported, adding that "when the M.W.I.U. were not allowed (a) seat in the Joint Marine Strike Committee (in San Francisco), by a majority vote of that body, their representatives threatened to send their 'scalers' out to SCAB on the strikers." The S.U.P. pointed out that the San Francisco Labor Council, over the signatures of Edward D. Vandeleur, president, and John A. O'Connell, secretary, had adopted a resolution strongly condemning Communist attempts to take over the maritime movement, particularly through the "so-called M.W.I.U." The resolution was duly endorsed by the S.U.P.

General Strike Call

In anticipation of violent action by the employers and government, as in Toledo and Minneapolis, and as foreseen in the Northwest, the maritime strikers in the Bay Area realized they must widen the strike. On June 27, the Joint Marine Strike Committee set up a subcommittee to communicate with the rest of the regional unions, for discussion of a general strike. Furuseth had arrived from Washington and participated in that morning's deliberations. On June 29, the Sailors' strike committee instructed Selim Silver to discuss with the Labor Council a general strike proposal to be supported by the S.U.P. in the event of force being used to "open the port." The Sailors' *Strike Bulletin* that day revealed a J.M.S.C. decision to combine all pickets into joint lines, with each picket provided three meals per day, in lieu of the previous two. Four "wharf captains" were to be posted, two on each side of the Ferry Building. The Sailors' publication quoted from the I.L.A. publicity committee's strike bulletin of June 29: "Brothers! We are on the road to victory! Let us retain our unity and solidarity!" The response of the Sailors was clear: "O.K. I.L.A. — THE I.S.U. OF A. is with you ONE HUNDRED PERCENT!!"

The Sailors' bulletin also reported that the Texaco tanker *Arizona* had left Portland two days before, "with six machine guns holding our pickets back from the dock."

The competition with the Communists continued even as the Sailors girded for the waterfront war. The June 29 Sailors' bulletin pointed out that the M.W.I.U. now had only some 25 individuals in Portland, and was absent from San Pedro. They answered the M.W.I.U. agitation head on, arguing that while the M.W.I.U. claimed to be controlled by its rank-and-file it could not and did not assert that it actually represented the rank-and-file of the striking seamen. The working sailors cleaved to the S.U.P.

The Sailors listed the following five demands which the M.W.I.U. accused the S.U.P. of *refusing* to support: a joint settlement of all the striking unions, no discrimination, abolition of the fink halls, "a seamen's hiring hall . . . to be controlled by democratically elected committees of seamen on the beach," and a joint negotiations committee. The Sailors answered that they did *not* refuse the first three points, and they already had a joint negotiating committee. But they concentrated fire on the idea of a "beach-controlled" hiring hall. This was a threat that had existed in the seamen's labor movement since the 1880s — that the union could fall into the hands of men who did *not* go to sea for a living. Either the M.W.I.U. did not realize this, or did, and hoped to utilize a shore-based structure to control the usually-absent seamen. The latter construction was applied to the issue by the S.U.P., which declared "we will never recognize a hiring hall run by farmers and coal miners!" All seamen's unions must contend with the problem of having the bulk of their members away from the hall, the meetings, etc. For the S.U.P. traditionalists this was a disadvantage; to the Communists, it was an asset.

The Sailors concluded this particular blast at the Communists by reminding their fellow-strikers that the M.W.I.U. "accuse our officers and officials of selling out. Remember that the I.S.U. is *still* on strike!" The Sailors held that "SCABS, treated accordingly, and rejected by the I.S.U., show up on the waterfront as members and followers of the publishers of the 'Focsleheadski.' It seems that the M.W.I.U. can easily 'spot' SCABS, but it is the I.L.A. and the I.S.U. who treat them as SCABS should be treated. As far as we can see, the M.W.I.U. wants these SCABS for membership."

In the same vein, an editorial by Herbert Mills, the S.U.P. strike committee chairman, said the M.W.I.U. was feeding only 350 men per day, the majority of them scalers, not seamen, while the S.U.P. was feeding 1,970 per day.

On June 28, Sam C. Telford, the main Bay Area M.W.I.U. leader, had wired the National Longshoremen's Board in San Francisco declaring the "in the name of twelve hundred striking marine workers we demand right of Marine Workers Industrial Union to participate in present negotiations for strike settlement." This called forth a written comment to the Board from Paul Scharrenberg that "by no stretch of the imagination can (M.W.I.U.) be called a union," to which he added a description of Telford's claims as "unfounded." This rather mild reaction was doubtless due to Scharrenberg's confidence in the Communists' inability to substantiate the obviously inflated figure of 1,200 members. The S.U.P. had already begun preparations for a post-strike election to be held by the federal authorities, to determine who would represent the seamen, and contested by the I.S.U. and M.W.I.U., and it is likely that Telford's provocative wire was intended as a first shot in anticipation of this balloting.

The attitude of Scharrenberg, seems particularly moderate considering the insults the Communists had directed toward him since the late 1920s, when he first enraged them by his forthright, though basically Socialist, criticisms of the Russian "workers' fatherland." Like Furuseth, he served as a rhetorical punching bag for the M.W.I.U.; the two men, along with others such as Victor Olander, were systematically branded as "finks" and "traitors." The reality, which latter-day historians have unfortunately helped obscure, was that the S.U.P. and I.S.U. leaders were unwavering fighters for labor's cause. As Larsen reported on June 30 to the S.U.P. strike committee, a visit by a Union delegation to the California state capitol had seen Scharrenberg, meeting with Governor Frank Merriam (who had taken over the post after the death of James Rolph in June), "present the strikers' case very ably," according to Larsen, "stating that the strike can be settled in 24 hours if the shipowners will listen to reason." Lynch, writing the same day, noted that Furuseth, having arrived only days before, and speaking briefly to a meeting of the I.S.U. joint strike committee, "said he likes the looks of things — that he has hoped and prayed for this strike for a long, long time, and when we declared it, he was very happy. He is glad that we went into it with our heads, instead of being dragged into it by our heels. He looks for victory and stated that his personal opinion is that the I.S.U. is 'coming back.' "

Lynch concluded by noting that the I.S.U. then had 9,018 men on strike on the Coast, a figure "increasing every hour." Broken down, the total showed 2,495 registered strikers in San Pedro, 451 in Portland, 2,368 in Seattle, and 4,604 in San Francisco. That day, three S.U.P. men and two Communists were arrested in Portland for stopping a Standard Oil tank truck. The press later reported that the judge had sentenced the Sailors — Bob Cooksey, Arthur Forrest, and Herbert Coster — to 30 days in jail each, but had released the Communists, recognizing that their participation in the incident had been verbal only.[2]

The morning of July 1, the strike was crowded out of newspaper headlines, with the attention of the entire West Coast momentarily drawn away from their immediate concerns, no matter how pressing, by gruesome news from Germany. Hitler had carried out his June 30 "blood purge," ordering, and himself participating in, the summary execution of some hundreds of Nazi leaders, nearly all commanders of his faithful storm troops. Ernst Röhm, national leader of the Brownshirt militia, was the best-known of the victims: Hitler's motives for the massacre were said to include outrage at the homosexuality prevalent in the Röhm circle and fear of a plot to overthrow his rule by "radical" Nazis linked to Röhm. The Brownshirts, mostly recruited from the ranks of the jobless, represented a "lower-class" segment of the Nazi movement and, having helped Hitler to power, were now considered a danger. Many of the murdered shouted "Heil

---

[2]Markholt, letter cited, on Seattle; Goldbloom, et al., op. cit., and Larrowe, op. cit.; Minutes, San Francisco Joint Marine Strike Committee, as cited, ibid; Minutes, San Francisco S.U.P. Strike Committee, June 1934, as cited, ibid; S.U.P. "Special Strike Bulletin," June 24, 1934, Strike-1934-HQ; *Pacific Shipper*, June 25, 1934; S.U.P. *Strike Bulletin* (San Francisco), June 26, 1934, 1934-GSS-Berkeley; Text of Roosevelt Orders, typed document, June 26, 1934, Strike-1934-HQ; S.U.P. *Strike Bulletin* (San Francisco), June 29, 1934, 1934-GSS-Berkeley; I.S.U. Joint Strike Committee, telegram, June 28, 1934, S.C. Telford, telegram, June 28, 1934, Paul Scharrenberg, typed letter, June 29, 1934, Carl Lynch, typed letter, June 30, 1934, and Synopsis of Work Done By the Strike Committee, S.U.P., Week Ending July 1, 1934, all in Strike-1934-HQ; *Oregon Journal* (Portland), July 2, 1934.

Hitler" as they were shot, in the belief that their *führer* had fallen in a coup. Like the February Paris riots and Vienna bombardment, the Hitler purge provoked worldwide dismay.[3]

The Storm Gathers

During the first two days of July, in San Francisco, the strikers awaited the attempt to "open the port." The "glad day" had been advanced by the Industrial Association to July 2, a Monday. Sunday, July 1, seemed quiet. The Sailors busied themselves with preparations to turn their *Strike Bulletin* into a *Joint Marine Journal* to be issued in 4,000 copies daily, and with other housekeeping matters. For example, the third daily relief meal had "pepped up" the picket line, but was an expensive luxury and could not be long maintained.

At headquarters on Monday, July 2, the regular meeting of the Sailors' Union noted "owing to reports that the port was to be opened by force the hall on two occasions today was completely emptied of men . . . no attempt was made, however, to get any trucks through the picket lines." There was reason: twenty thousand strikers and sympathizers had blocked the Embarcadero.

In the Northwest, the situation was equally tense, and watchful. The strikers occupied themselves with those vessels that had been left outside the strike: the Alaska ships and the non-striking oil tankers. In Seattle, as noted, after June 21 the Alaska commerce that had been released by agreement with the strikers had once again been halted. The Union now informed Mayor Charles L. Smith that "he had shown great favors to the shipowners by placing hundreds of armed policemen at Pier 40 to assist in importing strikebreakers, and that if he would agree to take his private army from Pier 40, the Alaska fleet would again be manned." Although this suggestion was ignored, a vote of over 2,000 longshoremen had called for resumption of the Alaska agreement and the S.U.P. was under pressure to comply. At the July 2 Seattle branch meeting, members were warned to show caution on the picket line; I.L.A. leader Shelby Daffron had been killed by Standard Oil thugs at Point Wells two days before.

The Portland branch meeting the same night discussed the problem of scab oil tankers. Carter noted that "due to the fact that the oil companies have had sufficient police protection, we have been forced to let the tankers alone. They have had our pickets outnumbered five to one, but we are changing our tactics, and are attacking from another angle . . . The mayor stated that we would only be allowed to have ten pickets in Linnton (the oil dock area), but so far it hasn't stuck. We have eighty there at the present time and intend to keep them there and the H--- with Mayor Carson." Perhaps influenced by reports from Germany, the Sailors' representative described the Mayor to reporters as a combination of "Mussolini, Hitler, and Stalin."

In the Bay Area, the decisive clash was close. On July 3, the San Francisco Joint Marine Strike Committee addressed a letter to all locals of the American Federation of Labor, pointing out that that day, San Francisco Police Chief William J. Quinn had ordered the public away from the waterfront. The Committee warned that "pickets of all striking unions who have maintained their lines solid for eight weeks are now being driven blocks away from the piers." The J.M.S.C. asked that unemployed members of all unions be sent to the waterfront "to stand shoulder to shoulder with our brothers in this struggle," and called on the A.F.L. unions to elect delegates to a conference set for Saturday, July 7, to prepare for a general strike in the Bay Area, "made necessary due to the avowed intention of the employers to break this strike through force and bloodshed."

Historian Felix Reisenberg, Jr., a witness to the unfolding strike, states that "police had cleared pickets from the Embarcadero outside of Pier 38 on the sunny morning of July 3. Longshoremen, armed with bricks, railroad spikes, and clubs, moved back slowly toward First Street and fell silent as noises came from within the dock. The Industrial Association of San Francisco had answered merchants' pleas by organizing the Atlas Trucking Company. They were about to break the strike, to open the port of San Francisco." These were tactics the Association had used to fight the Sailors' and Teamsters' unions three decades before, in the great strike battle of 1901.

Reisenberg continues, "Shouts inside the pier were answered by strikers nearest the entrance: 'come out, you dirty scabs! Come out and get it!' A cobblestone winged above the crowd, ringing against a corrugated iron door. A whistle blew. Then a break showed under the steel barrier. It was rising. Wild yells drowned out the racing of an engine as the door went up. The mob surged forward, sending a rain of missiles at the first truck. Policemen's nightsticks thwacked on unprotected skulls; curses, screams, and grunts rose from the milling crowd. In a cloud of dust the strikers were fighting furiously with every kind of weapon short of firearms, forcing back the law. Police lieutenants bawled new orders; a barrage of tear-gas bombs broke in the strikers' ranks. Choking, the men fell back, shaking their fists, hurling vile epithets at the policemen. On the fringes, cars full of strikers raced off after Atlas trucks, their running boards lined with shouting sailors, longshoremen, and radicals. Beaten by the tear gas, small parties stormed along Brannan, Townsend, and King Streets. Drivers without union buttons were pulled from their seats and beaten, men in side streets were roughly questioned. Five o'clock brought temporary peace. Casualties from that first day of open fighting numbered twenty-five, thirteen of them police."

In Portland, nearly 30 striking seamen, including a marine fireman named Frank Conner, were arrested at the Linnton oil dock. (Conner would soon become nationally-known as a defendant in the King-Ramsay-

[3]Konrad Heiden, *Der Fuehrer*, New York, Houghton Mifflin, 1944.

Conner case, which properly belongs to the history of the Marine Firemen.)

The next day, the Fourth of July, was comparatively tranquil in San Francisco, save for the explosion of Independence Day fireworks. However, the train crews on the Belt Railroad walked off the job and the I.L.A. strike committee noted they were now eligible to join the dock union. Attempts to secure replacements for them from the main-line railroads seem to have failed. Governor Merriam used the excuse of interference with the state-owned Belt Line to threaten the dispatch of the National Guard to San Francisco, but held off a day. Under heavy political fire from a left-wing Democratic gubernatorial candidate, writer Upton Sinclair, Merriam was committed to a public defense of law and order.

July 5, 1934: "Bloody Thursday"

The morning of July 5 found hundreds of pickets on the San Francisco waterfront between King and Mission Streets. Thousands of spectators had also turned out, lured by newspaper headlines. Many of the pickets carried guns. "Excited, swearing groups hustled past silent pier fronts, moving along like low-flying storm clouds," says Reisenberg. "Men stopped to pick up loose bricks, and strike cars raced by, carrying strategists." Policemen patrolled in gas masks. At eight a.m., the signal came when once again a truck drove out of Pier 38, and police began using gas and night sticks on the pickets. All witnesses agree that a shout rose from the crowd, and the strikers joined battle.

It was war. Boxcars on the belt tracks were set afire. Groups of strikers attacked policemen who continued firing gas grenades and swinging their long, brutal night sticks. Terrible wounds appeared, blood flowed, a haze of red seemed to settle on the battleground. The fighting continued through the fumes of tear gas. Ambulances tore back and forth along the Embarcadero. The enraged strikers were pushed into the downtown area. The spectators fled. This day, from then on, would be known as "Bloody Thursday."

Strikers, evading police clubs and gas, ran along First Street and up the promontory known as Rincon Hill, where more stubborn fighting broke out. The clouds of gas forced the strikers to the top of the hill. Combat raged until noon, when a sudden quiet fell, and a truce. In the afternoon fighting resumed with even greater ferocity. Says Reisenberg, a "new strategy was to avoid large gatherings. 'Then the gas won't be no good.' . . . A woman with disheveled hair was shrilling near the foot of Mission Street. 'The bloated scabherders aren't here,' she rasped." More freight car fires broke out close to Pier 38, although most of the pickets were now in the area of Mission Street near the Embarcadero, several blocks north. Tear-gas salesmen mingled with police.

The gas and clubs of the police had taken their toll, through the morning and early afternoon, on numerous innocent members of the public, as well as on strikers. Resentment grew, even among the bystanders. The police began to show fear. They began using their guns, and there were warning shots fired in the air. Then everything changed. "Protesting shrieks trembled the entire length of the waterfront," writes Reisenberg. " 'They're killing now! They're using guns!' " On Mission, at Steuart, outside the Audiffred Building, which housed the longshoremen's strike headquarters, police gunfire felled two men. Another man was shot down around the corner. One of the first two, a striking longshoreman named Howard Sperry died. The man around the corner also died. He was a Greek Communist cook named Nick Counderakis, who called himself Bordoise, and had been working in the I.L.A. relief kitchen. These deaths would not be forgotten. But the fighting did not cease. Uninvolved clerks fled the office buildings in the battle zone, sickened by the gas and carnage. Nausea gas doubled men over, leaving pools of vomit here and there. The strikers were covered with dust and sweat and blood, their clothing often in shreds.

Governor Merriam had called out the Guard, and by late evening they finally appeared in the streets of San Francisco. In Portland, July 5 had also seen long and bloody hours: strikers blocked the tracks of the Seattle, Portland, and Spokane rail system at the Linnton oil dock with their own bodies, threw rocks and jumped on locomotive units, daring the train crews to move over them.

That night Paul Nundstedt, S.U.P. picket captain in San Francisco, filed a report describing his own experience in the fray. At 8:00 a.m. he had proceeded to Pier 38, and had then gone to Pier 34, where policemen blocked the strikers in every direction. The sailors then tried to make their way to 3rd Street, but the police drove them back to Piers 30-32. At 9:40, an unknown man had attempted to get the pickets to force their way into Pier 36, but they had been pushed back to the foot of Main Street. At 9:45, the police hurled gas bombs. The pickets hid between the freight cars, with the bombs going off around them. They crawled over the cars and reached Harrison and Main, where they began throwing rocks. The police charged with gas. At 10:30, the police again attacked, at Rincon Hill and Harrison Street. The crowd headed for Main and Folsom, met by policemen coming down Folsom Street in open-doored squad cars, ready for throwing gas bombs. They pushed the strikers down to Main and Folsom where many were overcome by the gas. At 11 a.m. Nundstedt returned to the Union Hall for instructions.

To this report Carl Lynch added a summary written at around 5 p.m. Fighting was still continuing, with reports of eight to twelve dead and 44 wounded. Police were shooting directly into the crowds, and using a great deal of gas. The strike committee had decided to patrol the waterfront through the night, hoping to head off further confrontations. "Attempting to kill policemen isn't going to do our cause any good,"

Lynch noted. Meanwhile, the Union relief kitchen had been gassed out. No strike bulletin had been issued that day, as there was "no time to write one."[4]

Aftermath

July 6 was "very quiet" on the San Francisco waterfront; thoughts of the two dead, Sperry and Counderakis, hung over the City.

The general strike was now seen not only as a protest against the presence of the National Guard but as a memorial to the men struck down by police gunfire. Above all, a general strike could quickly resolve the situation by forcing the employers to back down.

Writing to Carter in Portland on July 6, Larsen reacted to Bloody Thursday with the following words: "Yesterday, was the worst yet; it was real war with two killed and a number wounded, many of them seriously. It was a complete change of tactics on the part of those sworn to uphold law and order; it seems to work only one way, and for one class."

On July 7, the new *Joint Marine Journal* appeared with an editorial titled "Unity." "Strikers — You put up a splendid battle in defense of your rights the other day, and since that battle, the general impression seems to be that the strike is won." But, the editors went on to warn, "our adversaries tried to split the I.L.A. by attacking certain of their leaders through the medium of newspapers. They failed. So they started on the I.S.U., only they are working a little bit differently . . . are you going to fall for it? Are your going to give up now after this long splendid fight?" The editorial added, "There isn't a man on any of your committees that wouldn't gladly resign . . . right now! Because we feel that some of the gang are swinging against us . . . we don't represent you anymore . . . but we are not going to quit under fire! And we are not going to stand by and see our union turned over to a bunch of irresponsible windbags! And we are not going to play the shipowners' game!" The editorial concluded, "Look before you leap . . . think before you act!"

An article in the same issue described the "strange opening" of the port of San Francisco. "The National Guard stands with fixed bayonets, in front of every pier . . . with machine guns on bridges, roofs, and other points of vantage. Pickets are restricted by a ring of steel . . . a half dozen trucks made furtive trips from one pier, to a warehouse three blocks away . . . and then the Industrial Association has the nerve to announce with pleasure, that the Port of San Francisco is now open to commerce . . . It would be funny if it weren't so serious . . . so stupid . . . And two of our comrades who came out to fight against the rotten conditions . . . are dead. Others are dying . . . Many are maimed . . . They won't fight any more . . ."

The bulletin called on all war veterans to report to the I.L.A. headquarters in uniform on the morning of July 9, a Monday, for the funeral of Sperry, himself a veteran, and Counderakis. On the afternoon of July 7, a mass meeting at Eagles' Hall, called by the J.M.S.C., heard from numerous union locals in the Bay Area, reporting votes for a general strike. In Portland, July 7 had seen "some excitement" between about 7:00 in the morning and the noon hour. The railroads had attempted to move freight into terminal 4, but the rails were oiled for several hundred yards, preventing the locomotives from maintaining traction. After chasing the pickets back and forth, the police gave up and sent the trains back out of the strike zone. The Portland branch strike committee reported to headquarters that "the boys up here have taken up an old pastime of their childhood days, slingshots; and from the looks of the windows of the pilot house of the police boat, the boys are getting very accurate." The Portland A.F.L. unions had scheduled a meeting for noon, on the 9th, to vote on a general strike.[5]

The funeral of Sperry and Counderakis was among the most dramatic public demonstrations ever held in San Francisco, and all commentators on the strike agree that it played an important role in bringing wavering elements in the public over to the strikers. The lineup for the funeral procession, distributed to the unions, called for silence and no placards in the march; only union banners were to be carried. The Spartacus Club, a Greek-speaking Communist group to which Counderakis belonged, was invited to march with the strikers. Carl Lynch reported to the Seattle, Portland, and San Pedro strike committees that "a conservative estimate gave 25,000 people" in the ranks of the marchers, taking an hour to pass a given point. Adding an ironic note to the grim event, Lynch pointed out that "the Marine Workers Industrial Union mustered about 900 men in their division, but they didn't look much like seamen to me. If they are seamen, I think I will retire."

Internal Conflicts Resume

Amid such great events, the problem of the M.W.I.U. had surfaced again. On the day Sperry and Counderakis were buried, 10 S.U.P. activists circulated a letter to the membership calling for Caves to be suspended from the union for his support of the M.W.I.U. One of the Communists' favored targets, Scharrenberg, in a statement before the National Longshoremen's Board that day, declared "it has been said

[4]Carl Lynch, Synopsis, Week Ending July 1, op. cit.;Minutes, San Francisco Joint Marine Strike Committee, op. cit.; Headquarters Minutes, July 2, 1934; Pete Gill, typed letter, July 2, 1934, Seattle-1934-HQ; Minutes, I.L.A. Joint Northwest Strike Committee, op. cit.; Carl Carter, typed letter, July 2, 1934, Portland-1934-HQ; San Francisco Joint Marine Strike Committee, typed letter, July 3, 1934, 1934-GSS-Berkeley; Minutes, San Francisco I.L.A. Strike Committee, July 4, 1934; Reconstructing the events of July 3 through July 5, 50 years later, is not easy; the main printed accounts do not agree on many points of detail. I have relied on Felix Reisenberg, Jr., *Golden Gate*, New York, Knopf, 1940, but have also utilized Quin, op. cit., along with Paul Nundstedt and Carl Lynch, Hour By Hour Report of the Battle, July 5, 1934, Strike-1934- HQ, *San Francisco Examiner*, July 6, 1934, and *Oregon Journal*, July 3 and July 6, 1934. I have minimized direct citations from the daily press inasmuch as their accounts are colorful but unreliable. Larrowe, op. cit., is useful as an outline of agreed-on "facts" from secondary sources. In effect, "Bloody Thursday" merits a full study that would correlate the various accounts. [5]Carl Lynch, typed letter, July 6, 1934, Strike-1934-HQ; George Larsen, typed letter [unsigned], July 6, 1934, Portland-1934-HQ; *Joint Marine Journal* (San Francisco), July 7, 1934, 1934-GSS-Berkeley; Minutes, Mass Meeting at Eagles' Hall, San Francisco, July 7, 1934, and Portland Branch Strike Committee [S.U.P.], Daily Strike Report, July 7, 1934, both Strike-1934-HQ.

that this strike is conducted by 'Reds.' That is not true! I admit that we have a few Reds but insist that the shipowners, too, have their Reds, their unreasoning Reds, dressed in broadcloth, but more arrogant than any Red among the strikers." Scharrenberg concluded, "This strike can still be settled by reason but not by the militia because the soldiers will neither load nor man the ships!"

The regular S.U.P. meeting held that night recorded "in Thursday's riots precipitated by the armed police force of San Francisco, two men were killed and numerous wounded and gassed, including many of our members. One of these killed was a striking member of the I.L.A. and the other a member of the Cooks and Waiters. The funeral was today, and was one of the most impressive affair(s) of its kind ever seen in San Francisco. The procession as it moved up Market Street was in complete charge of the strikers themselves no police being in evidence anywhere along the line of march."[6]

The next night, July 10, 1,500 striking seamen came to the S.U.P. Hall for a tumultuous meeting that revealed, anew, the basic dissensions within the Union. In his presentation to the National Longshoremen's Board, Scharrenberg had indicated that the Union would accept arbitration of its demands, "provided an agreement is also arrived at with the other Unions concerned." On this basis, Scharrenberg outlined a five-point settlement: recognition of the I.S.U. unions as employee representatives or, in lieu of immediate acceptance, a vote of the striking seamen to determine representation; abolition of the fink halls and no discrimination for strike activity; negotiation of a written agreement once the men had returned to work; arbitration if a contract could not be worked out within 30 days; and retroactivity, for wage improvements, to the first day of work after the strike.

These proposals were read to the mass meeting, with added comment on the definite wage and hour improvements to be demanded — specifically, $75 per month and the 8-hour day. They were met with disfavor. A healthy distrust of the officials, on which the Communists had capitalized, was very much in evidence. Speaking from the floor, members challenged the procedures through which the proposals had been put forward. They also complained at the removal of Caves and the involvement of C.W. Deal, an I.S.U. official representing the Ferryboatmen's Union, in the settlement. The Caves issue was brought up repeatedly but without action taken. The officials were accused of fraudulent polling practices and of excluding the rank-and-file from the business meetings. The mood of the strikers was exuberant to a point where, goaded by the Communists, they were prepared to push aside the S.U.P. leadership, regardless of the services they had rendered until then, and without a clear perspective for their replacement.

The situation was saved by Furuseth. The "old man" in his first major statement to the membership since his return from Washington on June 27, spoke long and emotionally, reciting incidents from the early history of the organization and discoursing on the past travails of seamen in America and Europe. He scornfully stated, according to the minutes, that "the shipowners might be willing, — do you get that wording? — they might be willing to arbitrate everything but the fink hall . . . if you were to tell me that you were willing to go to work through the fink hall for $75 per month and you asked me to go to the shipowners with that proposition — I'd tell you to go to Hell!" This was received by wild applause. "Wages can be arbitrated. Watches cannot be arbitrated," he insisted. "It is my conviction that the Industrial Association and the shipowners must be compelled to climb down . . . we must stand by the basic demands that are now in, in order to win now." The patriarch, speaking from the experience of a half-century of Union history, employed his admittedly-fading eloquence to good effect. The meeting ended with the members firmly united, once again, behind the Union. It was agreed that a vote would be taken on Scharrenberg's amended demands.

The next day, July 11, typed petitions began circulating among the strikers, to empower W.W. Caves as the seamen's representative before the N.L.B., and repudiating Scharrenberg and Furuseth. This effort seems to have originated with the Communists but it is impossible to determine how many men signed the forms.

Joint Marine Journal associate editor Charles Quentin was arrested that same day, July 11, while distributing the I.S.U. paper. But the next morning, Judge George J. Steiger dismissed the case, declaring "he thought we still have the freedom of the press and he was very glad that the working men still have a few rights . . . The Judge stated that this appears to be a very clean cut paper." The *Journal* expressed the dissatisfaction of the Union's members over the rumors that the strike would have to be ended through arbitration. "The main fight of the seamen is for the abolition of the infamous Fink Hall," the editors wrote. "Are we going to ARBITRATE that question? The Fink Hall must go, and all shipowners' employment bureaus must go with it. That includes these little shipping offices on docks, where the college boys (who are scabbing now) used to come with their letters . . . and get jobs . . . and go to sea . . . while we stood around all day and every day . . . waiting . . . waiting . . . chased away by police, if too big a crowd of hungry *seamen* gathered there."

The solidarity effort necessary to produce a general strike had come to occupy the Bay Area labor movement. On July 12, the California Federation of Labor addressed central labor councils and local unions throughout the state, calling on them to donate

[6]Funeral Procession Lineup, leaflet, n.d., Carl Lynch,typed letter, July 9, 1934, R.J. Evans et al., typed letter, July 9, 1934, Paul Scharrenberg, Statement to the National Longshoremen's Board, San Francisco, July 9, 1934, all in Strike-1934-HQ; Headquarters Minutes, July 9, 1934.

funds for strike relief, and stating that all labor organizations should "come to the aid of the men who have carried the banner in this momentous contest between entrenched wealth and the New Deal . . . While big business has obtained the aid of the militia, the soldiers will neither load nor man the ships." The Federation concluded, "This strike can and must be won!"

The tabulated results of voting on Scharrenberg's five-point settlement were also announced on July 12. Coastwide, 1,980 striking seamen had rejected the proposals, with 1,558 in favor and 34 disqualified. In San Francisco and Seattle, the Sailors, Firemen, and Stewards were polled separately, and the following results obtained: San Francisco Sailors, 258 in favor of the amended demands, 607 against, 4 disqualified; Seattle Sailors, 256 in favor, 23 against, none disqualified. In Portland, the Sailors and Firemen voted together, and showed 182 in favor, 5 against, none disqualified. In San Pedro, the Sailors, Firemen, and Stewards voted together, with 452 in favor and 540 against, none disqualified.

General Strike

On July 13, Robert Evans, Bennie Barrena, Thomas Hookey, and Albert Milbourne were sent as S.U.P. delegates to a general strike strategy meeting at the San Francisco Labor Council's headquarters in the Labor Temple at 16th and Capp Streets. The council had asked each of its affiliates, as well as the organizations linked to the Building Trades Council, to participate. Continuing sentiment against arbitration was to be heard. The I.L.A. in San Francisco issued a bulletin noting that although the striking Minneapolis truck drivers had agreed to arbitration on May 25, the national wire services revealed July 11 that the drivers had voted to resume their walkout, charging the employers with a "double cross." The S.U.P. negotiations committee was reported, on July 13, to have told the J.M.S.C. the Union would not consider voting on arbitration until a vote on representation of the seamen had taken place.

Although no official call for a general strike came that day, the San Francisco S.U.P. strike committee expected some such action momentarily. By July 14, the N.L.B. had indicated that plans were underway to hold a representation election, but the impending general strike, with the momentum of its approach, reduced this, temporarily, to a detail. That day L.H. Fry, Chris Craig, Lars Turner, M.J. Sheehan, and Hookey were named as S.U.P. delegates to the council's official general strike committee.

By July 16, Lynch could report "the alarming symptoms of a split that appeared last week, have disappeared." To reduce outside influence, the Union had reregistered its pickets and asked each to sign a non-communist disclaimer. This was complied with. Lynch noted with satisfaction that "regular meetings between the picket captains of all striking unions are held every morning at nine o'clock at the Sailors' Union hall. These men decide on joint orders for all pickets, and these meetings have been very successful in promoting harmony between the various striking unions. (This does not include the M.W.I.U. of course.)"[7]

On July 16, the general strike began. In its hysterical Red-baiting, the daily press now moved into higher gear, presenting readers with the specter of a revolutionary insurrection. Throughout the strike, the dailies had played an open anti-labor role, criminally confusing the situation by ascribing all strike leadership to the Communists. This scared the employers and less-knowledgable sectors of the public, but, above all, it *helped* the Communists, increasing their credibility among the strikers. Aside from the *Labor Clarion*, published by the San Francisco Labor Council, *Organized Labor*, issued by the Building Trades Council, and the shrill Communist weekly, the *Western Worker*, the only regular publication to support the strikers was the Catholic weekly *Leader*.

The second day of the general strike National Guardsmen and the police raided the M.W.I.U. meeting hall, first installing machine guns in front of the building. Communist writer Mike Quin admits that the "union" was unable to defend its headquarters with the tiny forces it could muster. One hesitates to imagine the bloodshed that would have taken place had the "forces of order" attempted such an action at the I.L.A. headquarters or the S.U.P. hall. But those who controlled the raiders knew very well who could or could not defend their facilities. Vigilantes found most of the Communist centers, including the offices of the *Western Worker* empty, for the functionaries, painfully aware that their actual forces did not match their inflated claims, had ordered them evacuated.

"A General Strike is a Desperate Remedy"

The *Joint Marine Journal* of July 17 summarized the outlook of the S.U.P. leadership on the second day of the general strike. Quentin, who had taken over the editorship after Carl Lynch had fallen victim to exhaustion and illness, wrote "we are fighting for decent living conditions, and the right to safe liberty and the pursuit of happiness. Our adversaries are the shipowners, and the San Francisco Industrial Association. We are not fighting against innocent women and little children! A general strike is a desperate remedy, and can easily lead to unforeseen terror, misery and starvation. It is intended as a gigantic mass protest of all labor, against unjust grievances. Let us take care that we are not carried away by our enthusiasm or our

[7]Carl Lynch, Minutes and Partial Transcript of the Meeting of the Blue Strike Card Men and Book Members of the S.U.P., San Francisco, July 10, 1934, Strike-1934-HQ; Scharrenberg, ibid.; Petition, July 11, 1934 [Heading only, no signatures], Strike-1934-HQ; *Joint Marine Journal*, July 12, 1934, 1934- GSS-Berkeley; California State Federation of Labor, printed letter, July 12, 1934, GC-1934-HQ; Tabulated Result of the Coastwide Ballot, July 12, 1934, Strike Strategy Committee, San Francisco Labor Council, mimeographed letter, July 12, 1934, George Larsen, typed letter [unsigned], July 13, 1934, I.L.A. Local 38-79 Publicity Committee *Bulletin* (San Francisco), July 13, 1934, Carl Lynch, typed letter [unsigned], July 13, 1934; Unsigned, Report of the Negotiations Committee, S.U.P., for the Week Ending July 14, 1934, Carl Lynch, Synopsis of Work Done by the Strike Committee, S.U.P., Week of July 9 to July 16, 1934, all in Strike-1934-HQ.

bitterness, to the extent of harming the innocent. A General Strike is aimed at the capitalistic interests . . . and not at our brothers of the working classes . . . Remember at all times to do *your own thinking*." Quentin jocularly listed the things that "because of the general strike . . . you can't do in town: Go to the movies, Call a taxicab, Get your trousers pressed, Buy gasoline, Eat in a hotel dining room, Get a shave or haircut, Buy fresh vegetables, Have your automobile repaired, Board a boat for Tahiti or even Los Angeles, Move your household goods, Get your shirt washed, Go to a night club."

Among the only wage workers not on strike were the San Francisco Municipal Railway carmen and the presumably newly-hired Belt Line personnel, both of whom were bound by civil service no-strike contracts. Personnel on the line-haul railroads had also continued working, although the J.M.S.C. addressed an appeal "To All Santa Fe and Southern Pacific Railroad Men," calling for solidarity and arguing that "the strikers in Toledo, Milwaukee, and Minneapolis won their demands when a general strike threatened." This last point, evidence of the impact of the dramatic Midwestern events on the West Coast workers, had been put forward in another appeal by the I.L.A., to all San Francisco trade unionists, with the statement that "the striking maritime groups have agreed to arbitrate everything — but the question of open shop *cannot* be arbitrated."

The Labor Council general strike committee had granted permits for 19 restaurants to operate in the city, and allowed food and milk deliveries to hospitals and other institutions. The only ominous note for the strikers was the success of the National Guard, by then, in driving pickets some four blocks from the actual waterfront, but this seemed almost irrelevant. Reflecting anger over the lies of the daily press, on July 17 the Sailors called on the San Francisco Labor Council to organize a boycott of the Hearst news chain.[8]

But the general strike proved to be of short duration. Already on July 18 Lynch reported to Seattle, Portland, and San Pedro that "our General Strike seems to be dissolving under our feet, and the leaders in our Central Labor Council have passed a resolution, advising us to submit to arbitration of all differences with the shipowners. Which goes to show what happens when you let someone else run your business. Our experience has been, during this General Strike, that we have nothing to say, anymore. The strike is now being run by other Unions, and the conservatives, having all the voting power, seem to be attempting to force us back to work immediately." In the same report, Lynch strongly criticized an East Coast I.S.U. official, Percy J. Pryor, for blocking measures taken by S.U.P. headquarters, at the urging of the Portland and San Pedro branches, to extend the strike to the East Coast and Gulf. On this issue, San Pedro had taken a strong lead. The branch there had come under the more or less spontaneous leadership of John Cooper, whom we met at the beginning of the previous chapter, writing from the East Coast, and Al V. Quittenton, an Australian-born rank-and-filer, who although later, at least, a Communist, seems to have been a sincerely dedicated supporter of the S.U.P.

General Strike Ends

On July 19, the general strike was called off. Within two days, the teamsters returned to work, moving cargo to and from the docks, although the marine unions were still on strike with no ships arriving or departing from San Francisco. *This action by the teamsters was a major setback for the movement.* Lynch bitterly scored the teamsters for their return to work, and wrote that he expected something similar from the I.L.A.; but, supported by Furuseth, he declared that "we must not weaken now." The Union was fighting to preserve its autonomy and its self-determination within the broad movement. The S.U.P. had told the J.M.S.C. that any "matters of vital importance" aside from negotiations would have to be brought before the S.U.P. strike committee before any binding decisions were carried out. Lynch wrote, "We have taken the stand that the Joint Marine Strike Committee, is in reality only supposed to be a committee of negotiators, and that any matters discussed or acted upon by that committee should be matters connected with Negotiations. If the Strike Committee of the Sailors' Union is not allowed to run our end of the strike, we might as well disband." An identical position was taken by the Firemen's and Stewards' Unions.

These statements by Lynch illustrate certain ironic aspects, little analyzed by historians, of the Battle of 1934. The general strike in San Francisco was not an unequivocally militant action: it seems to have been undertaken less to advance the strikers' cause then to transfer leadership responsibilities from rank-and-filers to the professional union officials of the Labor Council. Further, the Sailors, and not the longshoremen, were the most militant element within the movement, at least in San Francisco. With the sudden takeover of leadership by the Labor Council, the S.U.P.'s remarkable élan was threatened.

On July 23, the longshoremen began voting on a proposal that arbitration by the Presidential board be imposed in all matters still disputed, *with the strike to be called off.* This was a second important reverse for the strikers. Lynch noted in his report to the branches, "A committee of five longshoremen arrived here today from the Northwest Strike Committee to find out what the score is. It seems that the boys up there aren't

[8]Minutes, San Francisco Joint Marine Strike Committee, July 15, 1934; Unsigned, "The 1934 Strike and After," typed document, Anne Rand Memorial Research Library, I.L.W.U.; Carl Lynch, typed letter, July 17, 1934, Strike- 1934-HQ; Quin, op. cit.; *Joint Marine Journal*, July 17, 1934, Joint Marine Strike Committee, "General Strike! To All Santa Fe and Southern Pacific Railroad Men!," leaflet, n.d., I.L.A. Local 38-79, "To All Trade Unionists of San Francisco," leaflet, n.d. [July 6, 1934?], all in 1934-GSS-Berkeley. The Minutes of the San Francisco Labor Council General Strike Committee, held in the Anne Rand Memorial Research Library, I.L.W.U., were consulted but are of little interest on the S.U.P. Carl Lynch, Synopsis of Work Done by the Strike Committee, S.U.P., Week of July 16 to 23, 1934, Strike-1934-HQ.

getting any news from the San Francisco local. If the longshoremen elect to go back to work ahead of us, we can't stop them. Our negotiations committee believes that the seamen are in a relatively strong position, and that we will get a break no matter what the longshoremen do." He also warned that "many former Marine Workers are running over here now to ask for our strike cards. We are not accommodating any of these communist lads of course."

At the headquarters meeting that night it was revealed that the shipowners had a new weapon. On the *Dakotan*, which had left the coast before the walkout and was therefore declared "fair" although its crew consistently attempted to strike, the American-Hawaiian Steamship Company had circulated anti-union "yellow dog" affidavits, calling on the federal authorities to recognize the company as the employees' representatives. Apparently only one member each of the deck and engine departments had signed the forms; of the remainder, who refused, some had joined the Union.

On July 24, Furuseth spoke at an open meeting in S.U.P. headquarters, and reported on the federal preparations for a vote on union representation for the seamen. The voting scheme provoked dismay in Seattle and Portland, with the latter branch sending a wire to Larsen abusively ordering him to "keep us posted and don't crawl behind the bush." Controlling his temper at this unjustified rebuke, Carl Lynch declared with a certain despair, in his report to the branches on July 25, "I have learned the utter futility of trying to improve the lot of the average working stiff." Lynch informed the branches that the longshoremen had voted that day to return to work by a vote of 6,388 "yes" to 1,471 "no."

That evening, Furuseth again spoke to a strikers' assembly, which brought some 1,500 men to a San Pedro hall. Furuseth argued that interference with the State Belt Line had provided the authorities with the pretext they needed to send in troops, and that the Industrial Association had actually manipulated the strikers into a general strike. Furuseth felt that the effects of the general walkout had been to defuse, rather than strengthen, the maritime movement. Most importantly, he pointed out that with the vote of the dockers to end their strike, *the Sailors now stood alone.* The employers had taken the position that once the teamsters and longshoremen resumed work the strike was over. But the federal government had, it seemed, agreed with the I.S.U. that such could not be the case.

The "old man" emphasized the iniquities of the fink hall, or as he habitually called it, the "scab office." He declared "the bankers are the real culprits," and cited an article in a New York newspaper, quoting San Francisco banker William H. Crocker: "this strike is the best thing that ever happened to San Francisco. It's costing us money, certainly. We have lost millions on the waterfront in the past few months. But it's a good investment, a marvelous investment. It's solving the labor problem for years to come, perhaps forever . . . (when) the men have been driven back to their jobs, we won't have to worry about them any more. They'll have learned their lesson . . . Labor is licked." Furuseth commented that considering what the employers "said in their meetings about arbitration, considering what they did about their vessel(s), when they wanted to lay the foundation for a company union, it is not surprising that Crocker thinks it is over."

But the "old man" disagreed. "I do not think it is over," he insisted. "I know it is not over if you are men!" Furuseth, and not Crocker, was right. His remarks were met with prolonged applause. "Man after man came forward and shook Andrew by the hand," John Cooper wrote.

On July 26, a similar meeting was held in San Francisco, with some 2,000 in attendance. Representatives of the Joint Northwest Strike Committee assured the seamen that the North Country dockers would not return to work unless the demands of the seagoing unions were satisfied. That day, the *Joint Marine Journal* declared, "we did not strike in sympathy with the longshoremen. We struck independently with our own demands. Many of you seem to think that we are on a sympathy strike, and that if the longshoremen should go back to work, we would have to go back too. Get that idea out of your head *right now*." At a Sailors' strike committee meeting on July 27, the Union affirmed it stood on its basic demands, and would not return to work until the fink hall was done away with.

The Final Days

The movement was winding down, but the longshoremen seemed inordinately anxious to see it end. On July 28, at a special meeting of the J.M.S.C. held at the Fishermen's Hall in San Francisco, representatives of the I.L.A. called for an immediate return to work. The next day, July 29, a mass meeting of Sailors admitted the I.L.A. leaders for presentation of their proposals to the S.U.P. rank-and-file. Paddy Morris, I.L.A. official from Tacoma, argued that the general strike had failed, that the dockworkers had been forced to vote for arbitration, and that even removal of the fink halls would be made dependent on arbitration. Although the government had promised to do away with the fink halls pending the arbitrators' decision, the federal authorities had then reversed themselves and declared that the halls could continue to function under the stewardship of a federal representative. "The labor unions are tired of the fight," said Morris. "The return of the teamsters has weakened our position." Still, seeking to maintain the basic thrust of the movement in the face of possible defeat, Morris added combatively, "We don't feel the fight is over — it has just begun. This is merely a truce. The shipowners have lined up all Capital on their side, and it is a battle between Labor and Capital." But he admitted that a retreat at this point would be "more strategic than a continued advance." Another member of the longshore delegation from Seattle, named Craft, affirmed "we told you the other night that the northmen would stick, and we say it yet, but the time is limited. We know that the arbitration vote weakened all of us . . . We must all return together and make the Marine Federation a reality."

After further remarks by visitors from Portland and Seattle, Harry Bridges appeared before the Sailors. The longshore leader's remarks were not optimistic. "I think that the longshoreman is ready to break tomorrow. I don't think that they will last. They have had enough of it," he said. "They have their families to support. They are discouraged by the teamsters going back to work. They didn't get enough support from the council . . . I disagree with our officials in lots of things they have done. I agree on this point. I think they are right and my own judgment tells me they are right." Bridges had plainly washed his hands of the strike; he repeated several times his belief that at least a hundred of the longshoremen would return to work the next day. Curiously, the back-to-work trend of the longshore leaders appears as the product of a feeling of defeat. The dockers had gained promises of arbitration; for them, this and their exhaustion were, we must believe, sufficient reasons to, in effect, capitulate.

The longshore leaders left the Sailors' meeting. The Sailors listened as a letter was read from 42 steamship companies, expressing their willingness to discharge all strikebreakers, to not discriminate against strikers in future hiring, to accept a union representative in the fink hall, and to meet with a Sailors' representative for handling of any claims of unfairness. This had been answered by Scharrenberg: the joint I.S.U. strike committee would only recommend a return to work if the shipowners would agree to cease any use of the fink halls.

Furuseth then rose to speak. After a few moments, a recess was called. The meeting was resumed and Furuseth continued, when a communication was received from the Shipowners' Association of the Pacific Coast declaring their willingness to meet with the Union for the purpose of collective bargaining, with none of the strikers required to use the fink hall. Furuseth responded that the "scab offices" must be completely abolished. He read, as he had in San Pedro, from Crocker's quoted remarks about labor being "licked," and commented again on the *Dakotan* affidavits. The "old man" as often before, spoke long and eloquently, outlining the corruption and other abuses created by the fink halls, as well as problems involved in running a Union shipping office in the Union's first decades. Furuseth wanted to show the shipowners that any concession of the moment on the long-sought end of fink hiring was insufficient. Proposing a dramatic gesture, he said, "what you do now will be an answer to the fink hall . . . Your answer to them: It is an answer that will go like fire. It will wake up everybody. It will make the people realize that we came out of our own will, that you came of your own will because of the broken promises and that when we go back it is because the government knows our grievances . . .

"What do you think my proposition is? It is horrible and yet it is the most beautiful you can ever think of. We will build a fire in this lot nearby if we can get the police's permission to do it. We are going to build a fire. Alongside of that fire we will have a can of petroleum and each man who has got a fink hall book will come along there and he will dip it into that petroleum, and throw it on the fire.

"In doing this we will have moving picture men dare to take the picture of the fire. The newspapers will know about it . . . The pictures will be shown on the screens all over the country . . .

"The only thing I ask of you is first that you will endorse the answer to the letter . . . If you believe as I do and are willing to do as I suggest to you, bring your fink books and let us burn them — burn them — burn all of that." He asked, dramatically, "Will you do that?" The men answered by virtually unanimous cheers.

"The burning will begin tomorrow at 12 o'clock," the "old man" shouted.

The meeting voted for the burning of the fink books, plus communication with the branches for similar action in Seattle, Portland, and San Pedro, and submission of all other grievances to arbitration. On July 30, to "cheer after cheer," the hated fink books were reduced to ash, with Furuseth in proud attendance. The headquarters meeting, sure that the fink hall had been dealt a mortal blow, that night authorized a return to work at 8:00 on the morning of July 31, although a coastwide vote on the matter was still to be taken. Obviously, the seagoing crafts could not carry the strike on without the support of the dockers and teamsters. The greatest strike in the history of maritime labor in America had ended.

The fink book fire was lit again on July 31, "and God help anybody that flashes one of those slave market records around these parts again," Carl Lynch noted with satisfaction. A cross was erected to mark the grave of the fink hall. Lynch wrote, "We have a real fighting membership now, and thousands of men who have a little taste of unionism, will no doubt line up later. We have forced the U.S. government to realize that Seamen are human beings." Referring to the vote in progress, and emphasizing the positive, Lynch said, "The spirit here in Frisco is wonderful, and if the verdict is to stay out, we'll stick. If the longshoremen go back without us, they will no doubt clean out the rats on the ships and we'll have the much less work to do when we go back."[9]

[9]Carl Lynch, typed letter, July 18, 1934, Strike-1934-HQ; George Larsen, typed letter [unsigned], July 19, 1934, Portland-1934-HQ; on Cooper and Quittenton, see post-strike letters, GC-1934-HQ; *The Dispatcher* (San Francisco), April 6, 1984, on Quittenton's nationality; Carl Lynch, Synopsis, ibid.; Carl Lynch, typed letter, July 23, 1934, Strike-1934-HQ; Headquarters Minutes, July 23, 1934; Statement Which the Men on the S.S. *Dakotan* Were Asked to Sign, July 23, 1934, Minutes, San Francisco S.U.P. Strike Committee, July 24, 1934, Carl Lynch, typed letter, July 25, 1934, Unsigned stenographic report, Andrew Furuseth's Speech Before the I.S.U., San Pedro, July 25, 1934, John Cooper, typed letter, July 26, 1934, all in Strike-1934-HQ; *Joint Marine Journal*, July 26, 1934, 1934-GSS-Berkeley; George Larsen, typed letter [unsigned], July 27, 1934, Carl Lynch, Synopsis of the Work Accomplished by the Strike Committee, S.U.P., Week of July 23-30, 1934, Unsigned stenographic report, Meeting, San Francisco, July 29, 1934, Carl Lynch, typed letter, July 30, 1934, all in Strike-1934-HQ; Headquarters Minutes, July 30, 1934.

Strike Over

Post-strike cleanup work in Seattle included the election of a local patrolman to work with the agent, the need for which the branch had become convinced. At the July 30 meeting, Harry Lundeberg was the only nominee and was elected on motion, by acclamation. Another item of business remained to be taken care of in Seattle. Ole Helland, shot in the head by a gas-gun wielding policeman in June, died in August, and was buried by the organization. The great conflict had taken, in total, seven valiant lives: Dick Parker and John Knudsen, of the San Pedro I.L.A., Shelby Daffron, of the Seattle I.L.A., Howard Sperry of the San Francisco I.L.A., Nick Counderakis (Bordoise), the San Francisco Greek-speaking Communist, and Helland. The seventh, Bruce Lindberg, a 20-year old S.U.P. member, was stabbed to death by a scab in Hong Kong.[10]

For the S.U.P., the struggle was hardly over; it had merely entered a new phase, that of the contest over representation. The main enemy in this fight remained the Communist M.W.I.U. The Communists continued with their disruptive rhetoric. In June, the *Marine Workers' Voice* had falsely asserted that "forty or fifty" ships had been struck on the basis of the M.W.I.U. submission to the N.R.A. code hearings, namely three watches, expanded crews, the 1929 wage scale, and the right to join a union of their choice. They flatly declared "the I.W.W. refused to support the strike." In August, with the strike over, the line was unchanged: the *Fo'c's'le Head* referred to the S.U.P. officers as "finks and finkherders," "traitors and misleaders," charging them with "open scabbery," and naming Scharrenburg (sic) and Larson (sic) as grafters. But the top Communist leadership had already discovered a more devious method of confusing the Sailors, made possible by the daily press. They claimed the strike had been entirely led by them! And this legend, repeated in countless articles and histories, has come to be accepted by the majority of later commentators! In August, the "news service" of the Communist International, the sheet titled *International Press Correspondence*, reported that the I.S.U. "stood aside, expecting no strike, but the M.W.I.U. set up its own demands for the seamen and their strike became an independent one, not merely sympathetic;" further, "the M.W.I.U. became part of the Joint Marine Strike Committee."

A somewhat more rational approach to the struggle had been taken by the Communists' rivals, the Trotskyist members of the Communist League of America, who had distributed a leaflet during the strike calling on the workers to "place no confidence in mediation boards, arbitration and fact finding committees! Trust only in your own united strength — and use it!" Although the Trotskyists had been the leaders in the Minneapolis strike, which was still unresolved at the end of July, they made no attempt to impose their influence in the Bay Area.

The I.W.W., through its M.T.W. branch, hailed the West Coast struggle as "one of the greatest strikes of all time in the Marine Industry." While they offered the questionable interpretation that the "leadership of the I.S.U. in due time were forced to call a strike to save their faces," their main anti-A.F.L. comments were directed at the I.L.A's Ryan. They also stated that "on the whole East Coast the only place any action was taken in support of the West Coast strikers was in the Gulf district, where the Marine Transport Workers of the I.W.W. pulled the ships when the Gulf longshoremen struck. The seamen in the Gulf organized in the M.T.W. tied up all shipping including oil tankers and freighters and forced six of the largest oil companies and the largest singly owned fleet under one house flag to raise the wages to the Shipping Board scale (this was accomplished despite the disruptive influences of the Communist controlled M.W.I.U. who issued poisonous and provocateur leaflets during the strike attacking the M.T.W. and advising the men to go back to work.)"[11]

Nationally, the news was mixed for the resurgent labor movement. In late August, the Minneapolis strike ended in a victory for the truck drivers and warehousemen, who had suffered two dead on July 20, followed by martial law. August also saw a national convention of the United Textile Workers that carried motions for a walkout throughout the country in the first week of September. Battles between police and textile strikers took place in Massachusetts, Georgia, North Carolina, South Carolina, Rhode Island, and New Jersey, with at least a dozen, and probably more, deaths, and hundreds of wounded. Rhode Island, Connecticut, and Maine called out their state troopers. But little support in the textile strike came from the rest of the labor movement, and the strike ended on September 24, following promises of aid to the unions from the Roosevelt government. A wave of strikes also convulsed American agriculture.

Pacific Seaman

In September, Carl Lynch and Fred (Shanghai) Brown, responding to the needs of the upcoming representation vote, began publishing a San Francisco weekly, the *Pacific Seaman*, subtitled "A Square Rigged Paper — For Steamship Men." Surprisingly, the paper spent little space in attacking the M.W.I.U.; the emphasis was on news and editorials written in a positive, rather than a mean spirit, along with historical and humorous pieces and union business reports. (It was later retitled the *American Seaman.*)

[10]Pete Gill, typed letters, July 30, 1934, August 7, 1934, Seattle-1934-HQ. Unsigned, *The Story of the Marine Firemen's Union*, San Francisco, M.F.O.W., 1945. [11] Unsigned, "Strike Wave Sweeps Gulf & West Coasts," *Marine Workers' Voice*, June, 1934; Unsigned, "Insult to Injury" and "Try Something Else, Scharrenburg [sic]," in *Fo'c's'le Head*, August 3, 1934; A.G. Bosse, "The San Francisco General Strike," in *International Press Correspondence* (London), August 10, 1934; Oakland and San Francisco Branches, Communist League of America (International Communists), "Striking Longshoremen and Transportation Workers," leaflet, n.d., General Organization Committee, Marine Transport Workers' Industrial Union, Industrial Workers of the World, *M.T.W. Bulletin*, unnumbered, n.p. n.d. [Chicago, August 1934?], both in 1934-GSS-Berkeley.

On September 10, E.B. O'Grady, secretary of the Masters', Mates', and Pilots' Union in San Francisco, called on each of the marine unions to send two delegates to a meeting September 16, to begin practical work toward a Maritime Federation. At this meeting, the M.W.I.U. again sought admittance and was again rebuffed.

The attention of the world was distracted at mid-month by an incident that further dramatized the situation of seamen: the *Morro Castle*, a passenger ship serving the route between Cuba and New York, burned off the New Jersey coast, with great loss of life. An able-bodied seaman aboard the vessel, Morris Weisberger, would become a leading member, and finally President/Secretary-Treasurer, of the S.U.P. During the federal inquiry into the disaster, the *Pacific Seaman* demanded to know how a fire could make such progress without a report to the bridge, why no attempt was made to beach the ship, why the S.O.S. signal had been delayed, and, above all, the real truth about the crew, which had been falsely charged with leaving the passengers to their fate.

In the aftermath of the great strike, the militant spirit of the West Coast Sailors continued to show itself. On September 20, a one-day "unofficial" walkout on board three ships in San Francisco harbor, supported by the longshoremen and by union taxi drivers who refused to carry passengers to the piers, secured the removal of 17 scabs from the *President Taft*. In the East Coast and Gulf, the I.S.U. set a strike for October 8. The Communist M.W.I.U. announced they would strike the same day, although the *Marine Workers' Voice* continued to defame the I.S.U. In an attack on the *Pacific Seaman*, the Communists charged the Union with "a strikebreaking, class collaboration policy." The Communists asserted that the S.U.P.'s "chief concern is never the seamen's grievances (blacklisting and discrimination against militant seamen) but the shipowners' profits. They want to guarantee that every seaman is a faithful slave." They went on to assail "the sham and hypocrisy of 'voting to determine what union shall represent the seamen.' "

The Communist campaign to completely conquer the new maritime movement found classic expression in a pamphlet published in October, under the title *The Great San Francisco General Strike*, by William F. Dunne, a "Stalinist" Communist, disowned by his brothers, Vincent, Grant, and Miles Dunne, the Trotskyist leaders of the Minneapolis truck drivers. (William Dunne had the curious distinction of serving as a Soviet commissar in Outer Mongolia during the previous decade.) His literary effort included a few errors, but far more falsehoods. Dunne claimed that the Communist *Western Worker* "was the only voice of the embattled workers," and that leadership had "passed into the hands of a Left-wing group, working in fraternal cooperation with the M.W.I.U." A supplementary fictional work included in the pamphlet, a resolution adopted by the Communist Party central committee, said "the effort of the M.W.I.U . . . led to the tying up of every ship on the West Coast and many ships in other ports." Dunne's opus also contained a considerable amount of flattery toward Harry Bridges.[12]

The I.S.U. East Coast strike set for October was called off, with arrival of good news: 36 companies had agreed to recognize the Union. The Communists, meanwhile, had begun to realize they were falling behind, and resolved to press their infiltration of the I.S.U. and S.U.P. On the West Coast, in a spirit of reconciliation that may or may not have been appropriate, given their record, many were accepted, with each case judged individually in the membership meetings.

On October 22, the marine unions were able to secure the end of the federally-supervised seamen's representation ballot. Although the authorities only released the results of the voting on tankers, it was revealing of the emptiness of Communist propaganda. On the Standard Oil fleet, the only place the S.U.P. lost, but where lack of a majority caused the government to declare "no election," the vote was 217 for the Standard company union, 202 for the I.S.U., and 11 for the M.W.I.U. On Richfield Oil vessels, the total was 63 I.S.U., 2 M.W.I.U.; for Union Oil, 192 I.S.U., 5 M.W.I.U. On Associated ships, 130 I.S.U., 0 M.W.I.U.; on General Petroleum tankers, 87 I.S.U., 5 M.W.I.U.; on Hillcone Steamship, 35 I.S.U., 1 M.W.I.U. The total stood at 709 for the I.S.U. and 25 for the Communists.

An unarguable gain for the Communists, however, continued to be their use by the daily press as a means to frighten the employers and the public; this must have influenced many would-be "leaders" in the marine unions, who fell under the party's spell in the months following the 1934 strike. In October, the Communists abroad repeated their success in manipulation of public opinion when a working-class uprising broke out in the Asturias mining district of Spain. Although led by Socialists, Anarchists, and independent Marxists, the Asturian commune was presented in the world press as entirely a Moscow-inspired action.

"A Strike Which Has Worried the Capitalists of the Entire World"

Radical workers in Spain were clearly influenced by the events in February in Vienna and by the stirring example of San Francisco. *La Batalla*, a dissident Marxist weekly published in Barcelona, commented that San Francisco had been "the most impressive strike in the history of the U.S., a strike which has worried the capitalists of the entire world." The

[12]On Minneapolis, Goldbloom et al., op. cit., Preis, op.cit., and Dobbs, op. cit.; file of *Pacific Seaman* (San Francisco), S.U.P. central Archive; on Maritime Federation, see "E.B. O'Grady — 1934" file, S.U.P. central Archive; on the *Morro Castle* incident, *Pacific Seaman*, September 15, 1934; *President Taft* incident, *Pacific Seaman*, September 22, 1934; Eastern and Gulf strike call, *Pacific Seaman*, September 29, 1934, and Headquarters Minutes, October 8, 1934; Unsigned, "New I.S.U. Paper Carries On Old Lying Campaign," *Marine Workers' Voice*, October, 1934; William F. Dunne, *The Great San Francisco General Strike*, New York, Workers Library Publishers, 1934. On Dunne in Mongolia, see Robert Rupen. *How Mongolia Is Really Ruled,* Stanford, Hoover Institution, 1979.

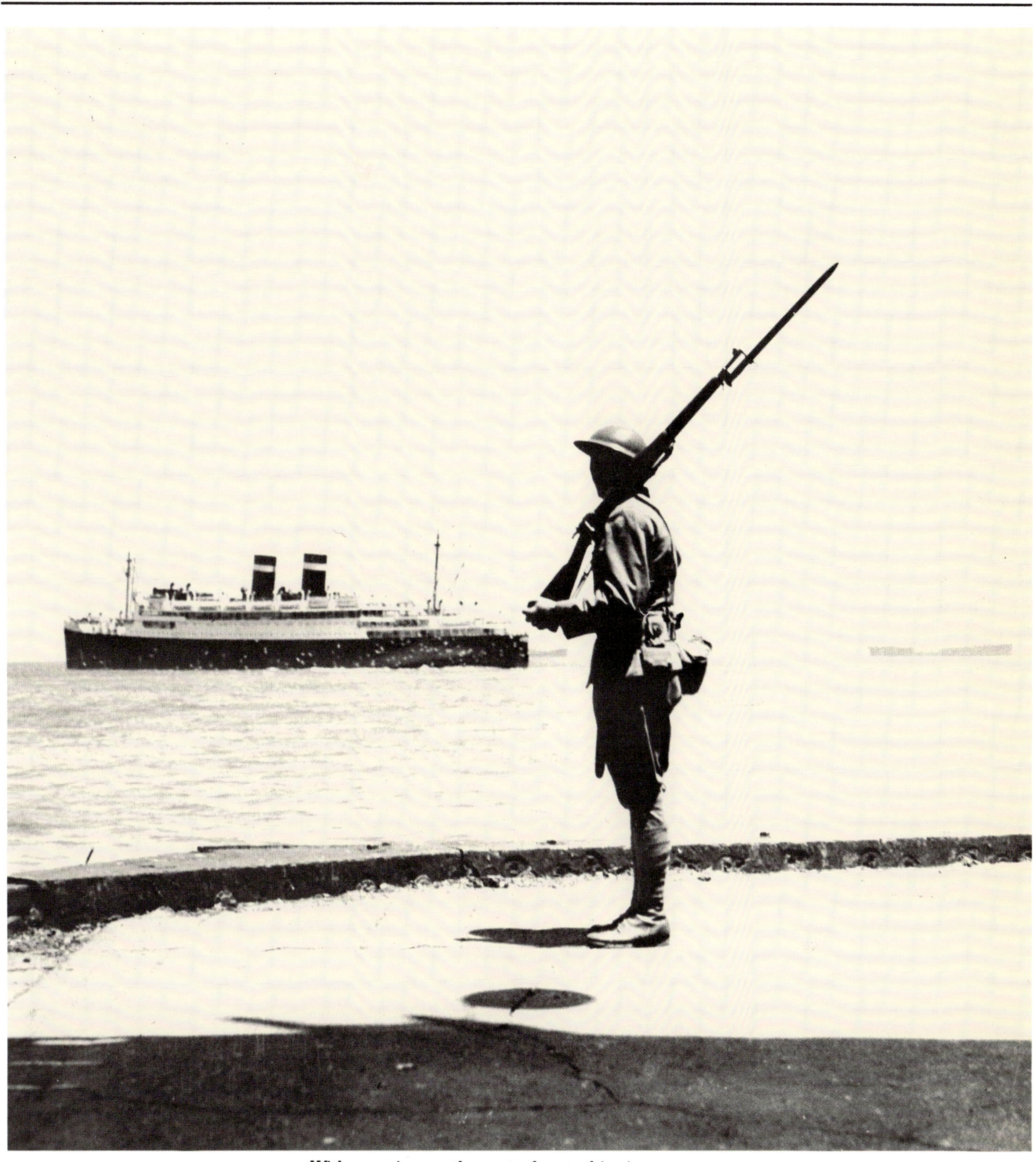

With sentries on the waterfront, shipping resumes
(S.U.P. Archive)

Police attack strikers

(Hugh Crandall Collection)

Seconds later

(Hugh Crandall Collection)

Tear gas on the San Francisco waterfront

(S.U.P. Archive)

National Guard on the Embarcadero

(S.U.P. Archive)

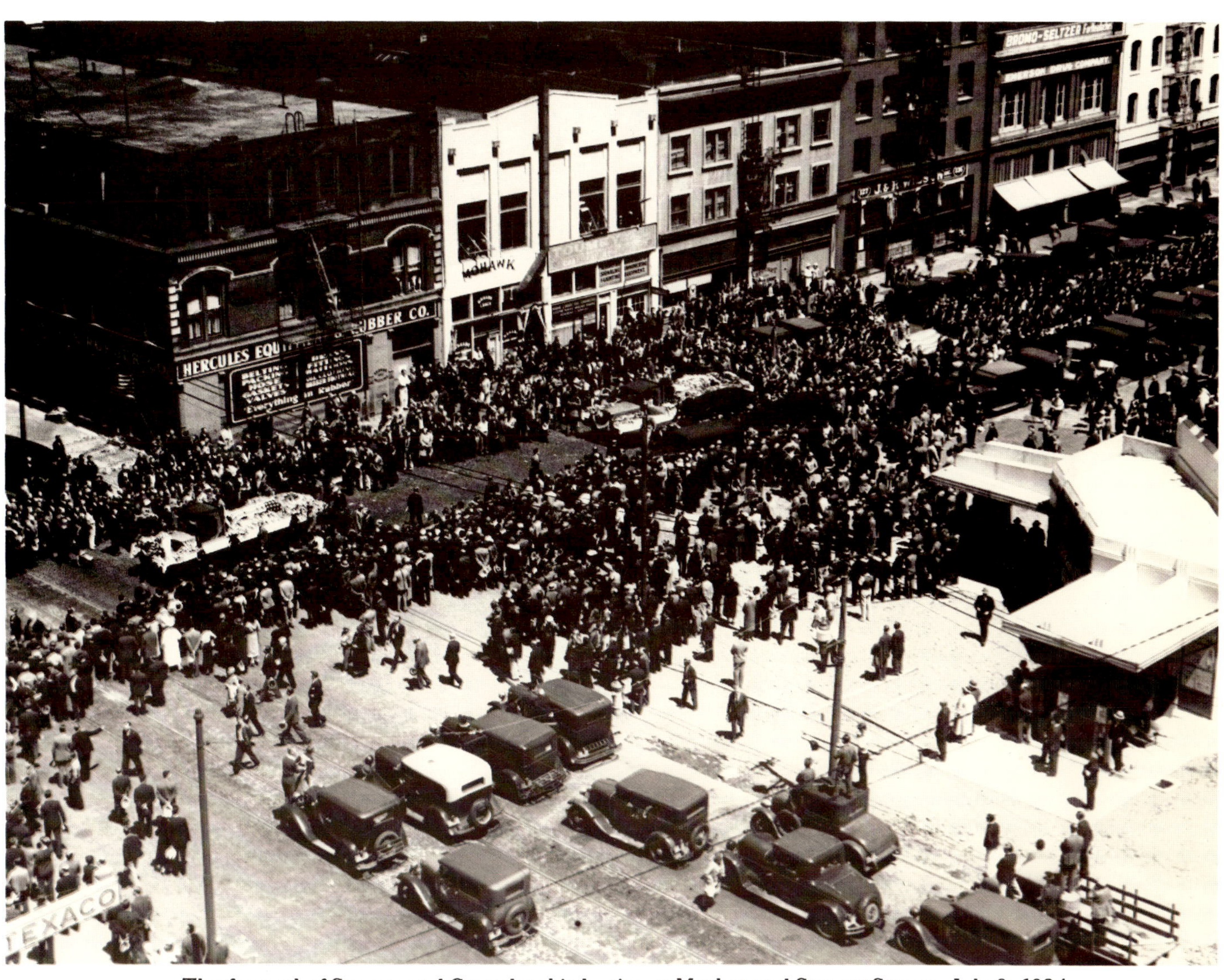

The funeral of Sperry and Counderakis begins at Market and Steuart Streets, July 9, 1934

(S.U.P. Archive)

Washington, D.C.

Feb. 6 1936

"I pledge myself to fight to keep the Charter of the Sailors' Union of the Pacific in the A. F. of L. and to uphold its present constitution and to resist any and all attempts by certain officials of the I. S. U. to reorganize our Union or take away our fundamental democratic rights as Union men."

Name Ed Coester

Book No. 2614

No. 5000

S.U.P. fights for its charter

(Edward Coester Papers — S.U.P. Seattle Archive)

PROTEST--

THE COPELAND BILL

No. 3001

Date JUL 16 1936

I, Ed. Coester, Book No. 2614

member of the Sailors' Union of the Pacific, hereby assert my unqualified opposition to the use of the Continuous Discharge Book imposed upon us by the provisions of the Copeland Bill, and I declare that I will never accept the book as a condition of employment.

Ed. Coester

A remembrance of the Copeland fight

(Edward Coester Papers — S.U.P. Seattle Archive)

"Lundeberg takes a walk" — leaving a hearing of the Federal Maritime Commission, November 1936

(Associated Press — S.U.P. Archive)

The old San Francisco waterfront: Clay Street in 1936. Three-story building at right is the old S.U.P. hall (with decorative twisted columns on second floor)

(Hugh Crandall Collection)

Harry Lundeberg in action: The Shepard Line Beef, 1938
(S.U.P. Archive)

Landscape soon to pass: the Richmond Long Wharf, hub of West Coast tanker shipping, in the 1940s — in the background, an as yet underpopulated Marin County

(Capt. Tony Horton Collection)

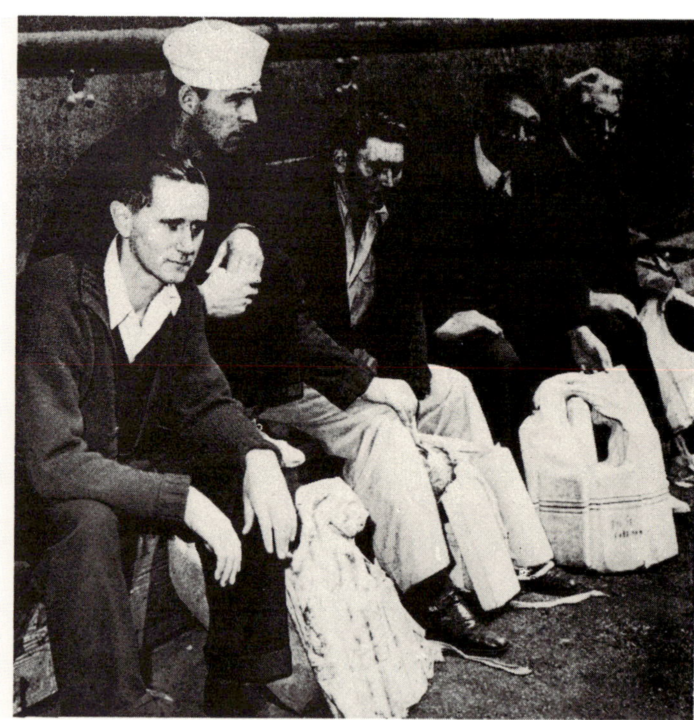

Survivors of a Japanese sub attack off the Pacific Northwest coast during the second world war (left to right): Bentley O'Brien, oiler, George Croff, A.B., Hans Waage, second mate, Pete Kalani, fireman, Frank Purviance, steward. Men were aboard the S.S. Arcata, *sunk in July, 1942*

(S.U.P. Archive)

Seamen offered great sacrifices during the second world war

(S.U.P. Archive)

With the end of the second world war, a great strike wave shook the U.S. This photo shows picket assignment at the Seattle S.U.P. hall during the maritime strike of 1946. Right foreground is Joe Voltero, a prominent S.U.P. militant

(S.U.P. Archive)

San Francisco's Embarcadero in the 1950s: S.U.P. members confront Communists over the M.V. Aleutian

(S.U.P. Archive)

APL's two-stacker President Cleveland, *in service until the 1970s*

(S.U.P. Archive)

Matson's Lurline, *a well-known vessel of the Pacific passenger trade*

(S.U.P. Archive)

Morris Weisberger

(S.U.P. Archive)

"A wall of sailors" — S.U.P. pickets Pacific Far East Line, 1975

(San Francisco Chronicle)

Pat Geraghty, Australian Seamen's Union (left), with Paul Dempster

(West Coast Sailors)

S.U.P. Headquarters, San Francisco. Opened in 1950; design by William Gladstone Merchant

(West Coast Sailors)

journal explained that 200,000 workers had become involved in the general strike in the California city to support the dockers and sailors in their fight for control of hiring. But in Spain as on the Pacific, the political outcome would prove identical: as the historian Murray Bookchin points out, "on the basis of my own researches and personal recollections of this period, I can say that the Communists in America as well as in Spain described the entire (Asturias) insurrection as Communist-led and depicted its goal as the establishment of a 'soviet republic.' None of these claims even remotely corresponded to the facts."

The Communists' claims to control in the Pacific, in Spain, and elsewhere went, at least temporarily, unchallenged by the mass of workers. Why? The answer is, I believe, complex and sobering. Some of the newly radicalized workers were young, and viewed older organizations like the I.S.U. as their natural generational opponents. In addition, most had little or no authentic education in unionism. And, finally, at this historical juncture, afflicted by a deep Depression, many were attracted by the totalitarian movements, both Communist and fascist, that seemed to be gaining headway in a doomed world. Whatever the reason, the Communists temporarily succeeded in largely annexing to themselves many leaders of the new labor upsurge, although one can strongly doubt that great numbers of the rank-and-file supported this trend. It seems very possible that a tiny but loud, aggressive, and ambitious political element projected a much greater impact than they actually had.

A barely-perceptible change, in addition, had taken place in overall Communist strategy during the course of the year. The Communists had begun 1934 violently condemning all unionists, radicals, or simple protesters not under their own control, as "fascists" or "social-fascists." In the West Coast maritime movement (and the October uprising in Spain), they appeared to have acquired enough wisdom to maintain a *dual* policy, of alliances where advantageous (as with the I.L.A. longshore rebels), along with unrestrained attacks where they could not easily claim a foothold (as in the S.U.P.) Also, Russia had begun to sense the danger from Germany and was moving slowly toward a policy of public support for socialist and liberal elements. Many socialist and labor leaders around the world welcomed this change; only in Norway did the Labor Party "consistently refuse to accept unity of action with a party led from Moscow, because they regarded Russia as something very near a fascist state," as Franz Borkenau put it. The Norwegian Labor Party was, as we have seen, the movement in which the new S.U.P. rank and file leader, Harry Lundeberg, had been educated.

But the Communists were already approaching an agony that would end up destroying some of the advantage they had accumulated in the worldwide labor movement. A madness had begun to overtake Moscow: the great purges were about to begin. Following after the deaths of at least 10 million peasants in the anti-Kulak campaign of the early 1930s, Joseph Stalin would now add some five million Communists and ordinary workers to the total of victims. In 1937, he would purge the officer corps of the Red Army, making possible Hitler's nearly-successful invasion of Russia in 1941. Hitler, opposing a decapitated army, had a free hand to carry out the destruction of 20 million Slavic and Jewish human beings.

Stalin was jealous of Hitler's June 30 "blood purge;" he felt the Austrian had displayed greater manhood in brutally destroying his enemies. Stalin was unprepared to actually liquidate his opponents gun in hand. But he could order others to kill for him. On December 1, Sergei Mironovich Kirov, Stalin's apparent successor, was shot down in a party office in Leningrad.

The year 1934 was also significant for Stalin's opponent, Trotsky. From his exile in France, observing the political turbulence that had gripped the world, he suggested a turn back from Bolshevism to the Socialist parties and the mainstream trade unions. Both the rage of Stalin and the maneuvering of Trotsky would find later echoes on the West Coast, within the Sailors' ranks.

Federal 'Award'

In the meantime, October had seen a significant ruling affecting the West Coast maritime movement. The National Longshoremen's Board announced its decision, or "award," for the dockers. The Board decreed a six-hour basic work day and 30-hour week, with joint maintenance of longshore hiring halls by the I.L.A. and the employers, the dispatcher to be selected by the union. The federal "award" for the seagoing employees would wait until January, 1935.

In November, with the California gubernatorial elections, Frank P. Merriam, the candidate of business, handily beat the socialistic Upton Sinclair.

As the year drew to a close, numerous "unofficial" or "quickie" ship strikes occurred in Seattle and Portland, to raise wages and clear off remaining finks. This revival of the old weapon of "the oracle," as it was known in the last decade of the 19th century, or "job action," as it was dubbed by the Wobblies, was eloquent proof that the new militancy of the Union was anything but temporary. The Sailors were prepared to resist whatever might be thrown against them, from the shipowners as well as from self-appointed Communist saviors. In many instances, as we shall see, these two enemies would, curiously, combine against the S.U.P.

The impact of the 1934 maritime movement, both in tandem with the rest of the year's panoply of events and in its own right, is unmistakable. The West Coast maritime workers and their organizations now stood as the leading force for labor solidarity in the region. Already, in December, the Sailors began putting forward lines of communication to other workers. At mid-month, a committee from the Union reported to Pete Gill in Seattle on the status of a mine strike in Juneau, Alaska, in which an embargo by the maritime workers served as the strikers' main advantage in dealing with the mine bosses. Although the situation of the Juneau miners was grim, the Sailors stood ready to assist.[13]

The year 1934 saw other important events we have so far left outside of our review. Bruno Hauptmann, the accused kidnapper of the Charles Lindbergh baby, was arrested, bandit John Dillinger was killed, a terrible drought heavily punished American agriculture, the world marvelled at the birth of the Dionne quintuplets, the Samuel Insull financial empire crashed, Dizzy and Daffy Dean won the world series for St. Louis, over Detroit. The F.D.R.-led Democrats increased their political edge in the nation, in off-year voting. In France, Yugoslav King Alexander was assassinated in full view of press and newsreel cameras. In October, in the Chinese hinterland, unreported by the world press, a "Red Army" began the "Long March" out of its former bastion in Kiangsi.

But the center of attention throughout the remarkable year was consistently held by labor. For only the month of July, in addition to the struggle on the West Coast we have chronicled, we could mention, among many similar conflicts, the Milwaukee streetcar strike, which had almost become another general strike, and an important walkout by 6,000 mine and smelter workers in Butte, Montana: on the international scale, rioting by Christian unionists, supported by construction workers, had shaken the Jordaan district of Amsterdam, with demonstrators burning bridges and spreading nails across the streets to stop police motorcyclists. In August, in Costa Rica, a massive banana strike seized the attention of the whole of Central America and the Caribbean.

But the West Coast maritime strike, then and now, was the peak experience, the crest of a mighty wave.[14]

---

[13]Eastern and Gulf I.S.U. strike cancellation, *Pacific Seaman*, October 8, 1934; examination of various M.W.I.U. members recorded in Headquarters Minutes, beginning October, 1934. Representation vote, George Larsen, Report to the Membership, mimeographed, December 28, 1934, Strike-1934-HQ, and unsigned, untitled summary of the relations between tanker operators and the Union, n.d., in the S.U.P. Seattle Branch Archive. The latter document presents slightly differing figures on the vote, but because it is more complete than Larsen, I have followed it. The literature of the Spanish Revolution and Civil War of 1931-39, which is enormous, includes a great deal on the Asturias events. See Murray Bookchin, *The Spanish Anarchists*, New York, Free Life Editions, 1977, Franz Borkenau, *The Spanish Cockpit*, London, Faber, 1937, Paul Preston, *The Coming of the Spanish Civil War*, New York, Methuen, 1983, and Adrian Shubert, "The Epic Failure: The Asturian Revolution of October 1934," in Paul Preston, ed., *Revolution and Civil War In Spain,* New York, Methuen, 1984. On the impact of the West Coast movement internationally, see the following, unsigned, in *La Batalla* (Barcelona): "Violentas Huelgas en el País de Roosevelt," June 2, 1934, "La Huelga General en San Francisco," July 20, 1934, "Los Grandes Movimientos de Clase en los Estados Unidos," July 26, 1934, "Las Huelgas en los Estados Unidos," September 6, 1934 [collection in Hoover Library, Stanford University]. On the changing tactics of the Communists, see Paul S. Taylor and Norman Leon Gold, "San Francisco and the General Strike," *Survey Graphic*, September, 1934 and Borkenau, op cit. On the Kirov assassination, N.S. Khrushchev, Speech to the 20th Congress, Communist Party of the Soviet Union, February 24-25, 1956, *The New Leader* (New York), July 16, 1956; on Trotsky's shift to the Socialists, known as the "French turn," Leon Trotsky, *Writings 1934-35*, New York, Pathfinder Press, 1971 and *Writings, Supplement 1934-40*, New York, Pathfinder, 1979. On the National Longshoremen's Board "award" to the longshoremen, see Lampman, op. cit. On the 1934 gubernatorial election in California, H. Brett Melendy and Benjamin F. Gilbert, *The Governors of California*, Georgetown, California, Talisman Press, 1961. On the end-of-year "job actions" in the Northwest, *Pacific Seaman*, December 29, 1934. On the Juneau mine strike, unsigned, typed letter, December 17, 1934, in the S.U.P. Seattle Branch Archive. [14]For a review of the year's main events, see *Proletarian News* (Chicago), February, 1935 [collection in Hoover Library]; on the "Long March," see Dick Wilson, *The Long March 1935*, New York, Penguin, 1971; on the Milwaukee strike, *Daily Worker* (New York), June 27-30, 1934, July 2, 1934; on the Butte strike, *Daily Worker*, July 13, 1934; on the Amsterdam riots, H.L. Van Zurk, "Las Batallas de Amsterdam," *La Batalla*, August 2, 1934; on the Costa Rican strike, see "1934," collection of articles, *La Nacion Internacional,* August 16-22, 1984.

CHAPTER VIII
Rebel Workers
(1935-1950)

In its depth of consciousness, regional impact, and audacity, the West Coast maritime strike movement of 1934 clearly stands apart from other notable chapters in the epic of American labor. The 1934 maritime movement was genuinely industrial: all the workers in maritime joined together for common as well as sectoral goals, as in the great railroad uprising of 1877 and the national steel strike of 1919. But unlike these forerunners, the 1934 movement impressed itself on the community from which it sprang in a special way. The waterfront workers came out of the battle as standard bearers for all of labor, the length of the coast.

Aftermath of 1934

1934's gains emerge as key achievements: the weapon of job action, most notably, was recovered by the Sailors, who began utilizing "the oracle" with a vigor and intensity that had probably never been seen even in the glory days of Andrew Furuseth's leadership. The at-first-unfulfilled emphasis on the Union hiring hall promoted a renewed belief in the Union as an autonomous institution in society, not limited to on-the-job issues such as pay and conditions. The maritime movement seemed to herald a trend toward the laboring-class hegemony over the productive process that had been the aim of the socialist movements since the early 19th century, and which survives today as the theory of "workers' control" and "self-management."

But, above all, the post-1934 movement *remained* a movement for an intense, if brief, time. The energies of the maritime workers did not dissipate with the end of the strike, as had so often happened: rather, they seemed to become replenished, as the workers increasingly understood their power in public affairs.

The impact of the movement outside the maritime industry was enormous. 1934 had stimulated solidarity throughout the West Coast union organizations, on the water and inland. But more, it created a completely new atmosphere in regional politics. Notwithstanding the defeat of the socialist Sinclair in the California gubernatorial race, the entire coast was moving in an unmistakably progressive direction. In many areas, particularly in rural counties of Oregon and California, reaction against the new tendencies was also intense, and even violent.

Post-1934 developments reached their height with the founding of the Maritime Federation of the Pacific, under the slogan "An injury to one is an injury to all." The Maritime Federation, set up by the dockworkers and seamen, simultaneously represented a fulfillment of the traditional sympathies in that direction evinced by the longshoremen, and a return to the ideals of the Knights of Labor and the I.W.W. It was also a harbinger of the Committee for Industrial Organization (C.I.O.), in gestation at that time. The goal of the Federation was a single coastwide maritime contract with a single expiration date, so that the workers could continue to present the kind of common front that had proven effective in the big strike. But the Federation was short-lived.

There was much cause for celebration; but, as we shall see, there was also cause for watchfulness and worry in labor's ranks. Understanding the contradiction between the great victories and the great weaknesses of 1934 is almost as difficult now as it must have been then.

Unfortunately, the great upsurge inaugurated by the 1934 strike and exemplified by the Maritime Federation began its decline within less than three years. By early 1937 the Federation was doomed. The post-1934 movement succumbed to the destructive effects of a political polarization that further divided the unionists between a "left wing" faction controlled by the Communists, and groups that eventually came together on nothing more than anti-Communism. The anti-Communists seemed to have little to offer in the way of a positive program. In an atmosphere of fears of world war and unease over fascism, tendencies too critical of the Communists could easily be perceived as "reactionary." The Sailors' Union, as we shall see, in order to protect its *fundamentally radical* program for the protection of the workers' interests, eventually found itself at violent odds with the Communists.

In January 1935 the federal authorities, acting through the arbitration board for coastwise shipping, issued an "award" for the deck, engine, and stewards' departments in the coast trade. The document established hiring preference for members of the S.U.P., the Marine Firemen, and the Marine Cooks and Stewards. The "award" also legally did away with the fink halls, although it preserved non-union shipping "off the dock" alongside the Union hiring hall. Wages were set at $70 per month for sailors and firemen, with an 8-hour day, and overtime at 70 cents per hour.

The next month, the board released its decision for the offshore trades. Union preference, the hiring hall, and "off-the-dock" shipping were established as in coastwise shipping. In April, Alaska Steamship Company, Northland Transportation, and Wills Navigation signed union contracts.

The involvement of the federal authorities in settling labor disputes was not universally applauded in S.U.P. ranks. The Rooseveltian concept of benevolent intervention "on the side of the people" was still a novelty and ran against longstanding A.F.L. principles. And the award itself was resented for the absence of a clause legally establishing *primacy* of the hiring hall.[1]

50th Anniversary

March 1935 marked the fiftieth anniversary of the founding of the Coast Seamen's Union. For those surviving pioneers, including Pete Gill, Nick Jortall, and Furuseth, who had manned the vessel of the Union from practically its first voyage, prospects must have seemed bright. The Union had regained its position as the leading labor organization for America's seamen, and on uncompromised terms. After years of Depression, American labor was forging ahead.

However, on the West Coast as well as on the Atlantic and Gulf, some basic grievances continued to fester. Crimping had blossomed in the wake of the 1921 defeat, and it was still common on the East and Gulf Coasts for men to find jobs through seamen's hotels and boarding houses that demanded rent in advance, with no refund if the man was shipped out immediately. Clothing dealers and other parasites continued to prey on the seaman in his quest for work. The crimps maintained contracts with the shipping companies or vessels, and received compensation at the rate of so much per head, exactly as in the 19th century.

Without the Union hall, the East or Gulf Coast sailor who shunned the crimps could only avail himself of visits to ships' officers or other company representatives in the personnel offices. The point was visibility; eventually, if one hung around and introduced oneself, discharges could be presented and a job secured. A similar process took place at the docks themselves. Shortly after arrival, one might board the vessel, find the chief mate, first assistant engineer, or steward, and ask for work. One could also wait outside the dock gates for an officer to appear, look the crowd over, and pick certain men or solicit certain ratings. And there were the bars and "sporting" houses as points of contact.

One anonymous militant in both the I.W.W. Marine Transport Workers and S.U.P. recalled in recent notes the main point in all such transactions: to have one's discharges ready, and to be submissive during interrogation.

Once aboard the vessel, the sailor was still expected to work hard, prove one's skills, and remain silent about such matters as long hours, small pay, poor food, bad quarters, and dangerous conditions. Any seaman could be fired in any port, for any reason, "real or imaginary." Seamen could still be forced to work off debts for wages paid in advance if hired on the East or Gulf Coasts.

After 1934 the situation changed, but only after further struggles. Once union hiring was erected as an unchallengable practice the solidarity of the men in fighting for shipboard conditions could be secured by elimination of non-union finks. It was not until after the second "big strike," in 1936-37, that Union hiring halls were established throughout the nation and many of the old practices were discontinued. "Enraged seamen ganged up and in their own fashion put many places out of business through violence and vandalism," an S.U.P. observer recalls. Many abuses on the East and Gulf Coasts were finally done away with through legal and political influence, as well as by direct action.[2]

The part of the picture that alarmed certain elderly S.U.P. stalwarts, particularly Furuseth, was the growing hold of the Communists over young militants. The ability of the Muscovites to develop such an audience among the newer ranks has, I think, been adequately explained in this narrative. As months and years went by, many criticisms they made of the Communists that marked men like Furuseth, Scharrenberg, and Larsen as so-called "reactionaries" would seem to be proven correct. The Communists, by then, did not represent a force *within* the labor movement, but a political faction bent on control of the workers *from outside*. Had the Communists been content to work within the Sailors' Union as one among many factions, defending their program on its merits, they might have retained support, far longer than they did. But particularly in the S.U.P., they were dissatisfied with such a role. They wanted much more. They tasted a certain power in the longshoremen's union, and wanted the same in the S.U.P. When they could not gain full control over the Sailors, they were prepared to destroy the organization.

Tanker Strike — Scharrenberg Expelled

On March 9, 1935, the S.U.P. and the other I.S.U. affiliates committed themselves to a gambit that would prove very risky for the Union. This was a short-lived attempt to unionize the non-union tanker fleets (led by Standard Oil) by strike action. Although S.U.P.

[1]Lampman, op. cit. Also see *Strikes Under The New Deal*, op. cit. [2]M. K. (further identification declined), notes, n.d. n.p., (San Francisco, April 1984), in S.U.P. central Archive.

members threw themselves valiantly into the tanker fight, the obstinate attitude of the employers proved too resistant. The strike was called off, with the unions left in some disarray. During the tanker strike, an incident in which eight members of maritime unions were charged with organizing a dynamite attack on a hotel housing scabs, came to national attention as the "Modesto Boys" case. The maritime workers had been framed in a plot involving Standard Oil company guards and private detectives.[3]

April, 1935, saw a conference in Seattle formally set up the Maritime Federation of the Pacific as an umbrella organization for the I.S.U., marine officers', and longshore unions. Harry Lundeberg was chosen as the first president, a representative of the shipping crafts, although the latter were a minority in the Federation. Historians have interpreted the choice of Lundeberg as an action by the Communists and Bridges to gain Lundeberg's allegiance. At the time, Lundeberg was clearly seen as a "progressive patrolman" by the left-wing forces. The dominant elements in the Federation sought a surrender to the Federation leaders of the power to strike, but the Sailors refused to give up this decision-making right.

The left continued to grow in authority. Former members of the Communist Marine Workers Industrial Union were officially allowed to transfer into the S.U.P. after June, 1935, and the *Voice of the Federation*, organ of the coastwide M.F.P., which included many attacks on Furuseth, Scharrenberg, and the other I.S.U. leaders, became the official publication of the S.U.P.[4]

Three months later, in July, came a bombshell: Paul Scharrenberg was tried and expelled from the S.U.P. Scharrenberg, who had served the organization for many decades, had, it was charged, seriously faltered in his responsibilities. He was blamed with loss of the tanker strike, and accused of issuing public statements supporting a war with Japan to improve shipping employment, as well as with support for the pre-1933 "blue book" company union of San Francisco dockers. Scharrenberg did not attend his trial, and claimed in response to the proceeding that he was a victim of an alliance between Harry Bridges and Lundeberg.

The I.S.U. international leadership under Furuseth could not but protest the expulsion of Scharrenberg, and between summer 1935 and the beginning of 1936 relations between the international and the S.U.P. became increasingly strained. In January, 1936, the international took steps to organize a new divisional office for the West Coast sailors, but this move was roundly repudiated by the rank-and-file. The men on the Pacific were sure in their instincts and their new leaders, and had grown extremely suspicious of the old generation of I.S.U. functionaries.[5]

The international was collapsing. The reborn S.U.P. had mobilized enough strength and enthusiasm among the "class of 1934" to forge a new, independent course for the historic West Coast Union. Increasingly, the rank-and-file perceived the group around Furuseth, including Victor Olander, Percy Pryor, and Scharrenberg, as inept and out-of-step with events. On the Atlantic, the Communists were taking daily advantage of the confusion in the I.S.U. to establish the groundwork for a new organization, which would eventually become the National Maritime Union.

The worst mistake of the I.S.U. leadership was to lump all the Pacific Coast "radicals," including Lundeberg, with the Communists. But the very militant Lundeberg, perhaps best compared in spirit and character to two men we have already discussed, his fellow-Norwegian Martin Tranmael and the Dutch Edo Fimmen, was much closer to the I.W.W. in his militancy than to the Communists. These were distinctions that Furuseth, repeating his 1921 error, again failed to make. It may therefore be argued that, as in 1921, Furuseth's undifferentiated anger at radicalism helped bring defeat for the I.S.U. Within a few brief years, the international had disappeared, with the S.U.P. and N.M.U. left to fight over the field.

Communists Vs. Lundeberg

That the Communists were not long happy with Lundeberg, an erstwhile candidate for their affections, was shown as early as November, 1935, when the *Western Worker* denounced him as "individualistic." But Lundeberg's Wobbly-style "individualism" had struck a deep chord in the S.U.P. membership. In December 1935, he was elected Secretary-Treasurer of the union, with Al Quittenton as Assistant Secretary-Treasurer, A. J. "Whitey" Probert and Charles Cates as San Francisco patrolmen, Ole Olsen as dispatcher, Carl Tillman as assistant dispatcher and Pete Gill as Seattle agent. Lundeberg resigned from the post of Maritime Federation president in order to devote himself completely to the S.U.P.[6]

Nationally, 1935 had seen other evidence of radical changes in the outlook of American workers. At the October convention of the American Federation of Labor, held in Atlantic City, John L. Lewis of the United Mine Workers presented the assembled delegates with forceful arguments against a continued attachment to the older, craft-based form of union organization, demanding a full pledge to industrial organization. The A.F.L. leaders opposed Lewis, who then began the process that would culminate in the emergence of the C.I.O. as the nation's second major labor grouping.[7]

"Anarchosyndicalism" — Charter Revoked

In 1936, turbulence within the Sailors' Union reached an explosion point, as the organization faced

---

[3]On the Modesto Boys, see Marine Firemen's Union, *From Hell Hole to High Tech*, San Francisco, M.F.O.W., 1983. [4]Lampman, op. cit. On Lundeberg, conversation with Walter Stack, Communist maritime leader, San Francisco, August 1983. [5]Lampman, op. cit.; Publicity Committee, Sailors' Union of the Pacific, *The True Story About The Expulsion Of Paul Scharrenberg From The S.U.P.*, San Francisco, 1935. [6]Lampman, op. cit. [7]*Report of the Proceedings of the 55th Annual Convention of the American Federation of Labor, Atlantic City, N.J., 1935*, Washington, Judd & Detweiler, 1935.

challenges from the employers, the I.S.U. international leadership, and the government. The temper of the rank-and-file was so militant at this point that commentators of the time as well as labor historians have identified the S.U.P. of 1936-37 with the "anarchosyndicalism" of the I.W.W. "Quickie" strikes, became the rule. Since federal authorities were seen as remiss in their guarantees of the organization's rights, there seemed to be only one way to secure full respect for the Sailors: direct action on the vessels, "the oracle."

In January, 1936, the 33rd international convention of the I.S.U. revoked the S.U.P. charter, thus expelling the Sailors from the I.S.U. and A.F.L. The Pacific Coast organization was represented at the convention by Al Quittenton and Edward Coester, a militant from Seattle. In an interview several decades later, Coester stated that Quittenton "made no bones about being a commie." A major basis for the revocation of the S.U.P. charter was the Union's admission of former members of the Communist M.W.I.U.[8]

Lundeberg and the West Coast militants replied to the revocation of the S.U.P. charter by putting the Union on an "emergency program" footing. Substitute membership books were printed, in which each member signed a pledge to support the "expelled" Union's elected officers. Thousands of sailors responded to the emergency call, and the now-independent S.U.P. was able to maintain its strength as the representative of the West Coast seamen. Distinguished figures from the early days of the Union, including Pete Gill, Nick Jortall, and Walter Macarthur, strongly supported the "new" S.U.P., against Furuseth and Scharrenberg.[9]

With the "expulsion" of the S.U.P., the decay in the I.S.U. could no longer be denied; in the face of the new and more modern spirit alive in the rank-and-file, the philosophy of the Furuseth age was obsolete. Furuseth's trust in a paternalistic government to look out for the sailors' interests received a further rebuff in 1936, when the fight over the "Copeland fink book" emerged. The fink book struggle was a chapter in the history of the S.U.P. nearly as important, in its way, as the 1934 strike.

The Copeland fink book, officially known as the Continuous Discharge Book, had been introduced into the Congress through H.R. 8555, the Merchant Marine Act of 1936, passed into law under the style of the Copeland-Bland Act. The Act called on seamen, in lieu of discharge certificates for each voyage, to carry a permanent identification booklet on the British model, in which a man's entire record of voyages and conduct would be revealed to each new employer. This was simply the old "grade book" the Union fought in the 1880s. It was obvious that conservative interests, alarmed at the upsurge of the post-1934 maritime movement, sought a means to reinstitute blacklisting of known militants. The fink book was met by deep anger among the sailors; over 50,000 throughout the U.S. signed pledge cards refusing to take the book.

The fink book campaign became the basis of a new conflict between the S.U.P. and the Communists. By 1936, the latter had exploited their spurious record in 1934 and growing labor unrest to attain a national position of some power in unions, including the East Coast maritime industry. After 1935, the Communist International had, in response to the Hitler threat, changed its line with regard to liberals and left-leaning non-communists. While the Party had previously attacked all possible "competitors" as capitalist and fascist agents, the emphasis was now on a "people's front" that would unite all "antifascist" elements. In the U.S., this meant working with the "liberal-left" elements in the Roosevelt administration, and therefore quieting criticism of the New Deal, which had previously been assailed as a "fascist scheme." Although the Communists at first supported the fight against the fink book, it became apparent they were unhappy opposing something that had the backing of F.D.R. and his cabinet. Their new attitude was that since the fink book was the product of the "progressive" Roosevelt administration, it must therefore be a "progressive fink book." The Sailors did not concur with this reasoning.

Early 1936 saw an effort to forge a Maritime Federation of the Gulf Coast, parallel to the Pacific Coast organization, and mainly based on the Gulf longshore locals. However, the Gulf federation, like many other projects of the time, was also undermined by political factionalism involving the Communists and their critics.[10]

1936-37 Strike

The undercurrent of conflict over the fink book was to prove an issue in the second maritime "big strike" of the 1930s, the 100-day walkout of 1936-37, in which a split between Lundeberg and the S.U.P., and the Communist "ruling cadre" in the West Coast maritime movement, came into the open. On October 1, 1936, the longshore and seagoing contracts expired. In the strike that followed the Sailors hoped to make up what they had not gained in 1934, for although the longshoremen had come out of the first "big strike" with a joint union-employer hiring hall and some control over conditions, the status of the Sailors' hiring hall was still ambiguous. The employers announced that after October 1, 1936, all hiring would be done by shipping "off the dock," unless disputed matters were submitted to arbitration. What followed was, therefore, as much an employer lockout as a strike. The Maritime Federation, acting as the leadership in the strike, formulated five demands:

• Union employment preference for ships' officers.

---

[8]Edward Coester, interview, Washington State Oral/Aural History Program, Washington State Archives, Olympia, June 9, 1975; *Seamen's Journal*, April 1, 1936. [9]Lampman, op. cit., and files in the S.U.P. central Archive on the "emergency program." [10]Wytze Gorter and George H. Hildebrand, *The Pacific Coast Maritime Shipping Industry, 1930-1948*, Berkeley and Los Angeles, University of California Press, 1954; Frederick J. Lang (Frank Lovell), *Maritime*, New York, Pioneer Publishers, 1945 (second edition). On the Maritime Federation of the Gulf Coast, see J.G. Mers. letter, August 24, 1985, in S.U.P. Central Archive.

- All unlicensed crew members to be shipped through the hiring halls.
- Sailors' overtime to paid in cash, rather than in time off.
- A work day of eight out of a spread of 12 hours for the stewards' department.
- The six-hour day and the hiring hall for dock workers, reaffirming what had been set up in 1934.

The strike began on October 30, 1936. Unlike the Battle of 1934, it was peaceful on the West Coast, although attempts to widen the strike into a national action, by extending it to the East and Gulf Coasts, saw violence on the Atlantic. The strike was on its way to being won, when its course was severely deflected, as political differences emerged pitting Harry Bridges against Harry Lundeberg.

The split in the maritime movement came over a number of issues. First, Bridges declared that if the strike could not be settled without the Sailors accepting the Copeland fink book, they should take the book. Then, a controversy broke out over the *Voice of the Federation*, the weekly newspaper of the Maritime Federation, now edited by one Barney Mayes. Mayes, a Trotskyist, was charged with undermining the strike by truthfully printing in December that the S.U.P. was near a settlement with the shipowners. Although the strike was universally felt to be the Sailors' game, in that it was their turn to win a firm hiring hall, Harry Bridges and his allies refused to brook any action that might distract from their central role as West Coast maritime labor leaders. Success with the newspapers in 1934, plus the support of the Communist machine, had bestowed an exalted status upon them.[11]

The political infighting in the unions had bizarre effects, of which the Mayes controversy is a striking example. The Russian government was just then executing Trotskyists and supposed Trotskyists in large numbers, and the name of the old, dissident revolutionary himself was a curse in Communist circles. The hue-and-cry over Barney Mayes became enormous, culminating, after the strike, in a Maritime Federation hearing in which Mayes was subjected to a range of accusations and insinuations worthy of the Moscow Trials themselves. "Archbishop" Roy Hudson, commissar of the Communist maritime forces, over the signature of the Waterfront Section, Communist Party, U.S.A., issued a declaration headed "TROTSKYITES Plot to Disrupt U.S. Maritime Unions," in which he charged that the Trotsky partisans had "worked together with stool pigeons and the fascist agents of Germany and Japan to prepare a war against the Soviet Union, murdered Kirov . . . and plotted the death of Stalin and other leaders of the Workers Republic." Turning to the *Voice of the Federation* and the S.U.P., Hudson claimed that "Barney Mayes and Norma Perry, his co-worker," had "tried to smuggle . . . into the unions in a concealed form" an "anti-working class policy." As the secret controller of the conspiracy, Hudson named James P. Cannon, a Trotskyist leader active in the California state Socialist Party, which the Trotskyists had joined. Hudson maintained that *"Mayes and other Trotskyite rats make their main task the splitting of the progressive forces by trying to mobilize and incite others against the Communists,"* (emphasis in the original). He labelled the Trotskyists agents of "Hearst, the shipowners, . . . Hitler and all the forces of reaction." Finally, quoting fellow Communist leader Jack Stachel, Hudson's splenetic declaration revealed the real source of conflict: the followers of Trotsky had opposed "the great Stalin, whose stature rises with every achievement in the building of socialism, with the rising people's front the world over."

It was undeniable that the Trotskyists were critical of Stalin and his followers in the Communist Party. As to the charge that they were agents of Hitler, not even the most avid partisan of the Communists would wish to defend this slander today. (The labor journalist Benjamin Stolberg later referred to the attack on Barney Mayes as the first 'Moscow trial' in America.) But that Mayes and other Trotskyists, including Cannon, were involved in the affairs of the S.U.P., was also undeniable.

At one point during the 1936-37 strike, just before Christmas, the anger of the S.U.P. rank and file at the maneuvers of the Communists brought about the publication of a special S.U.P. bulletin, #32, that roundly scored the Muscovites as a "disruptive faction." Bulletin #32 declared that "since 1935 — when the 'party' discovered they couldn't dictate to Lundeberg, this disruptive faction launched every vile, whispering, character assassination campaign they could think up against us. Against Lundeberg, and against every progressive policy which the Sailors' Union launched in order to protect the interest of its membership . . . We will continue to expose this faction from now on every way we know how — and we say to them flatly *You will not succeed in sacrificing the interests of the Sailors to the interests of a narrow political faction*" (emphasis in original).

Evidence of the infiltration and influence of Communists within the Union then came, as the Communists utilized Lundeberg's temporary absence from San Francisco to launch a brief *putsch* in which the S.U.P. "officially" repudiated Bulletin #32. However, the euphoria of the Communists at this audacious act was to prove short-lived. Cannon, writing in the California Socialist newspaper *Labor Action*, described the Muscovite "raid" as "a field day for the dry-land sailors, the meddling lawyers, and the framers of crooked headlines," the latter a reference to pro-Communist elements then associated with the San Francisco dailies. "The Sailors Union of the Pacific had been 'captured,'" Cannon noted. But then, he wrote, "Lundeberg came back to town roaring like a bull about the dirty tricks played in his absence . . . The

[11]Lang, ibid., Lampman, op. cit.; *Voice of the Federation* (San Francisco), 1937 issues on Mayes, at Anne Rand Memorial Research Library, I.L.W.U., San Francisco.

union was 'uncaptured,' the real militants were back at the helm."[12]

Trotskyists in S.U.P.

Mayes, Cannon, and other Trotskyists had been brought to the S.U.P. "by (a) fluke," according to Frank Barbaria, a leading Trotskyist militant in the maritime field. Many years later, Barbaria stated that one John Brum, a Trotskyist working on an academic thesis, had visited the S.U.P. offices, seeking an interview on technical matters. There he encountered Norma Perry, working as Lundeberg's clerical helper. Perry, who was to become the target of a long and particularly vile slander campaign by the Communists, had been a party militant herself, along with members of her family. However, she had grown disaffected, and warned Lundeberg, who was being wooed by the Communists, not to join, as they would use and discard him. (He never joined, although many contrary stories have circulated over the years.) Perry, aware of the violent hatred of the Communists for the Trotskyists, had concluded that a tactical alliance was worthwhile, if the latter could aid the S.U.P. and Lundeberg against Bridges and the Communists. Perry then met Barney Mayes, who proved to be a talented journalist, and soon Barbaria and a certain Frank Lovell, another Trotskyist of whom we shall hear more, entered the S.U.P., just before the 1936-37 strike began.

According to Barbaria — and the Trotskyists at that time — the struggle between the S.U.P. and the Stalinists was simple. Barbaria underscored the Communist Party's outrage that its "monopoly" control of the West Coast maritime unions was being challenged, and that its fight to gain acceptance of the "progressive fink book" was not succeeding. Barbaria affirms that the Communists had chosen, in the interest of the People's Front with Roosevelt, to hold down any and all militant action by the workers; eventually, the Communists hoped to integrate the merchant mariners into a fully governmentalized institution. As good followers of the Russian model of "state socialism," the Communists seemed to think they could similarly use the Roosevelt state to effectively militarize the seamen and submit them, through political wire-pulling, to their "progressive" ends. The main goal was to have a pro-Soviet intelligence and action force operating alongside the U.S. army and navy in time of war.

Barbaria puts it bluntly: the 1936-37 strike "was fought in the Maritime Federation Councils up and down the coast, not on the picket lines. The shipowners' side was being fought for by the the C.P. in these councils," he has written, pointing out that Bridges sought to exempt perishable and military cargoes from the strike, weakening the impact of the walkout. "The Kremlin must have been putting tremendous pressure on the U.S. Communist Party to get rid of this Trotskyite editor (Mayes) and to get on with cooperating with Roosevelt."

In the event, the 1936-37 strike ended with victories for both competing factions in the Maritime Federation. When the men went back to work in January 1937, the Sailors had won a guarantee for their hiring hall and a $10 per month wage increase. On the other hand, the Communists secured the removal of Barney Mayes and other Trotskyists, including one Joseph Hansen, from the *Voice of the Federation*. The real casualty of the strike was the Maritime Federation itself. Now fully controlled by the Communists, the Federation would never again act in the interest of the noble aim of maritime unity. In 1938 the S.U.P. left the Federation, which died at the beginning of the second world war.

From this point on, Lundeberg proved a determined enemy of the Communists. Nearly every S.U.P. publication in the twenty years until his death in 1957 reflected his disgust with them, hammering into the membership the lessons of Kronstadt and the R.I.L.U. "seamen's clubs," and the outlook of Tranmael's anti-Moscow Norwegian Labor Party.

The alliance between Lundeberg and the Trotskyists was destined to survive for some time; clearly, the S.U.P. could not do without specialized help in its struggle for independence from Communism. Frank Barbaria would become a union organizer in the fish cannery field under Lundeberg's direction, while another Trotskyist, Tom Kerry, worked with Lundeberg in the struggle against the Communists in the Marine Firemen's Union. Writing of Kerry in 1940, Lundeberg would state that, for himself, he was "not a Trotskyite, or any other form of political emancipator, and never will be," adding "my policy is strictly trade-union; along militant lines." However, he insisted Kerry was "sincere . . . capable . . . (and) has had experience directly with me here at San Francisco for four years now, and he knows the S.U.P. slant and he'll work night and day."

The Trotskyists were allowed to remain within the S.U.P. until the end of the 1940s (as we shall see), but they never gained positions of real leadership, and once the circle around Lundeberg had perfected its own leadership style, the Trotskyists fell out of prominence. Only Mayes, who eventually went to work with the California Federation of Labor, retained some influence within the S.U.P. (It should be here noted that Mayes was the author of an exceptionally significant manuscript of highly detailed memoirs. This untitled manuscript, of great relevance to students of the early history of the U.S. Communist Party, the Trotskyist movement, and the S.U.P., is currently held by Paul Dempster, President/Secretary-Treasurer of the S.U.P.)

Lundeberg and his colleagues in the S.U.P. leadership repaid their political debts to the Trotskyists in a

[12]Roy Hudson, *Trotskyites Plot to Disrupt U.S. Maritime Unions*, New York, C.P.U.S.A., n.d.; Benjamin Stolberg, "Communist Wreckers in American Labor," *Saturday Evening Post* (New York), September 2, 1939; Sailors' Union of the Pacific, *West Coast Sailors*, Official Bulletin #32, December 22, 1936, in S.U.P. central Archive (this is a mimeographed strike bulletin and should not be confused with the printed newspaper of the same title, begun in 1937); James P. Cannon, "Four Days That Shook the Waterfront," *Labor Action* (San Francisco), January 2, 1937, reprinted in James P. Cannon, *Notebook of an Agitator*, New York, Pioneer Publishers, 1958.

number of ways. They allowed them membership and employment in the S.U.P., and in addition, they performed such small acts as the endorsement, by S.U.P. San Pedro patrolman H.J. "Blackie" Vincent and San Pedro dispatcher Joe Voltero, of a "counter-trial" launched in Mexico, in April 1937, under the presidency of the philosopher John Dewey, to clear Trotsky of the Stalinist charges aired in Moscow. For at least a decade the "fraction" in the S.U.P. played a leading role in the Trotskyist movement, and it was in maritime that the U.S. Trotskyists gained their only chance to compete head-to-head with the Communists for mass leadership of workers. Above all, the Trotskyists, however useful they may have been to the S.U.P., succeeded no better than the Communists in establishing themselves at the S.U.P.'s "vanguard."

In the fight against Communist control, Lundeberg also depended for support on elements in the I.W.W., Marine Transport Workers' Union No. 510. In the aftermath of Mayes' removal from the helm of the *Voice of the Federation*, the newspaper had briefly been run by Wobbly poet Ralph Chaplin. Although not a Trotskyist, Chaplin was equally hostile to the Communists and supportive of Lundeberg and the S.U.P.

Chaplin's own interpretation of the situation on the West Coast was significant, and pregnant with meaning for the future. He found a parallel in Europe. A civil war had begun in Spain in July 1936, when an attempt by military and fascist elements to overthrow a left-wing elected government had provoked massive resistance by the working class. Spain divided into a fascist and a revolutionary zone. In the latter area, the Communists were fighting for total control, seeking to liquidate their critics on the left — also portrayed as "Trotskyite agents of fascism." For Chaplin, the comparison between Spain and the U.S. West Coast was obvious, and ominous.

(The Spanish civil war saw at its commencement the last of the great cycle of naval revolts in the first half of this century. In the first days of the military uprising, anarchist-syndicalist and socialist cells organized by the lower ranks and non-commissioned officers acted to secure the bulk of the Spanish fleet — then, surprisingly, the largest in the world outside the major powers — for the Republic. A special role was played by radio personnel, including a communications officer, Benjamín Balboa, who coordinated the emergency response by leftists in the fleet, from the naval ministry in Madrid. The anti-fascist forces were able to gain control of the battleship *Jaime Primero*, the cruisers *Libertad*, *Miguel de Cervantes*, and *Méndez Núñez*, and numerous destroyers, submarines, and patrol boats. The Spanish action was emulated in September 1936, with a brief and unsuccessful rebellion, in Lisbon, of the crews of the Portuguese vessels *Afonso de Albuquerque*, a sloop, and the *Dão*, a destroyer. The rebels attempted to join their Spanish comrades. Unfortunately, the combination of poor Republican strategic thinking in the early stage of the conflict, and less-than-competent advice from Soviet naval advisers later on the scene, dissipated the tremendous military advantages represented by the ships and bases held by the forces of the Spanish Republic.)[13]

Beginning in 1937, the S.U.P. was forced to chart a risky course between its opponents among the conservative forces in the union movement and the Communist enemy. Of course, the general labor public seldom clearly saw the reality of the situation. The Communists gained major influence in the new C.I.O. movement and in the Roosevelt administration's National Labor Relations Board, as well as in the daily press and at large. It was relatively easy for them to label Lundeberg as a "conservative," only a little more credible than the claim linking Trotsky and Hitler. Lundeberg and the S.U.P. remained anything but conservative, as their future actions on rank-and-file issues would prove. In mid-1937, the S.U.P. investigated entry into the C.I.O., then seen as the radical pole in the union movement. However, this effort proved unsuccessful after the top leadership position in the California C.I.O. was given to Harry Bridges by C.I.O. leader John L. Lewis.

The S.U.P. criticism of the Communist Party was, to emphasize, anything *but* conservative. During the controversy over entry into the C.I.O., for example, the S.U.P. issued a notable *Open Letter to Harry Bridges, C.I.O. Director,* in which the Sailors developed a far-sighted analysis of the limitations of C.I.O. "industrial unionism." Among other points, they noted that although C.I.O. unions were organized on an industry-wide basis, they did not bargain industry-wide, in the main.

Steady As She Goes

Perhaps the best statement of the position of the S.U.P. at this time is included in a short pamphlet, titled *Steady As She Goes*, issued to the membership late in 1937. The leaders of the Union affirmed that "today there is a bitter struggle going on between the old-line craft leaders of the A.F.L. who constituted themselves into the C.I.O., and are engaged in a quarrel with their former associates over respective fields of influence and jurisdiction in the American trades-

[13]Frank Barbaria, letter, October 16, 1983, in S.U.P. central Archive. The most substantive and despicable recent example of the Communist slander campaign against Norma Perry, which incredibly continues after fifty years, is to be found in Estolv E. Ward, *The Gentle Dynamiter*, Palo Alto, Ramparts Press, 1983. On Lundeberg's non-existent C.P. membership, Stack, conversation cited. On related matters, see Harry Lundeberg, letter, March 15, 1940, in S.U.P. central Archive; Farrell Dobbs, *Trade Union Problems*, New York, Pioneer Publishers, n.d. (1941?); Lang, op. cit.; James P. Cannon, *The History of American Trotskyism*, New York, Pioneer Publishers, 1944; and *Notebook of an Agitator*, ibid; Art Preis, *Stalinists on the Waterfront*, New York, Pioneer Publishers, 1947; *The Case of Leon Trotsky, Report of Hearings on Charges Made Against Him in the Moscow Trials*, New York, Merit Publishers, 1969; Leon Trotsky, *Writings, 1939-1940*, New York, Pathfinder Press, 1973; Barney Mayes, untitled manuscript, n.d.; Tom Kerry, *Workers, Bosses, and Bureaucrats*, New York, Pathfinder Press, 1980; Mary-Alice Waters, "Tom Kerry — Proletarian Fighter," *The Militant* (New York), January 28, 1983. Also, file of *I.W.W. Seaman* (New York), 1937, in S.U.P. central Archive; Chaplin, op. cit.; Thompson and Murfin, op. cit. On the naval revolt at the beginning of the Spanish civil war, see Willard C. Frank, Jr., *Sea Power, Politics, and the Onset of the Spanish War, 1936*, doctoral dissertation, University of Pittsburgh, 1969, and "Naval Operations in the Spanish Civil War, 1936-1939," in *Naval War College Review* (Annapolis), January-February 1984.

union movement. It is inevitable, therefore that the S.U.P., while having no quarrel with the rank and file of either the A.F.L. or the C.I.O. should be drawn into the riptide created by this bitter struggle." The pamphlet went on to underscore a rejection of the C.I.O's "industrial union" pretensions, comparing them to Hitler's use of the word "socialism" in his "National Socialist" program.

The pamphlet contained a list of the achievements won by the S.U.P. and its new leaders in the post-1934 period, affirming that the union had:

- Defeated the I.S.U. leadership.
- Established 100 percent control of shipping through the hiring hall.
- Doubled wages and abolished optional overtime.
- Done away with blacklisting.
- Added some 1,000-1,500 jobs on the West Coast.
- Established its own strike-and-lockout fund, with the result that the union was the only one with its own strike fund in the 1936-37 strike.
- Beaten the Copeland fink book.
- Reestablished its branch in Honolulu, and set up new branches in Aberdeen, Washington and Vancouver, British Columbia, and an office in New York.
- Established a shipwreck benefit, a hospital benefit, and a large burial plot.
- Accumulated no debts, had a bank account of $30,000, and owned its own building in San Francisco, worth $60,000, and a lot in San Pedro worth $10,000.

It should be added that in May 1937 the Union gained a valuable further weapon in the form of a weekly newspaper, the *West Coast Sailors.*

The pamphlet concluded by stressing the greatest asset of the S.U.P.: "*control (of) our destinies. No top committees: no executive boards can tell us what to do. The membership runs the union, and we are our own masters!* (emphasis in original)." Although sympathetic to the aims of the mass of C.I.O. members, the S.U.P. was clearly disturbed by the anti-democratic, "top-down" methods established by the Communists inside the National Maritime Union (N.M.U.), which, set up in the ruins of the East Coast I.S.U., was finally granted the C.I.O. charter for organization of seamen. In addition, with the final disappearance of the I.S.U., the A.F.L. had shown interest in a rapprochement with the S.U.P.[14]

S.U.P. vs I.L.W.U. — "Shepard Line Beef"

Intertwined with the political fight between Lundeberg and the Communists, jurisdictional conflicts between the S.U.P. and the Communist-lining West Coast longshoremen, now organized in the C.I.O. International Longshoremen's and Warehousemen's Union, began to flourish. The West Coast longshoremen had long looked with hungry eyes at the work done by Sailors loading and unloading cargo on the steam schooners, and as the factional fight became open war, the steam schooner controversy turned uglier than it had been in decades. The I.L.W.U. commenced a concerted effort, to raid the steam schooners away from the S.U.P., that did not cease until the literal disappearance of steam schooner operations from the coast years after the second world war. The Communist propaganda machine had begun a war on Lundeberg and the S.U.P. that would reach pathological dimensions, and raiding of the S.U.P. by another union came to be considered a legitimate political weapon in the struggle. The breaking point was reached in 1938 with the "Shepard Line beef."

The Shepard freighter *Timber Rush* had spent the winter of 1937-38 on the East Coast, where its S.U.P. crew was paid off and discharged. In springtime, when the ship once more crewed up, the S.U.P. found that it had been replaced on board the vessel by members of the N.M.U., which had been granted jurisdiction over Shepard Line employees after an election held by the National Labor Relations Board in which the S.U.P. had not been on the ballot. The N.L.R.B. was then a center of Communist influence in the Roosevelt administration.

The *Timber Rush* arrived in Seattle in April, with its N.M.U. crew, considered scabs by the S.U.P., and I.L.W.U. dockworkers broke through S.U.P. picket lines to work the ship. When the ship moved to Tacoma, however, S.U.P. men drove the N.M.U. off the vessel. The refusal of Tacoma longshoremen, who sided with the S.U.P. and had stayed out of the I.L.W.U., to work the ship, brought closure of the Port of Tacoma by the employers after the *Timber Rush* stood idle for 10 days. At the same time, Portland police helped I.L.W.U. and N.M.U. members bust S.U.P. picket lines around another Shepard vessel, the *Sea Thrush*. A third vessel, the *Windrush*, was picketed in New York.

The *Sea Thrush* came to San Francisco, and was met by an S.U.P. picket line. An attempt by the I.L.W.U., again supported by police, to break the line, turned into a long-remembered free-for-all, producing a distinctive photographic image of Lundeberg in action, urging on his members. Similar incidents involving the vessel *Sagebrush* in San Pedro, provoked confusion and dissension among the longshoremen there, who were I.L.W.U. members but were unenthusastic about confronting the Sailors. Several months, and extensive negotiations in Washington and elsewhere, would pass before the Shepard Line returned to S.U.P. control.[15]

The I.L.W.U action in crossing S.U.P. picket lines marked the end of an era for the Sailors. It was now clear that the Communist elements in the union movement would stop at nothing in their quest for total dictatorship. The S.U.P. leaders had gone on the assumption that, aided by the Trotskyists and Wobblies, and working through the Maritime Federation, they might be able to out-maneuver the Communists while maintaining their own independence. This was now, it

---

[14]*An Open Letter to Harry Bridges, C.I.O. Director*, San Francisco, S.U.P., 1937; *Steady As She Goes*, San Francisco, S.U.P. 1937. [15]Magden and Martinson, op. cit.; *West Coast Sailors*, issues on the Shepard Line controversy, 1938.

seemed, impossible. In the Shepard controversy the Communist faction in the C.I.O. had united with the employers, and with the police, to fight the S.U.P. The Maritime Federation was a shell of its former self.

The Sailors had courageously attempted to pursue an independent course that won them the affection and admiration of many workers, and not only Trotskyists and Wobblies. But the time had come to admit that the course must be changed. In October, 1938, in a momentous decision that would provoke dissension and argument lasting until today, the S.U.P. accepted a new charter from the American Federation of Labor, and organized the Seafarers' International Union as a structure to meet the Communist challenge on a national and international scale.

Ed Coester had claimed credit for naming the new organization (a Seafarers' Industrial Union of Wobbly-like sympathies had previously existed in British Columbia.) The S.U.P. would remain autonomous within the S.I.U., and in the years to come the two unions would face differing fortunes; but it is the task of this narrative to tell the tale of the S.U.P. The history of the S.I.U. must await another pen.

The year that saw the I.S.U. in essence reborn also had seen the passing of Andrew Furuseth, its main pioneer. His honorary pallbearers included Paul Scharrenberg, Carl Lynch, Walter Macarthur, George Larsen, and Pete Gill. On January 23, 1938, his body lay in state in the auditorium of the Department of Labor Building in Washington, D.C. On January 24, his eulogy was delivered by U.S. Senator Robert M. LaFollette, Jr., son of the author of the 1915 Seamen's Act. Furuseth's years had been filled with contention, fulfillment, and disappointment, and many of the S.U.P. partisans must have felt a certain sadness at the 1936 split between the "old man" and the Union. In honor of his achievements in the legal field, the Union commissioned a bust of Furuseth, which was first erected on the San Francisco Embarcadero and which today stands before the S.U.P. headquarters building in the city that saw the founding of the Coast Seamen's Union.[16]

A Spanish Interlude

1938 saw another chapter in S.U.P. history transpire far from the West Coast, in war-torn Spain. Because the incident in question illumines the histories of the Union and of the Spanish Republic, it is worth recounting.

Sam (Lloyd) Usinger, veteran S.U.P. militant and I.W.W. follower, had shipped aboard the S.U.P.-contracted vessel *Oregon,* chartered by Bulk Carriers Corporation for a voyage to deliver supplies to the Spanish Republican forces. Usinger arrived in the Republican port of Barcelona as an active supporter, like all radicals, of the Republican government. But what he saw in Spain deeply disturbed him. Some thousands of idealistic young Americans had volunteered to fight in Spain in the Russian-organized "international brigades." Usinger found that these young enthusiasts were "getting butchered for the party, when you haven't even a dying man's chance to live. We call them 'cannon meat'," he added.

Usinger learned that the Communists were succeeding, for the moment, in the campaign for control of the Spanish left that had provoked the unease of Ralph Chaplin. And he discovered that aboard the vessel *West Harshaw* N.M.U. crew members were prepared to sail from Barcelona to the fascist ports of Cádiz and Sevilla without protest. The C.I.O. union had ostensibly arranged a war bonus to be paid to the men. The *Oregon,* by contrast, had been chartered to visit *only* the Spanish Republican ports, with a $25,000 bond to be paid by the employer to the West Coast crew if any Spanish fascist port was called.

Usinger urged the S.U.P. membership, in a letter published in the *West Coast Sailors,* to discourage contributions to the Communist-controlled North American Committee to Aid Spanish Democracy, declaring that the volunteers he had encountered in Spain were without food, clothes, blankets, or tobacco, and intimating that the contributions would remain in the hands of the Communist Party network in the U.S. Usinger went on to comment bitterly on the presence in Spain of "Mink the Fink," the former M.W.I.U. head, G.P.U. gunman, and stewpot proprietor, who had first been reported on the scene a year before. After the bloody "May events" of 1937, in which the Communists in Barcelona provoked anarchist and independent Marxist workers into a violent showdown, Mink had been named as a killer of workers by the New York Spanish syndicalist newspaper *Cultura Proletaria.* This newspaper had been supported decades before by the I.S.U.

Mink's fellow M.W.I.U. activist, William C. McCuistion later gave an admiring eyewitness account of the S.U.P.'s Usinger as a major participant in the Barcelona anti-communist underground during the period the *Oregon* was in port; McCuistion had fled the international brigades after some time as a guard in a brigade prison. As he left, he freed the prisoners, who were apparently political dissidents marked for liquidation, rather than mere deserters.

Usinger was finally arrested and threatened with death by Communist police. Apparently, he and other members of the *Oregon* crew became involved in a tragic incident, when they attempted to help one of the American volunteers, Albert Wallach, escape from Spain. Wallach was taken off the *Oregon* and killed. McCuistion said this was the excuse for Usinger's arrest and the order for deportation of the S.U.P. militant, on charges of endangering the morale of the international volunteers.

Usinger's conclusion following his experience in Spain was eloquent. Speaking of the Communists, he warned "do not let them get a foothold in your Unions; drive them from your unions, and keep rank and file

[16]Coester, interview cited; on the British Columbia S.I.U., files in S.U.P. Seattle Branch Archive; on radical sympathizers of S.U.P., Herbert Brandon, interview, July 1983.

representation in your industry by organization." The San Francisco Communists replied by claiming Usinger had never been to Spain, which was easily disproven. Within a short time, the S.U.P. had followed Usinger's advice, and allowed a number of prominent Communist-lining members who had gone to Spain, including M.W.I.U. "hero" Joe Bianca, to effectively remove themselves from the Union. Lundeberg, in commenting on the departure of these "comrades," joined Usinger in assailing the willingness of the N.M.U. to sail U.S. ships into the Spanish fascist ports.[17]

Coming of Second World War

The final incident marking the year 1938 in the historical calendar of the S.U.P. involved an attempt by the federal authorities to set up government-controlled fink hiring halls for seamen. The U.S. Maritime Commission under Admiral Emory S. Land had dictated a policy on the East Coast whereby ships operated under the account of the Commission could only be crewed by sailors who signed articles before a shipping commissioner, with men from union hiring halls barred from service. Once Admiral Land attempted to transfer his policy to the West Coast, where Maritime Commission ships had previously not operated, the S.U.P. met the challenge in a forthright way, supported by the Pacific Coast Marine Firemen and the I.W.W. Marine Transport Workers. The N.M.U. refused to oppose the new government fink halls, since, like the Copeland continuous discharge book, they purportedly represented "progressive" Rooseveltian policies. The S.U.P. won the dispute, and the government withdrew its fink hall from the West Coast until the onset of the second world war.[18]

In February, 1939, Pete Gill, who had been the S.U.P.'s pioneering leader in the Northwest for so many decades, retired, although he remained on full pay from the Union until his death in 1945. During his retirement, he worked with Ottilie Dombroff (later Markholt), a young woman labor historian married to S.U.P. activist Bob Dombroff, on the manuscript history, *The Sailors Union of the Pacific, 1885-1929.*

By 1939, the indicators of a new war, in which the U.S. would almost certainly become involved, had become overwhelming. In September, war began between Hitler's Germany and an allied Britain and France. The immediate cause was the German invasion of Poland, which Hitler carried out with the support of Stalinist Russia, as the two dictatorships were then allied in the notorious Hitler-Stalin pact. Soon Russia invaded Finland. Although Finland was allied in principle with Germany, many radical workers in the U.S., including Scandinavians in the S.U.P., reacted to the Russian attack on Finland with indignation. Still, a reading of the *West Coast Sailors,* shows that few in the Union were enthusiastic about a war, whoever might wage it. But when war finally came to the United States, in December, 1941, following the Japanese attack on Pearl Harbor, S.U.P. members served their country loyally. Many lost their lives on vessels sunk by submarines as well as in battle. 6,000 American seamen died in the conflict; the merchant marine casualty rate (2.8 percent) was higher than that of any U.S. service except the Marine Corps (2.9) but the men who manned the ships have, even at the time of this writing, received no recognition from the U.S. Veterans Administration. An argument that is often put forward to justify the denial of veterans' benefits is that the seamen enjoyed Union wages and conditions. But when a ship went down, the survivors, if such there were, who suffered days and weeks of exposure on floating wreckage or in lifeboats (if they were lucky) received no pay for time after the ship was sunk. A soldier or naval seaman or marine drew pay for every day he was in uniform.

Five months before the Japanese attack on Pearl Harbor, Hitler's invasion of Russia had changed the U.S. Communist line to frenzied calls for the defense of the Russian motherland, from their previous praise for the Hitler-Stalin pact and violent attacks on Britain and France. During the war, the Communist-lining unions called for a ban on strikes, and imprisonment of workers such as the coal miners and railroad workers who struck during the hostilities. They avidly supported the imprisonment of 18 Trotskyists who had been active in Minneapolis, and who had opposed the war. Most importantly, through the N.M.U. the Communists called on the seamen to accept a regulation of the merchant marine undreamt of even during the days of the government fink hall. With an eye to United States aid for Russia, they asked the seamen to become, in effect, a completely regimented service arm comparable to the army or navy.

Although more genuinely patriotic than the Communists, Lundeberg and the S.U.P. strongly opposed the surrender of union rights and the militarization of shipping the Muscovites demanded. While prepared to die for their country, the members of the S.U.P. wished to meet their fates as free men. This partial refusal to accept pseudo-patriotic appeals led to grumbling in various circles during the war, but the S.U.P. remained faithful to its tradition of independence and autonomy as well as to its national loyalty.

One element in the governmental program for militarizaton of the seamen, in the mold of the Copeland fink book and the government fink hall, came through

[17]Sam Usinger, "American Seamen in Spain," *West Coast Sailors*, July 15, 1938; the first identification of Mink in Spain seems to be that included in unsigned, "La Cheka Bolchevique en Barcelona," *Cultura Proletaria*, (New York), September 25, 1937; in the massive literature of the Spanish civil war there is a great deal on the Barcelona "May events," but the classic account remains George Orwell, *Homage to Catalonia*, London, Secker & Warburg, 1937; on the *Oregon* incident, see Cecil Eby, *Between the Bullet and the Lie*, New York, Holt, Rinehart & Winston, 1969, and McCuistion, testimony cited; also, unsigned, "Calmrats Be — Calmed!," *West Coast Sailors*, August 12, 1938. On the dropping of Bianca and others, letter signed by seven volunteers in Spain, July 15, 1938, S.U.P. central Archive; Harry Lundeberg, "S.U.P. Membership Makes Short Shrift of Attacks by Renegade Stooges," *West Coast Sailors*, September 23, 1938, George Kaye, "'We couldn't believe it. . . ,'" *Volunteer for Liberty* (Barcelona), October 6, 1938. On the Bulk Carriers charter to Spain, Marine Firemen's Union, *The Story of the Marine Firemen's Union*, San Francisco, M.F.O.W., 1945. [18]Lang, op. cit.; Lampman, op. cit.

a scheme to promote governmental training and qualification of seamen. The S.U.P. countered with the creation of the Andrew Furuseth School of Seamanship, through which seamen would be trained by the Union. This facility exists today, as an apprenticeship program for personnel entering the merchant marine. It is currently headed by Thomas F. Zee.

Another way in which the S.U.P. leadership affirmed their faith in the dignity of free men came when some 35-40 ethnic Japanese members of the union were interned by the federal government, following the Pearl Harbor attack. At a time when the anger and bias of the American population was running strongly against all things associated with Japan, Lundeberg and New York S.U.P. agent Morris Weisberger distinguished themselves with an act of extreme courage and principle. Weisberger went to the highest levels of the U.S. military, insisting that all Japanese S.U.P. members were of proven loyalty, and that whatever the deeds of the Tokyo regime, American sailors of Japanese ethnicity should not be consigned to the miserable conditions in the concentration camp at Santa Anita, the Southern California race track where they were housed in the horse stalls.

The authorities finally acceded, and all the S.U.P. men of Japanese ancestry were released and permitted to sail in the Atlantic theater. While a very few trade union and civil liberties figures had defended the interned Japanese Americans' constitutional rights, most of their actions had been verbal or limited to the courtroom. Morris Weisberger, in typical S.U.P. style, took the initiative and confronted the issue directly. Some today might consider this the greatest single moment in the history of the Union, reminiscent of Sigismund Danielewicz's lone defense of the Chinese, described in Chapter II. This incident has remained unknown to the general public, and even to the specialized legal and political science scholars who have, in the past decade, spent so much time reviewing the wartime relocation controversy and its consequences for the Japanese Americans. It should be noted that the record of the S.U.P. on this matter not only contrasts strongly with that of the majority of the American labor and liberal communities, who viewed the problem of the interned Japanese Americans with disinterest, but reflects especially well on the Union when compared with the position of the Communists. The latter, so often touted as defenders of minority rights, were among the loudest persecutors of the Japanese.

Wartime Sacrifices

Much could be written about the sacrifices of the seamen during the war. With the beginning of U.S. involvement, the shipowners, handsomely paid by the federal government for their contribution to the military machine, secured the denial of war bonuses for seamen shipping between the U.S. West Coast and Hawaii, on Pacific or Atlantic coastwise voyages, or to Alaska, the West Indies, and South America. In all these trades shipping was menaced by enemy submarines; eventually a federal Maritime War Emergency Board granted one-hundred percent bonuses for most offshore voyages, including West coast to Hawaii, with forty percent bonuses to Alaska and the West Coast of South America.

Without doubt the most gallant action by a U.S. merchant marine crew in the second world war was that of the *Stephen Hopkins*, a Liberty ship.

The *Stephen Hopkins* was built by the Kaiser shipyard at Richmond, California. She was operated by the Luckenbach Gulf Steamship Co. According to Fred Klebingat, as interviewed by Karl Kortum, the *Hopkins* had wooden booms, an oddity, perhaps reflecting a wartime shortage of steel and the availability of long spars of Douglas fir on the Pacific Coast, steam schooner style.

The *Hopkins* was one of the first 20 Liberty ships to be built — in all there were 2,750 ultimately launched in the United States. The new Liberty shipped an S.U.P. deck crew for her maiden voyage, and the engine room gang was hired through the San Francisco Marine Firemen's hall.

The ship left San Francisco on May 25th, 1942, loaded with valuable war cargo, as well as army personnel. Part of the cargo was discharged at Bora Bora, and there was a possibility of the ship being ordered to Guadalcanal. But instead the *Hopkins* went to Wellington, New Zealand, to take on water and supplies, and then continued to Melbourne, Australia to discharge its deck load of army trucks and the remaining military cargo. The *Stephen Hopkins* then proceeded to Port Lincoln in South Australia, loading point of the last surviving square-rigged ships before the war and loaded a full cargo of both bulk and sacked wheat for South Africa.

The vessel left Australia and, after a 32 day voyage to the west, bucking heavy gales, arrived at Durban. During the heavy weather the lifeboats were smashed and much gear carried away. So bad was the weather that beams running fore and aft were cracked and in many places the welding of the plates gave way. The deckhouse tore loose, the welding having let go where it was attached to the deck. The forward ammunition hold was flooded and the bow stove in. The forward gun mounts were wrecked.

After eight days in Durban, discharging grain and having the welders repair the breaks and strains to the deckhouse, deck plating and hull plating, and with the life boats replaced, the Liberty ship left Durban with two thousand tons of sugar for Capetown. After discharging the sugar, the *Hopkins* left in a few days light for Paramaribo, Dutch Guiana, to load bauxite.

Four days out of Capetown, the *Stephen Hopkins* saw two vessels emerge from the morning mists. Some members of the San Francisco-shipped crew thought that they recognized a style of fast merchant ship familiar on the Pacific Coast before the war; the reefer ships *Oregon Express* and *Washington Express* were good examples of the type.

But there was no look of peacetime about this drab and sinister pair. When an unescorted American freighter encountered strange ships in the South Atlantic in 1942, her captain knew that within minutes he would probably face a bitter decision: to surrender and have his ship scuttled — or to fight and be sunk.

Captain Paul Buck of the *Stephen Hopkins* had not long to wait. The German colors were run up on both vessels and gun flashes blazed fore and aft on one of the ships. The flashes were simultaneous (indicating central fire control) and they came from six guns, it was later determined, of 5.9 inches. Each shell weighed four times as much as the shell that could be fired by the lone four-inch gun on the stern of the *Stephen Hopkins*. The Liberty ship had stumbled on what British and American naval intelligence were calling *Raider "J"*.

Captain Buck, who was to die and become one of the historic Americans for whom a Liberty ship was named (with his chief mate), had declared earlier that if he met a German raider he was going to fight. He ordered the general alarm sounded and called for hard left rudder to bring the ship from her heading of 310° true to 260°, directly away from the danger. He was going to offer the smallest possible target, his stern. And the stern was where the four-inch gun was located — a gun left over from the first world war, its recoil chamber in bad order and rifling worn out, but which would sink the German raider.

The first salvo slammed into the *Stephen Hopkins*' superstructure. Shrapnel whistled. Jagged holes opened in thin, unarmored bulkheads. Fires started from shorted electric wires. Men in the watch below, in their bunks, were killed. The ocean on either side churned with shellfire from the raider's lesser guns, 20-mm and 37-mm, as they sought the range and then closed in on the Liberty ship. Both enemy vessels (the second and somewhat larger vessel was a lightly armed freighter keeping a rendezvous with the raider to take off captured prisoners) appeared to have ten machine guns mounted. They rained machine gun bullets on the *Stephen Hopkins*, attempting to keep the crew from manning the Liberty ship's armament.

The raider was only a thousand yards away. But the spirit of Captain Buck was the spirit of the whole crew. The fire from the *Stier* and the *Tannenfels*, for those were their names, was now intense, but instead of producing the panic that German captain Horst Gerlach intended, it moved the merchant seamen and the armed guard to action. The second mate hurried forward and manned a 37-mm gun there and immediately hit the *Stier*. Amidships a 50-mm machine gun joined the battle. One by one, five other machine guns started to chatter at the Germans, the scattered bursts growing into a steady roar as tracer bullets guided the aim of the gunners. A storm of machine gun bullets was now falling on the enemy.

The chief mate, Richard Moczkowski, manned a machine gun amidships. Another machine gun amidships was blown completely off the ship by an enemy salvo. Moczkowski's gun was wrecked and he was wounded. Chief Steward Ford Stilson was in his room making out a menu when the first salvo struck. He later wrote:

"At the end of this first minute or so word was passed to me that the Chief Mate had been wounded. I went back to my room, secured bandages and antiseptics and proceeded to the bridge deck, where I found the Chief Mate reclining on the deck in the thwartship passageway adjacent to the wheelhouse but very active in shouting orders and advising the Captain to keep her turning with her stern bearing on the enemy. The Mate was shot high in the chest and in the left forearm. I applied a tourniquet and bandaged both wounds. I started below to get more material ready for the next casualty, but returned up the ladder at the sound of severe groans.

"He [Moczkowski] had gotten to his feet with the aid of one of the ordinary seamen, Piercy, and had turned [to] the opposite passage where he was again struck, this time in the leg, by a fragment. All this time shells had been riddling the superstructure . . ."

The merchant seamen stepped without flinching into the places of the gun crew as man after man was killed by the enemy shrapnel. The two 37-mm guns forward put between fifty and sixty shells into the larger enemy vessel, slowly crippling her.

We now turn to the only ordnance of consequence aboard the *Stephen Hopkins*, the four inch gun in the gun tub aft. Because of its age and deficiencies this had been fired only three times in practice during the voyage. On the boat deck Ensign Kenneth M. Willett, U.S.N.R., commander of the naval armed guard, was running to his station at the stern gun when he was hit by a high-explosive shell burst. He gasped in pain, badly struck in the stomach by a shell fragment. The experience of one of Willett's crew, Paul B. Porter, is recounted as follows in the book *German Raiders of World War II*:

"Porter had not been asleep very long when something like a sledgehammer hit the deck. He looked out the porthole of his starboard midship cabin and saw two ships, one of which was blazing away at *Hopkins*, and he could hear his own guns opening up. He grabbed a pea coat, sweater, and helmet — the gun crew slept in their clothes — and rushed aft to his 50-caliber mount, passing a deckhand whose buttocks had been shot off. But since his gun, wet under its canvas cover, would not function, he joined the four-inch crew who were being cut down man by man, the dead and dying being replaced by volunteers (ordinary seamen). Piercy had seen two ships flying signal flags when 'suddenly we received a blast and knew they were no friends of ours.' "

Author Robert L. Vargas has described the climax of the battle:

"On the *Stephen Hopkins*' stern Ensign Willett had reached his battle station at the 4-inch gun. With one hand clutched to his stomach wound, he rallied his young armed guard crew. His orders were short and crisp. Reacting, one seaman grabbed a shell from the ready magazine and shoved it into the breech.

Another relayed the range, one thousand yards. Willett ordered his gunners to fire at the raider's waterline. The 4-inch gun roared. Seconds later the shell exploded inside the *Stier*.

"Again and again the gun crew loaded and fired. A fourth, then a fifth shell hit the *Stier*. Very soon white smoke was pouring from holes near her waterline. Willett, straining to see his target through the smoke yelled for the pointer and trainer to keep aiming at the hull.

"Engineer Cronk no longer needed his headphones to hear the battle. Explosions echoed down the funnel into the engine room. Like every other man there, Cronk dreaded the shell that might explode a boiler. Then the deck shuddered and the lights went out. Cronk stood rigid, watching the boiler fires, until dim emergency lights flickered on, casting eerie shadows.

"Topside, a high-explosive shell hit the freighter's bow. As the smoke drifted away, Captain Buck could see the 37-mm gun platform wrecked and burning, the gun handlers killed or wounded. Another shell wrecked the radio room, ending the radioman's frantic SOS signals. Lifeboats along the port side dangled, splintered and torn, from their davits. The accurate German gunnery continued to rip gaping holes in the hull, and incendiaries started new fires.

"But Buck still commanded a fighting ship. His machine-gun fire peppered both the *Stier* and the *Tannenfels*. When the raider tried to maneuver into position for a six-gun broadside, Buck saw to it that the helmsman kept his ship stern on. At regular intervals, above the din, he could hear the 4-inch gun crack.

"At 1,000 yards' range Ensign Willett's crew furiously loaded and fired. In less than twenty minutes they had fired thirty-five 4-inch rounds, most of which had hit the *Stier* near the waterline. Between shots Willett praised his men or leaned down the ammunition hoist and shouted encouragement to the seamen passing powder and shells up from the magazine. Through the smoke he could clearly see the effects of his gunnery. The raider was listing slightly to port and settling by the stern. Fires burned from her bow to her stern.

"On Gerlach's bridge, the hope of a quick, easy victory had vanished. A shell from the merchantman's lone gun had disabled his torpedo tubes, and a fire was threatening his magazine. Below decks his men struggled in waist-deep water to plug holes below the waterline. The *Stier* was fighting to stay afloat, but with his vastly superior firepower Gerlach had no intention of breaking off the battle. He ordered his gun director to silence the enemy's 4-inch gun.

"Her power plant crippled, the *Stephen Hopkins* lost headway until she was finally lumbering along at one knot. All Buck's signals for more speed remained unanswered. Instead, out of passageways and escape tunnels the burned and choking survivors of the engineroom inferno began to stumble onto the open decks. Among them was George Cronk.

"With their target almost dead in the water, Gerlach's gun crews sent salvo after salvo into the *Stephen Hopkins*, turning the stern into twisted, burning wreckage. Still the 4-inch gun fired back. One by one, the armed guard crew were killed or wounded, until Willett manned the gun alone. He was struggling to load again when a shell hit the magazine below the gun tub.

"The harried German captain, seeing the explosion, must have assumed the gun was out of action and that he could at last finish off his adversary. His own ship was settling at the stern, and a telephone talker relayed a story of fires fore and aft, one dangerously near a magazine. Moreover, the sea was rising, a light, intermittent rain was falling, and visibility was deteriorating. Gerlach ordered his gun crews to hurry and sink the merchantman. But he had barely turned his attention to saving his ship when the *Hopkins'* 4-inch gun fired again.

"It must have seemed impossible. The Germans had seen the gun tub explode. But through the mist the 4-inch gun on the *Stephen Hopkins* now fired a second time. Aboard the shattered Liberty ship, the concussion of the magazine explosion had hurled Willett to the deck of the gun tub, wounding him again. He was struggling to his feet when the youngest member of the *Stephen Hopkins* crew, eighteen-year-old Engineering Cadet Midshipman Edwin J. O'Hara, took over the gun.

"O'Hara, who had escaped the blazing engine room, had learned the basics of naval gunnery at the United States Merchant Marine Academy at Kings Point, New York, and from his friend Willett. Quickly examining the gun, he found it damaged but in firing condition. In the ready magazine lay five live rounds. O'Hara shoved one into the breech, pointed the gun, and yanked the firing lanyard. The barrel jumped and a 4-inch shell hit the *Stier*.

"With the magazine below the gun tub in flames, O'Hara manned the gun alone, loading and firing the four remaining rounds at 900 yards' range, and scoring hits on the *Tannenfels* and the *Stier*. Only when the shells in the ready magazine were expended and no others were to be found did he leave the gun tub and help his wounded friend look for a lifeboat.

"The fight had lasted twenty minutes. On the *Stephen Hopkins'* bridge Paul Buck surveyed the blazing wreck. Besides exploding the starboard boiler and demolishing the radio shack and the mast, the *Stier's* shells had wrecked the engine steering room and shattered the deckhouse and hull. With the superstructure afire and his command sinking beneath him, he reluctantly gave orders to abandon ship.

"Buck, now joined by George Cronk, found only one lifeboat still serviceable. Together they struggled to lower it into the water as shellfire continued to demolish the *Stephen Hopkins*. They then separated and, except for a fleeting glimpse of him on a life raft, no more is known of Paul Buck, the freighter captain who had fought a warship to the death."

The rest of the story falls to Engineer George Cronk as senior American survivor and commander of the only *Stephen Hopkins* lifeboat to make land.

" 'The raider was using shrapnel and incendiary shells,' he reported. 'I lowered the after-fall of boat Number One, which was about five feet from a roaring inferno of flames. A shell burst along the boat on the way down, killing two and wounding four men. The remaining crew was putting over rafts when I jumped overboard. I was later picked up by this boat, and with all the able men in it we got out the oars, and among the dying we got several men from the water and from rafts.

" 'Then the wind started rising and the sea running high, the visibility becoming very bad. All sighted the Third Mate in one of the smashed lifeboats that had been blown off the *Stephen Hopkins* by shellfire. He had it bolstered up at one end by a doughnut raft, but row as hard as we could, we could not get to him on account of the wind and seas.

" 'A doughnut raft went by with at least five men on it. We rowed for two hours until our hands were blistered, and still we could not pick up the men. The wind and seas were getting higher all the time, and at last poor visibility blocked out everything.'

"Cronk, hoping to rescue more survivors, put out his sea anchor and drifted in the vicinity until noon the next day, but he found only floating wreckage. He was in command of a lifeboat 1,000 miles from the nearest land. Ordering his able-bodied men to rig a sail, he headed northwest."

Writer Peter Stanford has told about the aftermath: "Only after the war was over did the 15 survivors of the ship's complement of 57 learn that the *Stier*, flooding from many holes punched by the four-incher (later Liberty ships were given a 5-inch stern gun) had to be abandoned and sunk, her crew and captives taken aboard the *Tannenfels*." The two foes, *Stier* and *Stephen Hopkins* settled to the bottom where the ocean is two miles deep. The *Tannenfels*, although damaged, made Bordeaux, carrying Gerlach and his officers, men, and prisoners."

Stanford continues, "The Germans were stunned by the loss of their auxiliary cruiser. Captain Gerlach of the *Stier* refused to believe that the *Hopkins* had not been secretly rearmed as a cruiser herself. But Ludolf Petersen, another of the *Stier*'s officers spoke the true epitaph for the *Hopkins* and her people: 'We could not but feel that we had gone down at the hands of a gallant foe . . . that Liberty ship ended a very successful raiding voyage. We could have sunk many more ships.' " They had sunk twenty six ships in a four month's cruise; only one other, the tanker *Stanvac Calcutta*, had fought back. Fourteen of her crew died to shell fire before she went down.

Raiders like the *Stier* depended on their innocent appearance to get near to unsuspecting merchant ships. A few months earlier her sister ship, the *Kormoran* (*Raider "G"*) played the innocent and apparently consented to come alongside the Australian cruiser *Sydney* to be boarded and searched. Then at point blank range she and the *Sydney* shot each other out of the water. Not a man in the Australian crew of 645 survived.

So much for the first part of the epic — what of the second part, nineteen men, four of them severely wounded, in a shrapnel riddled lifeboat, with 2,200 miles to land?

Seven S.U.P. men were in the boat with the other twelve survivors. Three of them were to die of their wounds before the boat made land. These included able seaman William Joseph Adrian and able seaman George E. Papas.

Six S.U.P. men had died in the battle. They were the boatswain, Allyn Davenport Phelps, the carpenter, Hugh Markle Kuhl, able seaman Karl Gustave Leggren, able seaman Tony Moran, ordinary seaman, James Henry Burke, and deck engineer Nick Makres.

Of the ship's officers only George Cronk was still alive. He was an engineer, not a navigator, but by all reports a quietly capable leader for the disparate company in the lifeboat. Moreover, he had a quintessential Sailor, the old Cape Horn windjammer veteran August Reese, known aboard the *Hopkins* as "Sails", to back him up. Reese was a Dane who had joined the S.U.P. in Portland in 1935. He was nearly sixty years of age. He had lost his glasses, but he went about his sailorly duties anyway. In a boat that depended on constant patching to keep afloat it was old Reese who kept the sail patched enough to catch the wind. He had been A.W.O.L. two days in Capetown to have a good time; it would be a little while before he had another one.

An account published in the *San Francisco Chronicle*, not mentioning the *Stephen Hopkins* by name, gives some idea of the scene in the lifeboat:

"The night was pitch black — so black that none of the 19 men could see the others. There was no sound except the slap, slap of the waves against the hull of the shrapnel-riddled, 32 foot lifeboat.

"Suddenly a seaman screamed . . . a long, eerie wail.

" 'Kill me!' he cried. 'I can't stand the pain!'

"The other shipwrecked men stirred momentarily.

"George Cronk, in command, gritted his teeth and mumbled to the helmsman.

" 'Watch your course, mister.'

"Then, as an afterthought: 'He's delirious. Pay no attention.'

"The men settled down again, trying to catch precious sleep.

" 'I checked our compass with the sun,' (Cronk) said. 'It was 22 degrees off. We used a lamp to see the compass at night and steered by the sun in the daytime.

" 'We took care of our four wounded men first. They screamed from pain and cold. The first three days we had bad blows. Terrific blows.

" 'It was so cold,' Cronk continued . . . 'Finally we got into warmer weather. It was more comfortable, but never really comfortable.

" 'I put the men on shifts of watches. I had to keep them busy or they'd have gone nuts. They were either bailing — we had plugged the shrapnel holes, but they leaked continually — or taking care of the wounded.

" 'One by one the wounded men died. We waited until night to bury them, so their bodies would sink and not follow us around.

" 'As their bodies slipped into the water at night, I told the men they could pray. Nobody prayed out loud, but I think everybody prayed to himself.

" 'We got weak and we felt slimy. We had food, pemmican, sea biscuits, malted milk tablets, rationed water. We were thirsty sometimes.

" 'On the eleventh day Wallace Ellsworth Breck of Oakland was complaining about his shoulder. I found he had been wounded by a machine-gun bullet. I took a rusty pair of tweezers and got the bullet out.

" 'Once we saw a star signal on the horizon. We answered but got no reply. We decided it was a submarine trailing us and using us for bait to get another ship when it came to our rescue.' "

Schools of whales alarmed the survivors. They were afraid the whales would capsize the boat. The following entries come from the log of the lifeboat:

"*October 23rd* Poor breeze. Just steering way. Sun hot, everybody kind of weak. Cut ration in half 4 days ago. Now getting 1 oz. of pammicon, 1 oz. of chocolate, ½ oz. of malted milk tablets, 1 type C ration biscuit per man per day, water ration 20 oz. per man per day due to rain water caught . . .

"*October 24th* Been becalmed for 24 hours. Very hot, everybody very weak. Some kind of sediment floating in water. Saw a butterfly and 2 moths . . . Very poor visibility . . . Fair breeze at sunset. Steering west.

"*October 25th* . . . Seen a yellow moth. Makes us think we are near land . . .

"*October 27th* Hurrah, sighted land 4 a.m. Landed at the small Brazilian village of Barra do Itabopoana."

Besides August Reese, ordinary seaman Roger Piercy of Hayward, California, able seaman Walter Manning of Los Angeles and ordinary seaman Archie Carlson of San Francisco were the surviving S.U.P. members who came ashore that October day.

Cronk arranged for word to be sent to Rio de Janeiro that a boat load of survivors had landed at Barra do Itabopoana and Lt. Joseph Rich of the United States Navy hastened to meet them. He reported: "*One could not help but feel the deepest admiration for these men who had faced such odds and were never for one moment beaten. After thirty days of being battered together in a cramped lifeboat, they were still lavishing praise on one another, helping one another.*"

That spirit, which contributed so much to the wartime cause of the democracies, is the spirit of West Coast merchant mariners, S.U.P., and others.

A number of ships with S.U.P. deck crews were captured by the Japanese, including the *President Harrison* owned by American President Lines, and the *Admiral Y.S. Williams,* owned by the American Trading Company. Some West Coast seamen were captured after their ships were sunk; others were interned in Japanese-held territory on the Asian mainland. The *Coast Farmer's* crew operated their ship from Australia to the Philippines, running the Japanese blockade, at the height of enemy strength in the area.

In the fight for Dutch Harbor, Alaska, in June, 1942, the crew of the *President Fillmore* assisted navy deck gunners and army antiaircraft artillerymen in preventing Japanese bombing planes from carrying out their raids on the port. The crew of the Liberty ship *O. Henry*, operated by Moore-McCormack, was commended by the War Shipping Administration for fighting its way through German dive bomber raids and bringing down one bomber, while losing not a single man, in its run to besieged Malta. Two brave West Coast Liberty ships were the *Mark Hanna* and the *James Smith*, both attacked in a Caribbean convoy by enemy submarines. After barely surviving a destructive raid, the two vessels drifted for days, but their crews declined to abandon them, and eventually they returned to the U.S. for repair and new voyages.

One of the most terrible stories to come out of the second world war is that of the *Jean Nicolet*, a Liberty ship operated by Oliver J. Olson & Co. of San Francisco for the War Shipping Administration. On July 2, 1944, the vessel, with a West Coast crew, was attacked and sunk south of Ceylon (now Sri Lanka) by a Japanese submarine. All crew members got off the ship safely; the submarine crew picked up 95 of the 100 survivors, leaving five men in one life raft. The captive American seamen were herded on deck, then shot, stabbed, beaten to death, and drowned, before the arrival of a U.S. plane caused the submarine to crash-dive, allowing a grim escape for a few, who faced the sharks. Of 100 men aboard the ship, only 23 came back.

Special note must be made of the men who crewed ships on the "Murmansk run," supplying war materials to the nation's Russian ally. Many seamen sacrificed their lives in the waters of the North Atlantic, so close to German submarine and air bases. The Soviets, although grateful for the aid, were terrified that American Trotskyists, would, through the S.U.P. and S.I.U., infiltrate subversive literature into Russia, and maintained a clandestine Soviet intelligence agent, Floyd Cleveland Miller, on the national staff of the Union organization. Some Trotskyists indeed claim they lost seagoing members to the Murmansk secret police.

West Coast union ships served in every theatre of the war, proving once again that when called by their country, the seamen were prepared to show courage and honor. Today, the very least Americans can do is to honor these men as they honored their flag, by granting them full veterans' benefits.[19]

Postwar Changes

With the coming of peace in 1945, the mood of the country's working class changed perceptibly. The veterans who returned from a war fought for freedom

[19]Lang, ibid; on the Japanese American internment case, see Gunner Lindstrom, "Man at the Helm," *Trade Union Courier* (New York), August 23, 1957; *Stephen Hopkins* account assembled by Karl Kortum (see errata, p. 155); on the case of Floyd Cleveland Miller, and related matters connected with Trotskyists and the "Murmansk run," author's personal files; Jesse Calhoon, Marine Engineers' Beneficial Association, speech, Washington, DC, May 23, 1983.

streamed into jobs old and new, with impatience their nearly-universal attitude. In the period between 1945 and 1947, the nation's trade unions were pushed into action by members whose expectations were dramatically higher than those of workers even a decade before. The unions gained improvements in living standards and an increased role in decision-making both in the workplace and in the society at large. Basic industries were shaken by transforming strikes.

The dean of American labor reporters, A.H. Raskin of *The New York Times*, has trenchantly described the postwar strike movement centering on the then-heart of U.S. industry, automotive and steel production:

"When V-J Day brought quiet to the fighting fronts in 1945, war between labor and management broke out all across the production front. During World War II, when the United States was the arsenal of democracy, a no-strike pact to which the still divided AFL and CIO had committed themselves maintained a high level of peace in industry. That peace enabled unions, particularly the infant CIO unions spawned by Franklin D. Roosevelt's New Deal and by the magnetic leadership of John L. Lewis, to consolidate their position under the benevolent mediatory eye of the War Labor Board.

"The uncertainties of the postwar period of reconversion to a civilian economy represented a time of testing for both unions and employers. President Truman sought to head off a collision by convening a summit conference of union and industry chiefs in Washington on November 5, 1945, but it accomplished nothing. Two weeks later the most serious of the conflicts that developed out of the pentup animosities began with a walkout of 175,000 workers at General Motors (GM).

"The strike was led by Walter P. Reuther, then a vice president of the United Automobile Workers (UAW), who had come to prominence as a firebrand in the 1937 sit-down strikes at GM that gave organized labor its first foothold in the open-shop citadels of the auto industry. He sought to turn the 1945-46 shutdown, which dragged on for 113 days of siege, into the jumping-off point for an extension of the concept of collective bargaining beyond the boundaries traditional under business unionism. Reuther's idea was that unions performed a disservice to the community if their sole concern was to win higher wages and improved conditions for their members and if they then allowed the cost to be passed on to the consumer. As a token of the union's reluctance to enter into any contract that might feed postwar inflation, Reuther offered to keep his members at work if GM would let an arbitration board inspect its books and decide how much of a pay increase the company could reasonably afford without raising the price of its cars and trucks.

"To General Motors management the Reuther proposal meant not arbitration but abdication. It denounced as Socialism and profit-control any suggestion that it allow a board appointed by the President or anyone else inquire into ability to pay as an index of what the company ought to give in wages. So profound was GM's resistance on this point that its officials boycotted hearings before a presidential fact-finding panel after Harry Truman had sent the company chairman a telegram putting the White House on record in favor of a study of the relationship between wages and prices.

"The fact finders, proceeding in the absence of testimony from GM, recommended a wage increase of nineteen and one-half cents an hour, with no increase in car prices. Reuther accepted at once, but GM spurned the recommendation on the ground that it embodied the 'unsound principle' that a prosperous enterprise should pay higher wages than a less profitable competitor.

"The union's ranks held firm, but developments elsewhere in the labor front eroded Reuther's bargaining position as week upon week of payless paydays piled misery on his members. Philip Murray, president of both the CIO and the United Steelworkers of America, had made little secret from the start of his irritation at Reuther for having called out the GM workers instead of letting Murray's steel union set the pattern for the first postwar negotiating round. Murray was equally disapproving of what he considered the folly of the UAW leader's effort to bargain for consumers as well as auto workers.

"Smoldering under these twin annoyances, Murray set January 14, 1946, as the deadline for a strike of 750,000 workers in steel and related industries. When President Truman made an eleventh-hour proposal that both sides agree on a compromise settlement of eighteen and one-half cents an hour, Murray postponed the walkout for a week in the hope that the industry would join the union in acquiescing.

"The steel companies refused to go along unless the White House guaranteed a relaxation of price controls that would permit them to offset the wage boost with higher prices for steel, a reverse twist on the Reuther position at GM. Their stand touched off the biggest strike in the nation's history — a strike that ended after four weeks, with the companies granting the eighteen and one-half cent increase in hourly wages in exchange for a green light from Washington to raise steel prices by five dollars a ton.

"Even before the CIO president thus undercut Reuther, both economically and philosophically, political enemies within the UAW — an unholy alliance of pro-Communists and 'pork-choppers' eager to prevent Reuther from using the GM strike as a springboard to the union presidency — put a banana peel under him by negotiating strike-free arrangements at Ford for eighteen cents an hour and at Chrysler for eighteen and one-half cents (one cent below the Truman panel's recommendation). The left-wing leadership of the United Electrical, Radio, and Machine Workers held secret talks with GM and settled for an eighteen and one-half cent increase covering 30,000 employees in the company's electrical division. When the same pattern spread to the United Rubber Workers and other key unions, GM bluntly informed Reuther that he could strike forever but that it was determined not to give the UAW the extra penny an hour . . . much less a guarantee of stable car prices.

"With the strike sixteen weeks old, Reuther felt he could not ask his membership to make a further sacrifice in what was clearly a lost cause. The members went back to work with a raise of eighteen and one-half cents and no promise from the company to hold the line on prices. By August, the government had approved three price increases for GM and before the end of 1946 Congress abolished the last vestige of the war-time machinery for price-wage controls.

"Many of Reuther's critics in the executive suites of industry and labor alike openly gloated at the prospect that in a pragmatic, results-oriented labor movement the humiliation from the outcome of the marathon strike represented a death knell for Reuther's personal ambitions and for his brand of social engineering, as distinct from the virtues of 'bread-and-butter' unionism.

"That adverse judgement, it quickly developed, was not shared by the UAW membership. At the auto union's convention, which opened just after the long shutdown, Reuther challenged R.J. Thomas, the organization's jolly but bumbling president, for the top spot. Reuther squeaked through to a hairbreadth victory; then, a year later, solidified his control by winning a top-heavy majority in the international executive board.

"Within General Motors, these events in addition to the solidarity its unionized employees had exhibited through the long strike, prompted a review of the company's approach to collective bargaining. GM finally recognized that the UAW was there to stay and that the sensible course for management was a live-and-let-live relationship rather than endless confrontations.

"In the 1948 bargaining round, Charles E. Wilson, GM's chief executive, launched the new program by proposing the most ambitious step any major corporation had ever taken toward injecting some element of science into the hagglemaster environment that normally surrounded negotiations. The proposed formula, called 'progress sharing' took much of its inspiration from the anti-inflationary principles that underlay the Reuther initiative of 1945-46.

"It had two main features. The first was an 'annual improvement factor' designed to give the workers a tangible stake in industry's advances in technology and productivity by raising basic hourly wages each year in line with the long-term growth in the gross national product. The second was a cost-of-living escalator, under which the purchasing power of the wage bargain would be kept steady by automatic increases or decreases reflecting fluctuations in the Consumer Price Index.

"Over the next decade the GM formula became the pattern for wage determination affecting millions of workers in auto, steel and other industries in which a relatively few corporate giants exerted oligopolistic control over markets and prices. Out of that formula grew an *entente cordiale*, under which dominant elements in big business accepted the somewhat heretical notion that strong, secure unions could be of advantage to management by combating wildcat ("quickie") strikes and fostering cooperative relations in the workplace. Not the least of the attendant benefits, in the view of many, was the standardization of wage rates so that one company did not get an advantage on its competitors through lower labor costs.

"From the standpoint of unions, the dividends of this new-found amity were even more concrete. Outside of the South and Southwest, where all forms of compulsory union membership were prohibited by 'right-to-work' laws, management became much more amenable to signing union-shop contracts under which all workers in the bargaining unit were required to join the majority union as a condition of holding their jobs."

Communist Maritime Ploy

Communist-lining C.I.O. maritime elements, headed by the I.L.W.U.'s Harry Bridges, had changed their line with the end of the war. During the hostilities, they had demanded that the unions simply accept whatever the government and employers might dictate, in the interest of victory. Now, with the U.S.-Russian war alliance crumbling and expanding confrontation around the world between the "big two" powers, the Communists began a new program of "militant" actions to disrupt the U.S. economy and body politic. In January, 1946, Bridges patched together an alliance styled the "Committee for Maritime Unity," or C.M.U., bringing together his I.L.W.U., the N.M.U., the then-Communist-dominated Marine Cooks and Stewards, the Marine Firemen, which were not Communist-controlled but had a strong party presence, and other wavering unions. The C.M.U. set itself up as a national strike strategy center and made a great show of preparing for battle. Although the S.U.P. promised to respect any C.M.U. picketlines, the S.U.P. was basically excluded from the planned strike action. Lundeberg strongly attacked the C.M.U. for its turning of union decision-making power over to the top C.M.U. executives. This later point represented a dangerous threat to the Union autonomy the Sailors had always defended.

The S.U.P. pursued its own course, avoiding the Washington-based political negotiations sought by the C.M.U., in favor of direct bargaining with the ship operators. In June 1946, a series of day-to-day strikes by the S.U.P. gained a wage hike of $22.50 per month, reduction of the straight-time week in port by four hours, and the eight-hour day at sea. In the meantime, the C.M.U. had settled in Washington for an increase of only $17.50 per month, with various improvements in hours. In the words of West Coast maritime historians Wytze Gorter and George H. Hildebrand, by this action "the S.U.P. . . . won the contest for prestige with the maritime rank and file."

However, the federal government soon rescinded the $5.00 "S.U.P. differential," and on September 4,

1946, the Sailors called the first of the postwar national maritime strikes. On September 11, the C.M.U.-affiliated Marine Firemen joined as well. The strike lasted 21 days, and "was an impressive show of power by the maritime unions, especially the S.U.P. and S.I.U.," Gorter and Hildebrand aver. The "S.U.P. differential" was won back. In the following months Bridges and his cadre carried out a fumbling attempt to match the Sailors' gains, but with little success. The C.M.U. fell apart, and the honeymoon between the I.L.W.U. and the N.M.U. soon ended as well, with N.M.U. head Joseph Curran, a long-time ally of the Communists, suddenly attacking the Muscovites for their campaign against the S.U.P.

As pointed out by Frank Barbaria, the 1946 strike was the occasion for the last "glorious page" of collaboration between Lundeberg and the Trotskyists. As it became clear that C.M.U. politicos were attempting to climb aboard yet another strike movement, Barbaria and another Trotskyist prepared an "open letter" titled *An Appeal to Reason!,* outlining the absurdities of the Communist position. Lundeberg ordered the text printed on poster-sized sheets and distributed the length of the West Coast waterfront, and asked Barbaria to speak at meetings of the firemen's and stewards' unions.[20]

In 1947, Congress passed the Taft-Hartley Act. Judicial decisions interpreting "T-H" held that it outlawed employment of workers through hiring halls run exclusively by unions. To preserve the S.U.P. hall, Lundeberg met personally with Senator Robert Taft, Republican of Ohio, who had sponsored the legislation, and the S.U.P. secured an exemption from the ruling. The Communists, particularly those in the I.L.W.U. (whose hall was jointly run with the employers and therefore not threatened by the legislation), leaped on this incident to paint Lundeberg as a reactionary more at home with the likes of Taft than with ordinary working men. The simple reality was, however, that the hiring hall, a historic cornerstone of the Union's strength, had been saved.

End of Communist Influence — Expulsion of Trotskyists

In effect, although it went almost unnoticed at first, the breakup of the C.M.U. was the end of the Communist hold on West Coast maritime workers. The party stalwarts had been beaten in a fair competition over wages and conditions by Lundeberg and the S.U.P. The S.U.P. continued to face the missionary task of routing Communist manipulators out of the Marine Firemen and Marine Cooks and Stewards unions. From then on the S.U.P. was clearly on the offensive in this thankless and not-inconsiderable campaign.

As millions around the world increasingly became aware of the new threat of war between Russia and the U.S., the old appeals of the Communist-lining left began to lose their mass attraction. Russia was now generally seen as a nation bent on an aggressive course of worldwide conquest and disruption. Particularly in the U.S., the opinion of the majority of workers changed from disinterest or benign curiosity about the "Soviet experiment" to active hostility. The Communists inside the unions and out could no longer count on the susceptibility of the workers to propaganda. Their popularity fading, the Communists hysterically charged that the U.S. government was about to set up fascism and that a third world war was imminent.

Curiously, the old adversaries of the Communists, the Trotskyists, had changed their attitudes toward the Russian regime. Where before the second world war the Stalinists had had no opponents more convinced than the Trotskyists, the attitudes of the latter softened with the new division of the world between U.S. and Russian power blocs. The Trotskyists began to see the Russians as the underdog; in addition, they interpreted the growing dislike of millions of U.S. citizens for the Communists as an attack on the "left," of which the Trotskyists considered themselves a loyal section.

For these reasons, in 1949-50, the rupture between Lundeberg and the Trotskyists, which was probably inevitable, finally took place. The immediate cause of the break was a strike called by the Communist-controlled Canadian Seamen's Union. The Canadian group had originally been an affiliate of the Seafarers' International Union, although this link was only sought by the group in an attempt to undermine the S.U.P. In 1949, the Canadian Seamen's Union leadership called a worldwide strike of Canadian ships, without consulting its membership and without putting forward legitimate strike demands. The goal was the disruption of North Atlantic shipping to Europe; the strike was supported by dockworkers in Britain, and troops were sent by the ruling Labour government to the British waterfront cities. The Canadian seamen, dragged into a political strike many among them did not support, began leaving the "C.S.U." and joining the S.I.U.

The Trotskyists had decided that between the Communists and Lundeberg, they were more comfortable with the Communists. They used the Canadian controversy to brand the S.U.P. leadership as strike-breakers, although at least one Trotskyist participated actively in the anti-"C.S.U." struggle. In the meantime, an undercurrent of feeling had emerged in the Seattle branch of the S.U.P., in which the Trotskyists enjoyed their greatest strength, for a splitting away of Seattle from the rest of the Union. Under the slogan "Seattle ships for Seattle men," local dissidents sought to set up a regional union, depending on the Alaska Steamship Corporation as their major employer. John Mahoney, a prominent gadfly in the Seattle branch, touched

[20]A.H. Raskin, "Labor: Movement In Search of a Mission," in *Journal of Contemporary Studies* (San Francisco), Summer-Fall, 1985; Gorter and Hildebrand, op. cit.; Barbaria, letter cited; Sailors' Union of the Pacific, *An Appeal to Reason!*, poster, San Francisco, 1946, in S.U.P. central Archive.

off this potential bomb by attacking the S.U.P. leadership, repeating the charges of anti-Canadian "strike-breaking." In the conflict that followed over the next months, the Trotskyists, who supported Mahoney, found themselves outside the Union; the expelled included Frank Lovell, the main Trotskyist leader in maritime, and Jack (Shaun) Maloney, a veteran of the Trotskyist-led 1934 Minneapolis Teamsters' strike. Lovell left the maritime industry, while Shaun Maloney and several others went to work in the I.L.W.U. (Shaun Maloney eventually became the well-known president of the Seattle longshore local.)

The so-called "Mahoney beef" may be taken as the final chapter in the immediate post-1934 period of the S.U.P. history. The Sailors were no longer seriously threatened by the Communists, and no longer needed the assistance of the Trotskyists, who had, in the end, proven unreliable as allies. The Trotskyists, in later years, chose largely to forget their involvement with the West Coast maritime unions, although Joseph Hansen, Tom Kerry, and Frank Lovell all were prominent figures in the main American Trotskyist group, founded in 1938, the Socialist Workers party.

Perhaps most importantly, the Sailors in the fifteen years between 1935 and 1950 demonstrated that a union could successfully follow a path of militant and aggressive action without benefit of any kind of leftist ideological guidance, whether Communist or Trotskyist. The Sailors had beaten the employers and government over wages; they had maintained their independence and autonomy, as well as a sense of united struggle for fundamental goals, undiverted by political or other issues without meaning for the rank and file.

In addition to its record of dynamic action in the maritime field, the S.U.P. had also shown a commitment to the concept of *solidarity* with the rest of labor, S.U.P. pickets played major roles in two seminal incidents of the post-war period; these were the Oakland general strike of 1946 and the Wall Street financial employees' strike of 1948. Neither conflict originated in waterfront issues; but in both the intervention of the Sailors was crucial to labor's side of the battle. Both saw the Communists forced to acknowledge the correctness and commitment of the S.U.P.'s leadership. Both are worthy of a more adequate examination by historians than they have so far stimulated.[21]

---

[21]On the Canadian seamen, John Stanton, *Life and Death of a Union: Canadian Seamen's Union, 1936-1949*, Toronto, Steel Rail, 1978; Unsigned, "Le *Searchlight*, Journal Exemplaire de L'Union des Marins Canadiens," in *Stratégie* (Montreal), Spring-Summer 1976; files on the "Mahoney beef" in S.U.P. central Archive; important files on the C.S.U. are held at the Brooklyn S.U.P. hall, in New York; for important Trotskyist commentary, see the collection of documents on the C.S.U. strike at the Tamiment Institute Library, New York University, New York; also, Al Burton (Jim Kiernan), "In the Shadow of the Blackjack," *American Socialist* (New York), March 1955, and Richard Kirk (Richard Fraser), "A Letter to American Trotskyists," *Revolutionary Age* (Seattle), supplement 1, 1975, both strong and essentially dishonest Trotskyist attacks on Lundeberg. For a more balanced view, see two essays by Stan Weir: "The Informal Work Group," in Alice and Staughton Lynd, eds., *Rank and File*, Boston, Beacon Press, 1973, and "American Labor on the Defensive; A 1940s Odyssey," *Radical America* (Somerville, Massachusetts), July-August 1975.

CHAPTER IX
"The Fight Goes On"
(1950-1985)

The years from 1950 to the present, in the history of the S.U.P., are probably best symbolized by the classic headquarters building that stands on Rincon Hill in San Francisco. Within site of the bloody battle that raged in July '34, when the Sailors joined the rest of the labor movement to win back a measure of dignity, the imposing hilltop structure was opened for use in June 1950.

The building's plans were drafted by William Gladstone Merchant, who also designed the theme building of the 1939-40 San Francisco international exposition, "Pacific House." The S.U.P. headquarters is considered a specially-fine example of the art deco "streamlined moderne" style, and on the basis of esthetic excellence alone, the choice of this particular architect does credit to the Union.

Lundeberg's Legacy

The headquarters building project was a beloved one to Harry Lundeberg, and its construction reflected Lundeberg's own pride in the Union, its members, and its ideals. Even today, the structure is an impressive one, with a sense of grace both within and without. It is a good place to be, whether one is waiting for a job or handling Union business. It was built to last, as the Union itself was created.

A 1984 study by the San Francisco Department of City Planning, commissioned to examine proposals for development of 12 blocks of Rincon Hill for high-rise apartments, recommended that the S.U.P. headquarters be preserved, along with the Union Oil building across the street, the Hills Brothers coffee plant structure at the end of Harrison Street (slated for conversion to offices, shops, and housing), the Klockars blacksmith shop, and the Apostleship of the Sea. The city study pointed out that in addition to its architectural value, the S.U.P. building is "a most appropriate memorial to seamen and the maritime character of the neighborhood, and to a significant degree, the labor movement in San Francisco."

Merchant's design produced a building reminiscent of the ships on which the Union's members have earned their livelihood. The front portico resembles a ship's foredeck, while the columns were drawn to resemble sails. But, the S.U.P. building program of the time was oriented toward serving the members, and not simply architectural values. The large auditorium, for example, was conceived as a possible relief station for strikers. Under the same program, apartments for retirees were built into newly-constructed Seattle and Wilmington halls, erected and financed, like headquarters, through assessment of the membership. California Governor Earl Warren was present at the headquarters' final unveiling.

The decades of the 1950s through 1970s have been somewhat quieter in the maritime industry than those preceding them. We have outlined how, with the marked decline of interest in political leftism in the labor movement, the rhetoric of the Communists and Trotskyists became irrelevant. The grievances that once had fuelled labor radicalism and driven millions of American working people to the left seemed to have been replaced during the 1950s by a prosperity that improved the lives of all, but especially of wage workers. The extreme abuses of the old bucko system at sea had been abolished fifty years before; this great achievement may be credited directly to, and only to, the Sailors' Union. However, broader changes had come to America, at least temporarily. Labor disputes no longer featured bloody confrontations between armed thugs and strikers; massive unemployment and poverty no longer struck far and wide, as during the 1930s' depression.

In the struggles of three generations — the "classes" of 1885, 1915, and 1934 — the seafaring workers had gained most of what they had set out to win when a relative handful of men first gathered on the Folsom Street Wharf in San Francisco. The seamen came to enjoy wages and benefits comparable or superior to those of nearly every shoreside wage worker. With economic improvement came greater social stability, and opportunities to raise families and function as normal members of society. The seamen no longer had to wait on the margins of civilized life for some slender bit of recognition. Dignity, self-respect, and acceptance as equals had finally been won, thanks to the struggle we have recounted here.

But, with the end of the second world war (as in the aftermath of the first) the U.S. merchant fleet, which had been greatly enlarged to accommodate war needs, shrank. From around 7,500 U.S. registered vessels in 1946, the roster has declined to some 500 today. Hundreds of ships were given away to foreign operators. Although the unions battled on the docks, the real fight was lost in Washington.

In the era of the steamship, America failed to maintain itself as a maritime power, unlike Britain or the Scandinavian countries. Northern Europe's internal markets are tiny, and its business interests have traded mostly outside their own borders. America's gigantic internal market has traditionally dominated our commerce, with railroads therefore dominating the U.S. transportation industry. For this reason, a large merchant fleet was seen as unnecessary, except in wartime. A related problem for the maritime industry, connected with the influence over American business of the internal market and the power of the railroads, became evident during the 1940s and 1950s, when the railroads, through manipulation of interstate tariffs, forced the intercoastal ship traffic out of business.

The 1950s also brought an important economic setback for the S.U.P. with the final disappearance of the steam schooner trade along the West Coast. As we have noted, the "steam schooner boxheads" (Scandinavians) had long served as the iron-strong backbone of the organization. The phasing-out of steam schooner operations brought a sad feeling to many dry-land enthusiasts of the old vessels, who viewed them as a romantic remnant of an earlier technology, but the loss was worse for Union members, who felt it in terms of income. A related negative effect at this time was the ending of operations by Coastwise Line, which had hauled paper products.

A major factor in the post-1945 downturn in U.S. merchant shipping was the transfer of ship registry to "flags of convenience," through which a major share of American-owned bottoms went from the national flag to such nations as Liberia, Panama or Honduras. During the 1970s, the "runaway" shipping nations grew to include a number of new, small nations in the less-developed world, such as the Bahamas.

"Runaway" shipping is a simple game, and a profitable one, seemingly, for the less-scrupulous shipowner. By registering in a small nation one avoids the burden of U.S. or European standard wages, conditions, social welfare payments, and taxes. Maritime laws in "runaway" nations may be either nonexistent or unenforced. The rise of "runaway" operations struck deeply at employment for U.S. seamen after 1945. Since the primary task of a Union, aside from that of preserving its members' existing rights and dignities, remains that of protecting jobs, the maritime unions, including the S.U.P., found the postwar period to be one of almost-unrelieved crisis.

The S.U.P. responded to these challenges boldly and courageously, given the circumstances, by lobbying federal authorities for maximum support to the nation's merchant fleet, and by undertaking campaigns, both in the U.S. and through the International Transportworkers' Federation which Lundeberg's S.U.P. rejoined, to organize "runaway" seamen. But neither of these campaigns gained much success. In 1950, the S.U.P. succeeded in permanently organizing a Panamanian-flag gypsum carrier, the *Pho Pho*, owned by Henry Kaiser, which once it was organized was renamed the *Harry Lundeberg*. (This was in fulfillment of a bet Henry Kaiser had made with Lundeberg; that if Lundeberg could organize the ship it would be renamed for him.) Greek-born members of the Union played a special role in the *Pho Pho* events, picketing and talking to the Greek crew in Redwood City, California. The *Pho Pho* organizing campaign represented a major step forward for the S.U.P. in that it was the first vessel to be entirely crewed, top-to-bottom, by the Union: S.U.P. members filled every job from master to messmen, at the then-highest scale of wages, although the ship remained under the Panamanian flag. The goal of "one union" on board ship had been explicit in S.U.P. organizing efforts beginning in the early 1940s, when the Union first began signing up all three unlicensed departments (deck, engine, stewards) on West Coast tankers. S.U.P. tanker contracts continue to reflect this comprehensive unlicensed representation policy. (The first *Harry Lundeberg* was wrecked in 1954, but a second, new vessel with the same name was christened in 1957, and decades later renamed the *Mar de Cortez*. The S.U.P. later crewed two more Panamanian-flag gypsum ships for Kaiser, the *Ocean Carrier* and *Western Ocean*.)

In 1950 hostilities broke out in the Asian nation of Korea, divided between a Communist regime in the north and a pro-U.S. government in the south. The Korean conflict briefly improved the situation for hiring of seamen, but soon ended, throwing thousands of U.S. mariners out of work once again. The S.U.P. served honorably in the Korean crisis as it had in previous wars. During the Korean War, the S.U.P. established the first offshore U.S. Union hall, in Yokohama under Richard Kim, a well-known Union activist. S.U.P.-manned shuttle services operated extensively between Japan and Korea, dispatched from the Yokohama hall.

Two years later, in 1952, came the last of the major West Coast offshore maritime strikes, lasting 63 days, until July 26, 1952. The S.U.P. went into the action with a thoroughly combative attitude, facing down the Pacific Maritime Association, a reorganized employers' group that had become well-known for its adoption of a "new look" of sympathy and understanding for Harry Bridges, the longshore leader. The S.U.P. demanded wage improvements and a 40-hour week at sea and, once again, as in the Shepard Line "beef" of 1938, saw its enemies on the left — Bridges and Co. — and the shipowners, on the right, seemingly united to fight the Sailors. But the 1952 strike was won, and the

PMA contract that emerged from the battle may be said to have changed the situation of the West Coast seamen once and for all. Under the "status quo of 1952," many issues of control over the job were finally resolved in favor of the Union.

September 1952 saw a struggle centering on another "runaway"-registered ship, the *Riviera*. Built in the U.S., owned by Greeks, and registered in Liberia, the *Riviera* arrived in Portland, Oregon, where its crew chose to strike against their bad conditions. The sailors were dismissed from the ship without pay and their personal effects were held by the officers. The strikers were then arrested and jailed by the U.S. Immigration and Naturalization Service, although regulations permitted foreign seamen to come ashore in search of work on foreign vessels.

The S.U.P. picketed the *Riviera*, and the ship remained in Portland until it made its escape some four months later, with scabs brought across the border from Canada. The Union obtained release of the imprisoned seamen and payment of wages. However, the ship's Greek proprietors sued the S.U.P., along with the S.I.U. and the Masters, Mates, and Pilots, and the courts found against the unions. The U.S. Supreme Court, with a single dissenting ballot by Justice William O. Douglas, upheld the lower court action, and the S.U.P. was forced to pay a settlement totalling $23,750 to the Greek company. This decision, in effect, deprived the Union of the picketing weapon in cases involving "runaway" vessels.

In 1953, Lundeberg appeared as a representative of the S.U.P. before the U.S. Senate subcommittee on maritime subsidies. In his testimony, the Union's chief executive stressed a variety of important aspects of S.U.P. history. He pointed out that strikes could not simply be decreed by the picking up of a telephone, at least not in the S.U.P., where a coastwide two-thirds vote was constitutionally required to authorize strike action. Lundeberg strongly criticized the shipowners for their habit of blaming "everyone but themselves" for the ills of the maritime industry. "We've had to fight every inch of the way" for improvements in wages and conditions, he emphasized. He pointedly characterized the amateurish and improvisational way in which the West Coast shipowners' representatives pursued the supposed science of "labor relations," and spoke out aggressively against the "runaway" ship swindle.

Lundeberg and the National Maritime Museum

These years in Lundeberg's life also saw him become seriously committed to the growth of the Maritime Museum built in San Francisco through the efforts of Karl Kortum. Kortum, chief curator of what is now the National Maritime Museum, has described his relationship with Lundeberg in the following way:

"Harry Lundeberg five times saved the *Balclutha*, the square-rigged Cape Horner now in the National Maritime Museum. The first time was in 1942. (Largely on his own, by directly contacting Admiral Land in Washington, he had blocked certain zealous military types in San Francisco who wanted to cut down the sailing ship into a barge) . . . Harry saved the *Balclutha* again, twelve years later. The Board of State Harbor Commissioners had turned down the Maritime Museum's request for the berth the ship now occupies at Fishermen's Wharf. Without it we could not proceed with our plan to buy the ship. I asked Harry to intercede with Governor Knight. His letter to the Governor straightened the matter out. Governor Knight had his eyes on the presidency of the nation at this point in history, on the Republican side. And Harry Lundeberg was that rare creature, a Republican labor leader.

"Harry saved the ship a third time, in that same year 1954. He had become a Museum trustee but seldom attended meetings. I asked him to come to a meeting of the board and take care of a rebellion in the ranks. After a year of unsatisfactory negotiations with the owner by the Ship Committee, powerful elements in the board were ready to throw in the towel, including the most vociferous voice on the Ship Committee — loudest *for* the ship up until the present, but a voice that was now beginning to express doubts. Dangerous!

"At this point in the history of our fledgling organization it was a lot easier to stick with ship models, safe in their little glass cases. After all, the rusty old sailing ship being contemplated was the same size as the museum building that held the models. One of the many holes corroded through the side of the ship was big enough to put your head through. The *Balclutha* was a bizarre project for a small historical society. There was only $15,000 in the bank, little more than a tenth of what was required to put her back in shape. . . .

"An account in *Venture* magazine, February 1965, tells about the meeting of the full Board.

" 'The morning of that day found Kortum pleading his cause in the office of Harry Lundeberg, then secretary-treasurer of the Sailors Union of the Pacific and probably the most powerful man on the waterfront. Lundeberg, who had been a militant union organizer most of his life, was not noted for his charm. He listened glumly to Kortum's account of the difficulties over the *Balclutha*, then, without committing himself, promised to attend the meeting that afternoon. He showed up on time, brushed past the startled shipping magnates who were present and sat silently by while the leader of the *Balclutha* opposition made a speech suggesting that it was silly to spend all that money for an old ship that didn't even have any scrap value.

" 'When Lundeberg finally stood up to speak it was in a vein that none of the steamship men had ever heard from him. 'The scrap value is no way to set a price for the last great sailing ship left on the Coast,' he said softly. Then he went on to point out that the *Balclutha* was a reminder of the city's maritime history, of what the port had once been, of the spirit that would make it that way again. He said he had spent twelve years in sail and had a deep personal interest in the whole project.

" 'Then Lundeberg sat down, there was a stunned silence, and the man sitting next to Kortum whispered, 'Have you got this guy wired?' Kortum was too relieved to answer. The committee (Board) voted to continue the chase. . . .' "

"A few weeks later, the Museum acquired the *Balclutha* for $25,000 — borrowed.

"Harry was crucial to Museum affairs a fourth time, in 1955, when he sent a letter to Governor Knight launching the "schooner projects," to bring in the three master *C.A. Thayer* and the steam schooner *Wapama*. . . .

"The *fifth time* Harry stepped in was when the crunch was coming in the State Capitol about whether a Ferry Building Park project or the schooner bill was going to pull into favored position. The matter was going to be decided on April 29, 1955, in a meeting in Sacramento . . . Harry couldn't go but he gave me permission the day before to sit down with Miss Lentz, his secretary, and work up a batch of Lundeberg-type telegrams to the Governor and to half a dozen assemblymen and our state senator. Dave Nelson, my colleague, was aghast at my militant wording but I figured it might have an effect on the opposition the following day. The point is: Lundeberg was willing to send them.

"Harry Lundeberg and I got along because we both had a love of sailing ships. It was plain that Harry looked back on his forecastle days with pleasure, but his stories about those years were wry rather than sentimental.

"He occasionally leaned back in his chair, behind the big desk, and reminisced during our visits to his office in the formative days of the Museum. In 1949 the Sailors Union of the Pacific was still located on Clay Street, the city's "sailor town" of bygone days.

"One day not long after the *Balclutha* had been purchased, Harry was moved to describe the tween-decks forecastle of the *Great Britain*. This came up because we were discussing the forecastle arrangements aboard the *Balclutha* — yet to be recreated because the Alaska Packers had substantially changed her for salmon packet use.

"The *Great Britain* forecastle was buried deep in the ship and was primitive in the extreme. Lundeberg had gone aboard her in Port Stanley (Falkland Islands) in 1921, when she was a wool storage hulk. The bark *Oaklands*, in which he was a sailor, was alongside, loading from her.

"How he got into Port Stanley made another story . . . He had been sent up from New York to a lumber port in Canada to join the *Oaklands*, then under Norwegian flag. The crew forward consisted of eight men. The lumber was discharged in Bahia Blanca, Argentina, and the *Oaklands* then stood down the South Atlantic to the Falkland Islands with a charter to load wool there for London. But she struck bad weather and during two weeks of standing off and on outside the entrance of Port Stanley, the charter time had almost run out. The problem was that the tug had broken down and there was no way to negotiate the narrow entrance except to sail in.

"Finally, to save his charter, Captain Pederson decided he would have to try it. Watching for a favorable slant he closed with the narrow gap between broad Port William and the sheltered inner harbor, Port Stanley.

"Harry was at the wheel. The thousand-ton bark was sharp up, barely making her course as she headed in. Once in the entrance, 'I could have spit on the rocks from where I was steering the ship,' Lundeberg recalled. It did not look as if she were going to weather the lee headland.

"The captain could do no more. He paced from side to side of the ship in front of the helmsman muttering, under his breath, an unhappy litany:

" 'F--- this! F--- this! F--- this. . . .'

"But the *Oaklands* slipped through, barely, and the harbor inside opened up. The charter was saved. The Pilot came aboard, full of congratulations:

" 'You are the first ship to sail in that anyone can remember.'

" 'Nothing to it,' Harry quoted the master."

Controversial to the End

The year 1955 saw important further developments for the Union. Early in the year the S.U.P. announced an agreement with International Shipping Co., operators of the vessel *Tonsina*. The *Tonsina* agreement provided for a reduced manning scale, and increased the basic work-week from 40 to 44 hours, with improvement in the overtime rate and a boost to the base rate by incorporation of penalty time for weekend sea watches.

Later in 1955, the membership ratified a new contract pattern first negotiated with American President Lines and Pacific Far East Lines, and then accepted by the Pacific Maritime Association. The negotiations secured significant pay increases and, on the *Tonsina* model, permanent inclusion of penalty pay in the base rate. With penalty pay thus standardized, each member now received the same basic wage rate, eliminating the necessity for men to wait for jobs aboard ships with preferable penalty pay rates.

The same year brought another appearance by Lundeberg at congressional hearings, this time before the Committee on Merchant Marine and Fisheries of the House of Representatives. He reviewed the history of the S.U.P., highlighting the fight for passage of the Seamen's Act, but also outlining the degradations of the post-1921 period: $25 per month on the "western ocean run" between Europe and New York, $32 per month on intercoastal vessels, "no such thing as overtime, food . . . pretty rotten and the quarters . . . real bad," the blacklisting rule of the fink hall or "slave market", under the stewardship of the ex-policeman Captain Petersen and of the U.S. Shipping Board. The long climb upward was marked, he noted, by the years of the big strikes: 1934, 1936, 1946, 1952. An important subject at the hearings was the provision for the establishment of a federal board for automatic settlement of maritime strikes, which Lundeberg tenaciously opposed, identifying federal interference in the labor-management bargaining process as the beginning of a trend comparable to Nazi and Communist totalitarianism. "The Government steps in and settles all disputes," he stated, "and records show that means the finish of independent labor organizations and their free collective bargaining rights."

The issue of "runaway" shipping was attacked once again late in 1956 when Crown Zellerbach Corporation began operating a Japanese-built pulp carrier between Canada and Antioch, California. This vessel, the *Duncan Bay*, was manned by 28 Okinawan seamen, and flew the Liberian flag. By October, picketing by the S.U.P., with the support of construction workers at Crown Zee's unfinished Antioch facility, resulted in the transfer of the *Duncan Bay* to S.U.P. jurisdiction, still under Liberian registry. It, like the *Harry Lundeberg*, was 100 percent S.U.P. crewed.

The strife between the Sailors and the leaders of the West Coast longshoremen did not end until the death of Lundeberg in 1957. In the early '50s, the S.U.P. undertook to bring the West Coast Marine Firemen's Union into the Seafarers' International Union, Pacific District. The West Coast Firemen had been fought over for years by Communist and anti-Communist factions, and had remained independent of the A.F.L. and the C.I.O., (the A.F.L. and C.I.O. merged in 1955) Under their leaders, Vincent J. Malone, Sam Bennett, Harry Jorgensen, William Jordan, and, currently, Henry "Whitey" Disley, the Firemen came to forge with the Sailors the closest and warmest working relationship in the Pacific Coast maritime labor scene. In a time of need, and facing in the 1980s, a deeply troubled maritime industry, these two brother organizations have come to present a common front. Many believe this relationship can only get better over time.

A similar and more acrimonious S.I.U. affiliation effort took place in the West Coast Marine Cooks and Stewards' Union, which had been under the Communist thumb since the late '30s, except for a brief period during the second world war.

The Communist bureaucrats in the Stewards' union had long been reckless in their political activities, and violent in their denunciations of Lundeberg. With the ebbing of leftism, and with announcement of the S.U.P. intent to reform the Stewards' organization (which had been run in a flagrantly undemocratic way by the Communists), the tone of Communist propaganda became almost unbelievably abusive. Lundeberg was portrayed as nothing more than a "goon," a "fink-herder," and an outright agent of the employers. Since many of the Stewards were ethnically non-white, the Communists endeavored to exploit racial conflicts, painting the S.U.P., falsely, as "anti-Negro." The Coast Seamen's Union had invited Black seamen on the West Coast to join in 1885, while the old I.S.U. had been among the first unions in the nation to actively organize Blacks; the S.U.P. had *never* included a race standard in its constitution, unlike many American unions in which Communists acted as officials. To the extent Blacks were underrepresented in West Coast shipping, this was a consequence of employer, rather than Union practices. While the S.U.P. rejected the idea that any ethnic group should be brought into the union and given work on their race alone, the "anti-Negro" charge was a vicious smear.

The proof of the emptiness of Communist slanders against the S.U.P. came when, finally, the Marine Cooks and Stewards chose to affiliate with the S.I.U. by democratic ballot. The Communists had, at last, been driven out of leadership positions in the seagoing unions. At the end, when it became obvious that the M.C.S. Communists could not maintain control over the Stewards, the West Coast longshore union had made an attempt to reorganize them, but this failed ignominiously.[1]

Harry Lundeberg in 1956 authored a short essay on the history of the Union that may stand as his testament. This text began with the proud words, "The foundation of all the gains that have been made by the American seamen and European seamen today was laid down by the early American trade unionists in the seamen's field, . . . who established the unions and fought for and changed the legal status of seamen from slaves on ships to free men." The S.U.P. had "at all times been the leader in the fight for better economic and legislative conditions for the American seamen." Lundeberg granted credit to Furuseth, as well as to the earlier and lesser-known, such as Ed Crangle, the Union's first waterfront dispatcher in the hiring hall set up in San Francisco in June 1886.

After reviewing the legal and other controversies waged by the S.U.P. and the I.S.U. in the period before 1934, Lundeberg underscored the Union's resistance to the Communist threat, but also heaped derision on the shipowners who, he claimed, advanced the fortunes of the Communists by their mistreatment of the seamen; "the seamen had to battle the Communist leeches on the waterfronts as much as they battled the shipowners," he recalled. After hammering repeatedly at the leftists, Lundeberg enumerated the positive achievements of the union at the time of his writing:

- The S.U.P. had preserved a clean hiring hall, without employer interference.
- The S.U.P. had established the first welfare plan and the first pension plan for seamen. (At present, the monthly pension is available to any member who has accumulated 20 years' sea time, regardless of age.)
- Wages and conditions had improved far beyond the dreams of the men who had struck in '34.

[1]Material on post-1950 problems is derived from *West Coast Sailors*, Scharrenberg, op. cit., Harry Lundeberg, testimony, Senate Committee on Interstate and Foreign Commerce, Subcommittee on Maritime Subsidies, *Hearings*, Washington, D.C., Government Printing Office, 1953, and House Committee on Merchant Marine and Fisheries, *Hearings*, Washington, D.C., Government Printing Office, 1955. Karl Kortum, "Harry Lundeberg Has Been Heard From," *Sea History* (Brooklyn), Fall 1980.

• The Union had established congressional lobbying and related activities to monitor actions by the federal authorities.

"Fidelity, determined resistance to subversive influence and faithful observance of contracts, ratified and agreed to by the membership, (have) been the cornerstone of success," Lundeberg concluded.[2]

On January 28, 1957, Lundeberg died, mourned by thousands of seamen around the world. The helm of the organization passed to Morris Weisberger, an associate of Lundeberg in the S.U.P. leadership since the late 1930s. Weisberger, who was born in Cleveland, Ohio, on August 10, 1907, had first shipped out as an ordinary seaman in 1926. In 1936, he became front office clerk of the S.U.P. He served as Secretary-Treasurer for the Union from March 1957 to March 1978, when he was forced to relinquish the post by bad health (in 1976, the top executive's title was changed from "Secretary-Treasurer" to "President/Secretary-Treasurer" by vote of the membership.)

Morris Weisberger

Although not as contentious as his predecessors Furuseth and Lundeberg, Weisberger proved an active leader for the Union, serving in many labor and governmental capacities. He has said that he had no desire for office, and has expressed regrets that he came into the Union's top position at a bad time for the industry. The operators had become dependent on federal subsidies to a previously-unimagined degree; ships showed a poorer rate of return on profit than a regular bank account. In addition to the impossibility of securing new West Coast jobs, Weisberger felt the S.U.P. was handicapped by its traditional reliance on the deck department as the center of organization. But, above all, he notes, the operators showed a tragic lack of vision. Perhaps the single most eloquent bit of evidence in this regard is the collapse of the West Coast passenger-liner trade during the 1970s. A decade which began with the *President Wilson* and *President Cleveland* operating under the banner of American President Lines, with the *Mariposa* and *Monterey* sailing for Matson, then for the ill-fated Pacific Far East Line, and with a number of other passenger-carrying vessels under S.U.P. contract, ended with *no* passenger liners on the West Coast. An important job resource for the Union was gone. In addition to the actual seagoing jobs generated by the passenger ships, the fleet had also provided many shore-gang jobs, with over 200 men on each of the passenger-ship steady gangs at A.P.L., Matson, P.F.E.L. and States Line.

Although, as stated before, the S.U.P. had not excluded non-white seamen from membership, with the rise of the Black civil rights movement in the late 1950s and early 1960s came pressure for special measures to promote Black representation in the Union's ranks. Although Weisberger shared the concerns of Black leaders, little could be done in an industry where there were so few jobs available for those already working. What could be done was done, in terms of increased Black entry into the organization; when the 1965 Civil Rights Act was passed, the S.U.P. was among the first unions to offer full compliance. Entry of more Blacks depended on expansion of U.S. shipping; the latter has so far proved painfully elusive.

A related expression of the same problem, which Weisberger faced during his tenure in office, was the cutting of manning scales, demanded by the shipowners, and failure to secure a reform of the pay base that would help counteract this problem. Traditionally, the Sailors' pay was based on man-days worked, and with smaller crews, Weisberger sought unsuccessfully to change the standard to a tonnage basis.

The same period saw the emergence of a major technological change in shipping that would prove detrimental for the Sailors, although there seemed to be no way to combat it: containerization. With the great increase in shipping cargo in containers, the Sailors' work on deck required even fewer men, since cargo is now handled by giant dockside or shipboard container cranes, rather than by cargo booms, winch drivers and lashing gear set up by hand. On the other hand, the larger size and lowered manning on container vessels seems to have facilitated some improvement of crew conditions.

Finally, according to Weisberger, a consistent obstacle to improvement of the Sailors' fortunes was represented by the higher wages traditionally paid on the West Coast. With all the maritime unions competing for the loyalty of the seamen, no union wishes to settle for a wage-rise percentage lower than that of any other union. But where, at East Coast wage rates, a six percent improvement in base pay for the members of the National Maritime Union might equal, say $60 per month, on the West Coast 6 percent would reach $100 per month. Room for bargaining with the employer shrank accordingly.[3]

A dramatic modernizing trend also took place during this period in the worldwide tanker industry, with predictable effects on the West Coast. This book has tended to avoid closer study of the Union's many organizing campaigns, some of which involved employers no longer in business. However, it should be noted that the successive tanker campaigns of the 1930s and afterward were an important testing ground for individuals as well as for innovations in Union policy, such as the previously-mentioned concept of the 100 percent S.U.P. crew. With the coming of supertankers and of further automation, the numbers of tanker men, Union or not, was destined to decrease. The time was not far off when offshore drilling, offshore mooring, unloading while underway, and such political effects as worldwide tanker operator competition and pressures from the environmental movement would transform the tanker business even more.

---

[2]Harry Lundeberg, "The Seafarers' International Union of North America," typescript, October 19, 1956, in the S.U.P. central Archive. [3]Morris Weisberger, biographical synopsis, January 19, 1983, and interviews, May, 1984 through November, 1985.

All of these changes were first felt during Weisberger's tenure in office.

Perhaps the most dramatic action taken by the S.U.P. during the 1960s came under the presidency of Weisberger, when the Union, along with the Marine Firemen and the Cooks and Stewards, struck Pacific Maritime Association employers in 1962. The work stoppage began in March of that year after seven months of negotiations had produced an employer offer of wage improvements of less than 1 percent. Within a week, 45 vessels were shut down in S.U.P.-covered ports.

The 1962 strike went on for a month, and was suspended after President John F. Kennedy imposed an 80-day truce on the Union and the shipowners, under the Taft-Hartley Act. The 80-day period saw continuation of a standoff between the contending parties. The S.U.P., M.F.O.W., and M.C.S. arrived at eight points considered essential:

- Improvement in vacation allowances.
- Pension improvements, with reduction of the retirement age to 62.
- Wage and overtime boosts.
- Guaranteed benefit payments.
- A work stabilization fund.
- A joint maritime industry committee fund.
- Work rule adjustments.
- Guaranteed unemployment benefits.

Although by June the unions were again legally permitted to strike, an agreement was reached in time with P.M.A., and was duly ratified by the membership, in which all of the basic demands were achieved.

Weisberger presided over the Union during the Vietnam war, which like Korea, temporarily bolstered U.S. shipping activity, and briefly improved the S.U.P. employment picture. Here again, the S.U.P. seamen served at war. More than 100 vessels went into service during the hostilities. However, a major problem for the maritime Unions, in crewing them, was the revived competition, between the S.I.U. and N.M.U., over the unlicensed jobs.

Weisberger was responsible for efficiently managing the Union's pension, welfare, and deferred income plans, leaving them in excellent condition at the end of his term. An important aspect of the Lundeberg legacy, as carried on by Morris Weisberger, consisted of the role of the S.U.P. in the AFL-CIO Maritime Trades Department, grouping all affiliated unions with members in the industry. In a sense, the M.T.D. finally fulfilled the hopes of Lundeberg's youthful I.W.W. associates, who sought "one big union." Lundeberg's himself was succeeded in the top position in the M.T.D. by Paul Hall, head of the S.I.U.; with Hall's passing two decades later, the position was assumed by S.I.U. head Frank Drozak.

In 1975, the relationship between the S.U.P. and its Pacific district S.I.U. co-affiliate, the Marine Cooks and Stewards, was marred by conflict in the wake of Pacific Far East Line's sale of four vessels serving the U.S.-Australia trade to Farrell Lines. The *Thomas E. Cuffe* sailed and made a complete voyage with a non-S.U.P. deck gang, recruited from the National Maritime Union. The S.U.P. and Marine Firemen then refused to dispatch crew members to the rest of P.F.E.L.'s ships. S.U.P. and Firemen's pickets were ordered away from the ships by a federal court decision. The striking unions strongly condemned the Marine Cooks and Stewards, which continued manning the *Cuffe*, and which soon afterward became a fully-merged affiliate of the S.I.U. Atlantic and Gulf District, without the autonomy enjoyed by the Sailors and Firemen within the S.I.U. Pacific District.

In fighting for its side in the P.F.E.L. conflict, the S.U.P. encountered a new legal problem. In the P.F.E.L. case, the existence of an N.M.U. hiring hall in San Francisco since the second world war was judged by the courts to invalidate the S.U.P.'s claim of West Coast jurisdiction. The legal principle of "accretion" had hit the waterfront.

Paul Dempster

In 1978, Weisberger was succeeded as S.U.P. chief executive by Paul Dempster. Dempster, born in Honolulu, Hawaii, on October 12, 1928, had joined the Union in 1948, becoming tanker business agent in February 1966.

In President Dempster's first year in office he faced what proved to be some of the most difficult problems in the history of the Union, for 1978 saw the loss of three major West Coast shipping contracts: the remainder of Pacific Far East Line, Prudential-Grace Lines, and States Line.

In the cases of both P.F.E.L. and States, the companies went into bankruptcy leaving the Union virtually bereft of any serious means to defend the interest of members there employed. In the Prudential case, which turned into a notable controversy, the Union fought through the year to protect its jurisdiction, for rather than bankruptcy and the complete layup of the vessels concerned, Prudential had sold its ships to Delta Line, which transferred them to East Coast jurisdiction. The S.U.P. first reacted to the proposed sale of Prudential ships to Delta by filing an unfair practices suit aimed at protecting the pension fund.

Once the vessels were actually operating under the Delta house flag, the S.U.P. followed through by picketing Delta for refusing to take employment applications from former Prudential employees. Picketing was stopped by a court order, but the S.U.P. in the meantime had filed charges with the National Labor Relations Board, in response to Delta's manifest refusal to bargain in good faith. Unfortunately, the federal authorities supported Delta's decision to replace the S.U.P. with East Coast personnel.

The following year again saw troubled waters for the Union when the integrated tug-barge *Valerie F.*, formerly under West Coast contract, was turned over by her owners, Intercoastal Bulk Carriers, to the Rice Growers Association. The Rice Growers signed a new hiring agreement with the Masters, Mates, and Pilots organization to cover licensed officers, but hired unlicensed crew through newspaper advertisements in Florida.

The *Valerie F.* arrived in the Bay Area and was met by West Coast Union pickets. The company first argued that the conflict was strictly jurisdictional, but a court decision held the picket lines to be legitimate. The employer then announced that it was prepared to offer top-to-bottom jurisdiction to the M.M.P. A 48-day picketing action by the S.U.P. and its allies included extensive water-borne action involving the picket boat *Malabar,* operated by Hal C. Banks, a former S.U.P. member and head of the S.I.U. in Canada, who died as this book was in preparation. The West Coast unions won the "beef," forcing the *Valerie F.*'s operators to discharge the M.M.P. "replacement workers" and return the original crew members to their jobs, under S.U.P. contract.

A similar fight, beginning the same year, involved the American Pacific Container Company. AMPAC, which had formulated pre-hiring agreements with the M.M.P. and the N.M.U., found its attempt to get around West Coast unlicensed jurisdiction severely complicated by the protests of a coalition of labor and political figures organized by the S.U.P. On November 16, 1979, the West Coast unions commenced picketing two vessels acquired by AMPAC from Farrell Lines. AMPAC filed in court against the West Coast unions, and the unions responded by charging, in their own suit, that AMPAC, Farrell, the M.M.P., and the N.M.U. had conspired to exclude West Coast union workers from legitimate employment.

The AMPAC battle temporarily took a more dramatic turn in 1980, after the federal government ruled against the West Coast unions and in favor of the N.M.U. Legal representatives for the West Coast organizations introduced clear evidence of an unfair prehiring agreement between the N.M.U. and AMPAC, but the courts continued to support AMPAC, while the opposing unions continued to picket. Late in 1980, after almost a year of picketing, AMPAC went into bankruptcy.

Among the many changes rung in the maritime industry over the most recent decades, we must cite the close relationship that has developed, in the struggles of the 1970s and 1980s, between the S.U.P. and a union that was once its chief adversary, the I.L.W.U. Today, under the leadership of International President James R. Herman, the West Coast longshoremen's organization works in close partnership with the S.U.P. and President Dempster. This reconciliation between the often-brawling waterfront brothers is a key element in labor's overall strategic strength in the region and the nation. President Dempster and other S.U.P. representatives have affirmed their trust and affection for International President Herman and his membership on many occasions. The unity that has appeared anew is a positive harbinger for the future, and today's S.U.P. stands ready to "turn to" whenever needed to maintain it.

Both Morris Weisberger and Paul Dempster have been prominent in general labor and political affairs. At the time of this writing, S.U.P. President Dempster stands among the most respected labor activists on the West Coast, thanks to his active involvement in the defense of labor's rights during the series of conflicts that have marked the region since 1980: particularly in the Qantas lockout in which San Francisco Airport employees saw their union rights grossly denied, and in the dramatic Greyhound strike of 1983. Dempster has been on the front line whenever needed by the labor movement.

"Out in front" has always been the attitude of the S.U.P., fulfilling its 1885 promise as the "lookout of the labor movement." As these words are being written, the U.S. faces uncertainty in the labor field, perhaps as great as at any time in the past. Union membership has suffered a decline throughout the nation; union members seem confused about their loyalties and about the ability of their representatives to protect their rights. Many employers have come to the conclusion that unions no longer merit a share in the affairs of the workplace. The next few years will show whether or not the ideals and the sacrifices of the pioneers of American unionism will have been sown on ground turned, with time, to sterility. No modern society can survive without guarantees for labor's rights, as embodied in the unions. We may well see, once again, great and terrible conflicts in the economic field; on the other hand, new and more sophisticated strategies and tactics may emerge, on the side of labor as well as that of the employer.

Already, at the time of this book's writing, sinister warning signs had appeared. A severe blow had come in the early 1980s, when the Reagan administration cut off funding for the Public Health Service marine hospitals, destroying an institution that had been set up by federal mandate in 1793. The S.U.P. argued unsuccessfully for the hospitals' retention, before the U.S. Supreme Court. In mid-1984, a maneuver by a group of tanker companies led by Trinidad Corporation, an East Coast-based company, against the Masters, Mates, and Pilots union, saw union licensed officers arrested and removed from vessels.[4] This case, reminiscent of the pivotal *Arago* incident, shows that many shipowners are fully prepared to provoke a battle to restrict union representation. Truly, the Sailors must remain strong and prepared for action, no less vigilantly than at any other time in the past hundred years.

"The fight goes on," says President Dempster, "and the end is not yet in sight."

The S.U.P.: Its First Hundred Years

The year 1985 included the celebration of the Union's first century at a gala held March 9, in the

[4]Thomas J. O'Hara, "Are Maritime Officers' Unions Under Siege?" *The Professional Mariner*, August 1984.

Grand Ballroom of San Francisco's Fairmont Hotel, with parallel observances in each of the ports where branches are maintained. As President Dempster noted, the Union had come a good deal further than many would have predicted a century before. Symbolically, the seamen had made the long haul from the Folsom Street Wharf to the top of Nob Hill, from despair at their outcast situation to equality and influence in the leadership of the Pacific Coast community.

The March 9 dinner saw a guest list, mostly of members and pensioners, exceeding 1,500 in numbers. Honored participants included the lieutenant governor of California, Leo McCarthy, U.S. Representatives Sala Burton and George Miller, Commodore Tom Patterson of the U.S. Merchant Marine Academy at Kings Point, and representatives of the other maritime unions: Frank Drozak, Ed Turner, and George McCartney, for the Seafarers, Shannon Wall, N.M.U., Henry "Whitey" Disley, Pacific Coast Marine Firemen, Jesse Calhoon and Gene De Fries, Marine Engineers, Robert Lowen, Masters, Mates, and Pilots, and Jim Herman from the West Coast longshoremen.

In his remarks, President Dempster noted:

"This is a special occasion for American labor, for seamen the world over, for the West Coast, and for the city of San Francisco. One hundred years ago, on March 6, 1885, the Coast Seamen's Union, the predecessor of our organization, was founded on the old Folsom Street Wharf in this great city. The first formal meeting of the union was held on a lumber pile on that fateful evening. Two hundred and twenty-two men were enrolled and $34.60 was collected.

"The times were turbulent back in 1885 as the labor movement fought for recognition, better wages and conditions and, for shoreside workers, the eight-hour day. The situation was not easy, particularly for the men who went to sea for a living. Seamen did not even have the rights enjoyed by so-called 'wage slaves' ashore. If a seaman quit his ship without the permission of the employer, he could be arrested and imprisoned for the crime of desertion.

"Terrible grievances existed in the ships: quarters were cramped, crowded, cold and wet. The food was far below civilized standards and the men were physically abused by bucko mates and skippers. The public was deaf to the seamen's complaints until a scandal was raised by publication of *The Red Record*, a pamphlet detailing the worst incidents of shipboard brutality, prepared by the gifted Walter Macarthur, editor of our former Union newspaper, the *Coast Seamen's Journal*.

"The men who mustered at Folsom Street Wharf on that rainy night one hundred years ago were pioneers. They were courageous and convinced their cause was just, but the going was rough. Within a year, the Coast Seamen and their allies had called the big strike of 1886. The Union noted in their minutes that the spirit was one of complete determination. But the strike was lost. The following year Andrew Furuseth took over the helm and the Union had a man who would turn defeat around, who would never rest until the seaman could serve his calling as a free man, emancipated from servitude and bondage.

"We call March the 'Sailor's Month' for four reasons:

- March 4, 1915: the signing into law of the Seamen's Act,
- March 6, 1885: the founding of the S.U.P.,
- March 12, 1854: the birthdate of Andrew Furuseth,
- March 25, 1901: the birthdate of Harry Lundeberg.

"Andrew Furuseth was a true Viking, Norwegian born. He had sailed in the off-shore square-riggers and he knew first hand the injustices suffered by seamen. He was a great speaker and an inspiring leader of men. In 1891, he led the Coast Seamen's Union into unity with the Steamship Sailors, establishing the Sailors' Union of the Pacific. During the great transportation strike of 1901, when employers attempted to snuff the light of unionism in San Francisco, Andy and the City Front Federation fought them to a standstill. In 1892 he was largely responsible for the establishment of the old International Seamen's Union.

"In the long, complicated campaign that saw passage of the Maguire Act and the White Act and finally produced the Seamen's Act in 1915, Andy first used the slogan 'Tomorrow is also a day,' to remind the seamen that the battle would be long, as indeed it was, but also to affirm that there was reason for hope. At one point, he responded to the threat of an injunction with the words that today grace his statue in front of our headquarters building: 'You can put me in jail; but you cannot give me narrower quarters than as a seaman I have always had. You cannot give me coarser food than I have always eaten. You cannot make me lonelier than I have always been.'

"Andy was called the 'Abraham Lincoln of the seas' in recognition of the task he accomplished in securing passage of the Seamen's Act, which he called 'the dawn of a new day.' The Act, signed by President Woodrow Wilson, finally freed the seaman from the servitude of centuries. When Andy died in 1938, his body lay in state in the Labor Department Building in Washington, D.C. before his ashes were scattered at sea.

"Harry Lundeberg was another Norwegian with a Viking temperment. He was known as a Sailor's Sailor. He fought with distinction in Seattle during the 1934 strike and afterwards was named to lead the short-lived Maritime Federation of the Pacific. Loved by friends and respected by opponents, Lundeberg fought any group that threatened the maritime union movement. He was a vice president of the California Labor Federation for many years and supported every AFL union that asked for help. He established the Seafarers' International Union and the AFL-CIO Maritime Trades Department and pioneered many important benefits — welfare, pensions, vacations — in the maritime industry. His death at age 56 was mourned by seamen around the world.

"In 1957, the leadership of the Sailors' Union passed to Morris Weisberger, who continued the fight to better the lives of the membership. He served with dedication and distinction until he left office in 1978. He was a valued vice president of the California Labor Federation and president of the Bay Area Maritime Trades Department. He remains active here in San Francisco and is with us here tonight.

"Thanks to the leadership of men like Furuseth, Lundeberg and Weisberger, seamen were able to better their position in life, to marry and to raise families, and truly become first-class citizens.

"In the founding days of the republic, when the early patriots were taking on the 'establishment,' Ben Franklin said to his cohorts, 'We must all hang together, gentlemen, or surely we will all hang separately.' The S.U.P. has echoed that sentiment through all its difficult years of development and growth. We are not against the shipowners *per se* (although that may not always be apparent), for together we make up the maritime industry. If they fall, we fall, and one of our earliest declarations, in the preamble of our constitution, documents that commitment by stating that 'We are conscious of corresponding duties to those in command, our employers, our craft and our country.'

"We believe in the cause of labor, just as our founding members believed in it a century ago, and we have remained faithful to that cause. We are proud to have held up the banner of labor for one hundred years. We are joined here tonight by other century-old maritime unions: the Marine Firemen's Union, the Marine Engineers Beneficial Association, and the Masters, Mates and Pilots. These unions, along with the Seafarers, the National Maritime Union, the Longshoremen and the Teamsters on the waterfront, face with us today a formidable array of problems: a tight economy, political shenanigans in Washington and, in maritime, fierce competition for the remnants of a merchant marine that finds itself in the worst shape it has been in since it was first set up in the wake of the American Revolution.

"But as Andy used to say, tomorrow is also a day, and we will overcome the problems of the present as we did those of the past by using the one great asset that has remained constant over the years, an informed and dedicated membership willing to stand up and be counted. We are guided and inspired by the sacrifices of those who came before us. The men who fought on the picket lines were true heroes, like the men who paid the ultimate sacrifice in the second world war and other conflicts to defend our country's freedom.

"This union was founded by men of spirit and is continued by you, the members who are gathered here tonight. We would never be able to continue our struggle without the spirit that this membership has so often shown, the spirit that made it possible to win all the big strikes, that did away with the fink halls and the crimps. It is that spirit that bought us here to our centennial year.

"Members and friends of the Sailors' Union of the Pacific, I salute the first hundred years of a great organization. Let us go forward through the next century with our spirit strong and our ideals bright. The fight goes on!"

Weisberger Speaks

President Dempster's predecessor, Morris Weisberger, spoke in a similar vein:

"An event like this gives us old-timers a terrific excuse to ramble on about how far we've come, to congratulate ourselves, to reminisce a little about the bad old days, and to recall the struggles which got us to where we are. We started out on a pile of lumber down at the pier, and here we are at the Fairmont Hotel. We're entitled to crow a little. We earned it.

"There are some people who need remembering, who gave their life's blood so that we could be here tonight. Of course, we'll all talk about Andy Furuseth, and about Harry Lundeberg; and maybe someone will have a few kind words about old Morris Weisberger. We owe at least that much to people who gave us their whole lives. But over the years, many other people worked with the S.U.P., and deserve recognition as well tonight — and if I leave anyone out, it's surely not intentional.

"First of all, there was the national AFL and AFL-CIO leadership: Bill Green, George Meany and Lane Kirkland, who over the years were trustworthy allies and supporters of the S.U.P. and could always be counted on for help. Locally here on the Coast, we always have looked for and found similar support from the State Federation of Labor, from Neil Haggerty, Jack Henning and Al Gruhn, and from the Labor Council's Jack Crowley and Dick Groulx. It would be a mistake as well not to mention Jim Herman and Curtis McClain of the ILWU, who have done so much to end the years and years of unnecessary warfare between our two unions, and to the various officers of ILWU Longshore Local 10 here in San Francisco who came through for us when we needed them. We owe a great deal as well to outstanding Teamster leaders.

"Within the maritime industry, let us also remember the role of the leadership of the S.I.U.-Atlantic and Gulf District, people like Paul Hall, Frank Drozak, Lindsey Williams, Joe Di Giorgio, Al Kerr, George McCartney, Roy Mercer, and Ed Turner; from the S.I.U. Canadian District, we worked closely with people like Hal Banks and Roman Gralewicz. Other maritime leaders; from M.E.B.A. Districts one and two, Ray McKay, Gus Guzelian, Jesse Calhoon, Gene DeFries, Frank Lauritsen and Henry Borello; also: Whitey Disley, Whitey Shoup, Vince Malone, Sam Bennett, Harry Jorgensen and Bill Jordan of the Marine Firemen who have been very special friends of the S.U.P. over the years. We owe a great deal as well to Pete McGavin, Harry O'Reilly, Jack McDonald and Jean Ingrao of the national Maritime Trades Department.

"Captain Charlie May and Captain Durkin of the M.M.P. also deserve our thanks, as well as Al Clem, Dale Marr, T.J. Stapleton and James Ivey of the Operating Engineers, and Brandon Tynan of the Marine Staff Officers Association. Also, Capts. Art Thomas and William Meyer, Port Agents of the S.F. Bar Pilots.

"I would be making a terrible mistake to omit mentioning a couple of the staff people who have made such a contribution over the years — the late Rose

Lentz, who was my secretary during my many years as President of the S.U.P.; Jack Dwyer, who I worked with for 40 years, and the current editor of the *West Coast Sailors,* John Hill, who also served when I was in office.

"It is also a time for us to look back and try to see what it all meant. What was the single most important contribution the S.U.P. made in these last 100 years? Some would argue for Andrew Furuseth and his incredible legislative record, which effectively released the American sailor from centuries of peonage and set the standard for maritime workers all over the world.

"Others would point to the strikes of the 1930s which made the West Coast into Union country, and unionized not only the waterfront but made possible the unionization of so many other workers. Others would look at World War II, and the truly heroic record of the members of the S.U.P. during the war for democracy, as the outstanding achievement of these last 100 years. I won't argue it one way or another. All these achievements deserve the strongest possible recognition.

"But let's add to that list of outstanding achievements the creation and the continued defense of the Sailors' hiring hall. The hiring hall was a trade union answer to favoritism, corruption and violence on the waterfront. It was a unique method of expressing the solidarity of workers and their refusal to be played off against one another as they had been since time immemorial.

"Harry Lundeberg deserves to be remembered for many things, but if you ask me, Harry's defense of the hiring hall, against the Copeland Fink Book first enacted into law in 1936, against the Maritime Commission's so-called 'recruitment and manning office' of the World War II years,and finally, against the anti-hiring hall provisions of the Taft-Hartley Act — these efforts stand right in there among the great achievements of this Union. That the hiring hall today remains the cornerstone of our Union is a tribute to Harry Lundeberg and all who worked with him on these issues."[5]

Summing Up — To Asia, Australia, and Beyond

Looking to the future, it is the opinion of the author of this book that the Sailors' Union of the Pacific may best be summed up by describing its three pillars: its resources in terms of human character, its contract, and its spirit of cooperation with the rest of the labor movement.

The first of these pillars hardly needs elaboration. The story of this Union has consistently been that of strong, principled individuals, in the leadership and in the rank and file.

But an institution, and particularly a union, is more than simply the human material that makes it up. A union functions through a contract, and the S.U.P. contract remains one of the sturdiest models for a labor agreement in force in the U.S. At the time this book was completed, the 1984-1987 document was in effect. Even a cursory review of the S.U.P. contract shows the careful work that has gone, for decades, into rules and practices designed to protect the rights and dignities of seagoing workers.

A keystone of the S.U.P. contract is included in part II of the contract, headed *Work Rules*. This is section 4, the "scope of work" clause, which remains unique in U.S. maritime union contracts. This clause reserves certain work to the Sailors, and is remarkably extensive, including "the recognized and customary duties of the Deck Department," plus other maintenance and handling of cargo equipment, rigging, and other elements of shipboard work.

Naturally, as a document covering all aspects of a seafarer's life aboard ship, the contract also includes specifications for serving of meals, coffee time, and amenities in crew quarters. Suitable heating and ventilation, "medicine cabinets with mirrors," doors with adequate locks, desks and chairs, lockers, fumigation services, and careful standards for mattresses, linen, laundry facilities, recreation rooms, ship's hospitals, night lunches, all reflect the militance of the Union in past struggles for better conditions. In addition, the contract goes so far as to specify brands and quality of food.

The Sailors' Union has come a very long way in its first hundred years. Its recent leaders have often pointed out the progress achieved in the years since 1950: the seagoing workers went from steel bunks bolted to the deck, to built-in bunks, and eventually to current accommodations, including individual sleeping rooms, swimming pools, and video players aboard ship. However, improvements for the shipowner in profits have largely surpassed those for the Sailors in conditions. In 1984, the Sailors' Union began crewing two vessels with a new model for manning, the *President Eisenhower* and *President Roosevelt*, operated by American President Lines. These two *Presidents* require no more than a 21-man crew from top-to-bottom, with six sailors on deck, three members of the engine department (represented by the Pacific Coast Marine Firemen's Union), three stewards, and one less mate than formerly carried. The scheduling for the new *Presidents* is extremely tight, with a turn-around in port so fast that sailors may enjoy no more than 10 hours off after a 42-day trip. The strain is, obviously, extreme.

In the area of inter-union cooperation, the S.U.P. can be expected to remain fully committed to its active stance. Toward the end of 1985, two separate events showed the S.U.P.'s high profile in this area, with particular respect to the interests of the Pacific Basin in which the Union's employment opportunities have always been centered.

In the summer of 1985, President Dempster joined a team of maritime union, employer, and government representatives on a two week fact-finding tour

[5]Speeches by Paul Dempster and Morris Weisberger, in *West Coast Sailors*, March 22, 1985.

through Asia. Other union representatives on the 12-man Labor-Management Committee (L.M.C.) included Clyde Dodson, executive vice president of the Marine Engineers, David York, vice president of the Pacific Coast Masters, Mates, and Pilots, Ed Turner, head of the S.I.U. Marine Cooks and Stewards, and Sterling Barrymore of the Radio Officers. In a published report following the trip, President Dempster included the following observations on the situations he encountered:

"Day 1: Labor Management Committee has joint meeting with the All Japan Seamen's Union (A.J.S.U.), with the Japan Shipowner's Associations, and with the Japanese government's Ministry of Transport. L.M.C. was scheduled to meet with each organization separately so we held back on questions that Japan was having and still has, to some extent, with their maritime industry as a whole. These problems concerned the loss of ships and business to foreign competition and Third World countries with reduced crews which had affected their business to the extent that they as a maritime nation had lost almost 50 percent of their ships. One thing we all found out: Japanese seamen and their industry are suffering the same fate as the United States' maritime, a declining industry, competition from foreign flags-of-convenience, rate wars in the Pacific Basin, and older seamen who remain in the industry and whose average age is 39 years.

"We were surprised to learn that there were no female 'seamen' in their ships, licensed or unlicensed. They explained there were no plans at this time to employ or train any females. The company will hire a new employee who will work for them until age 55 when the seamen must retire on a pension plan that is below his earnings in the industry. The average Japanese seaman earns approximately $3,000 (U.S. currency) per month. When he retires, almost in the prime of his life, he has great difficulty in getting another job so he is practically forced to find low-paying work wherever he can find it. No one gets laid off. Whenever they lose ships due to sale or to reductions in crew size, they put their employees either on shoreside standby-type of work, relief crews in port, or other jobs within the company. The Japanese government subsidizes training and the retraining of seamen. They also support new ship construction by low interest rates. Thus, the Japanese shipowners are able to build new ships and they now have 45 ships under five years old.

"The greatest change in the Japanese maritime industry is reduction in crew size and new ratings which cross over to the different unlicensed departments in the ships. They started the first phase around ten years ago, a crew reduction down to 24 or 21 top-to-bottom and a non-watchstanding engine room. . . .

"Day 2: At A.J.S.U., Takeshi Kawamura, Vice President of A.J.S.U., and his staff gave a brief history of their union. They were established in 1945 by organizing both officers and unlicensed men into one union. The membership is about 134,000 as of 1984. The captains and a third of the radio officers are not in the union.

"All of their members on contracted vessels (mate, engineer and the crews) are guaranteed lifetime jobs until they are 55 years of age. Then they are pensioned off. The average age of the seamen is 40 years.

"A.J.S.U. said they go along with the effective manning policy with shipowners and government as a way of maintaining jobs and the security for Japan.

"Regarding Dual Purpose Crew (D.P.C.) rating, re-training and new training for officers was started at the Japan government school. The re-training of crew members who traditionally worked in the engine or deck department was hard, as it was difficult for them to cross over departmental lines. The mates and engineers had the same problem but, because of better education and training, were able to adjust to the change more readily. . . .

"Our last meeting on the Asian trip which was with Leow Ching Chuan, General Secretary of the Singapore Organization of Seamen and Thomas Tay, General Secretary of the Singapore Maritime Officers' Union.

"The officers' union six years ago had 400 members and now has 4,200 members. They have increased their wages 100 percent within six years. The unlicensed seamen number about 5,000. They have a no-strike clause but can go out if they follow strict procedures. They have 20 contracts, the terms and conditions of which are about the same except for the expiration dates. The officers have seven days' vacation on tankers and 10 days' on containerships, whereas the unlicensed seamen have four days' vacation on all ships.

"Their members do not like reduced manning. The officers are used to service, having bunks made and their own messroom. Unions invite the company representatives to speak to their membership to make them aware of maritime problems.

"The unions are losing their jobs to cheaper labor from the Philippines and from India and have signed an agreement with the Koreans, who will not sign on any Singapore ships without the approval of the Singapore unions."[6]

The attitude of cooperation and inquiry expressed in this report was visible at S.U.P. headquarters late in September 1985, when the Union participated in a colloquium with a 12-man labor-management delegation from Australia, including Pat Geraghty, head of the Seamen's Union of Australia. Australian and United States union people at the conference came together on such issues as defense of food standards aboard ships, with the Australians, for example, warning the U.S. unionists of moves toward "airline-type" feeding of crews, a concept that had, fortunately, not yet made an appearance on this side of the Pacific.

[6]Paul Dempster, "Labor/Management Scrutinizes Far Eastern Methods," *Transport 2000* (San Francisco), September 1985.

The year 1985 has seen a number of such events, stressing the Union's strong sense of what is right for the working people and its commitment to labor cooperation. In a sense, these global inter-union meetings are as important an observance of the Union's first hundred years as any banquet. That's the S.U.P. way.

The history of union organization in the United States and around the world is complex. Building on the social traditions of the guilds, in which skilled craftsmen protected their share of the market through collective action, the unions were forced by the terrible situation of the mass of wage workers in the industrial age to go beyond simple economic self-help. The unions became fighting organizations in what most participants and observers saw as a war of the classes, a war far more socially destructive and divisive than the past competitive conflicts of guilds. More than an apparatus for securing a high price for their labor, the unions came to embody the deepest aspirations of working people on a whole range of social issues. The unions became the main force in the historic movement, at the end of the 19th century and the first half of the 20th, toward a better, more just, more equal society.

Both the function of unions as a means to compete adequately in the labor market, over wages, and their role as a bulwark of genuine social progress have forced the unions to accept great responsibilities. In the wake of the 1930s' depression, with the virtual reorganization of the Western industrial nations on an extensive social-welfare basis, unions found themselves entwined with governments in a new kind of relationship. Where previously the political state structure stood, largely, on the side of employers against the unions, as, for example, in the 1921 case of the War Shipping Board, governmental authorities now endeavored to reconcile the interests of capital and labor through action of the political state. As we have noted, the dangers in this phenomenon were indicated with particular acuity by Lundeberg. Unlike the totalitarian regimes of Lenin, Mussolini, and Hitler, the democracies did not impose government-*controlled* unions on the workers. But unions *supported and monitored* by government as are now universal in the democracies, have tended to find their autonomy and militancy limited by a government-capital-labor "alliance." For this reason, a revitalized, more-independent unionism, a "new labor spirit," has become, to many, increasingly necessary.

In our review of the S.U.P.'s history, we have touched on many features that merit a much more extensive discussion. The Union has proved to be an especially durable and perhaps unique product of the combative outlook identified with the so-called "Chicago idea" in the 1880s — a labor organization wary of governmental interference, responsive to the needs of its members, and prepared for hard struggle based on militant action. If we ascribe this special and admirable attitude to the Union's human resources, we must understand that these have been regional as well as ethnic and vocational. The organization was toughened by the experience of its members in the sailing schooner and later steam schooner fleets and in the hard school of the Alaskan trade, where sailing time between the many Alaskan ports (almost a hundred) was short, longshoremen were non-existent, and the Sailors worked long and difficult hours, with little time to sleep or even to eat. Most of the Sailors who passed through this experience were Scandinavians, prepared for it, as we have emphasized, by the tradition of working-class solidarity they brought with them from Europe.

To this "educational" background we must add the often-noted hardships of the seamen's life everywhere on the globe, since the time of the Phoenicians. The sailor has been isolated from and often has totally lacked a home. In addition, Sailors share a special sense of trust and cooperation in the face of a sea that may always turn angry. The labor historian Stan Weir, a former S.U.P. member, has identified the Union's tradition of independence with the role of members of the deck department as an "informal work group," in which decisions are formulated collectively and expressed through the boatswain and the Union delegate, who have had the power to hold the licensed officers at a distance. These factors have broken down national and social barriers. In the S.U.P. this is especially visible in the contribution of the Hawaiians, with their multi-ethnic identity.[7]

Certainly, it is because of the special human aspects of the West Coast Sailors' experience that the Union has maintained its distinctive character, from the time of the "Chicago idea" through the period of I.W.W. influence and the struggle for freedom from Communist dictation.

However the history of the S.U.P. may be debated, of one thing we may be sure: the Union has stood out, historically, from others in the U.S. labor movement, for its dedication to principle and its courage. When men and women take up the labor banner in defense of their rights, whether today, tomorrow, or in the future, they will find in the history of the S.U.P. an exceptionally important and necessary example of the best traditions in Unionism. In this respect, the spirit of the men on the Folsom Street Wharf, of Furuseth, of Lundeberg, of Weisberger, of the seamen who manned the ships from 1885 to the present, will never perish.

[7] Weir, "The Informal Work Group," op. cit.

Index

Errata

In the second folio of photographs, appearing between pages 112 and 113, the funeral of Sperry and Counderakis is incorrectly described in the caption as shown at "Steuart and Market Streets." The correct location is Steuart and Mission Streets.

Page 121, column 2, line 8, read "less-than-competent" for "less-then-competent".

Pages 126-127, the selection from Robert L. Vargas' article, "The Saga of an 'Ugly Duckling,' is copyright 1969 by American Heritage, Inc., taken from *American Heritage*, December 1969, by permission of the editor, *American Heritage*.

Karl Kortum is incorrectly described as "Director of the National Maritime Museum" in the dustjacket copy. Mr. Kortum is the Museum's Chief Curator, as noted in his introduction.

Sailors' Union of the Pacific Branches and Officers – 1985

Paul Dempster, President/Secretary-Treasurer
Jack Ryan, Vice President
Gunnar Lundeberg, Headquarters Business Agent #1
Duane Hewitt, Headquarters Business Agent #2
Knud Andersen, Headquarters Business Agent #3
Kaj Kristensen, Tanker Business Agent

Headquarters, S.U.P., 450 Harrison Street, San Francisco, CA 94105 (415) 777-3400
Tanker Office, S.U.P., 203 Tewksbury Avenue, Point Richmond, CA 94801 (415) 233-3713

John Battles, Seattle Branch Agent
Morris Secrest, Seattle Business Agent
Seattle Branch, S.U.P., 2505 First Avenue, Seattle, WA 98121-1377 (206) 448-0290

Ray Murphy, Portland Branch Agent
Portland Branch, S.U.P., 3811 S.E. Belmont, Portland, OR 97214 (503) 232-0778

Charles Russo, Wilmington Branch Agent
William Ahia, Wilmington Business Agent
Wilmington Branch, S.U.P., 505 No. Marine Avenue, Wilmington, CA 90744 (213) 835-6617

William O. Smith, Honolulu Branch Agent
Honolulu Branch, S.U.P., 707 Alakea Street, Honolulu, HI 96813 (808) 533-2777

Henry Johansen, New Orleans Branch Agent
New Orleans Branch, S.U.P., 630 Jackson Ave., New Orleans, LA 70130 (504) 525-7428

William Armstrong, New York Branch Agent
New York Branch, S.U.P., 675 Fourth Avenue, Brooklyn, NY 11232 (718) 499-0711

John C. Hill, Editor, *West Coast Sailors*

Author's Biography

Stephen Schwartz was born in 1948 and has lived in the San Francisco Bay Area since he was two. He published poetry and other writings while at Lowell High School, and attended the City College of San Francisco and the University of California, Berkeley. At the latter institution, he was awarded a scholarship and other honors.

However, like many of his peers in the turbulent generation of the 1960s, Mr. Schwartz turned away from an academic career to become an activist, in his case in the labor movement. After shipping out as a member of the Sailors' Union of the Pacific, he "swallowed the anchor" and served almost ten years as a railroad employee. He has been a leading member of AFL-CIO Railway Clerks' lodges 248 (Western Pacific) and 226 (Santa Fe).

Since 1980, Mr. Schwartz has concentrated on his work as a writer. In 1981-83, he was senior editor of *Pacific Shipper*, the leading West Coast maritime periodical, and he is now editor of the San Francisco-based quarterly *Journal of Contemporary Studies*. He participated in the massive 1986 study, *Unions in Transition*, edited by Seymour Martin Lipset with Herman Benson, Lane Kirkland, and others. Mr. Schwartz has extensively studied politics in the Hispanic world, a major preoccupation aside from labor, and is working with the eminent Spanish historian Victor Alba on a book about the Spanish civil war, to be published by Transaction Books.

Mr. Schwartz has published articles in Spanish and French as well in leading American periodicals such as *Commentary* and *The New Criterion*, and in earlier incarnations, in various far-left journals. He has also published two collections of poetic texts, *Hidden Locks* (1972) and *A SLEEPWALKER's Guide to San Francisco* (1983).

He is a member of Social Democrats, USA.

Colophon

This first edition of *Brotherhood of the Sea* consists of five thousand copies printed on Ardor paper, with duotone illustrations on Wedgewood Gloss. Graphic design is by Terry Crescenti; Mergenthaler Cheltenham typefaces are used throughout. Presswork was completed on a Harris 240 Omsca press at the Robert Mattoch Printing Company, San Francisco, in June 1986. All copies were bound in Roxite B linen by Cardoza-James Binding Company, San Francisco.

IN MEMORY OF OUR BROTHERS WHO LOST THEIR LIVES IN WORLD WAR II

CHARLES LANG
ROBERT E. LANG
CARL LANGEN
CHRISTIAN S. LANTZ
R. A. LANTZ
CARL H. LARSEN
WILHELM LARSEN
PEDRO LAURIANO
A. LAWMAN
GEORGE LAWSON
ISAIAH LAWSON
THEODORE LAYNE
E. T. LEBRON
ANGIE LECTORA
HORACE LEE
JAMES R. LEE
WILLIAM LEE
EUGENE W. LEGGETT
VINCENT LEGURO
KENNETH LEHR
KENNETH E. LEHR
JOSEPH LESNIAK
OTIS LESTER
CHARLES E. LEWIS
RICHARD F. LEWIS
JOSEH B. LIMA JR.
THOR A. LINDBERG
HENRY LINDSEY
VERNON LINDQUIST
WALLACE D. LINDQUIST
VICTOR F. LISKOYS
WALTER LITCH
GEORGE L. LITTEL
THOMAS LITTLE
THOMAS J. LIVELY
ALEXANDER LIVINGSTON
W. E. LOCKETT
GROVER C. LONG
FRANCISCO LOPEZ
JAMES C. LOTT JR.
JESSIE LOVITT
DENTON S. LOWE
CLARENCE C. LOWERY
MARTIN J. LUDWICK
DARWIN LUMBATTIS
ALBERT LUNDQUIST
JOHN A. LUNK
BRUCE LUPTON
JOSEPH LUSSIER
DAVID B. LYNCH
JOHN J. LYNCH
JULIUS LYNCH
LAWRENCE LYNCH
ARTHUR LYON
GEORGE LYSAGHT

M

CHARLES M. MacCASKILL
MARK MacDONALD
HARRY MACK
CAYTANO MacKENZIE
ANTHONY MCKSEY
MANUEL MADURO
ALFRED MAFFIA
JOSEPH E. MAHONEY
FRANK C. MALIZIA
THOMAS MALONE
WILLIAM MALONE
JOSEPH MARCINKEVIC
EDWARD MARK
OBDULIO MARTINEZ
CALVIN MANGUM
JOSEPH P. MANN
W. E. MANUEL
EDWARD W. MARKO
CLEMENT S. MAKOWSKI
WILLIAM MARLAND
MITCHEL MARQUESS
LINWOOD W. MARSHALL
ROBERT MARTEL
JAMES MARTIN
CHARLES MASON
E. G. MASON
ANTHONY MASSETTS
ALFRED E. MAYER
OSCAR K. MAYO
F. MEADOWS
ELMER MEHEGEN
NORMAN W. MEIRAN
WILLIAM MELL
E. P. MENDEZ
PRIMITIO MENDEZ
WILLIAM MERRYFIELD
WILLIAM MESSICK
ANTHONY MICH
JOSE MIGUEZA
A. W. MILLAY
CHARLES MILLER
F. J. MILLER
JOHN M. MILLER
JOSEPH MILLER
OLIVER J. MILLER
ROBERT E. MILLS
CLARENCE MISHLER
FILLMORE MITCHAM
BENJAMIN C. MITCHELL
LAWRENCE MITCHELL
JERRY MIXON
ANTONIO MONREAL
JOHN F. MONTEVERDE
GEORGE R. MOORE
MANUEL MORALIS
A. C. MORAN
ANTONIO MORAN
WALTER H. MORELLI
OSCAR M. MORGAN
THEO MORGAN
W. MORLAND
ALBERT MORRELL
WHITNEY MORRIS JR.
A. B. MOSES
J. MOYES
ERIC O. MUEHLE
THOMAS MULLANEY
JOHN MULLIGAN
ERASMO MUNEZ
HERBERT MUNGINS
ALAN MUNRO
JOSEPH MURILLO
HUGH MURPHY
JOSEPH MURPHY
K. W. MURPHY
ALBRYANT W. MURRAY JR.
THOMAS F. MURRAY
IRVIN MYERS

Mc

JOHN E. McCAFFREY
JOHN L. McCARLEY
WILLIAM McCLELLAND
ST. CLAR W. McCONNEY
ALEXANDER McCORMACK
JAMES McCULL
WILLIAM McCULLARD
THOMAS J. McDANIEL
ALBERT McDONALD
MARK D. McDONALD
DEWEY W. McDONOUGH
ARNOLD McDOWELL
EDGAR McDOWELL
WILLIAM McEVOY
ROY R. McFARLANE
CHARLES H. McGAHAN
FRED McGEE
FRANK McGEE
J. McGILLICUDDY
STEWART S. McGILLIVROY
JOHN McGINNETY
THOMAS W. McGOVERN
FRANK McGUIRE
MERLE McGUINNIS
WILLIAM McKEE
STEPHEN L. McKENNA
WALTER B. McKINNEY
JOSEPH McLAREN
R. E. McNALLY
JEREMIAH McNAMERA
ROY McNISH
JOHN G. McWILLIAMS
STEWART S. McGILLIVROY

N

HARRY E. NATHAN
ST. JULIAN NEVETTE
ANTHONY NICH
ROY M. NICKERSON
ALFRED K. NIELSEN
RUPERT NIELSEN
FRANK NIEMI
KARL NILSSON
CHARLES NOBLE
MANUEL NOBLE
EUGENE NOBLES
JAMES NORTH
WILLIAM P. NORRIS
ISAAC B. NORWOOD
TOM NUMME
F. H. NUMZIATA
FRANK H. NUNGIATO
CARL W. NYMAN

O

ALTON O'BERRY
EDWARD O'BRIEN
ROBERT J. O'BRIEN
THOMAS P. O'BRIEN
JOSEPH M. O'CONNER
TIM J. O'DONOGHUE
CYRIL OGLE
ARTHUR O'LIGNY
FRANK J. OLCHESKIE
R. A. OLIVER
RAFAEL OLIVERO
EINAR OLSEN
JENS F. OLSEN
CLARENCE OLSON
KENNETH OLSON
LAWRENCE A. J. OLSON
JOHN B. OLSZEWSKI
JOHN OLSZEWSKI
S. V. OLUFSON
WILLIAM ORAN
HERBERT O'REILLY
CARROL A. ORLANDO
RICHARD D. ORSBORNE
ANTONIO M. ORTIZ
FRANK OSTERMAN
MARVIN OSTROM
FRANK J. OTREMBA JR.

P

JOSE A. PABON
JUAN PABON
WILLIAM PACETTI
CRISTOBAL PADRO
CARLOS PAGAN
FRANCESCO PAGAN
DON D. PAGE
THOMAS PAINTER
FRANK PALMER
HARRY PANE
ALEXANDER PANKO
GEORGE PAPAS
VASIL PAPATHAMAS
VICTOR J. PAPINEAU
JAMES PARESES
EDWARD PARKER
MOSE PARKER
MOSES G. PARKER
MACK PARKS
MARIANO M. PARROCHA
WILLIAM PARSLEY
HERMAN PAS
VICTOR J. PATROLA
JAMES E. PATTON
HARRY PAUL
STEPHEN PAVELKO
FRANK P. PAVIA
JOHN PAVILONIS
EDWARD PEART
CLARENCE F. PECK
RODERICK PECOT
DEMETRO PELAYO
CLARENCE E. PELLERIN, JR.
IGNACIO P. PENARANDA
JOAO E. PENEDA
ROY W. PENNINGTON
THEODORE VON PENTZ
GERMAN PEREZ
MARCELINO PEREZ
DWIGHT PERKINS
JOHN PERKINS
MORRIS PERLIS
JOSEPH E. PERRANT
KASTON F. PERRY
RICHARD PERRY
STANLEY PESHEN
GILVERT E. PETERSON
R. S. PETTERSON
CHARLES PETITTI
WILLARD PHILBRICK
ALLYN D. PHILIP
W. PHILLIPS
LOREN PICKETT
CHARLES A. PIEDRA
RALPH PIEHET
JOHN PIERCE
PHILLIP B. PIERCE
WILLIAM J. PIKE
B. D. POEDING
EMMET L. POIRRIER
RICHARD POLOMS
RAY E. POTTER
L. A. POTTHOFF
FREDERICK W. POTTS JR.
JOHN C. PRESTON
GILBERT PRINCE
JOSEPH PROCTOR
JOSEPH W. PROCTOR
GEORGE PROSCHASKA
CHARLES F. PUCKETTE

Q

EDWARD QUINN

R

ORVILLE W. RADDEN
ROBERT F. RADEL
J. RADIGAN
EUGENE F. RAITT
ROBERT RAMIREZ
EDWARD RAMSEY
DEAN RANK
STEVE M. RAPCHAK
LOUIS RAY
LOUIS J. RAY
LUCIANO RAYCO
JOHN A. REA
WREN REAGAN
ORVILLE REDDEN
CLYDE REED JR.
HALLOWAY REED
WALLACE REED
GEORGE REEVES
CHARLES E. REGAN
W. M. REID
FRANK REILLY
GERARD F. REILLY
JOHN REILLY
THOMAS J. REILLY

IN MEMORY OF OUR BROTHERS WHO LOST THEIR LIVES IN WORLD WAR II

CHARLES REIP
ANTONIO REY
OREN REYNOLDS
CECIL RHODES
HERBERT J. RHODES
ELMER RICHARDSON
SMITHMAN C. RICHARDSON
WILLIAM J. RIDDLE
FRANK RILEY
ALBERTO RIVERA
JOAQUIN RIVERA
JUAN RIVERA
MANUEL RIVERA
HOWARD STANLEY RIVET
R. D. ROBERTSON
HARRY ROBERTS
HENRY ROBINSON
TORIBIO RODENAS
BURTON RODGERS
J. L. RODGERS
MARION RODGERS
B. L. RODMAN
P. I. RODRIGUES
PEDRO V. RODRIGUES
ANGEL M. RODRIGUEZ
F. D. RODRIGUEZ
HARRISON RODRIQUE
MANUEL RODRIQUEZ
PEDRO RODRIQUEZ
CANDELARIO ROJAS
GEORGE C. ROLY
JESUS ROMERO
JOHN B. RORIE JR.
VIRGILIO ROSARIO
FELIX ROSARIO
ARTHUR ROSE
JAMES E. L. ROSE
CARL ROSS
ISADOR ROSS
RICHARD ROSS
SAMUEL ROUCHERON
ALLEN J. ROUNDS
ARANT ROUNDTREE
THOMAS J. ROVERE
JULIO ROZENFELD
MICHAEL RUBIN
MARIANO RUBIO
JOHN RUEDA
LEONARD RUEDIGER
HANS RUNSTAD
MACK RUTHERFORD
THOMAS P. RYAN
J. RYAN

S

DANIEL SABIO
LOUIS SABO
WILLIAM L. SAGE
JUAN SALAMO
LOUIS SALUS
CARL F. SALZMAN
NICOLAS SAMILLANO
RAMON SAN AUGUSTIN
ELADIO SANCHEZ
JUAN SANCHEZ
JOHN SANDOVA
AARON C. SANGSTER JR.
EUGENIO SANTANA
ESTEBAN SANTIAGO
MATIAS SANTIAGO
NICK SANTIAGO
DEWEY SAUNDERS
ROY SAUNDERS
ALEXANDER C. SCHENCK
DOUGLAS SCHERMER
BRUNO G. SCHIBOLD
VICTOR SCHULE
EMIL SCHULER
WOODROW E. SCHWETER
H. W. SCHWETERS
EDMUND P. SCULLY
KENDRICK SEARLESS
NORMAN S. SEELY
EUGENE J. E. SEFFRINGER
B. R. PRETON SELF
SAM SELLERS
ADOLPH SEPPA
SOTERO D. SERENCIO
MAYNARD A. SHANOWER
CEIL SHAW
CHARLES H. SHAW
RICHARD C. SHEPHERD
PATRICK M. SHERIDAN
WILLIAM T. SHERIDAN
ELLIOT I. SHERRIS
J. H. SHERROD
CHARLES SHIPLIS
SAMUEL J. SHUGARS
VALENTINE B. SIEBERT
LOUIS SIERRA
LAWRENCE S. SILBERGER
JOSEPH SIMMONS
FRANK A. SIMPSON
EDWIN E. SMARLING
WILLIAM V. SMEDLEY
HENRY SMITH
JIM SMITH
MARVIN D. SMITH
MATTHEW SMITH
WILLIAM SMITH
HAROLD SMITHSON
EDGAR SOBERBERG
LOUIS SOBO
KARL G. SORENSON
MANUEL SOUSA
EMANUEL SPATHAROS
FRANK E. SPENCER
CLAYTON SPIVEY
DONALD E. SPRAGUE
JOSEPH SQUIRES
P. A. SQUIRES
JAMES STANLEY
RAY N. STALKER
WILLIAM S. STANFORD
ORVILLE STARLIN JR.
WILMER STARNS
HENRY STATZELL JR.
FRED STEBBINS
L. STEELING
CHARLES STEPHENS
JAMES STEVENS
CHARLES STEWART
JOHN B. STEWARDT
MASON STILTNER
WILBUR L. STINE
DONALD R. STITH
MELVIN STOKES
MELVIN W. STOKES
GEORGE L. STROEMPLE
RUFUS STROUGH
STEPHEN STRACHEN
LEONARD STRECHARTZ
HENRY STROM
STANLEY STUPINSKI
ARTHUR STYPCZYNSKI
DENNIS J. SULLIVAN
KOKOMO SULLIVAN
SYDNEY SULLIVAN
LEONARD M. SUNDERBERG
HENRY SURLES
MELVIN SUTHERLAND
WILLIAM SUTHERLAND
WAYNE SWEARINGEN
BERNARD E. SWISHER
COSIMO R. SYLVESTER
WILLIAM S. SZPARKOWSKI

T

WILLIAM M. TAIT
GUISIPPI N. TANGORA
BENJAMIN TANNER
EDWARD J. TARKA
JAMES TATE
ALFRED TAYLOR
FRED TAYLOR
JAMES TAYLOR
JOHN TAYLOR
JOSEPH TAYLOR
LESLIE TAYLOR
RICHARD TAYLOR
ROBERT TAYLOR
STANLEY TAYLOR
RONALD J. TEARSE
JOHN TEREZA
D. H. THOMAS
JOHN THOMAS
THOMAS J. THOMAS
CECIL THOMPSON
OHLMIER THOMPSON
JOHN THORNTON
LEO G. THORP
F. H. TILLEY
THOMAS S. TINGLE
TOBIAS TOBIASSEN
R. M. TODD
ARCHIE A. TOMLINSON
ALEXANDER TOMM
MERRITT TOMPKINS
CARROL TORKELSON
GREGORIO TORRES
PEDRO TORRES
RUDOLPH F. TORSTENSON
EDWARD B. TOUT
GEORGE W. TOWNER
JOSEPH TRALIE
WALTER D. TRUAX
GLEN TRAWEEK
LOUIS TRYMERS
JULES TUBENS
RUBIN TUBIN
ROBERT TUOHY
IEMUEL TURNER
GEORGE TURNER
CLIFFORD B. TWISS
FRANK TYMULA
THOMAS TYRRELL
MICOZYSLAW TYSZKOWSKI

U

DAVID H. UDELL

V

EDWIN H. VANDEGRIFF
CHARLES VAN NAMEE
JESUS VARELA
MANUEL VASQUEZ
PEDRO VELEZ
MANUEL VERLARINO
SPENCER G. VERRETT
JOSEPH VILA
FRANK VILBISAS
THOS. VINCENT
JOHN VINECK
DANIEL VOLIVA
ANTHONY J. VON DOLTEREN
THEODORE VON PENTZ

W

WILTON W. WADE
ROBERT A. WAHYAHNTEETAH
J. A. WALCOTT
JOHN WALDMAN
PHILIP R. WALDON
FLOYD M. WALER
FLOYD WALKER
JOHN WALKER
WALTER WALKER
WILLIAM F. WALLDEN
JAMES D. WALSER
JOHN W. WAPON
J. S. WARD
THOMAS F. WARE
BERTRAM WARNER
JAMES N. WARREN
R. P. WATERS
RAYMOND WATERS
DONALD WATTS
GEORGE WATTS
JOHN WAYSO
JOHN W. WAYSON
WILLIAM WEAVER
DAVID WEBSTER
LEONARD A. WEEDAN
DONALD C. WEIGART
GEORGE P. WEIGART
JOSEPH WEIR
ROBERT O. WEIR
WILLIAM WEISS
THOMAS W. WELSH
GEORGE WEST
H AL WESTOVER JR.
HAROLD M. WHALMAN
JAMES WHEELER
CHARLES T. WHITE
EARL WHITE
HAROLD WHITE
HAROLD P. WHITE
JAMES T. WHITE
THOMAS WHITE
THOR WHITE
H. D. WHITEHEAD
G. M. WHITNEY
HAROLD WHITNEY
GEORGE WHYTE
G. M. WICKENHISER
FRANK A. WICKMAN
HENRY WIERA
JOHN H. WILCOX
RALPH WILKINSON
A. WILLIAMS
ASHLEY WILLIAMS
FLOYD J. WILLIAMS
EDWARD WILLIAMS
FRANK WILLIAMS
HUGH WILLIAMS
JAMES WILLIAMS
JARVIS WILLIAMS
JOHN B. WILLIAMS
STANFORD E. WILLIAMS
GEORGE WILLIS
CHARLES WILSON
FRANK T. WILSON
ROBERT R. WILSON
WARREN L. WILSON
EDDIE B. WILTZ
EDWARD WISNIEWSKI
WALTER J. WODARCZYK
PAUL WOLFE
JOHN WOLOSZ
ALFRED SOLTJEN
FRANCIS D. WOOD
FRANK L. WOOD
JAMES E. WOODWARD
ALLEN E. WORTHY
JAMES WRIGHT
NATHANIEL WRIGHT
WILLIAM W. WRIGHT
LEWIS WYNN
BEN A. WINTER

Y

THOMAS YATES JR.
DESSO YEOMAN
JOSEPH H. YOUNG
ALBERT S. YOUNGBERG

Z

JOSEPH ZALESKI
OSCAR ZAYES
JOS. C. ZUGOWSKA
HUBERT ZUMPFT
DONALD M. ZOOK

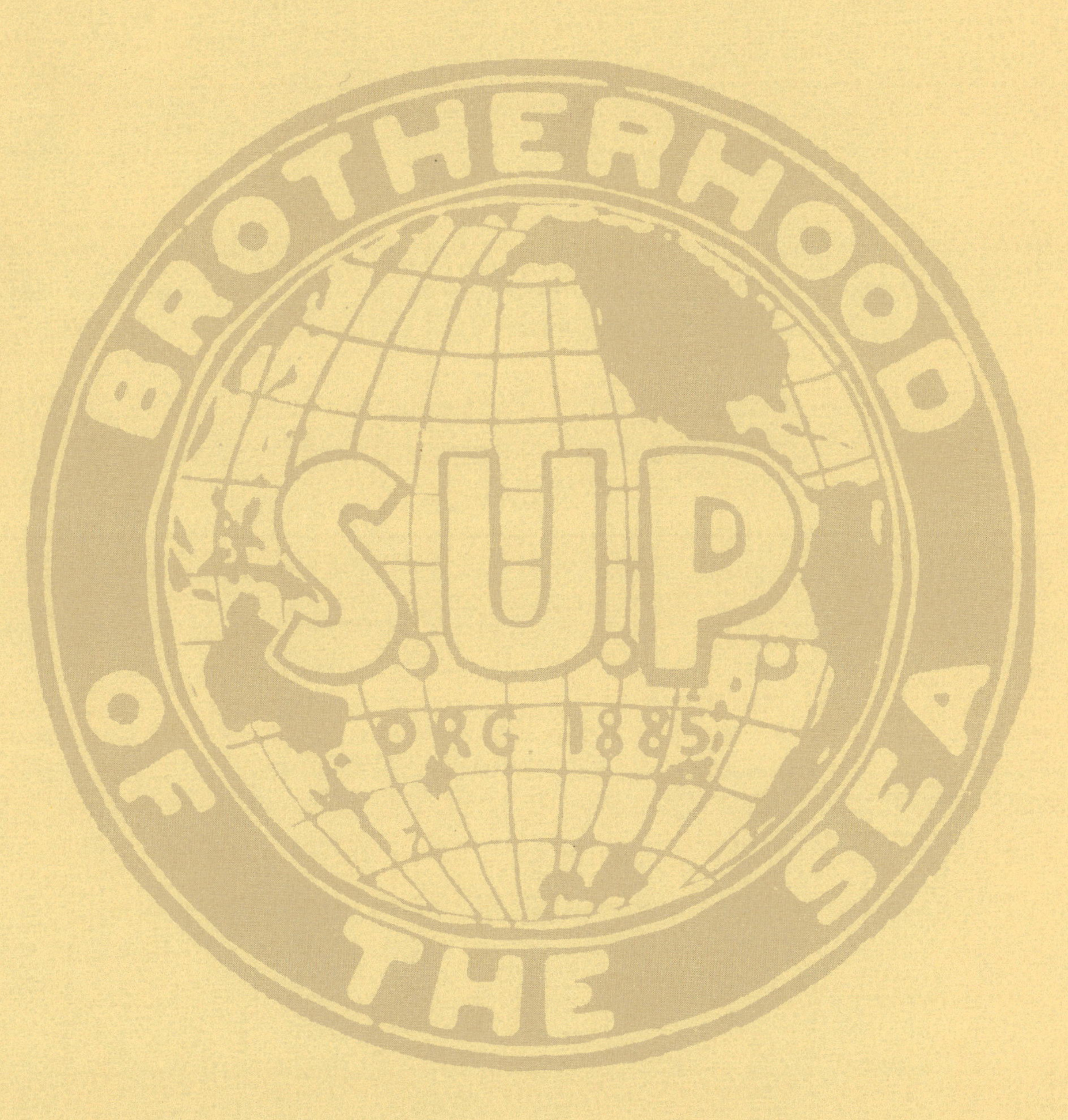
BROTHERHOOD
S.U.P.
ORG 1885
OF THE SEA